Oh! 365 Homemade Puff Pastry Recipes

(Oh! 365 Homemade Puff Pastry Recipes - Volume 1)

Kathy Terry

Content

CHAPTER 5: AWESOME PUFF PASTRY RECIPES 140

Chapter 1: Puff Pastry Appetizer Recipes

***

1. Artichoke Spinach Pinwheels

Serving: 2 dozen. | Prep: 20mins | Cook: 20mins | Ready in:

Ingredients

- 1 can (14 ounces) water-packed artichoke hearts, rinsed, drained and chopped
- 1 package (10 ounces) frozen chopped spinach, thawed and squeezed dry
- 1/2 cup grated Parmesan cheese
- 1/2 cup mayonnaise
- 1/2 teaspoon onion powder
- 1/2 teaspoon garlic powder
- 1/2 teaspoon pepper
- 1 package (17.3 ounces) frozen puff pastry, thawed

Direction

- Mix the first seven ingredients in a small bowl. Roll out the puff pastry. Scatter the artichoke mixture on each sheet within 1/2 inch of edges then in a jelly roll style, roll up the pastry. Use plastic to wrap and keep in the freezer, about 30 minutes.
- Slice each of the rolls into 12 pieces each of the rolls with a serrated knife. Transfer on a greased baking sheets, seam side down. Bake for 18 to 22 minutes at 400 degrees F until golden brown.

Nutrition Information

- Calories: 150 calories
- Protein: 3g protein.
- Total Fat: 10g fat (2g saturated fat)
- Sodium: 168mg sodium
- Fiber: 2g fiber)
- Total Carbohydrate: 13g carbohydrate (0 sugars
- Cholesterol: 3mg cholesterol

2. Asparagus Wraps

Serving: 2 dozen. | Prep: 20mins | Cook: 15mins | Ready in:

Ingredients

- 3 tablespoons butter, softened
- 1 tablespoon Mrs. Dash Onion & Herb seasoning blend
- 1/4 teaspoon garlic salt
- 1 package (17.3 ounces) frozen puff pastry, thawed
- 1 cup crumbled feta cheese
- 3 ounces thinly sliced prosciutto or deli ham
- 24 thick fresh asparagus spears, trimmed

Direction

- Preheat oven to 425°F. Combine garlic salt, butter and seasoning blend. Roll out puff pastry on a lightly floured work area. Cover it with 1 1/2 tablespoons butter mixture and scatter 1/2 cup cheese on top. Place prosciutto over cheese, pressing a bit to stick.
- Cut each sheet into 12 1/2-inch strips using a sharp knife or pizza cutter. Wrap each asparagus spear with a strip of pastry, filling side in. Transfer to baking sheets lined with parchment paper.
- Bake for about 15 minutes or until golden brown. Serve while still warm.

Nutrition Information

- Calories: 139 calories
- Sodium: 248mg sodium
- Fiber: 2g fiber)
- Total Carbohydrate: 12g carbohydrate (0 sugars
- Cholesterol: 11mg cholesterol
- Protein: 4g protein.
- Total Fat: 8g fat (3g saturated fat)

3. Asparagus In Puff Pastry

Serving: 28 servings. | Prep: 30mins | Cook: 10mins | Ready in:

Ingredients

- 2 cups water
- 24 fresh asparagus spears (about 1 pound), trimmed
- 1 package (8 ounces) reduced-fat cream cheese
- 1/2 teaspoon salt
- 1 package (17-1/4 ounces) frozen puff pastry dough, thawed
- 1/4 cup egg substitute

Direction

- Boil water in a large nonstick skillet. Toss in asparagus and cook with cover, about 3 minutes. Remove water from asparagus and quickly add in ice water. Remove asparagus from ice water and pat it to dry. Whisk salt and cream cheese in a bowl until mixture is smooth. Put on one side.
- On the lightly floured work area, roll out dough and slice each of the sheets into half, widthwise. Spread the cream cheese mixture lengthwise on top of half of the dough within 1/2 inch of edges, for each rectangle. Put 3 asparagus spears assembled into two rows lengthwise in a single layer on top of the cream cheese.

- Brush some of the egg substitute over the dough edges, then fold the dough over the filling. Seal by pressing the edges together. Keep in the refrigerator while covered, about 1 hour.
- Slice into 1-1/4-inch slices, widthwise. On a baking sheet coated with cooking spray, transfer pastry and arrange them 1 inch apart. Brush with the rest of the egg substitute. Bake for 8 to 12 minutes at 425 degrees F until golden brown. Serve while warm.

Nutrition Information

- Calories: 87 calories
- Total Fat: 6g fat (3g saturated fat)
- Sodium: 156mg sodium
- Fiber: 1g fiber)
- Total Carbohydrate: 6g carbohydrate (0 sugars
- Cholesterol: 9mg cholesterol
- Protein: 3g protein. Diabetic Exchanges: 1 vegetable

4. Aussie Sausage Rolls

Serving: 3 dozen. | Prep: 30mins | Cook: 20mins | Ready in:

Ingredients

- 1 medium onion, finely chopped
- 2 tablespoons minced fresh chives or 2 teaspoons dried chives
- 2 teaspoons minced fresh basil or 1/2 teaspoon dried basil
- 2 garlic cloves, minced
- 1/2 teaspoon salt
- 1/4 teaspoon pepper
- 1 teaspoon paprika, divided
- 1-1/4 pounds Jones No Sugar Pork Sausage Roll
- 1 package (17.3 ounces) frozen puff pastry, thawed

Direction

- Preheat oven to 350 degrees F. Mix the first six ingredients and add a 3/4 tablespoon of paprika. Toss in the sausage and lightly mix until well blended.
- Roll each of the pastry sheets in an 11x10 1/2-inch rectangle on a lightly floured area. Slice into three lengthwise strips. Add 1/2 cup of the sausage mixture into each strip lengthwise down at the middle. Fold over the corners, and seal while pinching the edges. Slice each of the logs into 6 pieces.
- Place a 15x10x1 inch pan on a rack and transfer the pieces into the pan, seam side down. Season with the leftover paprika. Bake for 20 to 25 minutes until golden brown and the sausage is no longer pink.

Nutrition Information

- Calories: 116 calories
- Protein: 3g protein.
- Total Fat: 8g fat (2g saturated fat)
- Sodium: 198mg sodium
- Fiber: 1g fiber)
- Total Carbohydrate: 8g carbohydrate (0 sugars
- Cholesterol: 11mg cholesterol

5. Autumn Squash Tartlets

Serving: 32 tartlets. | Prep: 15mins | Cook: 15mins | Ready in:

Ingredients

- 1 package (17.3 ounces) frozen puff pastry, thawed
- 2-1/2 cups cubed acorn squash
- 3 tablespoons heavy whipping cream
- 4 teaspoons dry bread crumbs
- 1-1/2 teaspoons minced fresh rosemary
- 1-1/2 teaspoons minced fresh thyme
- 1/2 teaspoon salt

- 1/8 teaspoon pepper
- 2 ounces fresh goat cheese

Direction

- Roll out puff pastry, then slice sixteen pieces of 2-inch circle from each of the sheets. Prepare greased mini muffin cups; press pastry onto the bottom and up to the sides.
- Mix cream and squash in a food processor. Process with cover until smooth, about 1 to 2 minutes. Transfer the mixture into a large bowl and blend with thyme, pepper, bread crumbs, salt, and rosemary.
- Scoop mixture and place on the pastry cups. Bake for 15 to 17 minutes at 375 degrees F until golden brown. Sprinkle cheese on top; broil until cheese melts, about 1 to 2 minutes. Serve while warm.

Nutrition Information

- Calories: 92 calories
- Sodium: 98mg sodium
- Fiber: 2g fiber
- Total Carbohydrate: 11g carbohydrate (1g sugars
- Cholesterol: 3mg cholesterol
- Protein: 2g protein.
- Total Fat: 5g fat (1g saturated fat)

6. Beef & Onion Piroshki

Serving: 32 appetizers. | Prep: 30mins | Cook: 15mins | Ready in:

Ingredients

- 1 pound lean ground beef (90% lean)
- 1 cup finely chopped sweet onion
- 2 garlic cloves, minced
- 1/2 teaspoon salt
- 1/4 teaspoon pepper
- 1 cup chopped fresh spinach

- 1 cup (4 ounces) Havarti cheese
- 1/4 cup sour cream
- 2 tablespoons snipped fresh dill
- 1 package (17.3 ounces) frozen puff pastry, thawed
- 1 egg
- 1 tablespoon water

Direction

- Sauté onion, garlic, beef, pepper and salt in a pan over medium heat. Cook until beef is no longer pink. Drain and let it rest at room temperature.
- Mix in the cheese, spinach, dill and sour cream into the beef mixture. Roll a puff pastry on a lightly floured surface into a 12-inch square. Slice into 16 three-inch squares. Do again with the rest of the sheets.
- Place a tablespoon of the beef in the middle of each square. Fold the dough, to form a triangle, over the filling. Seal by pressing the edges using a fork. Put them on greased baking sheets. Beat egg and water and use to brush the tops. Bake for 14-16 minutes at 400°F, until golden brown.

Nutrition Information

- Calories:
- Sodium:
- Fiber:
- Total Carbohydrate:
- Cholesterol:
- Protein:
- Total Fat:

7. Beef Wellington Appetizers

Serving: 16 appetizers (1-1/2 cups sauce). | Prep: 45mins | Cook: 15mins | Ready in:

Ingredients

- 2 beef tenderloin steaks (8 ounces each), cut into 1/2-inch cubes
- 2 tablespoons olive oil, divided
- 1-1/4 cups chopped fresh mushrooms
- 2 shallots, chopped
- 2 garlic cloves, minced
- 1/3 cup sherry or chicken broth
- 1/3 cup heavy whipping cream
- 1/2 teaspoon salt
- 1/8 teaspoon pepper
- 1 tablespoon minced fresh parsley
- 1 package (17.3 ounces) frozen puff pastry, thawed
- 1 egg, beaten
- HORSERADISH CREAM:
- 1 cup sour cream
- 1/2 cup mayonnaise
- 2 tablespoons prepared horseradish
- 1 tablespoon minced chives
- 1/4 teaspoon pepper
- Additional minced chives, optional

Direction

- In a big pan, cook beef in 1 tablespoon oil until browned. Remove beef from the pan and keep warm.
- Using the same skillet and what remains of the oil, sauté shallots and mushrooms until tender. Toss in garlic and cook for another minute. Pour sherry and stir to loosen browned bits from bottom of the pan. Add in cream and season with salt and pepper. Bring mixture to a boil and continue cooking for 7 minutes until liquid is almost gone. Mix in beef and parsley then set aside and keep warm.
- Preheat oven to 400 °F. Spread out puff pastry on a lightly floured work area. Roll each sheet into a square, 12 inches in size, and divide each square further into 16 squares.
- On half of the squares, spread 2 tablespoonfuls of beef mixture in center. Cover each using the rest of the squares. Use a fork to seal the edges by pressing on it. Arrange filled squares on baking sheet lined with parchment paper. Slash slits on top then brush with egg. Bake until golden brown, about 14 to 16 minutes.

- While the pastry bakes, mix the ingredients for the horseradish cream in a small bowl. Serve pastries on the side. If desired, sprinkle with more chives as garnish.

Nutrition Information

- Calories: 315 calories
- Sodium: 231mg sodium
- Fiber: 2g fiber
- Total Carbohydrate: 19g carbohydrate (1g sugars
- Cholesterol: 45mg cholesterol
- Protein: 10g protein.
- Total Fat: 22g fat (6g saturated fat)

8. Crab Mornay

Serving: 6 servings. | Prep: 30mins | Cook: 0mins | Ready in:

Ingredients

- 1 package (10 ounces) frozen puff pastry shells
- 1/2 cup butter, cubed
- 1 jar (6 ounces) sliced mushrooms, drained
- 6 green onions, sliced
- 1 jar (4 ounces) diced pimientos, drained
- 2 tablespoons all-purpose flour
- 1 can (12 ounces) evaporated milk
- 2 cups shredded Swiss cheese
- 3 cans (6 ounces each) crabmeat, drained, flaked and cartilage removed
- 1 teaspoon salt
- 1/8 teaspoon cayenne pepper
- 1/3 cup minced fresh parsley

Direction

- Prepare pastry shells according to package instructions. Meanwhile, put butter in a 2-qt microwavable dish and cover. Put inside the microwave set on high for 20-30 seconds or until the butter melts. Add pimientos,

mushrooms and onions. Cover and cook in the microwave again on high temperature for another 2-3 minutes or until the vegetables are crispy-tender.
- Mix together milk and flour until smooth; slowly add to the vegetables. Without cover, put it in the microwave 2-3 minutes on high temperature until the mixture thickens, frequently stir. Add cayenne, crab, cheese, and salt.
- Cover and cook for another 30-60 seconds on high temperature until the cheese melts; then put mixture in the pastry shells. Garnish with parsley before serving.

Nutrition Information

- Calories: 627 calories
- Fiber: 4g fiber
- Total Carbohydrate: 35g carbohydrate (8g sugars
- Cholesterol: 117mg cholesterol
- Protein: 24g protein.
- Total Fat: 43g fat (22g saturated fat)
- Sodium: 1053mg sodium

9. Cranberry Bacon Galette

Serving: 9 servings. | Prep: 25mins | Cook: 20mins | Ready in:

Ingredients

- 1 carton (8 ounces) mascarpone cheese
- 1 tablespoon orange marmalade
- 1 tablespoon jellied cranberry sauce
- 2 tablespoons sugar
- 1 cup chopped red onion
- 1 cup dried cranberries
- 3/4 cup chopped fresh mushrooms
- 1 tablespoon olive oil
- 1/2 teaspoon lemon-pepper seasoning
- 1/4 teaspoon salt
- 1/4 teaspoon smoked paprika

- 3 tablespoons cranberry-tangerine juice
- 1 sheet frozen puff pastry, thawed
- 5 cooked bacon strips, crumbled
- 1/4 cup minced fresh basil

Direction

- Prepare the oven and preheat to 400 degrees F. To prepare the topping, combine the marmalade, cranberry sauce, and cheese in a small bowl. Keep in the refrigerator until serving time.
- On medium-high heat, cook sugar for 1 to 2 minutes in a large skillet until sugar starts to melt. Stir in onion and cook for 2 minutes more.
- Add in the mushrooms, lemon pepper, paprika, cranberries, oil, and salt; stir and cook for 2 minutes. Lower heat and pour juice. For 4 minutes, stir and cook until mushrooms tenderize, about 4 minutes.
- Use a rolling pin to form a 10-inch square from puff pastry on the baking sheet lined with parchment paper. Using a ruler, slice a 10x2 inch rectangle with the aid of a long sharp knife or a pastry wheel. Slice two 7x1/2-inch strips and two 10x1/2-inch strips from the 10x2-inch strip. Cut trimmings and discard. Using a fork, pierce all over the rest of the 10x8-inch pastry base. At the edges of the pastry base, brush water about a 1/2 inch. Form sides by placing the 7x1/2-inch strips and the 10x1/2-inch strips along the edges. Lightly press.
- Pour the cranberry mixture at the edges; top with bacon. Bake the pastry for 18 to 22 minutes or until golden brown; let cool for about 10 minutes and season with basil. Serve with the topping while warm.

Nutrition Information

- Calories: 355 calories
- Protein: 6g protein.
- Total Fat: 23g fat (9g saturated fat)
- Sodium: 299mg sodium
- Fiber: 3g fiber)

- Total Carbohydrate: 34g carbohydrate (15g sugars
- Cholesterol: 38mg cholesterol

10. Cranberry Orange Tartlets

Serving: 6 dozen. | Prep: 25mins | Cook: 15mins | Ready in:

Ingredients

- 1 package (17.3 ounces) frozen puff pastry, thawed
- 3/4 cup Mascarpone cheese
- 1/4 cup sugar
- 3 tablespoons finely chopped dried cranberries
- 3 tablespoons beaten egg
- 2 teaspoons grated orange zest
- 3 tablespoons finely chopped walnuts
- TOPPING:
- 1/2 cup whole-berry cranberry sauce
- 3 tablespoons plus 4-1/2 teaspoons water, divided
- 2 teaspoons cornstarch

Direction

- Roll out puff pastry sheets into 10-in. squares. Divide each sheet into 36 squares and press each square carefully into greased mini muffin cups. Bake for 10 minutes at 375°F. Create a hollow in the center of each cups using the end of a wooden spoon handle
- Combine egg, cranberries, cheese, orange zest and sugar in a small bowl. Scoop about 1 teaspoon filling into each muffin cup. Top with walnuts.
- Bake in the oven until golden brown, 6 to 8 minutes. Transfer on wire racks to cool completely.
- To make the topping, combine 3 tablespoons water and cranberry sauce in a small pot. Mix cornstarch with the remaining water and mix until smooth. Pour cornstarch mixture slowly into cranberry mixture. Stir and cook to a boil.

Continue cooking and stirring for another minute until sauce thickens. Put on top of tartlets.

Nutrition Information

- Calories: 63 calories
- Protein: 1g protein. Diabetic Exchanges: 1/2 starch
- Total Fat: 4g fat (2g saturated fat)
- Sodium: 26mg sodium
- Fiber: 1g fiber)
- Total Carbohydrate: 6g carbohydrate (1g sugars
- Cholesterol: 9mg cholesterol

11. Creamy Chicken Vol Au Vent

Serving: 6 servings. | Prep: 20mins | Cook: 20mins | Ready in:

Ingredients

- 1 package (17.30 ounces) frozen puff pastry, thawed
- 1 large egg
- 1 tablespoon water
- 6 bacon strips
- 2 medium leeks (white portion only), sliced
- 1 medium sweet yellow pepper, diced
- 1 cup shredded rotisserie chicken
- 8 ounces cream cheese, softened
- 1/4 teaspoon salt
- 1/4 teaspoon pepper
- Minced fresh parsley plus additional ground pepper

Direction

- Preheat oven to 400°F. Dust work area lightly with flour and roll out one puff pastry sheet. Cut out 6 discs using a 3 1/4 inch round cutter. Line a baking tray with parchment paper and arrange cut discs on top.

- Roll out the rest of the pastry sheet and cut six more circles of the same size using the 3/4 in. round cutter. Then, using a 2 1/2 inch cutter, carve the centers out of the circles. Place the rings on top of the discs that are on the baking tray then also put the carved-out center circles on the tray. In a small bowl, beat egg and water together then brush mixture over pastries. Refrigerate for 15 minutes. Bake in the oven for 20 to 25 minutes or until dark golden brown. Set aside on a wire rack to cool.
- While the pastry cools, fry bacon in a large pan set over medium heat. Cook until crisp then transfer onto paper towels so oil gets absorbed. Leave 1 tablespoon drippings on the pan and throw away the rest. Toss in pepper and leeks and stir-fry for 5 to 7 minutes over medium-high heat until tender. Turn down heat to low then add in chicken, bacon, cream cheese, salt and pepper. Stir as it cooks until blended then remove pan from heat.
- Once pastries are cool enough to hold, use a small knife to hollow them out. Stuff with chicken and bacon mixture. Coat with pepper and parsley. Add the small center pastries on the side when serving.

Nutrition Information

- Calories: 669 calories
- Sodium: 670mg sodium
- Fiber: 6g fiber)
- Total Carbohydrate: 47g carbohydrate (4g sugars
- Cholesterol: 108mg cholesterol
- Protein: 19g protein.
- Total Fat: 45g fat (16g saturated fat)

12. Crisp Caraway Twists

Serving: about 1-1/2 dozen. | Prep: 15mins | Cook: 15mins | Ready in:

Ingredients

- 1 egg
- 1 tablespoon water
- 1 teaspoon country-style Dijon mustard
- 3/4 cup shredded Swiss cheese
- 1/4 cup finely chopped onion
- 2 teaspoons minced fresh parsley
- 1-1/2 teaspoons caraway seeds
- 1/4 teaspoon garlic salt
- 1 sheet frozen puff pastry, thawed

Direction

- Beat water, mustard and egg together in a small bowl then set aside. Combine onion, cheese, caraway seeds, garlic salt and parsley in another bowl.
- Roll out pastry sheet and brush it with egg mixture. On a lengthwise motion, spread cheese mixture over half of the pastry. Fold pastry over filling and press the edges to seal. Use the rest of the egg mixture to brush the top. Slice crosswise into 1/2 inch strips then twist each strip many times.
- On greased baking sheets, arrange the strips 1 in. apart, pressing the ends down. Bake for 15 to 20 minutes at 350°F or until golden brown. Serve while still warm.

Nutrition Information

- Calories: 179 calories
- Sodium: 185mg sodium
- Fiber: 2g fiber)
- Total Carbohydrate: 16g carbohydrate (1g sugars
- Cholesterol: 32mg cholesterol
- Protein: 5g protein.
- Total Fat: 10g fat (3g saturated fat)

13. Garlic Onion Appetizer Rounds

Serving: 16 appetizers. | Prep: 30mins | Cook: 15mins | Ready in:

Ingredients

- 2 large sweet onions, chopped (about 4 cups)
- 2 tablespoons butter
- 2 garlic cloves, minced
- 1 sheet frozen puff pastry, thawed
- 1 large egg
- 1 tablespoon water
- 1/3 cup shredded Swiss cheese
- 1/4 cup grated Parmesan cheese
- 2 tablespoons minced fresh basil

Direction

- In a big pan set over medium-low heat, put butter and cook onions until golden brown while stirring frequently. Toss in garlic and cook for another minute. Take pan from the heat and let it cool at room temperature.
- Spread out puff pastry. In a small bowl, beat water and egg together. Brush pastry with the egg wash. Spread onion mixture to within 1/2 in. of edges and top with basil and cheeses. Using jelly-roll style, roll up the puff pastry then cut into 16 pieces.
- Arrange on greased baking sheets, 2 inches apart. Bake for 12 to 14 minutes at 425°F or until golden brown and puffed. Serve while still warm.

Nutrition Information

- Calories: 114 calories
- Total Carbohydrate: 11g carbohydrate (1g sugars
- Cholesterol: 20mg cholesterol
- Protein: 3g protein.
- Total Fat: 7g fat (3g saturated fat)
- Sodium: 91mg sodium
- Fiber: 1g fiber)

14. Greek Breadsticks

Serving: 32 breadsticks. | Prep: 20mins | Cook: 15mins | Ready in:

Ingredients

- 1/4 cup marinated quartered artichoke hearts, drained
- 2 tablespoons pitted Greek olives
- 1 package (17.3 ounces) frozen puff pastry, thawed
- 1 carton (6-1/2 ounces) spreadable spinach and artichoke cream cheese
- 2 tablespoons grated Parmesan cheese
- 1 large egg
- 1 tablespoon water
- 2 teaspoons sesame seeds
- Refrigerated tzatziki sauce, optional

Direction

- In a food processor, combine olives and artichokes. Cover and pulse into fine chops. Roll out puff pastry on a lightly floured work area. On one half side of the pastry, spread half of the cream cheese mixture then pour half of the artichoke mixture over it. Top with half of the Parmesan cheese. Fold plain half over filling, then seal by pressing carefully.
- Do the same with the rest of the pastry, Parmesan cheese, cream cheese and artichoke mixture. Beat water and egg together and brush pastry with the egg wash mixture. Dust with sesame seeds. Divide both rectangles into 16 strips, 3/4 inch wide each. Turn strips into spiral a couple of times and arrange on greased baking sheets, 2 inches apart.
- Bake for 12 to 14 minutes at 400°F or until golden brown. If preferred, you can add tzatziki sauce on the side, serve while warm.

Nutrition Information

- Calories: 101 calories
- Fiber: 1g fiber)
- Total Carbohydrate: 9g carbohydrate (0 sugars
- Cholesterol: 11mg cholesterol
- Protein: 2g protein.
- Total Fat: 6g fat (2g saturated fat)
- Sodium: 104mg sodium

15. Greek Pinwheels

Serving: 20 appetizers. | Prep: 20mins | Cook: 10mins | Ready in:

Ingredients

- 1 sheet frozen puff pastry, thawed
- 1 tablespoon beaten egg
- 3/4 teaspoon water
- 1/2 cup cream cheese, softened
- 1/3 cup marinated quartered artichoke hearts, drained and finely chopped
- 1/4 cup crumbled feta cheese
- 1 tablespoon finely chopped drained oil-packed sun-dried tomatoes
- 3 Greek olives, finely chopped
- 1 teaspoon Greek seasoning

Direction

- Roll out puff pastry. Beat together water and egg. Brush pastry with the egg wash mixture. Mix the rest of the ingredients together and spread over pastry to within 1/2 inch of edges. Roll up pastry, jelly-roll style, and cut into twenty slices, about 1/2 inch thick each.
- Arrange on greased baking sheets, 2 inches apart. Bake for 9 to 11 minutes at 425°F until puffed and golden brown. Serve while it's still warm.

Nutrition Information

- Calories: 92 calories
- Total Fat: 6g fat (2g saturated fat)
- Sodium: 142mg sodium
- Fiber: 1g fiber)
- Total Carbohydrate: 7g carbohydrate (0 sugars

- Cholesterol: 9mg cholesterol
- Protein: 2g protein.

- Cholesterol: 7mg cholesterol
- Protein: 3g protein.
- Total Fat: 9g fat (3g saturated fat)
- Sodium: 125mg sodium
- Fiber: 2g fiber)
- Total Carbohydrate: 13g carbohydrate (1g sugars

16. Gruyere & Caramelized Onion Tarts

Serving: 2 dozen. | Prep: 45mins | Cook: 15mins | Ready in:

Ingredients

- 1 large sweet onion, thinly sliced
- 2 tablespoons olive oil
- 1 tablespoon butter
- 3 garlic cloves, minced
- 1/4 teaspoon salt
- 1/4 teaspoon pepper
- 1 package (17.3 ounces) frozen puff pastry, thawed
- 1 cup shredded Gruyere or Swiss cheese
- 1/4 cup grated Parmesan cheese
- 2 tablespoons minced fresh thyme or 2 teaspoons dried thyme

Direction

- In a big pan, sauté onion in butter and oil until tender. Turn heat down to medium-low and continue cooking, uncovered, until deep golden brown, about 40 minutes. Stir occasionally. Toss in garlic and cook for another minute. Season with salt and pepper.
- Spread out each puff pastry sheet onto an ungreased baking tray. With a knife, create decorative lines around the pastry edges. Pour onion mixture and spread to within 1/2 inch of edges. Top with thyme and cheeses.
- Bake for 12-15 minutes at 400°F or until golden brown. Slice tart into 12 pieces. Serve while still warm.

Nutrition Information

- Calories: 142 calories

17. Ham & Dijon Puff Pastry

Serving: 15 servings. | Prep: 10mins | Cook: 25mins | Ready in:

Ingredients

- 1 package (17.3 ounces) frozen puff pastry, thawed
- 1/2 cup Dijon mustard
- 1/2 pound thinly sliced deli ham
- 1 large egg, beaten

Direction

- Roll out one sheet of puff pastry in a greased baking pan, with 15x10x1-inch dimensions. Pour mustard over pastry and spread to within 1 inch of edges. Top with ham.
- Spread out the rest of the puff pastry sheet and lay over ham. Using a fork, press edges to seal. Brush pastry with egg.
- Bake for 25-30 minutes at 400°F or until golden brown. Serve while still warm.

Nutrition Information

- Calories: 187 calories
- Fiber: 2g fiber)
- Total Carbohydrate: 20g carbohydrate (0 sugars
- Cholesterol: 21mg cholesterol
- Protein: 5g protein.
- Total Fat: 9g fat (2g saturated fat)
- Sodium: 445mg sodium

- Cholesterol: 20mg cholesterol

Serving: 32 appetizers. | Prep: 30mins | Cook: 15mins | Ready in:

Ingredients

- 4 cups frozen broccoli florets, thawed and finely chopped
- 1 carton (8 ounces) spreadable chive and onion cream cheese
- 1 cup shredded Swiss cheese
- 1/4 pound thinly sliced deli ham, finely chopped
- 1/2 cup finely chopped fresh mushrooms
- 1/4 teaspoon salt
- 1 package (17.3 ounces) frozen puff pastry, thawed
- 2 large eggs, beaten

Direction

- Mix the first six ingredients in a large bowl. On a lightly floured work area, roll out puff pastry. Form the sheet into a square with a 12-inch dimension. Slice each into 16 squares.
- Scoop a heaping tablespoon of the broccoli mixture into the middle of each square. Brush the pastry edges with eggs. Fold the opposite corner over the filling while pressing the seams to seal.
- Transfer pastries to ungreased baking sheets. Bake for 12 to 15 minutes at 425 degrees F, until pastries are golden brown. Serve while warm.

Nutrition Information

- Calories: 122 calories
- Protein: 3g protein.
- Total Fat: 8g fat (3g saturated fat)
- Sodium: 146mg sodium
- Fiber: 1g fiber)
- Total Carbohydrate: 10g carbohydrate (1g sugars

Serving: 12 servings. | Prep: 15mins | Cook: 20mins | Ready in:

Ingredients

- 2 cups chopped rotisserie chicken (about 10 ounces)
- 1 carton (8 ounces) spreadable chive and onion cream cheese
- 1 cup shredded pepper jack or Monterey Jack cheese
- 1 can (4 ounces) diced jalapeno peppers
- 1 sheet frozen puff pastry, thawed
- 1 large egg, lightly beaten

Direction

- Set oven to preheat at 425°F. Mix cream cheese, chicken, peppers, and pepper jack cheese in a bowl.
- Unfold puff pastry on a floured surface. Roll it into a 13-inch square. Transfer to a baking sheet lined with parchment paper. Spread the chicken mixture over a half of the pastry, up to half an inch of the edges. Fold the other half over the filling. Seal by pressing down the edges with a fork.
- Beat an egg and use to lightly brush the pastry. Make slits in the pastry. Bake until golden brown, for 20-25 minutes. Rest for 10 minutes before slicing and serving.

Nutrition Information

- Calories: 237 calories
- Sodium: 252mg sodium
- Fiber: 2g fiber)
- Total Carbohydrate: 13g carbohydrate (1g sugars
- Cholesterol: 58mg cholesterol
- Protein: 12g protein.

- Total Fat: 15g fat (6g saturated fat)

20. Lamb Pastry Bundles

Serving: 1-1/2 dozen (2 cups sauce). | Prep: 30mins |
Cook: 20mins |Ready in:

Ingredients

- 1 small onion, grated
- 2 teaspoons ground cumin
- 1 teaspoon paprika
- 1-1/2 pounds ground lamb
- 1 tablespoon olive oil
- 1 package (17.3 ounces) frozen puff pastry, thawed
- 2 logs (4 ounces each) fresh goat cheese, cut into 18 slices
- 1 egg, lightly beaten
- SAUCE:
- 3/4 cup mayonnaise
- 1 jar (24 ounces) roasted sweet red peppers, drained
- 1 garlic clove, minced
- Dash crushed red pepper flakes

Direction

- Mix the cumin, paprika, and onion in a large bowl. Crush the lamb into the mixture and blend well. Mold the mixture into eighteen mini patties, 1/2 inch thick each. Cook patties in batches; fry with oil in a large pan over medium heat, about 3 to 4 minutes per side until thermometer registers 160 degrees F and the juices turn clear.
- Roll out puff pastry onto a lightly floured work area. Form each of the sheets into 12x12-inch square by rolling. Slice each of the sheets into 9 squares. Put a burger in the middle of each square. Add cheese on top. Brush edges of the pastry lightly with egg. Take the opposite sides of the pastry over the burger and press the seams to tightly seal the pastry.

- Transfer pastry on a 15x10x1-inch baking pan, seam side up. Brush with egg. Bake for 18 to 22 minutes at 400 degrees F, or until golden brown.
- Toss in the sauce ingredients into a food processor. Process with cover until smooth. Serve along with the bundles.

Nutrition Information

- Calories: 318 calories
- Fiber: 2g fiber)
- Total Carbohydrate: 18g carbohydrate (1g sugars
- Cholesterol: 43mg cholesterol
- Protein: 10g protein.
- Total Fat: 22g fat (6g saturated fat)
- Sodium: 352mg sodium

21. Little Pigs In A Hammock

Serving: 1-1/2 dozen. | Prep: 15mins | Cook: 15mins
| Ready in:

Ingredients

- 1 package (17.3 ounces) frozen puff pastry, thawed
- 3 tablespoons seedless raspberry jam
- 1 tablespoon Dijon mustard
- 1 round (8 ounces) Camembert cheese
- 18 miniature smoked sausages
- 1 large egg
- 1 tablespoon water

Direction

- Preheat oven to 425°F. Spread out puff pastry and cut 9 squares out of each pastry. Slice each square diagonally to create two triangles. Combine mustard and jam in a small bowl, mix well. Spread mixture over triangles. Slice cheese in half crosswise; then cut each half into nine wedges.

- Put a cheese wedge and a sausage on top of each pastry triangle. Pull pastry edges over sausage and cheese and seal by pressing the edges together. Arrange pastry on baking sheet lined with parchment paper. Beat water and egg together in a small bowl and brush pastry with the egg wash mixture. Bake until golden brown, 15 to 17 minutes.

Nutrition Information

- Calories:
- Fiber:
- Total Carbohydrate:
- Cholesterol:
- Protein:
- Total Fat:
- Sodium:

22. Maple, Fennel & Squash Bites

Serving: 2 dozen. | Prep: 35mins | Cook: 15mins | Ready in:

Ingredients

- 2 tablespoons butter, divided
- 2 cups finely cubed peeled butternut squash
- 6 tablespoons maple syrup, divided
- 1 fennel bulb, quartered and thinly sliced
- 1/2 teaspoon salt
- 1 package (17.3 ounces) frozen puff pastry, thawed
- 1 large egg
- 1 tablespoon water
- 3/4 cup crumbled goat cheese
- 4 bacon strips, cooked and crumbled
- Minced fresh thyme, optional

Direction

- Preheat oven to 400 °F. In a big pan set over medium-high heat, heat 1 tablespoon of butter. Add 3 tablespoons maple syrup and squash.

Cook until caramelized and tender, 6 to 8 minutes, stirring as it cooks. Take squash out and heat the rest of the butter in pan. Pour remaining maple syrup and toss in fennel. Continue cooking and stirring cook for 6 to 8 minutes until caramelized and soft. Bring squash back to the pan. Sprinkle with salt and stir. Take pan off the heat and chill in the refrigerator.
- Spread out puff pastry sheets. Beat water and egg together in a small bowl and brush pastry with the egg wash mixture. Divide each pastry sheet into 12 squares and arrange on a baking sheet lined with parchment paper. Put 1 tablespoon squash and fennel mixture on the middle of each square. Top with bacon and cheese. Bake until golden brown, 15 to 18 minutes. Halfway through cooking, rotate the baking sheets. Garnish with fresh thyme leaves if desired.

Nutrition Information

- Calories:
- Sodium:
- Fiber:
- Total Carbohydrate:
- Cholesterol:
- Protein:
- Total Fat:

23. Mediterranean Palmiers

Serving: 40 appetizers. | Prep: 10mins | Cook: 10mins | Ready in:

Ingredients

- 1 package (17.3 ounces) frozen puff pastry, thawed
- 1/4 cup prepared pesto
- 1/2 cup crumbled feta cheese
- 1/4 cup chopped oil-packed sun-dried tomatoes, patted dry

- 1/4 cup finely chopped walnuts

Direction

- Take one sheet of puff pastry and roll it out. Spread 2 T. pesto to within 1/2 in. of the edges then top with walnuts, tomatoes and half of the cheese.
- Starting from the left and right sides, roll the pastry's edges toward the center, like a jelly roll. Roll at 1-in. intervals so that the sides meet in the center. Do the same with the rest of the ingredients then slice each pastry rolls into 20 pieces.
- Arrange on baking tray lined with parchment paper, cut side down and 2 inches apart. Bake for 10 to 12 minutes at 400°F or until golden brown. Serve while it's still warm.

Nutrition Information

- Calories: 77 calories
- Protein: 2g protein. Diabetic Exchanges: 1 fat
- Total Fat: 5g fat (1g saturated fat)
- Sodium: 68mg sodium
- Fiber: 1g fiber)
- Total Carbohydrate: 7g carbohydrate (0 sugars
- Cholesterol: 1mg cholesterol

24. Mediterranean Pastry Pinwheels

Serving: 16 appetizers. | Prep: 20mins | Cook: 15mins | Ready in:

Ingredients

- 1 sheet frozen puff pastry, thawed
- 1 package (8 ounces) cream cheese, softened
- 1/4 cup prepared pesto
- 3/4 cup shredded provolone cheese
- 1/2 cup chopped oil-packed sun-dried tomatoes
- 1/2 cup chopped ripe olives
- 1/4 teaspoon pepper

Direction

- Preheat oven to 400 degrees F. Roll out the puff pastry and form into a 10-inch square.
- Whisk the pesto and cheese until smooth and add in the rest of the ingredients. Place the cheese mixture onto the pastry within 1/2 inch edges, then in jelly-roll style, roll up the pastry. Keep in freezer for 30 minutes. Slice into 16 pieces, crosswise.
- Prepare a baking sheet by lining with a parchment paper and place pastry seam side down; bake for 12 to 15 minutes. For freezing option: Cover the unbaked pastry pieces and freeze on a baking sheet lined with waxed paper until pastry is firm. Place into a resealable plastic freezer bags, then put back in the freezer. To use: Preheat oven to 400 degrees F. Bake the pastries for 15 to 20 minutes until golden brown.

Nutrition Information

- Calories: 170 calories
- Sodium: 227mg sodium
- Fiber: 2g fiber)
- Total Carbohydrate: 11g carbohydrate (1g sugars
- Cholesterol: 18mg cholesterol
- Protein: 4g protein.
- Total Fat: 13g fat (5g saturated fat)

25. Mini Party Burgers

Serving: 8 servings. | Prep: 15mins | Cook: 15mins | Ready in:

Ingredients

- 1/2 pound ground beef
- 1 envelope ranch salad dressing mix
- 1 large egg
- 1 teaspoon water
- 1 sheet frozen puff pastry, thawed

- 4 slices Havarti cheese (about 4 ounces), quartered

Direction

- Preheat oven to 400 degrees F. In a small bowl, place the beef and season with the dressing mix; stir lightly but thoroughly. Mold 8 patties with 1/2 inch thickness each.
- On medium heat, fry burgers in a large nonstick skillet, about 3 to 4 minutes per side until the thermometer registers 160 degrees. Take off from heat.
- Beat water and egg in a small bowl. Roll out the puff pastry on a lightly floured working area. Form into a 12-inch square. Slice the pastry into four pieces of 6-inch squares. Cut the squares in half to create 8 rectangles. Put a burger on one end of each rectangle; sprinkle with cheese. Brush the edges of the pastry with the egg mixture. Fold the pastry over the burger to enclose then pinch the corners using a fork to seal.
- Prepare baking sheets by lining with parchment paper; transfer the pastries. Brush the surfaces with the egg mixture. Bake for 15 to 20 minutes until golden brown.

Nutrition Information

- Calories: 271 calories
- Total Carbohydrate: 20g carbohydrate (0 sugars
- Cholesterol: 54mg cholesterol
- Protein: 11g protein.
- Total Fat: 16g fat (6g saturated fat)
- Sodium: 488mg sodium
- Fiber: 2g fiber)

26. Miniature Shepherd's Pies

Serving: 4 dozen. | Prep: 40mins | Cook: 15mins | Ready in:

Ingredients

- 1/2 pound ground beef
- 1/3 cup finely chopped onion
- 1/4 cup finely chopped celery
- 3 tablespoons finely chopped carrot
- 1-1/2 teaspoons all-purpose flour
- 1 teaspoon dried thyme
- 1/4 teaspoon salt
- 1/8 teaspoon ground nutmeg
- 1/8 teaspoon pepper
- 2/3 cup beef broth
- 1/3 cup frozen petite peas
- 2 packages (17.3 ounces each) frozen puff pastry, thawed
- 3 cups mashed potatoes

Direction

- Preheat oven to 400 degrees F. Stir-fry onion, carrot, celery, and beef in a large skillet over medium heat until beef is no longer pink, then drain. Add in salt, nutmeg, thyme, pepper, and flour; stir until well blended, then slowly pour the broth. Allow to boil, cook and stir sauce until it thickens, about 2 minutes. Toss in peas and thoroughly cook. Set aside.
- Unfold the puff pastry and cut out 12 circles per sheet with a floured 2 1/4-inch round cutter (reserve the scraps for later use). In ungreased mini muffin cups, press circles onto the bottoms and up to the sides.
- Add 1 1/2 teaspoon of beef mixture to fill each cups then pipe or top 1 tablespoon of mashed potatoes. Bake for 13 to 16 minutes until cooked thoroughly and the potatoes turn light brown. Serve while warm.

Nutrition Information

- Calories: 86 calories
- Sodium: 112mg sodium
- Fiber: 1g fiber)
- Total Carbohydrate: 10g carbohydrate (0 sugars
- Cholesterol: 4mg cholesterol
- Protein: 2g protein.

- Total Fat: 4g fat (1g saturated fat)

27. Mixed Mushroom Tartlets

Serving: 8 servings. | Prep: 40mins | Cook: 15mins | Ready in:

Ingredients

- 1-1/2 pounds sliced fresh assorted mushrooms
- 1 medium onion, chopped
- 1/2 cup butter
- 3 tablespoons olive oil
- 1/2 cup white wine or dry vermouth
- 1 teaspoon minced fresh thyme or 1/2 teaspoon dried thyme
- 1 teaspoon salt
- 1 cup heavy whipping cream
- 1 package (17.3 ounces) frozen puff pastry, thawed
- 1 egg yolk
- 1 teaspoon water

Direction

- Stir-fry the onion and mushroom in oil and butter by batches on a large pan until tender. Lower heat to medium and add the salt, wine, and thyme. Cook until wine is reduced to half then add the cream; stir. Continue to cook until mixture is thick, about 10 minutes. Take out from heat and put on one side.
- Roll out one puff pastry sheet; form into a 12x8-inch rectangle. Slice into 8 rectangle pieces. Mark 1/2 inch from the corner of each pastry with a sharp knife (don't slice through the pastry).
- Place into the baking sheets. Repeat procedure with the rest of the puff pastry. Scoop the mushroom mixture and spread at the middle. Beat water and egg yolk; brush onto the edges of the pastry.
- Bake for 13 to 16 minutes at 400 degrees F, until golden brown.

Nutrition Information

- Calories: 610 calories
- Protein: 8g protein.
- Total Fat: 44g fat (19g saturated fat)
- Sodium: 593mg sodium
- Fiber: 6g fiber)
- Total Carbohydrate: 42g carbohydrate (2g sugars
- Cholesterol: 96mg cholesterol

28. Mushroom Pastry Tarts

Serving: 1 dozen. | Prep: 50mins | Cook: 15mins | Ready in:

Ingredients

- 1/4 cup chopped walnuts or hazelnuts
- 3 tablespoons olive oil, divided
- 2 medium sweet onions, thinly sliced
- 1 garlic clove, minced
- 1 teaspoon brown sugar
- 1/2 teaspoon sea salt
- 1/4 teaspoon coarsely ground pepper
- 1/3 cup dry red wine
- 10 ounces sliced fresh shiitake mushrooms
- 1/2 pound sliced baby portobello mushrooms
- 2 teaspoons minced fresh thyme, divided
- 1 sheet frozen puff pastry, thawed
- 1 package (4 ounces) fresh goat cheese

Direction

- Toast walnuts in a pan for 5-7 minutes over low heat. Stir often. Cook until lightly browned. Turn the heat off and set aside.
- Heat 2 tablespoons of oil in a pan over medium heat. Sauté onions for 6-8 minutes until they are tender. Lower the heat to medium-low. Cook until the onions become a deep golden brown color, for 20-22 minutes more, stirring from time to time. Pour in a small bowl.

- Pour wine to the pan. Scrape down to free up browned bits. Let it boil. Stir while cooking for a minute. Pour this over the onions. Heat the rest of the oil in the same pan over medium-high heat. Add a teaspoon of thyme and mushrooms. Cook until the liquid is absorbed almost completely, for 8-10 minutes while stirring. Add onions. Turn the heat off. Put the lid on. Set aside.
- Set oven to preheat at 400°F. Unfold the puff pastry. Roll it on a floured flat surface, until you form a 12-inch square. Slice it into a 12x6-inch rectangles. Place them on a baking sheet. Score the pastries a half inch from the edges with a sharp knife, taking care not to cut through. Poke holes into the pastry with a fork. Bake until it's lightly browned and puffed, for 10-12 minutes. Take out of the oven. Use a spoon to press it down lightly if needed. Lower the oven heat to 350°F.
- Place the mushroom mix on top of the tarts. Garnish with cheese, walnuts, and the rest of the thyme. Bake until the cheese melts, for 5 minutes more. Slice each tarts into 6 pieces.

Nutrition Information

- Calories:
- Cholesterol:
- Protein:
- Total Fat:
- Sodium:
- Fiber:
- Total Carbohydrate:

29. Onion Tarts With Balsamic Onion Jam

Serving: 6 dozen. | Prep: 01hours15mins | Cook: 10mins | Ready in:

Ingredients

- 3 large sweet onions, chopped
- 1/2 cup butter, divided
- 5 bay leaves, divided
- 2 small sage sprigs, divided
- 2 fresh thyme sprigs, divided
- 4 garlic cloves, minced
- 1/4 cup balsamic vinegar
- 3 tablespoons brown sugar
- 2 tablespoons molasses
- 1 package (17.3 ounces) frozen puff pastry, thawed
- 3/4 cup grated Parmesan cheese

Direction

- In a big pan, sauté onions in 1/4 cup butter until tender. Toss in 1 sprig of sage, 1 sprig of thyme and 3 bay leaves. Turn heat down to medium-low and cook for 30 to 40 seconds until onions turned deep golden brown. Stir occasionally while it cooks. Stir in garlic and cook for another 2 minutes. Remove sage, thyme and bay leaves. Allow mixture to cool a bit.
- Transfer onion mixture to a food processor; cover and pulse until well-blended. Pour to a small pot and add brown sugar, vinegar, molasses and the rest of the butter, bay leaves, thyme and sage. Cook until it boils, then continue cooking for about 10 minutes until thickened. Remove sage, thyme and bay leaves.
- Roll our puff pastry and cut into squares, about 1 1/2 inches each. Arrange squares on greased baking sheets and put a little teaspoonful of onion mixture in the center of each square. Top with 1/2 teaspoon cheese.
- Bake for 10 to 15 minutes at 400°F or until golden brown. Serve while it's still warm or at room temperature.

Nutrition Information

- Calories: 57 calories
- Fiber: 1g fiber)
- Total Carbohydrate: 6g carbohydrate (2g sugars
- Cholesterol: 4mg cholesterol

- Protein: 1g protein.
- Total Fat: 3g fat (1g saturated fat)
- Sodium: 46mg sodium

- Total Carbohydrate: 8g carbohydrate (2g sugars
- Cholesterol: 13mg cholesterol
- Protein: 2g protein.
- Total Fat: 7g fat (3g saturated fat)
- Sodium: 178mg sodium

30. Pancetta, Pear & Pecan Puffs

Serving: 2 dozen. | Prep: 25mins | Cook: 10mins | Ready in:

Ingredients

- 1 sheet frozen puff pastry, thawed
- 6 ounces cream cheese, softened
- 2 tablespoons honey
- 1/8 teaspoon salt
- 1/8 teaspoon pepper
- 1/4 cup (1 ounce) crumbled fresh goat cheese
- 3 tablespoons crumbled crisp pancetta or crumbled cooked bacon
- 3 tablespoons finely chopped peeled ripe pear
- 2 tablespoons finely chopped pecans, toasted

Direction

- Preheat oven to 400 degrees F. Roll out the pastry dough onto a lightly floured work area. Slice the dough into 24 circles with 1-3/4-inch round cookie cutter. Place the circles into a baking sheet lined with parchment paper. Bake for 10 to 12 minutes, until pastries are golden brown. Transfer onto wire racks to completely cool.
- While waiting, whisk the salt, cream cheese, pepper, and honey until well incorporated. Add in the goat cheese, pecans, pancetta, and pear; fold.
- Split each cooled pastry in half and scoop the cream cheese mixture onto the bottom of pastry halves. Cover with the top halves and serve on room temperature.

Nutrition Information

- Calories: 105 calories
- Fiber: 1g fiber)

31. Pesto Twists

Serving: 12 servings. | Prep: 15mins | Cook: 10mins | Ready in:

Ingredients

- 1 package (17.3 ounces) frozen puff pastry, thawed
- 1/2 cup prepared pesto
- 1/2 cup shredded Parmesan cheese

Direction

- Prepare the oven and preheat to 400°.
- Place the puff pastry sheets on a floured surface and unfold it. Form each sheet into 12-inches square. Fill one pastry sheet with pesto and spread it to within 1/4-inch of edges. Sprinkle cheese on its top. Top the layer with the remaining pastry. Cut the sheet into 12 1-inch wide strips. Turn each strip 4 times. Arrange and press the strips into the parchment paper-lined baking pan, positioning them 2-inches apart from each other, pressing down ends.
- Let it bake inside the oven until golden brown, about 12-15 minutes. Serve while hot.

Nutrition Information

- Calories: 265 calories
- Sodium: 270mg sodium
- Fiber: 3g fiber)
- Total Carbohydrate: 24g carbohydrate (0 sugars
- Cholesterol: 6mg cholesterol
- Protein: 6g protein.

- Total Fat: 17g fat (4g saturated fat)

Serving: 2 dozen. | Prep: 15mins | Cook: 15mins | Ready in:

Ingredients

- 1 package (17.30 ounces) frozen puff pastry, thawed
- 1 large egg
- 1 tablespoon water
- 1/4 cup prepared pesto
- 1/2 cup feta or goat cheese, crumbled
- 1/4 cup oil-packed sun-dried tomatoes, patted dry and finely chopped

Direction

- Preheat oven to 400 degrees F. Roll out one sheet of puff pastry. Beat water and egg, then brush over the pastry. Use half of the pesto to spread. Season with 1/2 sun-dried tomatoes and 1/2 of feta.
- In jelly-roll style, roll up the right and left corners towards the middle until they meet at the center. Do the same procedure with the rest of the pastry sheet and other ingredients. Store in freezer until firm, about 30 minutes.
- Slice each of the rolls crosswise, making 12 pieces. Prepare baking sheets by lining them with parchment paper. Bake palmiers for about 15 minutes until crisp and golden.

Nutrition Information

- Calories: 121 calories
- Sodium: 126mg sodium
- Fiber: 2g fiber)
- Total Carbohydrate: 12g carbohydrate (0 sugars
- Cholesterol: 9mg cholesterol
- Protein: 2g protein.
- Total Fat: 7g fat (2g saturated fat)

Serving: 2 dozen. | Prep: 30mins | Cook: 15mins | Ready in:

Ingredients

- 1 package (17.3 ounces) frozen puff pastry, thawed
- 1 egg
- 1 tablespoon water
- 4 ounces cream cheese, softened
- 1 cup (4 ounces) crumbled feta cheese
- 1/2 cup minced fresh parsley
- 1/2 cup prepared pesto
- 24 pimiento pieces

Direction

- On a lightly floured working area, roll out the pastry sheets. Using a floured 3 1/2-inch leaf-shaped cookie cutter, carve out 12 leaves from each of the sheets. Prepare an ungreased baking sheet; transfer the leaves. Draw veins in leaves using a toothpick. Whisk the water and egg in a small bowl and brush mixture over the pastry.
- Bake for 12 to 14 minutes, at 400 degrees F or until golden brown. Transfer to wire racks for cooling.
- Mix the parsley, pesto, and cheeses in a large bowl. Divide the pastry leaves in half. Put 1 tablespoon of cheese mixture on the bottom halves; replace tops. For a holly berry, place a piece of pimiento on each. Keep leftovers in the refrigerator.

Nutrition Information

- Calories:
- Total Fat:
- Sodium:
- Fiber:
- Total Carbohydrate:

- Cholesterol:
- Protein:

34. Puff Pastry Stars

Serving: 10 appetizers. | Prep: 20mins | Cook: 10mins | Ready in:

Ingredients

- 1 frozen puff pastry, thawed
- 2 tablespoons canola oil
- 1 tablespoon ranch salad dressing mix
- 3 tablespoons shredded Parmesan cheese

Direction

- Roll out puff pastry. Combine dressing mix and oil in a small bowl. Brush pastry with the oil mixture. Carve out 10 stars from the sheet using a 3-inch star-shaped floured cookie cutter. Arrange stars on a greased baking sheet. Sprinkle cheese on top.
- Bake for 7 to 9 minutes at 400°F or until golden brown and puffy. Serve while still warm.

Nutrition Information

- Calories: 60 calories
- Protein: 1g protein. Diabetic Exchanges: 1/2 starch
- Total Fat: 4g fat (1g saturated fat)
- Sodium: 123mg sodium
- Fiber: 1g fiber)
- Total Carbohydrate: 6g carbohydrate (0 sugars
- Cholesterol: 1mg cholesterol

35. Puffy Lobster Turnovers

Serving: 16 appetizers. | Prep: 15mins | Cook: 10mins | Ready in:

Ingredients

- 1 cup chopped fresh lobster meat
- 1/4 cup finely chopped onion
- 1 teaspoon minced fresh basil
- 1 teaspoon minced fresh thyme
- 1 teaspoon paprika
- 1 garlic clove, minced
- 1 teaspoon tomato paste
- 1/8 teaspoon salt
- 1/8 teaspoon pepper
- 2 packages (17.3 ounces each) frozen puff pastry, thawed
- 1 egg, lightly beaten

Direction

- In a small pan, mix the first nine ingredients and sauté for 4 to 5 minutes over medium heat or until lobster is opaque and firm. Set side.
- Roll out puff pastry and carve out 4 circles with a 4-in. round cookie cutter. Place circles on greased baking sheet. Do the same for the rest of the pastries. In the center of each circle, place 1 tablespoon lobster mixture. Brush edges with egg and fold dough over filling. Seal the edges by pressing them together.
- Bake for 8 to 10 minutes at 400°F or until golden brown and puffed. Serve while it's still warm.

Nutrition Information

- Calories: 167 calories
- Total Carbohydrate: 18g carbohydrate (0 sugars
- Cholesterol: 20mg cholesterol
- Protein: 5g protein.
- Total Fat: 9g fat (2g saturated fat)
- Sodium: 160mg sodium
- Fiber: 2g fiber)

36. Puffy Sausage Mummies

Serving: 8 servings. | Prep: 15mins | Cook: 15mins | Ready in:

Ingredients

- 1 sheet frozen puff pastry
- 2 tablespoons honey mustard
- 4 fully cooked spicy chicken sausage links (3 ounces each), cut in half lengthwise
- 1 egg
- 1-1/2 teaspoons water
- Mustard

Direction

- Thaw the puff pastries for 40 minutes at room temperature. Unfold them on a surface that's been floured lightly. Roll them into a 16x12-inch rectangle. Apply mustard. Slice into eight 16x1 1/2 inch strips. Wrap each sausage with one pastry strip.
- Arrange them an inch apart on a baking sheet, ungreased. Mix egg and water in a bowl, and use this to brush over the pastries. Bake for 15-17 minutes at 400°F, until golden brown. Use mustard to add faces.

Nutrition Information

- Calories:
- Fiber:
- Total Carbohydrate:
- Cholesterol:
- Protein:
- Total Fat:
- Sodium:

37. Reuben Rounds

Serving: 16 appetizers | Prep: 10mins | Cook: 20mins | Ready in:

Ingredients

- 1 sheet frozen puff pastry, thawed
- 6 slices Swiss cheese
- 5 slices deli corned beef
- 1/2 cup sauerkraut, rinsed and well drained
- 1 teaspoon caraway seeds
- 1/4 cup Thousand Island salad dressing

Direction

- Preheat oven to 400°F. Roll out puff pastry and arrange layers of corned beef, sauerkraut and cheese to within 1/2 in. of the edges. Roll up the pastry like a jelly roll and shear off ends. Slice the roll crosswise into 16 pieces. Transfer rolls on greased baking sheets with cut side down. Dust with caraway seeds.
- Bake in the oven until golden brown, 18 to 20 minutes. Place salad dressing on the side when serving.

Nutrition Information

- Calories: 114 calories
- Cholesterol: 8mg cholesterol
- Protein: 3g protein.
- Total Fat: 7g fat (2g saturated fat)
- Sodium: 198mg sodium
- Fiber: 1g fiber)
- Total Carbohydrate: 10g carbohydrate (1g sugars

38. Sage & Prosciutto Pinwheels

Serving: 3 dozen. | Prep: 15mins | Cook: 15mins | Ready in:

Ingredients

- 1 package (17.3 ounces) frozen puff pastry, thawed
- 1/4 cup honey mustard
- 1 cup shredded Gruyere or Swiss cheese
- 8 thin slices prosciutto or deli ham, chopped
- 2 tablespoons chopped fresh sage

Direction

- Preheat oven to 400 degrees F. Roll out one sheet of pastry and add 2 tablespoons of mustard within 1/2 inch edges; spread. Top with 1/2 cup of cheese; spread with half of sage and chopped prosciutto. In a jelly roll style, roll up the pastry. Slice into 18 pieces, crosswise with a serrated knife.
- Transfer onto a greased baking sheet, placing seam side down. Do the same procedure with the rest of the ingredients. Bake for 12 to 15 minutes until golden brown. Serve while warm. For freezing option: Freeze with cover the unbaked rolls placed on a baking sheet lined with waxed paper until firm. Prepare resealable plastic freezer bag; transfer firm rolls and put back into the freezer. To use, leave rolls at room temperature for about 10 minutes. Slice and bake the pinwheels as directed; cook longer as needed.

Nutrition Information

- Calories: 90 calories
- Protein: 3g protein.
- Total Fat: 5g fat (2g saturated fat)
- Sodium: 131mg sodium
- Fiber: 1g fiber)
- Total Carbohydrate: 8g carbohydrate (1g sugars
- Cholesterol: 6mg cholesterol

39. Savory Pear Tarts

Serving: 50 appetizers. | Prep: 30mins | Cook: 10mins | Ready in:

Ingredients

- 2 shallots, thinly sliced
- 1/4 cup orange juice
- 1/4 cup balsamic vinegar
- 1/4 cup honey
- 2 tablespoons sugar
- 1 tablespoon lemon juice
- 1 garlic clove, minced
- 1/8 teaspoon salt
- 1/8 teaspoon pepper
- 2 Bosc pears, halved and sliced
- 1 package (17.3 ounces) frozen puff pastry, thawed
- 1/3 cup crumbled blue cheese
- Chopped glazed pecans, optional

Direction

- In a small pot, mix the first nine ingredients together. Cook to a boil over medium heat then continue cooking until half of the liquid evaporates. Stir in pears and cook for another 6 to 8 minutes or until pears soften.
- While the filling cooks, spread out puff pastry and roll each into a square, 10 inches in size. Carve out 25 discs from each of the squares using a 2-inch round cookie cutter. Arrange discs on a greased baking sheet and bake for 7 to 9 minutes at 400°F until golden brown.
- On each of the pastries, place a dollop of the pear mixture and top with cheese. You can also garnish with pecans if desired.

Nutrition Information

- Calories:
- Fiber:
- Total Carbohydrate:
- Cholesterol:
- Protein:
- Total Fat:
- Sodium:

40. Shrimp Napoleons

Serving: 3 dozen. | Prep: 20mins | Cook: 15mins | Ready in:

Ingredients

- 1 package (17.3 ounces) frozen puff pastry, thawed
- 6 ounces cream cheese, softened
- 1 tablespoon thinly sliced green onion
- 1 tablespoon Dijon mustard
- 1 teaspoon Worcestershire sauce
- 2-1/2 cups chopped cooked peeled shrimp
- 1/3 cup finely shredded carrot
- 4 bacon strips, cooked and crumbled

Direction

- Prepare 2 baking sheets and line them with parchment paper. Roll out puff pastry on a lightly floured work area. Divide sheet into 9 squares, about 3 inches, then cut each square in half, creating 18 rectangles.
- Arrange pastries on the prepared baking sheet. Bake for 12 to 15 minutes at 425°F or until golden brown and puffy. Transfer to a wire rack to cool.
- Combine onion, cream cheese, Worcestershire sauce and mustard in a small bowl. Stir until well blended. Toss in carrot, bacon and shrimp.
- When assembling, split each pastry across in half using a fork. Put a rounded tablespoonful of cream cheese mixture over the bottom halves and cover with the other half. Keep chilled until it's time to serve.

Nutrition Information

- Calories: 99 calories
- Total Fat: 6g fat (2g saturated fat)
- Sodium: 98mg sodium
- Fiber: 1g fiber)
- Total Carbohydrate: 8g carbohydrate (0 sugars
- Cholesterol: 21mg cholesterol
- Protein: 4g protein.

41. Shrimp And Pineapple Party Pizza

Serving: 24 servings. | Prep: 40mins | Cook: 20mins | Ready in:

Ingredients

- 2 sheets frozen puff pastry, thawed
- 1 pound uncooked shrimp (31-40 per pound), peeled and deveined
- 1 can (8 ounces) unsweetened pineapple tidbits, drained and juice reserved
- 6 thick-sliced bacon strips, apple- or maple-smoked
- 1 small green pepper, diced
- 1/4 teaspoon salt
- 1/4 teaspoon pepper
- 1/4 cup hoisin sauce
- 1 carton (8 ounces) spreadable chive and onion cream cheese
- 1 cup shredded Parmesan cheese, plus more for topping

Direction

- Preheat oven to 400 degrees F. Roll out and slice pastry sheet in half on a lightly floured area. Form each half into 10x6 inch rectangle then transfer on a baking sheet. Form a rim by folding under 1/4 inch of the edges. Use a fork to pierce the middle portion of the pastry. Do the same procedure with the rest of the pastry sheet. Bake pastry for about 12 minutes, until the crust turns golden. Meanwhile, marinate the shrimp in the juice of the pineapple tidbits.
- In the meantime, cook and stir the bacon occasionally in a large pan over medium-low heat until crispy, about 12 minutes. Use a slotted spoon to remove bacon from skillet and transfer onto paper towels to drain oil. Scoop 1 1/2 tablespoons drippings; set aside.
- Using medium-high heat, heat 1 teaspoon drippings in a pan. Toss in pepper and cook until crispy and tender for about 4 minutes. Take out from pan. Drain the shrimp and place into pan with the leftover drippings of

bacon. Season with the pepper and salt. Stir and cook shrimp until pink for about 2 minutes. Take out from the heat and pour in the hoisin sauce.

- Sprinkle puff pastries with cream cheese. Arrange shrimp evenly on top of the cream cheese. Add green pepper and bacon over the shrimp. Squeeze the pineapple tidbits with paper towels to dry; spread over the pizza. Top with Parmesan cheese.
- Bake for about 10 minutes, until crust turns brown and cheese melts. Set aside briefly then slice each of the pastry into six rectangles. Add more Parmesan cheese on top, if desired.

Nutrition Information

- Calories: 222 calories
- Protein: 8g protein.
- Total Fat: 14g fat (5g saturated fat)
- Sodium: 321mg sodium
- Fiber: 2g fiber)
- Total Carbohydrate: 16g carbohydrate (3g sugars
- Cholesterol: 38mg cholesterol

42. Smoked Salmon Bites With Shallot Sauce

Serving: 25 appetizers. | Prep: 15mins | Cook: 15mins | Ready in:

Ingredients

- 1 sheet frozen puff pastry, thawed
- SAUCE:
- 2 shallots
- 2 tablespoons Dijon mustard
- 1 tablespoon mayonnaise
- 1 tablespoon red wine vinegar
- 1/4 cup olive oil
- FINISHING:
- 1 cup fresh arugula or baby spinach, coarsely chopped

- 4-1/2 ounces smoked salmon or lox, thinly sliced
- 1/2 cup shaved Asiago cheese

Direction

- Preheat oven to 400 degrees F. Roll out the pastry and slice out 25 squares. Prepare greased baking sheets and transfer pastries. Bake for 11 to 13 minutes, until golden brown.
- While waiting, grate one of the shallots and finely slice the other. Mix the mustard, vinegar, shallots, and mayonnaise in a small bowl. Add oil gradually in a steady stream while beating. Scoop a small amount of the sauce onto each pastry. Add layers of salmon and arugula. Pour in the rest of the sauce and top with cheese.

Nutrition Information

- Calories:
- Protein:
- Total Fat:
- Sodium:
- Fiber:
- Total Carbohydrate:
- Cholesterol:

43. Smoky Pecan Puffs

Serving: 81 appetizers. | Prep: 30mins | Cook: 10mins | Ready in:

Ingredients

- 1 sheet frozen puff pastry, thawed
- 1 egg
- 1 tablespoon water
- 1 tablespoon poppy seeds
- 1 package (8 ounces) cream cheese, softened
- 2 tablespoons sherry
- 1/2 teaspoon liquid smoke, optional
- 1/4 cup finely chopped pecans

- 1 tablespoon finely chopped onion

Direction

- Roll out the puff pastry and slice into 1-inch squares. Prepare a baking sheet by lining with parchment paper and put the pastries on the surface. Beat the water and egg and brush onto the squares. Bake for 8 to 10 minutes at 400 degrees F until golden brown.
- Mix the sherry, Liquid Smoke (if desired), and cream cheese in a small bowl. Toss in onions and pecans.
- Divide each of the squares horizontally. Place 3/4 teaspoon of cream cheese mixture on the squares. Replace the tops.

Nutrition Information

- Calories: 29 calories
- Fiber: 0 fiber)
- Total Carbohydrate: 2g carbohydrate (0 sugars
- Cholesterol: 6mg cholesterol
- Protein: 1g protein.
- Total Fat: 2g fat (1g saturated fat)
- Sodium: 19mg sodium

44. Spanakopita Pinwheels

Serving: 2 dozen. | Prep: 30mins | Cook: 20mins | Ready in:

Ingredients

- 1 medium onion, finely chopped
- 2 tablespoons olive oil
- 1 teaspoon dried oregano
- 1 garlic clove, minced
- 2 packages (10 ounces each) frozen chopped spinach, thawed and squeezed dry
- 2 cups (8 ounces) crumbled feta cheese
- 2 eggs, lightly beaten
- 1 package (17.3 ounces) frozen puff pastry, thawed

Direction

- Stir-fry the onions in oil on a small pan until tender. Toss in the garlic and oregano and cook for another minute. Stir in spinach and cook for 3 minutes more until liquid has evaporated. Place into a large bowl and allow to cool.
- Add eggs and feta cheese into the spinach mixture until well blended. Roll out puff pastry. Place half of the spinach mixture on the surface to within 1/2 inch of edges. In jelly-roll style, roll up the sheets. Slice each of the sheets into 12 pieces, 3/4 inch in size. Transfer into the greased baking sheets, seam side down.
- Bake for about 18 to 22 minutes at 400 degrees F, until golden brown. Serve while warm.

Nutrition Information

- Calories: 197 calories
- Cholesterol: 39mg cholesterol
- Protein: 7g protein.
- Total Fat: 13g fat (5g saturated fat)
- Sodium: 392mg sodium
- Fiber: 3g fiber)
- Total Carbohydrate: 14g carbohydrate (1g sugars

45. Spicy Crab Salad Tapas

Serving: about 2 dozen. | Prep: 35mins | Cook: 20mins | Ready in:

Ingredients

- 1 can (16 ounces) lump crabmeat, drained
- 1/4 cup finely chopped sweet red pepper
- 1/4 cup finely chopped sweet yellow pepper
- 1/4 cup finely chopped green onions
- 1 jalapeno pepper, seeded and finely chopped
- 1 tablespoon minced fresh cilantro
- 1 tablespoon lemon juice
- 2 garlic cloves, minced

- 1 teaspoon ground mustard
- 1/2 cup mayonnaise
- 1/2 teaspoon salt
- 1/4 teaspoon pepper
- 1 package (17.30 ounces) frozen puff pastry, thawed
- 1 large egg
- 1 tablespoon water
- Minced fresh parsley and seafood seasoning, optional

Direction

- Preheat oven to 375 degrees F. Mix the first 12 ingredients together. Cover and keep in the refrigerator for 1 hour.
- While waiting, roll out the puff pastry onto the lightly floured work area. Roll each of the pastry into a 10-inch square. Slice pastry to make twenty-five 2-inch squares (fifty pieces in total). Carve out the middles of half of the puff pastry squares with a round 1 1/2-inch cookie cutter. Beat the water and egg then brush over pastry. Put the sliced-out squares over the solid squares and place into the prepared baking sheets lined with parchment paper.
- Bake for about 18 minutes until golden brown. Let them cool to room temperature. When already cool, scoop 1 heaping tablespoon of the crab salad onto the middle of each baked pastry. Sprinkle with minced parsley and seasoning on top, if desired. Serve immediately.

Nutrition Information

- Calories: 145 calories
- Total Fat: 9g fat (2g saturated fat)
- Sodium: 240mg sodium
- Fiber: 2g fiber)
- Total Carbohydrate: 11g carbohydrate (0 sugars
- Cholesterol: 25mg cholesterol
- Protein: 5g protein.

46. Taco Puff Pastries

Serving: 80 appetizers. | Prep: 45mins | Cook: 10mins | Ready in:

Ingredients

- 2 pounds ground beef
- 1 large onion, chopped
- 4 garlic cloves, minced
- 2 envelopes taco seasoning
- 1/2 teaspoon pepper
- 2 cans (8 ounces each) tomato sauce
- 2 cans (4 ounces each) chopped green chilies
- 2 packages (17.3 ounces each) frozen puff pastry, thawed
- 2 egg whites
- 1 tablespoon water
- 1/2 cup grated Parmesan cheese

Direction

- Preheat oven to 400 degrees. Cook the onion, beef, and garlic in a large skillet for 8 to 10 minutes over medium heat until the beef is no longer pinkish while crushing beef into crumbles. Drain the beef. Add in the tomato sauce, pepper, chilies, and taco seasoning. Allow to cool thoroughly.
- On a lightly floured work area, roll out a sheet of puff pastry. Form the sheet into a rectangle with a 15x2-inch dimension. Slice into twenty pieces of 3-inch squares. Scoop 1 rounded tablespoon of beef mixture into the middle of each square. Brush the pastry edges with water. Fold the pastry over the filling and mold over the filling, creating a triangle. Use a fork to pinch the edges to seal. Prepare ungreased baking sheets and transfer pastries. Do the same procedure with the rest of the filling and pastry.
- Beat water and egg whites into a small bowl; brush on top of pastries. Top with cheese and bake for 10 to 14 minutes until golden brown. Serve while warm.

Nutrition Information

- Calories: 86 calories
- Total Carbohydrate: 8g carbohydrate (0 sugars
- Cholesterol: 6mg cholesterol
- Protein: 3g protein.
- Total Fat: 4g fat (1g saturated fat)
- Sodium: 174mg sodium
- Fiber: 1g fiber)

Chapter 2: Brie Puff Pastry Appetizer Recipes

***

47. Brie Cherry Pastry Cups

Serving: 3 dozen. | Prep: 25mins | Cook: 5mins | Ready in:

Ingredients

- 1 sheet frozen puff pastry, thawed
- 1/2 cup cherry preserves
- 4 ounces Brie cheese, cut into 1/2-inch cubes
- 1/4 cup chopped pecans or walnuts
- 2 tablespoons minced chives

Direction

- Roll out puff pastry and slice into 36 squares. Press squares carefully onto the bottoms of 36 greased mini muffin cups.
- Bake for 10 minutes at 375 °F. Create a hollow in the center of each cups with the end of a wooden spoon handle, making a 1/2-inch deep dent. Bake for another 6 to 8 minutes until golden brown. Press the squares down again using the handle of a spoon.

- Scoop and round 1/2 teaspoonful of the preserves and place into each cup. Put cheese on top and sprinkle with chives and nuts. Bake until cheese is melted, 3 to 5 minutes.

Nutrition Information

- Calories: 61 calories
- Total Carbohydrate: 7g carbohydrate (3g sugars
- Cholesterol: 3mg cholesterol
- Protein: 1g protein.
- Total Fat: 3g fat (1g saturated fat)
- Sodium: 42mg sodium
- Fiber: 1g fiber)

48. Brie Puff Pastry

Serving: 10 servings. | Prep: 15mins | Cook: 20mins | Ready in:

Ingredients

- 1 round (13.2 ounces) Brie cheese
- 1/2 cup crumbled blue cheese
- 1 sheet frozen puff pastry, thawed
- 1/4 cup apricot jam
- 1/2 cup slivered almonds, toasted
- 1 large egg, lightly beaten
- Assorted crackers

Direction

- Preheat oven to 400 degrees F. Slice the Brie in half, horizontally. Spread blue cheese at the bottom half and replace the top.
- Roll the pastry into 14-inch square on a lightly floured working area. Form a circle by trimming the sides. Scoop the jam and spread at the middle of the pastry. Top with almonds over and sprinkle with Brie.
- Brush the sides of the pastry lightly with whisked eggs. Fold the pastry over cheese while pinching the corners to seal. Cut out excess pastry.

- Prepare an ungreased sheet and transfer pastry, seam side down. Brush the pastry with the whisked egg. Bake for about 20 to 25 minutes, or until golden brown.
- Quickly take out from the pan and transfer into a serving plate. Let cool for 45 minutes. Serve along with the crackers.

Nutrition Information

- Calories: 328 calories
- Sodium: 424mg sodium
- Fiber: 2g fiber)
- Total Carbohydrate: 20g carbohydrate (3g sugars
- Cholesterol: 64mg cholesterol
- Protein: 13g protein.
- Total Fat: 22g fat (10g saturated fat)

49. Brie In Puff Pastry

Serving: 8-10 servings. | Prep: 10mins | Cook: 20mins | Ready in:

Ingredients

- 1 sheet frozen puff pastry, thawed
- 1/4 cup apricot jam
- 1 round (13.2 ounces) Brie cheese
- 1 egg
- 1 tablespoon water
- Apple slices

Direction

- Roll puff pastry to create a square, about 14 inches. Place jam in the center of the pastry, up to about 4 1/2 in. circle. Top with cheese. Fold pastry around cheese, removing any excess dough. Seal edges by pinching them, then transfer pastry on ungreased baking sheet, seam side down. Beat water and egg together and brush pastry with the egg wash mixture.
- Create decorative shapes out of the trimmed pastry pieces and arrange them on top. If

desired, you can also brush them with egg wash. Bake for 20 to 25 minutes at 400°F until puffed and golden brown. Garnish with apple slices and serve warm.

Nutrition Information

- Calories: 272 calories
- Cholesterol: 59mg cholesterol
- Protein: 10g protein.
- Total Fat: 17g fat (8g saturated fat)
- Sodium: 326mg sodium
- Fiber: 2g fiber)
- Total Carbohydrate: 19g carbohydrate (5g sugars

50. Brie Apple Pastry Bites

Serving: 4 dozen. | Prep: 30mins | Cook: 15mins | Ready in:

Ingredients

- 1 package (17.3 ounces) frozen puff pastry, thawed
- 1 round (8 ounces) Brie cheese, cut into 1/2-inch cubes
- 1 medium apple, chopped
- 2/3 cup sliced almonds
- 1/2 cup chopped walnuts
- 1/4 cup dried cranberries
- Ground nutmeg

Direction

- Roll out the puff pastry and slice 24 squares on each sheet. Press squares gently on the bottoms of the 48 greased mini muffin cups.
- Mix the nuts, cheese, cranberries, and apples. Scoop mixture into the cups. Bake for 12-15 minutes at 375 degrees F, until the cheese melts. Top with nutmeg.

Nutrition Information

- Calories: 85 calories
- Protein: 2g protein.
- Total Fat: 6g fat (2g saturated fat)
- Sodium: 63mg sodium
- Fiber: 1g fiber)
- Total Carbohydrate: 7g carbohydrate (1g sugars
- Cholesterol: 5mg cholesterol

- Cholesterol: 27mg cholesterol
- Protein: 6g protein.
- Total Fat: 13g fat (5g saturated fat)
- Sodium: 193mg sodium
- Fiber: 2g fiber)
- Total Carbohydrate: 15g carbohydrate (2g sugars

51. Cranberry Brie Pecan Pinwheels

Serving: about 2 dozen. | Prep: 20mins | Cook: 15mins | Ready in:

Ingredients

- 1 pound Brie cheese, rind removed
- 1 package (17.3 ounces) frozen puff pastry, thawed
- 2/3 cup whole-berry cranberry sauce
- 1 large egg
- 1 tablespoon water
- 1/2 cup chopped pecans

Direction

- Preheat oven to 400 degrees F. On medium setting, beat the trimmed Brie until creamy and smooth for about 5 minutes.
- Roll out the puff pastry onto a lightly floured work area. Scatter half of the Brie within 1/2 inch of the corners. Pour half of cranberry sauce over Brie. In jelly-roll style, roll up pastry beginning with the short side. Slice into 12 pieces, crosswise. Transfer pastries into prepared baking sheets lined with parchment paper. Beat water and egg then brush over the pastries. Top with chopped pecans. Do the same procedure with the rest of the puff pastry. Bake for 15 to 20 minutes, or until golden brown.

Nutrition Information

- Calories: 193 calories

52. Fruit 'n' Almond Stuffed Brie

Serving: 8 servings. | Prep: 30mins | Cook: 30mins | Ready in:

Ingredients

- 2/3 cup sliced almonds
- 1/3 cup chopped dried apricots
- 1/4 cup brandy
- 1 sheet frozen puff pastry, thawed
- 1 round (8 ounces) Brie cheese, rind removed
- 1 egg, lightly beaten
- RASPBERRY SAUCE:
- 1/2 cup sugar
- 1 tablespoon cornstarch
- 1/2 cup cold water
- 2 cups fresh or frozen raspberries
- Assorted crackers

Direction

- Mix apricots, almonds and brandy in a small pot with high sides. Cook over medium-low heat, stirring occasionally, until liquid is almost gone. Take pot off the heat and set aside.
- Roll out puff pastry on a lightly floured work area into an 11-inch by 9-inch rectangle. Cut cheese across in half and put one half in the middle of pastry. Spread half of the almond mixture over it, sprinkle with the remaining cheese and top with the rest of the almond mixture.
- Pull edges of the pastry around cheese to enclose it. Cut off excess dough and seal edges by pressing them together. Set pastry on

ungreased baking sheet, seam side down. Brush with egg.

- Bake for 30 to 35 minutes at 375°F until golden brown and puffy.
- Mix in water, cornstarch and sugar in a small pot, and stir until smooth. Toss in raspberries and bring to a boil over medium heat, stir continuously. Cook for another minute, while stirring, until sauce thickens slightly. Pour through a strainer to remove the seeds then transfer sauce to a small bowl or pitcher. Serve crackers and stuffed Brie with the raspberry sauce on the side.

Nutrition Information

- Calories: 397 calories
- Total Carbohydrate: 40g carbohydrate (17g sugars
- Cholesterol: 55mg cholesterol
- Protein: 11g protein.
- Total Fat: 21g fat (7g saturated fat)
- Sodium: 292mg sodium
- Fiber: 6g fiber)

53. Ham & Brie Pastries

Serving: 16 pastries. | Prep: 15mins | Cook: 15mins |Ready in:

Ingredients

- 1 sheet frozen puff pastry, thawed
- 1/3 cup apricot preserves
- 4 slices deli ham, quartered
- 8 ounces Brie cheese, cut into 16 pieces

Direction

- Preheat oven to 400 degrees F. Roll out the puff pastry on a lightly floured working area. Form the pastry into a 12-inch square then slice in sixteen 3-inch squares. Add 1 teaspoon of preserves at the middle of each square, then add ham on top while folding as needed;

sprinkle with cheese. Overlap the two pastry edges over the filling and tightly press to seal.

- Prepare a baking sheet by lining with the parchment paper. Bake for 15 to 20 minutes until pastries are golden brown. Let pastries cool on the pan for 5 minutes. Serve. Transfer freeze cooled pastries into the freezer container and separate the layers using a waxed paper. To use, reheat the pastries on a baking sheet in an oven preheated to 400 degrees; bake until thoroughly heated.

Nutrition Information

- Calories: 144 calories
- Sodium: 192mg sodium
- Fiber: 1g fiber)
- Total Carbohydrate: 13g carbohydrate (3g sugars
- Cholesterol: 17mg cholesterol
- Protein: 5g protein.
- Total Fat: 8g fat (3g saturated fat)

54. Mummy Wrapped Brie

Serving: 10 servings. | Prep: 10mins | Cook: 20mins |Ready in:

Ingredients

- 1 package (17.3 ounces) frozen puff pastry, thawed
- 1/4 cup apricot jam
- 1 round (16 ounces) Brie cheese
- 1 large egg
- 1 tablespoon water
- Apple slices
- 2 dried cranberries or raisins

Direction

- Preheat oven to 400°F. Spread out one sheet of puff pastry on a lightly floured work area and roll it into a 14-in. square. Remove the corners to turn pastry sheet into a circle. In the center of the pastry, spread jam into a 4 1/2 in. circle. Put Brie on top then fold pastry over cheese. Seal edges by pinching it and trim as necessary. Whisk water and egg together and brush pastry with the egg wash.

- Transfer pastry on an ungreased baking sheet with seam side down. Roll the rest of the pastry into a square, about 14 inches. Cut into 1-inch strips, 4 pieces, then cut each strip across in half. Wrap strips around Brie, pruning as needed, discard any scraps. Bake in the oven for 10 minutes then brush again with egg wash. Continue baking for another 10 to 15 minutes until golden brown. Carve out two circles from apple slices and arrange on top of Brie to make the eyes. Put a dried cranberry on top of each circle. Garnish with apple slices and serve warm.

Nutrition Information

- Calories: 372 calories
- Total Fat: 24g fat (10g saturated fat)
- Sodium: 426mg sodium
- Fiber: 3g fiber)
- Total Carbohydrate: 28g carbohydrate (4g sugars
- Cholesterol: 64mg cholesterol
- Protein: 13g protein.

55. Mushroom Stuffed Baked Brie

Serving: 8 servings. | Prep: 30mins | Cook: 30mins | Ready in:

Ingredients

- 2 tablespoons butter
- 1 tablespoon olive oil
- 1/2 pound sliced fresh mushrooms
- 1 small onion, finely chopped
- 3 garlic cloves, minced
- 1 teaspoon dried thyme
- 1 teaspoon dried rosemary, crushed

- 1/8 teaspoon seasoned salt
- 1/8 teaspoon pepper
- 1 sheet frozen puff pastry, thawed
- 1 round (8 ounces) Brie cheese, halved horizontally
- 1 large egg, lightly beaten

Direction

- Preheat oven to 400°F. In a big pan set over medium-high heat, heat butter and oil. Toss in mushroom and onion and sauté until golden brown, 6 to 8 minutes. Stir in garlic and season to taste. Cook for another minute. Take pan off the heat then pour mixture to a bowl. Chill in the refrigerator.
- Roll our puff pastry on a lightly floured work area. Set one Brie half on pastry, with cut side up. Spread mushroom mixture and remaining Brie half on top, cut side down. Fold pastry up over cheese and press the edges on top to seal. Arrange pastry on an ungreased baking tray, seam side down. Brush egg on the sides and top of the pastry. Bake for 30 to 35 minutes until browned and puffed.

Nutrition Information

- Calories:
- Fiber:
- Total Carbohydrate:
- Cholesterol:
- Protein:
- Total Fat:
- Sodium:

56. Onion Brie Appetizers

Serving: 1-1/2 dozen. | Prep: 25mins | Cook: 15mins | Ready in:

Ingredients

- 2 medium onions, thinly sliced
- 3 tablespoons butter

- 2 tablespoons brown sugar
- 1/2 teaspoon white wine vinegar
- 1 sheet frozen puff pastry, thawed
- 4 ounces Brie cheese, rind removed, softened
- 1 to 2 teaspoons caraway seeds
- 1 large egg
- 2 teaspoons water

Direction

- In a big pan set over medium-low heat, cook butter, onions, vinegar and brown sugar. Cook and stir until onions are golden brown while stirring frequently. Use a slotted spoon to remove from the pan then let it cool to room temperature.
- Spread out puff pastry on a lightly floured work area into an 11x8-in. rectangle. Slice Brie into thin pieces and scatter evenly over pastry. Top with the onions and sprinkle caraway seeds over it.
- Take one long side of the pastry sheet and roll it up to the center of the dough. Roll up the other side until the 2 rolls meet in the middle. Cut into 1/2 inch slices using a serrated knife. Arrange rolls on baking sheets lined with parchment paper then press to flatten, about 1/4 in. thick. Chill for 15 minutes.
- Whisk water and egg in a small bowl. Brush slices with the egg wash mixture. Bake for 12 to 14 minutes at 375°F or until golden brown and puffed. Serve while it's still warm.

Nutrition Information

- Calories: 121 calories
- Total Carbohydrate: 11g carbohydrate (3g sugars
- Cholesterol: 23mg cholesterol
- Protein: 3g protein.
- Total Fat: 8g fat (3g saturated fat)
- Sodium: 109mg sodium
- Fiber: 1g fiber)

57. Peach Baked Brie

Serving: 8 servings. | Prep: 10mins | Cook: 20mins | Ready in:

Ingredients

- 1 sheet frozen puff pastry, thawed
- 1/2 cup peach or mango preserves
- 1/2 cup chopped pecans, toasted
- 1 round (8 ounces) Brie cheese
- Toasted cinnamon-raisin bread and assorted crackers

Direction

- On a lightly floured work area, spread out pastry into a 12-inch square. Remove the corners to turn it into a circle. Put the preserves in the center and spread to within an inch of pastry edge. Top with pecans then put Brie over it. Pull edges of the pastry to enclose the cheese filling. Press edges to seal.
- Transfer to an ungreased baking sheet, seam side down. Bake for 20-25 minutes at 400°F or until golden brown. Serve while still warm with toast and crackers on the side.

Nutrition Information

- Calories: 346 calories
- Total Fat: 21g fat (7g saturated fat)
- Sodium: 280mg sodium
- Fiber: 3g fiber)
- Total Carbohydrate: 31g carbohydrate (12g sugars
- Cholesterol: 28mg cholesterol
- Protein: 9g protein.

Chapter 3: Cheese

Puff Pastry Appetizer Recipes

***

58. Apple & Pecan Goat Cheese Pastries

Serving: 1-1/2 dozen. | Prep: 20mins | Cook: 15mins | Ready in:

Ingredients

- 1 large apple, peeled and finely chopped
- 1 log (4 ounces) honey-flavored fresh goat cheese
- 1/2 cup finely chopped pecans
- 1 package (17.3 ounces) frozen puff pastry, thawed
- 1/4 teaspoon ground cinnamon

Direction

- Set oven to preheat at 400°F. Mix goat cheese, apple and pecans in a bowl.
- Unfold the pastry. Slice them into 3-inch squares. Slightly separate the squares. Put four teaspoons of the apple mix in the middle of each square. Brush the edges of the pastry with water, lightly.
- Bring the 4 corners of the pastry together over the filling. Seal the seams and corners by pinching. Dust with cinnamon on top.
- Put them on greased baking sheets. Pop in the oven and bake for 15-18 minutes, or when they become golden brown. Serve while warm. Chill any leftovers.

Nutrition Information

- Calories:
- Cholesterol:
- Protein:

59. Fontina Asparagus Tart

Serving: 16 servings | Prep: 15mins | Cook: 20mins | Ready in:

Ingredients

- 1 pound fresh asparagus, trimmed
- 1 sheet frozen puff pastry, thawed
- 2 cups shredded fontina cheese
- 1 teaspoon grated lemon peel
- 2 tablespoons lemon juice
- 1 tablespoon olive oil
- 1/4 teaspoon salt
- 1/4 teaspoon pepper

Direction

- Set the oven to preheat at 400°F. Boil an inch of water in a pan. Add the asparagus and cook with cover, for 3-5 minutes, until crisp-tender. Once cooked, drain and blot dry.
- Flour a work surface lightly. Roll the pastry on the surface to make a 16x12-inch rectangle. Place it on a baking sheet lined with parchment paper. Bake for 10 minutes, until golden brown.
- Put 1 1/2 cups of cheese on top, up to within half an inch of the edges. Put the asparagus on top, and layer with the rest of the cheese. Combine the rest of the ingredients and drizzle on the pastry. Bake for 10-15 minutes more, until you have melted cheese. Serve while warm.

Nutrition Information

- Calories: 142 calories
- Sodium: 202mg sodium
- Fiber: 1g fiber)

- Total Carbohydrate: 10g carbohydrate (1g sugars
- Cholesterol: 16mg cholesterol
- Protein: 5g protein.
- Total Fat: 9g fat (4g saturated fat)

60. Goat Cheese & Onion Pastries

Serving: 1 dozen. | Prep: 30mins | Cook: 20mins |Ready in:

Ingredients

- 6 bacon strips, chopped
- 2 large onions, finely chopped
- 3 shallots, thinly sliced
- 1/2 teaspoon sugar
- 1/2 cup white wine
- 2 teaspoons minced fresh thyme or 1/2 teaspoon dried thyme
- 2 garlic cloves, minced
- 1/4 teaspoon pepper
- 1 sheet frozen puff pastry, thawed
- 1 egg white, beaten
- 1 log (4 ounces) fresh goat cheese, cut into 12 slices

Direction

- Preheat the oven to 400 degrees F. Cook the bacon on medium heat in a large skillet until crispy while occasionally stirring. Use a slotted spoon to remove bacon and drain onto paper towels. Reserve 2 tablespoons drippings in pan; discard the rest. Toss shallots, sugar, and onions into the drippings and stir for 15 to 20 minutes over medium heat until the vegetables turn golden brown.
- Pour wine and loosen the browned bits from the pan by stirring. Toss in the pepper, thyme, and garlic. Cook without cover for 2 to 3 minutes until the liquid evaporates. Add in bacon; stir.
- Roll out the puff pastry onto a lightly floured work area. Slice the puff pastry into 3

rectangles with a dimension of 9x3 inch. Place on a baking sheet lined with a parchment paper. Brush the dough with the egg white. Spread with onion mixture and goat cheese. Bake for 16 to 20 minutes until golden brown. Slice each of the rectangles into four appetizers.

Nutrition Information

- Calories: 168 calories
- Sodium: 186mg sodium
- Fiber: 2g fiber)
- Total Carbohydrate: 17g carbohydrate (2g sugars
- Cholesterol: 10mg cholesterol
- Protein: 4g protein.
- Total Fat: 9g fat (3g saturated fat)

61. Herbed Havarti In Pastry

Serving: 16 servings. | Prep: 15mins | Cook: 20mins | Ready in:

Ingredients

- 1/2 cup dried parsley flakes
- 1 teaspoon dried thyme
- 1 teaspoon dried rosemary, crushed
- 1/2 teaspoon dried oregano
- 2 tablespoons Dijon mustard
- 2 blocks (8 ounces each) dill Havarti cheese
- 1 sheet frozen puff pastry, thawed
- 1 egg, beaten
- Coarse salt, optional
- Assorted crackers and fresh fruit

Direction

- Mix parsley, rosemary, thyme and oregano in a shallow bowl. Place mustard over the cheese blocks. Dredge to coat with herbs.
- Roll pastry on a floured surface, to 13 inches long (should be long enough to accommodate

blocks of cheese end to end). Put the cheese on the pastry. Fold the puff pastry around the cheese. Remove excess dough. Seal by pinching edges. Put on an ungreased baking sheet, seam side down.

- Use egg to brush the pastry. Cut the scraps into decorative shapes using floured cutters if preferred. Place them over the top and apply more egg brush. Season with salt, if you wish. Bake for 20-25 minutes at 375°F, until golden brown and puffed. Serve while warm, with fruit and crackers.

Nutrition Information

- Calories: 188 calories
- Cholesterol: 40mg cholesterol
- Protein: 8g protein.
- Total Fat: 13g fat (6g saturated fat)
- Sodium: 261mg sodium
- Fiber: 1g fiber)
- Total Carbohydrate: 10g carbohydrate (1g sugars

---

spread half of cheese mixture. Fold the plain half over filling, and seal by pressing carefully.

- Do the same with the rest of the pastry and cheese mixture. Divide each rectangle into 12 strips, 3/4 inch wide. Turn strips into spiral a couple of times and arrange on greased baking sheets, 2 inches apart.
- Beat water and egg together and brush twists with the egg wash mixture. Dust with a bit of chili powder. Bake for 14 to 16 minutes at 400°F until golden brown. Serve while still warm.

Nutrition Information

- Calories: 242 calories
- Protein: 6g protein.
- Total Fat: 14g fat (5g saturated fat)
- Sodium: 230mg sodium
- Fiber: 3g fiber)
- Total Carbohydrate: 24g carbohydrate (0 sugars
- Cholesterol: 28mg cholesterol

---

62. Nacho Cheese Twists

Serving: 2 dozen. | Prep: 15mins | Cook: 15mins | Ready in:

Ingredients

- 1 cup shredded cheddar cheese
- 1/4 cup salsa
- 2 tablespoons finely chopped ripe olives
- 1 package (17.3 ounces) frozen puff pastry, thawed
- 1 large egg, beaten
- 1 tablespoon water
- 1/2 teaspoon chili powder

Direction

- Combine the salsa, olives and cheese in a small bowl. Roll out puff pastry on a lightly floured work area. On one half side of the pastry,

---

63. Paprika Parmesan Puffed Cheese Sticks

Serving: 3 dozen. | Prep: 10mins | Cook: 5mins | Ready in:

Ingredients

- 1 sheet frozen puff pastry, thawed
- 1/4 cup grated Parmesan cheese
- 1/2 teaspoon paprika
- 1/4 teaspoon salt
- 1/4 teaspoon dried savory

Direction

- Roll out puff pastry. Form the pastry to a 10-inch square onto a lightly floured work area.
- Mix together the rest of the ingredients in a small bowl and drizzle over the pastry. Slice

12 strips from the pastry, 3/4-inch wide each. Slice each strip into thirds, widthwise.

- Transfer on baking sheets lined with parchment paper, 1 inch apart. Bake for 5 to 7 minutes at 375 degrees F, until golden brown. Serve immediately.

Nutrition Information

- Calories: 36 calories
- Total Carbohydrate: 4g carbohydrate (0 sugars
- Cholesterol: 0 cholesterol
- Protein: 1g protein.
- Total Fat: 2g fat (1g saturated fat)
- Sodium: 47mg sodium
- Fiber: 1g fiber)

64. Parmesan Pastry Twists

Serving: 4 dozen. | Prep: 15mins | Cook: 15mins | Ready in:

Ingredients

- 1/2 cup grated Parmesan cheese
- 3/4 teaspoon coarsely ground pepper
- 1 garlic clove, minced
- 1 package (17.3 ounces) frozen puff pastry sheets, thawed
- 1 egg white, lightly beaten

Direction

- Mix the pepper, Parmesan cheese, and garlic in a small bowl. Roll out one pastry sheet on a lightly floured working area; brush with the egg white. Add in 1/4 of the Parmesan mixture and press lightly into the pastry. Turn the pastry sheet upside down and do the same procedure.
- Slice the sheet into 12 strips and slice each of the strips in half. Twist the strips a couple of times. Transfer on greased baking sheets. Do the same with the rest of the pastry sheet. Bake

for 14 to 16 minutes at 350 degrees F, until golden brown.

Nutrition Information

- Calories:
- Cholesterol:
- Protein:
- Total Fat:
- Sodium:
- Fiber:
- Total Carbohydrate:

65. Raspberry & Cream Cheese Pastries

Serving: 1 dozen. | Prep: 15mins | Cook: 20mins | Ready in:

Ingredients

- 2 packages (10 ounces each) frozen puff pastry shells
- 2 tablespoons sugar
- 5 tablespoons amaretto, divided
- 1/2 cup sliced almonds
- 1/2 cup seedless raspberry jam
- 1 package (8 ounces) cream cheese, softened
- 6 ounces white baking chocolate, melted and cooled
- 1 ounce semisweet chocolate, chopped
- 1 teaspoon canola oil
- 12 fresh raspberries

Direction

- Bake pastry shells as per package instructions. Let them cool completely.
- While waiting, mix 1 tablespoon amaretto and sugar in a heavy skillet. Stir and cook over medium heat until sugar caramelizes, about 3 to 4 minutes. Toss in almonds; cook for 2 to 3 minutes until golden brown. Prepare a foil and scatter almonds on surface to completely cool.

- Beat 2 tablespoons amaretto and jam in a small bowl until smooth. Scoop into the pastry shells.
- Whisk the leftover amaretto and cream cheese into a large bowl until smooth, then slowly stir in the cooled white chocolate. Scoop over the jam mixture. Top with candied almonds.
- Melt semisweet chocolate with oil in a microwave. Whisk until mixture is smooth. Pour over tarts and add raspberries for toppings. Keep in the refrigerator until ready to serve.

Nutrition Information

- Calories:
- Fiber:
- Total Carbohydrate:
- Cholesterol:
- Protein:
- Total Fat:
- Sodium:

66. Ricotta Puffs

Serving: 1-1/2 dozen. | Prep: 20mins | Cook: 15mins | Ready in:

Ingredients

- 1 package (17-1/4 ounces) frozen puff pastry, thawed
- 1/2 cup ricotta cheese
- 1/2 cup roasted sweet red peppers, drained and chopped
- 3 tablespoons grated Romano or Parmesan cheese, divided
- 1 tablespoon minced fresh parsley
- 1 teaspoon dried oregano, crushed
- 1/2 teaspoon pepper
- 1 teaspoon 2% milk

Direction

- Preheat oven to 400°F. Spread out puff pastry on a lightly floured work area and cut each sheet into 9 squares. Combine 2 tablespoons Romano cheese, ricotta cheese, red peppers, oregano, parsley and pepper.
- Brush the edges of the pastry with milk. On the center of each square, put 2 rounded scoops of the cheese mixture, about 2 teaspoonfuls. Fold the edges of the pastry to enclose the filling as you form a rectangle. Use fork to seal the edges. Slash slits in the pastry then brush with milk. Dust with the rest of the Romano cheese.
- On lightly greased baking sheets, place the pastries 2 inches apart. Bake for 15 to 20 minutes or until golden brown. Transfer to wire racks. Serve while they're still warm and put any leftovers in the refrigerator.

Nutrition Information

- Calories: 150 calories
- Sodium: 140mg sodium
- Fiber: 2g fiber)
- Total Carbohydrate: 16g carbohydrate (1g sugars
- Cholesterol: 4mg cholesterol
- Protein: 3g protein.
- Total Fat: 8g fat (2g saturated fat)

67. Sausage And Swiss Mini Quiches

Serving: 4 dozen. | Prep: 20mins | Cook: 15mins | Ready in:

Ingredients

- 1 package (17.3 ounces) frozen puff pastry, thawed
- 1 package (16 ounces) Jones No Sugar Pork Sausage Roll sausage
- 4 green onions, finely chopped
- 1/2 cup finely chopped sweet red pepper

- 1 garlic clove, minced
- 4 eggs
- 1 carton (8 ounces) Mascarpone cheese
- 1 teaspoon salt
- 1 teaspoon crushed red pepper flakes
- 1 teaspoon Worcestershire sauce
- 1/2 teaspoon dried sage leaves
- 1/2 teaspoon dried thyme
- 1/4 teaspoon ground mustard
- 1/2 cup shredded Swiss cheese

Direction

- Roll puff pastry to make it 1/8-inch thick. Carve out twenty-four pieces 2 1/2-inch circles. Prepare greased mini muffin cups; press pastry onto bottoms and up to the sides.
- Cook red pepper, garlic, sausage, and onions in a large pan over medium heat until the sausage is no longer pink, then drain. Transfer into the pastry cups.
- Mix the salt, Mascarpone cheese, Worcestershire sauce, pepper flakes, sage, mustard, eggs, and thyme in a small bowl. Scoop mixture over the tops and season the Swiss cheese.
- Bake for 10 to 12 minutes at 400 degrees F until a knife inserted at the middle comes out clean. Serve while warm.

Nutrition Information

- Calories: 101 calories
- Protein: 3g protein.
- Total Fat: 7g fat (3g saturated fat)
- Sodium: 134mg sodium
- Fiber: 1g fiber)
- Total Carbohydrate: 6g carbohydrate (0 sugars
- Cholesterol: 28mg cholesterol

68. Tomato And Corn Cheesy Pastry Bites

Serving: 8 pastries. | Prep: 25mins | Cook: 20mins | Ready in:

Ingredients

- 1 tablespoon olive oil
- 1/2 cup finely chopped onion
- 1 cup fresh corn
- 1 teaspoon garlic powder
- 1/2 teaspoon minced fresh parsley
- 1/4 teaspoon salt
- 1/8 teaspoon pepper
- 1 package (17.3 ounces) frozen puff pastry, thawed
- 1 large egg
- 1 tablespoon water
- 3/4 cup quartered cherry tomatoes
- 1/2 cup crumbled goat cheese
- 1/2 cup shredded provolone cheese
- 2 tablespoons minced fresh basil

Direction

- Preheat oven to 375°F. Heat oil in a big pan set over medium heat. Toss in onion and sauté for about 5 minutes until tender. Add in garlic powder, corn and parsley. Season with salt and pepper to taste. Continue cooking for about 2 minutes until corn is tender. Take pan off the heat.
- Roll out puff pastry sheets. Using a floured 4-in. round cookie cutter, carve out four circles out of each sheet and lay them on baking trays lined with parchment paper. Beat water and egg together. Brush pastries with the egg wash mixture. Scoop 2 tablespoons of the corn mixture and place them on each circle. Layer with cheeses and tomatoes on top.
- Bake for about 20 minutes or until cheese is melted and pastry has turned golden brown. Garnish with basil.

Nutrition Information

- Calories: 236 calories
- Fiber: 3g fiber)
- Total Carbohydrate: 22g carbohydrate (2g sugars
- Cholesterol: 37mg cholesterol
- Protein: 7g protein.
- Total Fat: 14g fat (5g saturated fat)
- Sodium: 279mg sodium

Chapter 4: Phyllo Puff Pastry Dough Recipes

***

---

69. "Tomato Time" Tart

Serving: Makes 2 servings | Prep: | Cook: | Ready in:

Ingredients

- 2 sheets frozen puff pastry, thawed
- 2 egg yolks
- 2 teaspoons corn oil
- 2 teaspoons water
- 4 medium-sized ripe tomatoes, sliced 1/4-inch thick
- 1/2 teaspoon extra-virgin olive oil
- 1/2 teaspoon sugar
- Freshly ground black pepper, to taste
- 1/2 cup Garden Pesto or store-bought pesto

Direction

- On a lightly floured surface, roll pastry out; use salad-size plate for guide to cut each sheet to 8-in. circle. Put on ungreased baking sheet; use fork to prick pastry all over.

- Whisk water, corn oil and egg yolks; lightly brush on pastry. In concentric circles, put tomatoes; leave 1/2-in. edge.
- Preheat an oven to 400°F; evenly drizzle pepper, sugar and olive oil on tarts. Bake till tomatoes are caramelized and tarts are golden or for 25 minutes.
- Immediately serve with a dollop of Garden Pesto.

Nutrition Information

---

70. 3 Ingredient Caramel Apple Hand Pies

Serving: Makes 9 | Prep: 20mins | Cook: 35mins | Ready in:

Ingredients

- 1 (14–17-ounce) box puff pastry (preferably all-butter puff), thawed according to package directions
- 1 large apple, cut into 1/4" pieces
- 1/3 cup caramel sauce
- Flaky sea salt

Direction

- Put a rack in the middle of the oven; preheat to 425°F. On flat work surface, unroll or unfold pastry; cut as many rounds out as you can with biscuit cutter or 3-in. circular cookie cutter to get 18 rounds.
- Put 1/2 of the rounds on a parchment-lined rimmed baking sheet, scoop 1 heaping tbsp. of apples in the middle of each round, leaving a 1/2-in. border. Put 1 heaping tsp. of caramel sauce then a pinch of sea salt over apples.
- Brush pastry brush dipped in water on pastry border; put 2nd pastry round over each filled round. Crimp edges together with a fork, sealing every pie well to prevent leakage.

- Use sharp knife to cut several small slits over each pie to let steam escape. Bake pies for 15 minutes till puffed and golden brown, rotating sheet halfway through; serve warm.

Nutrition Information

- Calories: 312
- Saturated Fat: 5 g(24%)
- Sodium: 199 mg(8%)
- Fiber: 1 g(6%)
- Total Carbohydrate: 33 g(11%)
- Cholesterol: 0 mg(0%)
- Protein: 4 g(8%)
- Total Fat: 19 g(29%)

71. 3 Ingredient Cinnamon Sugar Twists

Serving: Makes 12–18 twists | Prep: 30mins | Cook: 1hours | Ready in:

Ingredients

- 1 cup sugar
- 1 teaspoon ground cinnamon
- Pinch of kosher salt
- 14–17 ounces frozen puff pastry, thawed

Direction

- Put racks in lower and upper thirds of the oven then preheat to 400°F. Line parchment on 2 rimmed baking sheets. Mix salt, cinnamon and sugar on a big plate. Use cold water to fill small bowl or glass.
- Between 2 parchment sheets, roll pastry out till dough is 1/8-in. thick and short side is 10-in. long. Freeze for 5 minutes. Slice the dough to 1-in. strips crosswise with a sharp knife or pizza cutter; put 1/2 of the strips in the fridge. One by one, lightly brush the strip with water or use your fingertips. Put in sugar mixture immediately; turn to coat.

- Twist dough to the ends with both hands, beginning from the middle. Put, vertically arranging twists, on prepped sheet; repeat with leftover dough then freeze for 10 minutes.
- Bake twists for 18-20 minutes till starting to caramelize and golden brown, rotating sheets top to bottom and front to back halfway through. Lift twist from parchment immediately with tongs; cool with 1 end on baking sheet rim; be careful, sugar coating is very hot.

Nutrition Information

- Calories: 213
- Total Fat: 11 g(17%)
- Saturated Fat: 3 g(14%)
- Sodium: 81 mg(3%)
- Fiber: 1 g(2%)
- Total Carbohydrate: 27 g(9%)
- Protein: 2 g(4%)

72. Almond Glazed Pastries With Whipped Cream And Berries

Serving: Makes 8 servings | Prep: | Cook: | Ready in:

Ingredients

- 3/4 cup sugar
- 1/4 cup water
- 2 6-ounce packages red raspberries
- 6 dried hibiscus flowers*
- 1 teaspoon Sherry wine vinegar
- 1/2 17.3-ounce package frozen puff pastry (1 sheet), thawed
- 1 1/2 cups powdered sugar
- 3 tablespoons all purpose flour
- 1 large egg white
- Water
- 1 cup slivered almonds
- 1 6-ounce package red raspberries
- 1 6-ounce package golden raspberries

- 1 5.6-ounce package boysenberries
- 2 4.4-ounce packages blueberries
- 2 cups chilled whipping cream

Direction

- Raspberry-hibiscus sauce: Mix 1/4 cup of water and sugar till sugar dissolves in a heavy small saucepan on medium heat. Put heat on high; boil for 7 minutes, varies on pan size, swirling pan occasionally and brushing sides down with wet pastry brush till syrup is light golden. Add hibiscus flowers and 2 packages of raspberries, it will slightly harden; boil, constantly mixing to dissolve caramel bits. Lower heat to medium; simmer for 3 minutes, constantly mixing. Take off from heat; stand to blend flavors for 15 minutes. To remove seeds, strain raspberry sauce and press on solids; mix in vinegar.
- You can make this 2 days ahead, covered and refrigerated.
- Almond glaze pastry: On a lightly floured surface, roll out puff pastry sheet to 17x11-in. rectangle; put on a parchment lined baking sheet. Use fork to pierce dough all over; freeze for 1 hour.
- Meanwhile, preheat an oven to 400°F. Whisk egg white, flour and sugar till smooth and blended; to make this thick yet spreadable glaze, add water by 1/4 teaspoonfuls.
- Thinly spread glaze on frozen pastry with a small offset spatula; evenly sprinkle almonds on glaze. Bake for 35 minutes till almonds are toasted and glaze is dark golden; cool. To shape 16x10-in. rectangle, trim pastry; cut to 4 even strips crosswise. Cut every strip to 4 even pieces crosswise to create 16 4x21/2-in. rectangles.
- You can make this 4 hours ahead; stand at room temperature.
- Filling: Put blueberries, boysenberries, golden raspberries and red raspberries in a big bowl. Add raspberry sauce; fold gently to coat.
- Whip cream till peaks form in a big bowl. On each of 8 plates, put 1 pastry rectangle; on each pastry rectangle, scoop 1/4 cup of whipped cream. Scoop 3 tbsp. of berry mixture on cream; put leftover pastry rectangles over. Spread 1/4 cup of cream on each; scoop leftover berry mixture over. Immediately serve.

Nutrition Information

73. Alsatian Cheese Tart

Serving: Makes 36 hors d'oeuvres | Prep: 20mins | Cook: 50mins | Ready in:

Ingredients

- 1 puff pastry sheet (from a 17 1/4-oz package), thawed
- 1/2 cup whole-milk cottage cheese
- 1/4 cup sour cream
- 1/4 teaspoon salt
- 1/4 teaspoon black pepper
- 6 bacon slices (6 oz), cut crosswise into 1/2-inch pieces
- 1/3 cup packed thinly sliced onion
- 1 tablespoon freshly grated parmesan

Direction

- Place oven rack in center position; preheat the oven to 400°F.
- Use lightly floured rolling pin to roll pastry out to 12-in. square on a lightly floured surface; put in a big baking sheet.
- In a blender, blend pepper, salt, sour cream, and cottage cheese till smooth.
- Cook bacon in a 10-in. skillet on medium heat for 5 minutes till it just starts to brown, occasionally mixing; bacon should not be crisp, just tender. Take off from heat.
- Evenly spread cheese mixture on pastry; all around, leave 1-in. border. Scatter onion and bacon over; sprinkle parmesan. Bake for 20-25 minutes till pastry is golden brown. Cut to 36 pieces; serve warm.

Nutrition Information

- Calories: 66
- Saturated Fat: 2 g(8%)
- Sodium: 66 mg(3%)
- Fiber: 0 g(1%)
- Total Carbohydrate: 3 g(1%)
- Cholesterol: 5 mg(2%)
- Protein: 2 g(3%)
- Total Fat: 5 g(8%)

74. Amaranth And Feta Phyllo Triangles

Serving: Serves 4; makes 8 triangles | Prep: | Cook: | Ready in:

Ingredients

- 4 tablespoons (1/2 stick) unsalted butter
- 2 medium leeks, white and light green parts only, chopped
- 2 garlic cloves, chopped
- 4 ounces (2 cups packed) amaranth leaves, roughly chopped
- 1 to 1 1/2 teaspoons red pepper flakes, to taste
- Salt
- 4 ounces feta cheese, crumbled (1 cup)
- 2 large eggs
- 4 (16 x 12-inch) sheets frozen phyllo dough, defrosted
- 1/4 cup freshly grated Parmesan cheese (optional)

Direction

- Preheat an oven to 350°F.
- Melt butter in a big skillet. Pour off the half; put aside. Add garlic and leeks into pan; cook for 2 minutes on medium heat. Add 1/4 cup of water, 2 generous pinches of salt, red pepper flakes and amaranth; cook for 3 minutes on low heat or till liquid evaporates. Take off

from heat; put in a medium bowl. Add eggs and feta; stir to combine.
- On a smooth work surface, lay 1 phyllo dough sheet; halve to make 8x12-in. rectangle. Brush reserved melted butter on top surface of rectangle lightly; fold in half to make a double-layered 4x12-in. sheet, with buttered parts inside. Divide amaranth to 8 even portions, around 3 tbsp. each. Put 1 portion on bottom left corner of phyllo, 1-in. from end. Fold up corner over filling to create a triangle shape; to seal, press down. Keep folding up sheet like a flag; to seal, press end. Brush melted butter on top of triangle; if desired, sprinkle grated parmesan. Put on a baking sheet; repeat using leftover phyllo sheets.
- Bake till edges are golden brown or for 20 minutes; cool and freeze or serve warm. Defrost on baking sheet then bake to reheat.

Nutrition Information

- Calories: 331
- Total Fat: 23 g(36%)
- Saturated Fat: 14 g(70%)
- Sodium: 488 mg(20%)
- Fiber: 1 g(5%)
- Total Carbohydrate: 20 g(7%)
- Cholesterol: 157 mg(52%)
- Protein: 11 g(23%)

75. Anchovy Puffs

Serving: Makes about 24 anchovy puffs plus scraps | Prep: | Cook: | Ready in:

Ingredients

- a 2-ounce can flat anchovies, rinsed patted dry, and minced
- 3 tablespoons mayonnaise
- a 1-pound package frozen puff pastry sheets, thawed

- an egg wash made by beating 1 large egg with 1 tablespoon water

Direction

- Use fork to mash mayonnaise and anchovies in a small bowl. Roll both pastry sheets out to 14-in. squares on a lightly floured surface; trim edges to make 13-in. squares. Brush extra flour off; evenly spread anchovy mayonnaise on 1 pastry sheet. Use leftover pastry sheet to cover; gently press sheets together.
- Preheat an oven to 375°F.
- Cut pastry to shapes with 3-4-in. decorative cutter, like a fish. Reserve scraps; to bake separately, cut to bite-size pieces. Cut pastry to squares to eliminate scraps; don't do decorative shapes.
- On lightly greased baking sheets, put pastries; brush egg wash on tops. Score fish with back of sharp knife or edge of a cookie cutter. In oven, bake pastries for 12-15 minutes till golden and puffed.

Nutrition Information

- Calories: 299
- Total Fat: 22 g(33%)
- Saturated Fat: 5 g(26%)
- Sodium: 353 mg(15%)
- Fiber: 1 g(3%)
- Total Carbohydrate: 20 g(7%)
- Cholesterol: 25 mg(8%)
- Protein: 6 g(11%)

76. Apple Raisin Strudels

Serving: Makes 2 strudels | Prep: | Cook: | Ready in:

Ingredients

- 1/2 cup fine dry bread crumbs
- 7 1/2 tablespoons unsalted butter
- 1 1/2 pounds tart apples, such as Granny Smith, peeled, quartered, and sliced thin crosswise
- 1/3 cup granulated sugar
- 1/2 cup raisins
- 1/2 teaspoon cinnamon
- twelve 17- by 12-inch sheets of phyllo, stacked between two sheets of wax paper and covered with a dampened kitchen towel
- confectioners' sugar for dusting the strudels
- 1 cup well-chilled heavy cream
- 1/4 cup sour cream
- 1/4 cup confectioners' sugar
- 1 teaspoon vanilla

Direction

- Strudels: Cook breadcrumbs in 1 1/2 tbsp. butter in a small skillet on medium heat till golden, mixing; put in a big bowl. Add cinnamon, raisins, granulated sugar and apples into breadcrumbs; toss mixture well. Put 18-in. long wax paper piece with long side facing you on work surface; cover using 1 phyllo sheet. Lightly brush some leftover melted butter on phyllo. In the same manner, layer 5 additional phyllo sheets on top of the 1st sheet, lightly brushing with some of the melted butter on each sheet. Evenly mound 1/2 apple mixture along long side facing you; at each end, leave 2-in. border. Rolling away from you, tightly roll strudel up using wax paper for guide; to enclose filling, seam side down, fold ends under. Carefully put strudel on lightly buttered jellyroll pan; brush some leftover melted butter. In same manner, create another strudel with leftover apple filling, melted butter and phyllo; put in jellyroll pan. Bake strudels for 35-45 minutes in center of preheated 375°F oven or till golden; cool in pan on a rack to warm. You can make strudels 1 day ahead; kept at room temperature, loosely covered. Reheat strudels for 15 minutes in preheated 400°F oven. Carefully put strudels with slotted spatula to serving platters; dust confectioners' sugar over them.

- Whipped cream: Use electric mixer to beat vanilla, confectioners' sugar, sour cream and heavy cream till mixture holds soft peaks in a chilled bowl; put in a serving bowl.
- Sliced diagonally, serve strudels warm with whipped cream.

Nutrition Information

- Calories: 248
- Saturated Fat: 10 g(49%)
- Sodium: 45 mg(2%)
- Fiber: 2 g(8%)
- Total Carbohydrate: 26 g(9%)
- Cholesterol: 49 mg(16%)
- Protein: 2 g(3%)
- Total Fat: 16 g(24%)

77. Apple Tarts With Vanilla Ice Cream

Serving: Makes 12 | Prep: 40mins | Cook: 1.5hours | Ready in:

Ingredients

- 6 Gala apples (preferably red; 2 3/4 pounds)
- 1/2 cup water
- 1/2 cup sugar
- 1/2 vanilla bean, split lengthwise
- 1 (17 1/4-oz) package frozen puff pastry sheets, thawed
- All-purpose flour for dusting
- 1 1/2 tablespoons unsalted butter, melted
- Accompaniment: vanilla ice cream
- parchment paper

Direction

- In lower and upper thirds of oven, put oven racks; preheat the oven to 400°F. Line parchment paper on 2 big baking sheets.
- Peel apples; keep skins. Mix 6 tbsp. sugar and water in a 1-qt. heavy saucepan. Scrape in vanilla bean seeds; add pod. Put in the reserved apple skins; boil, mixing till sugar dissolves. Take off from heat; allow to stand for 10 minutes. Put through a medium-mesh sieve into a bowl; press on them hard. Discard solids.
- Roll 1 pastry sheet out with a lightly floured rolling pin on a lightly floured surface to 10-in. square; cut in half. Put on 1 of the baking sheets; repeat with leftover pastry sheet, putting onto 2nd baking sheet.
- Lengthwise halve apples; use a small spoon or a melon-ball cutter to core. Crosswise cut to very thin 1/8-in. thick or less slices; keep apple halves intact. Slightly fan apple slices; keep apple shape. On each pastry piece, put 3 halves in a row; leave 2/3-in. border on all the sides.
- Lightly brush syrup on border; fold over 1/3-in. to touch apple edges. Use fork to crimp edges; brush syrup on pastry edges and apples. Put leftover syrup aside. Fully brush melted butter on apples; evenly sprinkle leftover 2 tbsp. sugar.
- In lower and upper thirds of oven, bake tarts for 20 minutes; switch sheets positions. Lower oven temperature to 375°F then bake tarts for 15-20 more minutes till edges are golden. Rotate tarts on sheets 180° halfway through baking is pastry edges aren't evenly browning.
- Boil leftover syrup as tart bakes for 30-60 seconds till reduced to 1/4 cup on medium heat.
- Allow the tarts to stand for 5 minutes; brush leftover syrup on warm apples.

Nutrition Information

78. Apple, Goat Cheese, And Honey Tartlets

Serving: Makes 8 | Prep: | Cook: | Ready in:

Ingredients

- 2 17.3-ounce packages frozen puff pastry (4 sheets), thawed
- 1 egg, beaten to blend
- 6 ounces soft fresh goat cheese (about 3/4 cup packed)
- 1 tablespoon fresh lemon juice
- 1/4 teaspoon coarse kosher salt
- 3 medium Gala apples, peeled, quartered, cored, cut into 1/8-inch-thick slices
- 3 tablespoons unsalted butter, melted
- 3/4 cup honey (preferably dark), divided
- 1/2 teaspoon (scant) ground allspice

Direction

- Line parchment paper on 2 rimmed baking sheets. Roll each puff pastry sheet out to 11-in. square on lightly floured surface; cut 4 rounds out from each pastry sheet with 5-in. diameter cookie cutter or bowl to make 16 rounds in total. Divide 8 pastry rounds among prepped baking sheets; use fork to pierce rounds all over. Cut smaller rounds out from middle of leftover 8 rounds with 3 1/2-in. diameter cookie cutter or bowl to make 8 5-in. diameter rings; keep 3 1/2-in. rounds for another time. Brush beaten egg on outer 1-in. edges of the 5-in.rounds on the baking sheets; put 1 pastry ring over each. Freeze for 30 minutes minimum; you can make this 1 day ahead, kept frozen and covered. Before continuing, don't thaw.
- Preheat an oven to 375°F. In bowl, mix salt, lemon juice and cheese; spread mixture inside the rings on the frozen pastry rounds. Over cheese, overlap apple slices. Mix 1/4 cup honey and butter in a small bowl; brush on apples. Sprinkle allspice over; bake for 35 minutes till pastry is golden and apples are tender. Put tartlets on plates then drizzle 1 tbsp. honey on each; serve at room temperature or warm.

Nutrition Information

- Calories: 911
- Fiber: 3 g(14%)
- Total Carbohydrate: 91 g(30%)
- Cholesterol: 41 mg(14%)
- Protein: 14 g(28%)
- Total Fat: 56 g(86%)
- Saturated Fat: 18 g(89%)
- Sodium: 472 mg(20%)

79. Apricot Phyllo Napoleons

Serving: Serves 4 | Prep: 30mins | Cook: 8.5hours | Ready in:

Ingredients

- 1 cup nonfat yogurt
- 4 (17- by 12-inch) phyllo sheets
- 1 teaspoon unsalted butter, melted
- 1 teaspoon vegetable oil
- 6 teaspoons granulated sugar
- 1 vanilla bean, halved lengthwise
- 1/4 cup low-fat sour cream
- 1 tablespoon plus 1 teaspoon packed light brown sugar
- 6 fresh apricots (1 pound), pitted and each cut into 6 wedges
- 1/4 cup water

Direction

- Drain yogurt in a cheesecloth-lined colander or sieve above a bowl for 8 hours, chilled and covered.
- Preheat an oven to 350°F.
- Put phyllo stack on a work surface; use 2 overlapping plastic wrap sheets and damp kitchen towel to cover the stack. Mix oil and butter together.
- Put 1 phyllo sheet on a big parchment-lined baking sheet; use dampened pastry brush to spread 1/4 of the butter mixture. Sprinkle 1 tsp. of granulated sugar over. The same way, put 3 extra layers over the top with leftover 3 tsp. of granulated sugar, butter mixture and

phyllo. Cut stack to 12 rectangles, 3 crosswise, 2 lengthwise cuts. Bake for 10 minutes in the middle of the oven till golden brown and crisp; cool in the pan on a rack.

- Use a small sharp knife to scrape vanilla bean seeds into a bowl; mix in 1 tbsp. of brown sugar, sour cream and drained yogurt.
- Heat a big nonstick skillet on medium high heat; add apricots. Sprinkle with the leftover 2 tsp. of granulated sugar; toss gently for 2-3 minutes till apricots are tender and warm. Use slotted spoon to move apricots in a bowl.
- Add leftover tsp. of brown sugar and water to skillet; boil to deglaze on medium high heat till reduced by around half, scraping brown bits up; in warm syrup, toss apricots.
- Put 1 phyllo rectangle on plate; put 3 apricot pieces then 1 generous tbsp. of yogurt mixture over the top. Create 2 extra layers with yogurt mixture, apricots and phyllo squares; in same way, make 3 more napoleons.

Nutrition Information

---

80. Asparagus Custard Tart

Serving: Makes 8 servings | Prep: 1hours | Cook: 2.75hours | Ready in:

Ingredients

- 1 cup all-purpose flour
- 1/2 teaspoon salt
- 3/4 stick (6 tablespoons) cold unsalted butter, cut into 1/2-inch cubes
- 1 large egg, lightly beaten
- 1 medium leek (white and pale green parts only), quartered lengthwise, then cut crosswise into 1/3-inch pieces
- 1 lb medium asparagus, trimmed
- 1 tablespoon unsalted butter
- 1/2 teaspoon salt
- 1/2 teaspoon black pepper

- 1 1/3 cups heavy cream
- 3 large eggs
- 2 teaspoons finely chopped fresh tarragon
- 2 teaspoons water
- parchment paper; a 9 1/4-inch flan ring* (see cooks' note, below)

Direction

- Pastry: Use fingertips or pastry blender to blend butter, salt and flour till most of mixture looks like coarse meal with some pea-size small butter lumps or pulse in a food processor. Evenly drizzle egg; pulse in processor or gently mix with fork just till dough forms.
- Turn dough on lightly floured surface; divide to 4 portions. In forward motion, smear each portion 1 or 2 times to help distribute fat with heel of your hand. Gather dough to ball; flatten to 5-in. disk. Chill dough for 30 minutes minimum till firm, wrapped in plastic wrap.
- As pastry chills, make filling: In bowl of cold water, wash leek, agitating water. Lift leek out; pat dry.
- Cook asparagus in a wide 4-5-qt. pot with boiling salted water for 5 minutes till just tender, uncovered. Use tongs to put asparagus in bowl with cold water and ice to stop cooking; drain. Pat dry. Cut off then reserve tips; if asparagus is thin, leave more stalk. Crosswise slice stalks thinly.
- Heat butter in a 10-12-in. heavy skillet on medium low heat till foam subsides; cook leek and 1/4 tsp. salt for 6-8 minutes till soft, mixing. Mix in 1/4 tsp. pepper and sliced asparagus; take off heat.
- Assemble and bake tart and finish filling: Place oven rack in center position; preheat the oven to 375°F.
- Line parchment paper on baking sheet; put flan ring in middle of baking sheet. Roll dough with floured rolling pin to 11-in. round on lightly floured surface. Fit dough inside flan ring; press the dough against side and bottom edge of ring. To cut excess dough off, run rolling pin on top edge of ring.

- Whisk 1/4 tsp. pepper, leftover 1/4 tsp. salt, tarragon, 2 eggs and cream. Beat water and leftover egg in small bowl lightly; brush some egg wash all over tart shell. Scoop asparagus mixture in shell, evenly spreading; put cream mixture on asparagus.
- Bake tart for 20-25 minutes till filling is just starting to set yet loose on top; scatter asparagus tips on top; if needed, lightly press to help settle them into filling. Bake for 30 more minutes till custard is just set yet slightly wobbly in middle and golden; custard sets more while cooling.
- On baking sheet on rack, cool tart for 30 minutes till warm. Use a small sharp knife to loosen edge; lift flan ring off. Serve at room temperature or warm, cut to wedges.

Nutrition Information

- Calories: 338
- Saturated Fat: 16 g(82%)
- Sodium: 346 mg(14%)
- Fiber: 2 g(7%)
- Total Carbohydrate: 17 g(6%)
- Cholesterol: 174 mg(58%)
- Protein: 7 g(14%)
- Total Fat: 27 g(42%)

---

81. Asparagus Parmesan Pastry Rolls

Serving: Makes about 96 hors d'oeuvres | Prep: | Cook: | Ready in:

Ingredients

- 1 (17 1/4-ounce) package frozen puff pastry sheets, thawed
- 2 large egg yolks, lightly beaten with 2 tablespoons cold water
- 5 ounce finely grated Parmigiano-Reggiano (1 3/4 cups packed)
- 28 (3/4-inch-thick) asparagus (2 pounds), stalks trimmed to 6-inch lengths and tips reserved if desired
- 3 tablespoons white or black truffle oil (1 1/2 ounces; optional)

Direction

- Unfold pastry sheets; parallel to fold lines, halve each. Roll 1 half out; (keep leftover 3 halves, covered with plastic wrap, chilled) with a floured rolling pin on a well-floured surface to 20x7-in. rectangle. Brush extra flour off both pastry sides and work surface; use a sharp knife to trim all edges to make even. Cut to 6 6 1/2 x 3-in. rectangles crosswise.
- Brush some egg wash on rectangles; evenly sprinkle each with 1 packed tbsp. cheese, leaving 1/2-in. border on long sides. Along 1 long side, lay asparagus stalk; roll asparagus in pastry. Press the seam to seal; create extra rolls with leftover asparagus, cheese and pastry.
- Put rolls on lightly oiled baking sheets, seam sides down, 1-in. apart; brush egg wash lightly on sides and top. Chill rolls for 15 minutes minimum till pastry is firm.
- Preheat the oven to 400°F.
- In middle of oven, bake rolls for 16 minutes in batches till golden and puffed.
- Use a metal spatula to put on a cutting board; trim 1/2-in. from ends. Cut each roll in half crosswise; diagonally cut each section in half beginning 1/2-in. from either end. On end, stand asparagus rolls, 2 by 2 on platters; drizzle 1 drop of truffle oil (optional) on each; serve warm.

Nutrition Information

- Calories: 40
- Saturated Fat: 1 g(4%)
- Sodium: 33 mg(1%)
- Fiber: 0 g(1%)
- Total Carbohydrate: 3 g(1%)
- Cholesterol: 5 mg(2%)
- Protein: 1 g(2%)

- Total Fat: 3 g(4%)

82. Autumn Apple Strudel

Serving: Makes 6 to 8 servings | Prep: | Cook: | Ready in:

Ingredients

- 1 cup apple juice
- 4 ounces bittersweet (not unsweetened) or semisweet chocolate, chopped
- 1 tablespoon brandy
- 1/2 teaspoon vanilla extract
- 1 cup plus 2 tablespoons apple juice
- 1/2 cup dry white wine
- 3 whole star anise*
- 1 cinnamon stick
- 1 vanilla bean, split lengthwise
- 1/3 cup (packed) dried Bing cherries
- 1/3 cup (packed) pitted prunes, halved
- 1 1/4 pounds Braeburn apples, peeled, cored, cut into 1/2-inch cubes
- 1/3 cup (packed) golden brown sugar
- 1 1/2 tablespoons cornstarch
- 2/3 cup hazelnuts, toasted, husked
- 1/2 cup graham cracker crumbs
- 3 tablespoons sugar
- 9 17x12-inch sheets fresh phyllo pastry or frozen, thawed
- 1/2 cup unsalted butter, melted
- Vanilla ice cream

Direction

- Sauce: Boil juice for 6 minutes till reduced to 1/2 cup in small saucepan; take off heat. Add chocolate; stand for 1 minute; whisk till smooth and melted. Mix in vanilla and brandy; you can make sauce 4 days ahead, chilled and covered. Before serving, rewarm.
- Filling: Mix cinnamon, star anise, wine and 1 cup juice in big saucepan; scrape in vanilla bean seeds then add bean. Simmer; take off heat. Cover; stand for 10 minutes. Add prunes and cherries; cover. Simmer for 5 minutes till

fruit is plump; discard vanilla bean, cinnamon and star anise. Mix in sugar and apples; simmer for 45 minutes till liquid reduces to 3 tbsp. and apples are tender yet hold shape, occasionally mixing.
- Mix 2 tbsp. apple juice and cornstarch then add to filling; mix on medium high heat for 3 minutes till filling boils and thickens. You can make this 3 days ahead; slightly cool, cover then chill.
- Strudel: Preheat an oven to 375°F; butter big heavy baking sheet lightly. Blend initial 3 ingredients till nuts are ground finely in processor.
- On work surface, put dry kitchen then put 1 phyllo sheet over; use plastic wrap then damp towel to cover leftover phyllo. Lightly brush melted butter on phyllo. Put 2nd phyllo sheet over; brush butter. Sprinkle scant 3 tbsp. nut mixture; continue using 6 extra phyllo sheets, brushing butter on each then sprinkle scant 3 tbsp. nut mixture. Put leftover phyllo sheet over; brush butter. Put filling over phyllo stack in 12x3-in. log, beginning 2 1/2-in. from each short side and 2-in. from 1 long side. Fold short edges over filling. Roll strudel up jellyroll style, beginning at edge near filling and using towel as aid. Put strudel on prepped baking sheet, seam side down; brush butter on strudel. You can make this 4 hours ahead, chilled.
- Bake strudel for 45 minutes till golden, uncovered; cool for 30 minutes minimum. Cut room temperature or warm strudel to slices; put on plates. Serve with warm chocolate sauce and ice cream.

Nutrition Information

- Calories: 654
- Saturated Fat: 14 g(72%)
- Sodium: 183 mg(8%)
- Fiber: 7 g(28%)
- Total Carbohydrate: 87 g(29%)
- Cholesterol: 41 mg(14%)
- Protein: 7 g(13%)

- Total Fat: 33 g(51%)

83. Bacon Baklava

Serving: Makes about 24 servings | Prep: | Cook: |Ready in:

Ingredients

- 1/2 pound raw walnut pieces
- 1/2 pound raw pistachio meats
- 1 cup cooked and crumbled bacon (about 12 slices)
- 1/3 cup sugar
- 1 teaspoon ground cardamom
- 1 1/4 cup (2 1/2 sticks) unsalted butter, melted
- 1 package (16 ounces) phyllo dough, thawed
- 1 cup water
- 1 cup sugar
- 1 cup honey
- 1 cinnamon stick
- 1/4 cup orange flower water or rose water

Direction

- Preheat an oven to 350°F.
- Pulse nuts till ground yet not become into meal in a food processor. Add cardamom, sugar and bacon; pulse several more times till nut mixture is evenly blended and chopped finely.
- Layering baklava: Generously brush melted butter on a jellyroll pan or a sheet pan with sides. Unroll phyllo dough; use a piece of plastic wrap and a damp towel to cover sheets to prevent drying out sheets while layering baklava. For detailed handling instructions, read package.
- Put phyllo sheet on the sheet pan; brush with melted butter. Repeat using 6 extra phyllo dough sheets and butter to get a total of 7 sheets; you don't need to use butter to cover every inch of phyllo, just try to disperse between all layers evenly. Evenly spread 1/3 cup of the nut mixture on top of phyllo; put nuts then 2 extra buttered phyllo sheets over. Keep dusting with 1/3 cup of the nut mixture then adding 2 buttered phyllo sheets till you use all the nut mixture; put the final layer of 7 buttered phyllo sheets over the top.
- Cut uncooked baklava to 24 diamond shapes with a sharp knife; bake baklava for 30-35 minutes till crisp and brown.
- Slowly heat honey, sugar and water in a saucepan as baklava bakes till sugar dissolves. Add cinnamon stick; boil. Slightly lower the heat; simmer for 25-30 minutes. Take the pan off the heat. Add orange flower water; slightly cool. Evenly put syrup on baklava once it gets out of the oven, putting syrup in every crevice and crack; soak for a few hours. Serve it at room temperature and keep the leftovers in the fridge.

Nutrition Information

- Calories: 360
- Total Fat: 23 g(35%)
- Saturated Fat: 9 g(45%)
- Sodium: 194 mg(8%)
- Fiber: 1 g(4%)
- Total Carbohydrate: 34 g(11%)
- Cholesterol: 41 mg(14%)
- Protein: 7 g(13%)

84. Bacon And Egg Casserole

Serving: 8–10 servings | Prep: 45mins | Cook: 1hours35mins |Ready in:

Ingredients

- 1 (14- or 17-ounce) box of puff pastry (preferably all-butter puff), thawed according to package directions
- All-purpose flour (for surface)
- 14 large eggs, divided
- 9 strips bacon (about 8 ounces)

- 1 large onion, thinly sliced
- 8 ounces Gruyère, coarsely grated (about 2 1/2 cups)
- 1/2 teaspoon kosher salt
- 1/2 teaspoon freshly ground black pepper
- 1/4 teaspoon freshly grated or ground nutmeg
- 2 cups plus 1 tablespoon heavy cream, divided
- 1 medium Yukon Gold potato (about 5 ounces), cut into 1/2" cubes
- 5 ounces baby spinach

Direction

- Preheat an oven to 350°F. Roll pastry on a lightly floured surface to 18x13-in. rectangle if using 14-oz. puff pastry package with 1 pastry sheet; halve crosswise. Keep leftover piece for another time. Roll 1 sheet on a lightly floured surface to 13x9-in. rectangle if using 17-oz. 2 pastry sheet package; keep leftover sheet for another time. Slice pastry lengthwise parallel to 13-in. side to 14 strips, 1/2-in. wide. Put strips on parchment-lined rimmed baking sheet; while assembling casserole, chill.
- Boil a medium pot of water. Add 6 eggs then cover; cook for 7 minutes. Put eggs in a bowl with ice water; fully cool then peel eggs.
- Meanwhile, cook bacon in batches in a big skillet on medium heat for 10-12 minutes till crisp, occasionally turning; put bacon on paper towels. Put bacon fat in a small bowl. Cool bacon; chop coarsely.
- In same skillet, heat 2 tsp. bacon fat on medium heat and add onion; cook for 5-7 minutes till onion is translucent and soft, occasionally mixing.
- Use 1 tbsp. bacon fat to grease a 13x9-in. pan; discard leftover fat or keep for another time.
- In a big bowl, whisk 8 eggs. Add 2 cups cream, nutmeg, pepper, salt and cheese; whisk to mix. Add chopped bacon, onion, spinach and potato; mix to combine then put in prepped pan. Halve cooked eggs lengthwise; put on filling. Push down in order for egg's top edge becomes even with top of filling.
- Lengthwise, put chilled dough strips 1-in. apart on the diagonal; to fit flush against pan's edge, trim. On shorter sides, use trimmed dough. Going the other direction, lay extra strips on arranged strips to make lattice like yet not woven design. Brush leftover 1 tbsp. cream using small pastry brush on dough.
- Bake casserole for 50-55 minutes till pastry is cooked through and deep golden brown, rotating pan halfway through; before serving, cool for 15 minutes.
- You can cut pastry strips 1 day ahead; put on rimmed baking sheet, chilled and covered with plastic wrap. You can make filling 1 day ahead, covered and chilled. You can make baked casserole 1 day ahead, chilled and wrapped in plastic tightly; reheat for 20 minutes till warmed through in 350°F oven.

Nutrition Information

- Calories: 689
- Fiber: 1 g(5%)
- Total Carbohydrate: 12 g(4%)
- Cholesterol: 474 mg(158%)
- Protein: 30 g(60%)
- Total Fat: 58 g(89%)
- Saturated Fat: 29 g(145%)
- Sodium: 660 mg(28%)

85. Banana Chocolate Strudel

Serving: Makes 6 servings | Prep: | Cook: | Ready in:

Ingredients

- 4 (17- by 12-inch) phyllo sheets, covered with 2 overlapping pieces plastic wrap and then a damp kitchen towel
- 3 tablespoons unsalted butter, melted
- 2 firm-ripe bananas
- 2 oz fine-quality bittersweet chocolate (not unsweetened), finely chopped
- 1 large egg, beaten with 1 teaspoon water
- Confectioners sugar for dusting

- Accompaniment: lightly sweetened whipped cream

Direction

- Preheat an oven to 425°F.
- On a work surface, put 1 phyllo sheet with short phyllo side near you; keep leftover sheets covered. Brush with some butter. Put 3 extra phyllo sheets over phyllo; brush butter on each. One above the other, horizontally put bananas on lower third of phyllo; on both sides, leave a 1-in. border. If too long, trim the bananas. Sprinkle chocolate on bananas; fold phyllo sides toward center, over banana ends. Fold bottom phyllo edge over bananas; roll bananas up in phyllo.
- Put strudel on parchment paper-lined baking sheet or to a buttered baking sheet, seam side down; brush beaten egg on strudel. Diagonally cut 4 1/2-in. long steam vents with sharp knife along top of strudel. Bake in the middle of the oven for 12-15 minutes till golden; slightly cool on a rack. Dust confectioners' sugar.

Nutrition Information

- Calories: 184
- Saturated Fat: 6 g(29%)
- Sodium: 75 mg(3%)
- Fiber: 2 g(7%)
- Total Carbohydrate: 22 g(7%)
- Cholesterol: 46 mg(15%)
- Protein: 3 g(6%)
- Total Fat: 10 g(16%)

86. Beef Tenderloin And Vegetable Pot Pies

Serving: Makes 6 servings | Prep: | Cook: | Ready in:

Ingredients

- 1 tablespoon olive oil
- 3 1/2 pounds beef back ribs or short ribs
- 7 1/4 cups beef stock or canned beef broth
- 6 tablespoons tomato paste
- 2 bay leaves
- 2 cups chopped carrots (about 2 medium)
- 1 cup chopped onion
- 2 cups chopped zucchini (about 2 medium)
- 2 cups coarsely chopped mushrooms (about 6 ounces)
- 1 cup chopped tomatoes (about 2 medium)
- 3 tablespoons all purpose flour
- 3 tablespoons butter, room temperature
- 1 1/2 pounds beef tenderloin steaks, trimmed, cut into 1/2-inch pieces
- 1 17 1/4-ounce package frozen puff pastry (2 sheets), thawed
- 1 large egg, beaten (for glaze)

Direction

- Heat olive oil in a big heavy pot on high heat then add beef ribs; brown for 10 minutes on all sides. Add bay leaves, tomato paste and beef stock; boil. Lower the heat; simmer for 1 hour 15 minutes without a cover till liquid reduces to 4 cups. Discard ribs.
- Add onion and carrots to pot; simmer for 10 minutes till carrots are tender. Add tomatoes, mushrooms and zucchini; simmer for 8 minutes. Mix 2 tbsp. of butter and flour till paste forms in a small bowl. Mix paste into stock mixture; simmer for 3 minutes till gravy thickens. You can make this 1 day ahead, covered and refrigerated. Prior to continuing, rewarm on medium heat, frequently mixing.
- Preheat an oven to 400°F then butter 6 soufflé dishes or 1 1/4-cup custard cups. Melt leftover 1 tbsp. of butter in a big nonstick skillet on high heat; sprinkle pepper and salt on beef tenderloin pieces. Put beef in skillet; cook for 1 minute per side till outside of beef is brown. Put beef, evenly dividing, to prepped custard cups. Put vegetable gravy on beef in cups, evenly dividing. On a floured surface, roll 1 puff pastry sheet out to 12-in. square. Cut 3 5 1/2-in. rounds from sheet with a small plate as guide; repeat using leftover pastry sheet.

Brush egg glaze on pastry rounds edges; put 1 round over each filled custard cup, glazed side down. Firmly press overhang to outside of every cup. In every pastry round; cut 3 vents; brush leftover egg glaze on pastry.

- Bake beef tenderloin pies for 15 minutes till pastry is puffed and golden brown; serve warm.

Nutrition Information

- Calories: 1775
- Sodium: 1153 mg(48%)
- Fiber: 5 g(19%)
- Total Carbohydrate: 56 g(19%)
- Cholesterol: 331 mg(110%)
- Protein: 82 g(164%)
- Total Fat: 135 g(208%)
- Saturated Fat: 51 g(255%)

87. Beef Wellingtons With Gorgonzola

Serving: Serves 4 | Prep: | Cook: |Ready in:

Ingredients

- four 1 1/2-inch-thick center-cut filets mignons (about 6 ounces each)
- 4 large mushrooms (about 1/4 pound total)
- 1 tablespoon unsalted butter
- 1 tablespoon finely chopped shallot
- 1 tablespoon minced garlic
- 1 large egg
- 1 puff pastry sheet (from a 17 1/4-ounce package frozen puff pastry), thawed
- 4 tablespoons Gorgonzola cheese (about 2 1/2 ounces)
- 1 cup veal or beef demiglace
- 2 tablespoons Sercial Madeira

Direction

- Preheat an oven to 425°F.

- Pat dry filet mignons; season with pepper and salt. Roast filets in center of oven in a shallow roasting pan for 12 minutes or till meat thermometer reads 110°F for rare; cool. Filets get baked again after getting wrapped in pastry. Chill the filets for 1 hour till cold, covered.
- Slice mushrooms thinly; cook butter with pepper and salt to taste, garlic and shallot in a heavy skillet on medium heat till mushrooms are lightly browned, mixing. Put mushroom mixture in a bowl; fully cool. Beat egg lightly to create egg wash in a small bowl.
- Roll puff pastry sheet out to 14-in. square on a lightly floured surface; to make 13-in. square, trim edges. Cut square to 4 6 1/2-in. squares.
- In middle of 1 square, put 1 tbsp. gorgonzola; put 1/4 mushroom mixture over. Put a filet mignon over mushroom mixture; gently press down. Overlapping them, wrap 2 opposing puff pastry corners over filet; use egg wash to seal seam. Wrap leftover 2 pastry corners over filet; seal the same way. Use egg wash to seal any gaps; to fully enclose, press pastry around filet. Put beef wellington in a nonstick baking pan, seam side down; in same manner, create 3 more beef wellingtons. To brush on pastry before baking, chill leftover egg wash. Chill beef wellingtons for 1 hour minimum and up to 1 day, loosely covered.
- Preheat an oven to 425°F.
- Brush some leftover egg wash on sides and top of each beef wellington; bake till pastry is golden or for 20 minutes.
- As beef wellingtons bake, make sauce: Boil Madeira and demiglace for 1 minute in a saucepan; keep sauce warm
- Serve beef wellingtons along with sauce.

Nutrition Information

- Calories: 878
- Sodium: 889 mg(37%)
- Fiber: 1 g(5%)
- Total Carbohydrate: 31 g(10%)
- Cholesterol: 208 mg(69%)

- Protein: 45 g(90%)
- Total Fat: 62 g(96%)
- Saturated Fat: 23 g(117%)

88. Beef And Guinness Pie

Serving: Makes 4 main-course servings | Prep: 1.25hours | Cook: 6.5hours | Ready in:

Ingredients

- 2 pounds boneless beef chuck, cut into 1-inch pieces
- 2 tablespoons all-purpose flour
- 1 teaspoon salt
- 1/2 teaspoon black pepper
- 2 tablespoons vegetable oil
- 1 large onion, coarsely chopped
- 2 garlic cloves, chopped
- 3 tablespoons water
- 1 1/2 tablespoons tomato paste
- 1 cup beef broth
- 1 cup Guinness or other Irish stout
- 1 tablespoon Worcestershire sauce
- 2 teaspoons drained brined green peppercorns, coarsely chopped
- 2 fresh thyme sprigs
- Rough Puff Pastry
- 1 large egg, lightly beaten
- 1 tablespoon water
- 4 (14-ounce) deep bowls or ramekins (4 to 5 inches wide) or similar-capacity ovenproof dishes

Direction

- In center position, put oven rack; preheat the oven to 350°F.
- Pat dry beef. In a shallow dish, mix pepper, salt and flour. Add beef; turn to coat. Shake excess off; put on a plate. Heat oil in a 5-6-qt. wide ovenproof heavy pot on medium high heat till just smoking; in 3 batches, brown meat for 5 minutes per batch, occasionally turning, putting into a bowl.

- Add water, garlic and onion to pot; cook for 5 minutes till onion is soft, frequently mixing and scraping brown bits up from bottom of pot. Add tomato paste; cook for 1 minute, mixing. Mix in beef with juices accumulated in bowl, thyme, peppercorns, Worcestershire sauce, beer and broth; simmer. Cover. Put in oven; braise for 1 1/4-1 1/2 hours till sauce is thick and beef is very tender. Discard thyme; fully cool stew for 30 minutes, uncovered. If stew is warm while making pies, it'll melt the uncooked pastry top.
- On middle oven rack, put a shallow baking pan; put oven temperature to 425°F.
- Divide cooled stew between bowls; they won't be totally full. Roll pastry dough to 13-in. square, around 1/8-in. thick with a lightly floured rolling pin on a lightly floured surface. Trim edges; cut dough to quarters. Mix water and egg; brush 1-in. egg wash border around every square. Invert 1 square over each bowl; drape, lightly pressing sides to adhere. Brush some leftover egg wash over pastry tops; freeze to thoroughly chill dough for 15 minutes.
- In preheated shallow baking pan, bake pies for 20 minutes till pastry is golden brown and puffed.
- Lower oven temperature to 400°F; bake to fully cook dough for 5 more minutes.

Nutrition Information

89. Brie En Croûte

Serving: Serves 4 | Prep: | Cook: | Ready in:

Ingredients

- 6 ounces Brie, chilled
- 1 large egg
- a thawed 17 1/4-ounce package frozen puff pastry sheets (2 sheets)

- 3 tablespoons white-wine vinegar
- 1 teaspoon Dijon mustard
- 1 teaspoon chutney (preferably tomato)
- extra-virgin olive oil
- 2 vine-ripened tomatoes
- 4 cups mesclun (mixed baby greens; about 4 ounces)

Direction

- Discard brie rind; cut to 1/4-in. dice. Freeze the brie cubes for at least 1 hour and up to 3 days till hard, covered.
- Beat egg lightly in a bowl. Cut 4 rounds out from 1 pastry sheet with 3 1/2-in. round cutter; fit rounds in 4 1/2-cup muffin cups. Use frozen brie cubes to fill cups. Cut 4 rounds out from leftover pastry sheet with 2 1/2-in. round cutter; brush egg on 1 side of each round. Put 1 round on each filled cup, egg side down. Create steam vents in pastry tops with a sharp small knife; chill pastries for 30 minutes.
- As pastries chill, make dressing: Whisk chutney, mustard and vinegar in a small bowl; in a stream, add oil, whisking till emulsified. Season dressing with pepper and salt; you can make it 1 day ahead, covered, chilled.
- Quarter tomatoes; cut seed sections out. Cut the quarters to thin strips.
- Preheat an oven to 425°F.
- In middle of oven, bake pastries for 25 minutes till deep golden; cool Brie en croute in the cups for 5 minutes on racks. Keeping upright, lift from cups. Whisk dressing to combine. Toss pepper and salt to taste, enough dressing to coat, tomatoes and mesclun in a bowl; serve brie en croute while warm along with salad.

Nutrition Information

- Calories: 548
- Total Carbohydrate: 33 g(11%)
- Cholesterol: 89 mg(30%)
- Protein: 16 g(32%)
- Total Fat: 40 g(61%)
- Saturated Fat: 14 g(71%)

- Sodium: 466 mg(19%)
- Fiber: 2 g(9%)

90. Broccoli Rabe, Black Olive, And Smoked Mozzarella Pizza

Serving: Serves 8 as an hors d'oeuvre | Prep: | Cook: | Ready in:

Ingredients

- 1 puff pastry sheet (from one 17 1/4-ounce package frozen puff pastry sheets), thawed
- 1/2 pound broccoli rabe
- 1/3 cup drained Kalamata or other brine-cured black olives
- 2 garlic cloves
- 1 tablespoon fresh lemon juice
- 6 ounces smoked mozzarella
- 1 tablespoon extra-virgin olive oil

Direction

- Line parchment paper on a baking sheet. Unfold pastry sheet on a lightly floured surface; roll to 14x12-in. rectangle lightly. Put pastry on baking sheet; use fork to prick all over. Chill pastry for a minimum of 30 minutes and up to 1 day, covered.
- Preheat an oven to 400°F.
- Prep bowl with cold water and ice. From bottoms of broccoli rabe stems, trim 1-in. Blanch broccoli rabe in a saucepan with boiling salted water for 30 seconds; use tongs to put in ice water to halt cooking. In a colander, drain broccoli rabe well; pat dry. Slice broccoli rabe to 1/2-in. pieces; put in a bowl. Pit then chop olives and mince garlic. Add pepper and salt to taste, lemon juice, garlic and olives into broccoli rabe; toss well. Grate mozzarella coarsely in another bowl; cover and chill.
- In middle of oven, bake pastry for 15-20 minutes till golden. Evenly sprinkle cheese on pastry; on all sides, leave 1/2-in. border.

Evenly spread broccoli rabe mixture over cheese. Bake for 10 minutes or till heated through in middle of oven; drizzle oil on pizza.

- Cut the pizza to serving pieces.

Nutrition Information

- Calories: 261
- Sodium: 256 mg(11%)
- Fiber: 1 g(6%)
- Total Carbohydrate: 16 g(5%)
- Cholesterol: 17 mg(6%)
- Protein: 8 g(16%)
- Total Fat: 19 g(29%)
- Saturated Fat: 6 g(30%)

91. Camote Tartes Tatins With Pumpkin Seed Brittle

Serving: Makes 8 | Prep: | Cook: | Ready in:

Ingredients

- Nonstick vegetable oil spray
- 1/4 cup sugar
- Pinch of salt
- 1 cup raw shelled pumpkin seeds, toasted
- 1 tablespoon plus 1 teaspoon vanilla extract
- 1 teaspoon salt
- 2 large 3-inch-diameter yams (red-skinned sweet potatoes), peeled, cut crosswise into eight 1/2-inch-thick slices total
- 1 cup plus 1 tablespoon sugar
- 10 tablespoons unsalted butter, cut into 1-inch cubes, room temperature
- 1 17.3-ounce package frozen puff pastry (2 sheets), thawed
- 1 large egg
- Vanilla ice cream

Direction

- Brittle: Spray nonstick spray on a big rimmed baking sheet. Mix pinch of salt, 2 tbsp. water and sugar till sugar dissolves in a small saucepan on medium heat; put heat on high. Boil without mixing for 5 minutes till mixture is deep amber, swirling pan occasionally and using wet pastry brush to brush down sides. Mix in seeds; spread out on baking sheet immediately. Cool till hardened; break to pieces. You can make it 2 days ahead; keep at room temperature in an airtight container.
- Tartes: Boil 1 tsp. salt, 1 tbsp. vanilla and 8 cups water in a heavy big saucepan. Add yam slices and cook for 6 minutes till just tender; don't overcook. Put yam slices using slotted spoon on rack; cool.
- Preheat an oven to 375°F; spray nonstick spray on 8 3/4-cup ramekins or custard cups lightly. Mix 3 tbsp. water and 1 cup sugar in a small heavy saucepan on medium heat till sugar dissolves. Put temperature on high; boil without mixing for 5 minutes till syrup is deep amber, swirling pan occasionally and using wet pastry brush to brush down sides. Take off from heat. Add butter slowly, whisking till smooth and melted, it'll bubble; whisk in 1 tsp. vanilla. Divide caramel to ramekins; in each ramekin, put 1 yam slice on caramel.
- Cut pastry to 8 disks with 3 1/2-in. round cutter; use fork to pierce pastry all over. Put pastry disk on each yam slice. Beat egg to blend in a bowl; lightly brush egg on pastry. Sprinkle 1 tbsp. sugar; bake for 25 minutes till pastry is puffed and browned.
- On plates, invert tartes; serve warm with brittle and vanilla ice cream.

Nutrition Information

- Calories: 745
- Total Fat: 49 g(75%)
- Saturated Fat: 17 g(84%)
- Sodium: 398 mg(17%)
- Fiber: 3 g(11%)
- Total Carbohydrate: 69 g(23%)
- Cholesterol: 61 mg(20%)

- Protein: 11 g(22%)

92. Caramel Apple Pastis

Serving: 12 servings | Prep: 1hours | Cook: 2.5hours | Ready in:

Ingredients

- 3/4 cup sliced blanched almonds
- 8 Gala apples (3 1/2 lb), peeled, cored, and cut into 1/4-inch wedges
- 1 teaspoon fresh lemon juice
- 1 teaspoon cinnamon
- 1 stick (1/2 cup) unsalted butter, melted
- 1/2 cup honey
- 1/2 cup granulated sugar
- 1/2 cup confectioners sugar
- 10 (17- by 12-inch) phyllo sheets (from 1 package), thawed if frozen
- Accompaniment: vanilla ice cream or whipped cream
- a 9- to 9 1/2-inch (24-cm) springform pan

Direction

- In lower and upper thirds of oven, put oven racks; preheat an oven to 375°F.
- Keep 2 tbsp. almonds; spread leftover almonds on a baking sheet evenly. Toast for 5-8 minutes till golden in upper third of oven. Take out of oven.
- Put oven temperature to 400°F. Toss 1/4 tsp. cinnamon, lemon juice and apple wedges in a big bowl.
- Cook granulated sugar, honey and 1 tbsp. butter in a 12-in. deep heavy skillet on medium high heat for 6 minutes till mixture is deep golden, constantly and carefully mixing with a wooden spoon (it will foam).
- Add apples carefully; caramel will harden and liquefy. Gently mix from bottom of skillet so apples get coated with caramel. Cook for 10 minutes without a cover till apples are tender, occasionally mixing. In a colander above a big

bowl, drain apples; keep caramel. Put apples in another bowl; mix in toasted almonds. Put caramel through a fine-mesh sieve into a 2-qt. heavy saucepan; discard solids. Briskly simmer for 5-10 minutes till reduced to around 1/3 cup thick glaze; keep at room temperature or slightly warm.

- Mix leftover 3/4 tsp. cinnamon and confectioners' sugar; put in a sifter or a fine-mesh sieve.
- Brush some leftover butter on springform pan. Use plastic wrap and a dampened kitchen towel to cover phyllo stack. Keeping leftover phyllo covered, on a work surface, lay 1 sheet; brush using butter. Lightly dust cinnamon sugar over and lift the buttered phyllo; fit into pan gently with ends overhanging. Slightly rotate pan; butter then sugar another sheet. Put into pan; sheets shouldn't align. Repeat with 7 extra sheets, rotating pan every time so sheet overhang covers whole rim.
- Evenly spread apple mixture in phyllo sheet; smooth top.
- Brush butter on leftover phyllo sheet then dust some cinnamon sugar; lay on filling, slightly crumpling sheet gently to fit in pan. To enclose, bring overhanging bottom sheet edges up and over top sheet and filling; it'll appear rustic, but don't make tall peaks, they burn. Brush leftover butter on top; sprinkle reserved almonds. Generously sift cinnamon sugar on pastis; bake for 30-40 minutes till top is golden brown in lower third of oven.
- Put oven temperature to 425°F; bake for 15 minutes till top is shiny and deep golden brown. Edges might look very dark. Cool for 5 minutes in pan on a rack. Remove pan side carefully; cool for 5 minutes. Put on a platter; use serrated knife to cut into wedges. Serve with caramel sauce at room temperature or warm.

Nutrition Information

- Calories: 333
- Total Fat: 14 g(21%)

- Saturated Fat: 5 g(27%)
- Sodium: 81 mg(3%)
- Fiber: 4 g(16%)
- Total Carbohydrate: 52 g(17%)
- Cholesterol: 20 mg(7%)
- Protein: 3 g(7%)

93. Caramelized Bananas And Vanilla Cream In Phyllo Cups

Serving: Makes 6 servings | Prep: | Cook: |Ready in:

Ingredients

- 9 phyllo pastry sheets (each about 17x13 inches), stacked and halved crosswise, forming eighteen 8 1/2x13-inch rectangles
- 1/2 cup (1 stick) unsalted butter, melted
- 8 tablespoons (about) sugar
- 1/2 cup sugar
- 3 1/2 tablespoons cornstarch
- 2 cups whole milk
- 4 large egg yolks
- 1/2 vanilla bean, split lengthwise
- 3 large firm but ripe bananas, peeled, sliced thinly on diagonal
- Additional sugar
- Chocolate sorbet

Direction

- Phyllo cups: Preheat an oven to 350°F; butter every other cup generously in 12-cup muffin pan. On a work surface, put 1 phyllo rectangle; to avoid drying, use damp cloth to cover leftover phyllo. Brush melted butter on rectangle; sprinkle 1/2 tbsp. of sugar over. Put 2nd phyllo rectangle over 1st; brush using butter. Sprinkle 1/2 tbsp. of sugar. Repeat thrice; put 1 extra rectangle over. Brush using butter, creating stack of 6 rectangles. Cut out 2 6-in. round stacks with 6-in. diameter plate as guide and small sharp knife. In 1 buttered muffin cup, press each stack; repeat whole procedure twice, creating 4 extra phyllo cups,

6 in total. Bake cups for 15 minutes till crisp and golden. Lift cups carefully; to loosen, slightly twist and put on a rack. Fully cool; you can make this 2 days ahead, kept airtight at room temperature.
- Pastry cream: Whisk cornstarch and 1/2 cup of sugar to blend in a heavy medium saucepan; whisk in milk slowly then yolks. Scrape in vanilla bean seeds; add bean. Whisk on medium heat for 6 minutes till pastry cream boils and thickens. In a small bowl, strain pastry cream; directly on surface, press plastic wrap. Chill for a minimum of 3 hours and up to 2 days till cold.
- Preheat a broiler. On a small baking sheet, put phyllo cups; scoop 1/3 cup of pastry cream in every cup. Over pastry cream, overlap 5 or 6 banana slices in every cup; sprinkle extra sugar on bananas over. Broil pastries for 2 minutes, turning sheet for even browning, till sugar topping caramelizes. Put cups on a plate; spoon sorbet next to it.

Nutrition Information

- Calories: 518
- Saturated Fat: 13 g(64%)
- Sodium: 182 mg(8%)
- Fiber: 2 g(8%)
- Total Carbohydrate: 73 g(24%)
- Cholesterol: 172 mg(57%)
- Protein: 7 g(14%)
- Total Fat: 23 g(35%)

94. Caramelized Nectarine Almond Phyllo Cups With Frozen Orange Mousse

Serving: Makes 6 | Prep: | Cook: |Ready in:

Ingredients

- 6 large egg yolks
- 2/3 cup sugar

- 1/4 cup water
- 1 vanilla bean, split lengthwise
- 2 teaspoons grated orange peel
- 2 cups chilled whipping cream
- 1/4 cup Grand Marnier or other orange liqueur
- 1/2 cup (1 stick) unsalted butter, melted
- 4 sheets fresh phyllo pastry or frozen, thawed
- 1 cup apricot preserves
- 3 5-to-6 ounce nectarines, pitted, thinly sliced
- 1/3 cup almond paste (about 4 ounces), crumbled
- 1 large egg yolk
- 1 1/2 tablespoons unsalted butter, room temperature
- 1 1/2 tablespoons all purpose flour
- 1 teaspoon vanilla extract

Direction

- To prepare mousse: In a large metal bowl, whisk a cup of water, sugar, and yolks to blend. Set the bowl over a saucepan that has simmering water (be sure that the bottom of the bowl does not touch the water). Whisk the mixture constantly until it thickens and the candy thermometer registers at 170 degrees F, which is about 4 minutes.
- Remove the bowl from the simmering water then scrape the vanilla bean seeds into the egg mixture. Use an electric mixer to beat the mixture for about 5 minutes until it is thick and cool then mix in peel.
- In another large bowl, beat cream until it forms soft peaks. Add in Grand Marnier and beat until the cream mixture forms stiff peaks. Fold into the cooled mousse mixture. Cover and freeze for at least 6 hours or overnight until firm.
- To prepare phyllo cups: Use some melted butter to brush 6 3/4-cup sized custard cups. Place one phyllo sheet on a work surface, covering the remaining phyllo with plastic wrap, then a damp kitchen towel. Brush the sheet with melted butter and top with the second phyllo sheet. Brush again with melted butter and cut the stack of phyllo in to 6 5 1/2

to 6 inch squares. Press one squared stack into each cup with the butter side down. Repeat the buttering, stacking, and cutting with the remaining two phyllo sheets. Press one square stack on top of the first with the buttered side down in each cup. Position the corners at different angles and extend them over the edges of the cups, then brush the phyllo with butter. These cups can be made 4 hours ahead and let them stand in room temperature.

- Preheat a broiler and using a small saucepan over medium-low heat, stir preserves until they are melted. On a baking sheet, arrange nectarine slices and brush with some of the apricot preserves generously. Broil for about 2 minutes just until the glaze bubbles, moving the baking sheet to make sure they are broiling evenly. Cool the nectarines in a baking sheet. In a processor, combine vanilla, flour, 1 tablespoon of butter, yolk, and almond paste and process until smooth.
- Preheat an oven at 375 degrees F. Divide the almond filling between the phyllo cups in a thin layer. Place the cups on a baking sheet and bake for about 10 minutes until filling is set and the phyllo is golden. Cool for 15 minutes.
- Gently remove phyllo cups from the custard cups and place onto plates then, melt preserves in low heat. Arrange the nectarine slices on top of the almond filling and brush with the preserves. Then, place a scoop of frozen mousse along the side.

Nutrition Information

- Calories: 876
- Cholesterol: 352 mg(117%)
- Protein: 9 g(18%)
- Total Fat: 55 g(84%)
- Saturated Fat: 30 g(148%)
- Sodium: 125 mg(5%)
- Fiber: 3 g(11%)
- Total Carbohydrate: 88 g(29%)

95. Carrot Tart With Ricotta And Almond Filling

Serving: Serves 6–8 | Prep: 1hours10mins | Cook: 1hours35mins | Ready in:

Ingredients

- 1 1/2 cups sliced almonds (about 5 1/2 ounces)
- 2 pounds rainbow or orange carrots, peeled, cut into 3 1/2x1/4–1/2" sticks; plus 1 cup coarsely chopped tops
- 1 teaspoon finely grated orange zest
- 1/2 cup fresh orange juice
- 1/2 cup (1 stick) unsalted butter, divided
- 2 tablespoons sugar, divided
- 2 1/4 teaspoons kosher salt, divided
- 2 teaspoons red wine vinegar, divided
- 1/2 teaspoon ground allspice, divided
- 1/4 teaspoon plus 1/8 teaspoon freshly ground black pepper, divided
- 2 large eggs
- 1 1/4 cups whole-milk ricotta
- 2 tablespoons thyme leaves
- 1 (14–17-ounce) package frozen puff pastry, preferably all-butter, thawed
- All-purpose flour (for dusting)
- 1 tablespoon olive oil
- 1 small shallot, thinly sliced

Direction

- Preheat an oven to 400°F. On rimmed baking sheet, spread almonds; bake for 5 minutes till lightly toasted then cool.
- Meanwhile, cook 1 1/2 cups water, 1/4 tsp. allspice, 1 tsp. vinegar, 1 tsp. salt, 1 tbsp. sugar, 4 tbsp. butter, orange juice and carrots in big skillet on medium high heat for 10-12 minutes till crisp-tender, mixing occasionally. Put carrots on plate with slotted spoon. Keep liquid in skillet; cool.
- Put 1/4 cup almonds in small bowl; put aside. Process 1/4 tsp. allspice, 1 tbsp. sugar, leftover almonds, 1/4 tsp. pepper and 1 tsp. salt till finely chopped in food processor. Add leftover 4 tbsp. butter, orange zest, thyme, ricotta and eggs; process till smooth.
- Roll pastry to 18x13-in. rectangle gently on lightly floured parchment sheet; put along with parchment on rimmed baking sheet. Score 1/2-in. border around pastry lightly with sharp knife; make diagonal small shallow cuts within the border to make it decorative.
- Evenly spread egg mixture within pastry border; in geometric pattern, put carrots over. Shape 6 carrots to 3 even V shapes, points touching long border of crust, to create chevron/zigzag pattern. Fill using extra rows of V shapes; as needed, cut carrots to fit.
- Bake tart for 25 minutes till filling is golden brown and puffed. Put on cutting board; slightly cool.
- Meanwhile, heat saved carrot-cooking liquid in skillet on high heat; cook for 10 minutes till reduced to thick syrup, mixing. Brush syrup over tart while warm then cut to 12-16 pieces.
- Whisk 1/8 tsp. pepper, 1/4 tsp. salt, leftover 1 tsp. vinegar and oil in medium bowl then add reserved almonds, carrot tops and shallot; toss to mix. Put over tart to serve.

Nutrition Information

- Calories: 932
- Total Fat: 67 g(103%)
- Saturated Fat: 23 g(115%)
- Sodium: 883 mg(37%)
- Fiber: 9 g(38%)
- Total Carbohydrate: 66 g(22%)
- Cholesterol: 129 mg(43%)
- Protein: 21 g(42%)

96. Chai Spiced Crème Caramels With Raspberries And Pistachio Phyllo Crisps

Serving: Makes 2 servings | Prep: | Cook: | Ready in:

Ingredients

- 1/2 cup whole milk
- 1/2 cup heavy cream
- 6 green or white cardamom pods
- 1/2 teaspoon whole black peppercorns
- 1/2 teaspoon fennel seeds
- 3 (3-inch) cinnamon sticks
- 3 whole cloves
- 1/4 cup granulated sugar
- 1 large egg
- 1 large egg yolk
- 1/3 cup packed light brown sugar
- 1 cup fresh raspberries
- Pistachio phyllo crisps
- 2 (1-cup) ramekins (about 4 inches in diameter)

Direction

- Preheat an oven to 350°F.
- Boil cloves, cinnamon sticks, fennel seeds, peppercorns, cardamom, cream and milk in a heavy saucepan on medium heat. Take off from heat; stand for 15 minutes, covered.
- Meanwhile, in a dry small heavy saucepan, cook granulated sugar on medium heat, swirling pan to evenly melt sugar, till sugar melts to deep golden caramel. Put caramel into ramekins immediately; tilt to evenly cover bottoms.
- Whisk yolk and whole egg in a big bowl. Boil spiced milk again; in a slow stream, add to eggs, whisking. Put custard base through a fine sieve into a 2-cup measure. Add a pinch of salt and brown sugar; mix till sugar dissolves. Divide custard among ramekins.
- In a water bath, bake custards in center of oven for 30 minutes till set yet slightly trembling; custard sets while cooling. Take ramekins from water; cool crème caramels on

a rack. Chill for a minimum of 3 hours till cold, covered with plastic wrap loosely.
- Run a knife around inside ramekin edges before serving. Put raspberries, open ends up, on whole custard surface; gently press to adhere. Put a pistachio phyllo crisp on each ramekin; invert onto a plate. Remove ramekins carefully.

Nutrition Information

97. Cherry Hand Pies

Serving: Makes 9 pies | Prep: 25mins | Cook: 3hours | Ready in:

Ingredients

- 1 1/2 tablespoons cornstarch
- 2 cups fresh cherries, stemmed and pitted, or about 12 ounces frozen pitted cherries, unthawed
- 2/3 cup dried cherries
- 1/2 cup sugar
- 1 teaspoon vanilla extract
- 1/8 teaspoon kosher salt
- 1 14-ounce package all-butter puff pastry (preferably Dufour), thawed in refrigerator
- Flour (for dusting)
- 1 large egg white
- 1 1/2 teaspoon raw sugar

Direction

- Line parchment paper on a big rimmed baking sheet. Mix 1 1/2 tbsp. of cold water and cornstarch to blend in a small bowl. Cook fresh cherries and following 4 ingredients in a big saucepan on medium heat for 5 minutes till cherry juices are releases, occasionally mixing. Add cornstarch mixture; boil, mixing often. Take off from heat; cool, occasionally mixing, to room temperature.

- On a lightly floured surface, roll pastry out to 18x15-in. rectangle. Cut dough to 9 6x5-in. rectangles with a sharp knife or a pizza cutter. Whisk 1 tbsp. of water and egg white for egg wash in another small bowl.
- One pastry rectangle at a time, put on a work surface; brush egg wash on edges. On 1 side, scoop 3 tbsp. of cherry mixture; so short ends meet, fold dough over filling to make 5x3-in. packet. Use fork to crimp edges to seal; cut few slits over pie to vent with a sharp knife. Put on prepped baking sheet; repeat with leftover filling and dough.
- Brush egg wash on tops; sprinkle raw sugar then chill for 30 minutes. Preheat an oven to 375°F; bake pastries for 30-40 minutes till bottoms and tops are golden brown. Cool on baking sheet for 10 minutes. Put on wire racks; fully cool. You can make this 1 day ahead; stand at room temperature.

Nutrition Information

- Calories: 379
- Protein: 5 g(9%)
- Total Fat: 17 g(26%)
- Saturated Fat: 4 g(21%)
- Sodium: 144 mg(6%)
- Fiber: 2 g(9%)
- Total Carbohydrate: 53 g(18%)

98. Chicken And Mushroom Pie With Phyllo Parmesan Crust

Serving: Makes 6 servings | Prep: | Cook: |Ready in:

Ingredients

- 1 1/2-ounce package dried porcini mushrooms
- 1 cup hot water
- 9 tablespoons butter, divided
- 1 pound assorted fresh mushrooms (such as crimini, stemmed shiitake, and button mushrooms), sliced
- 3 garlic cloves, minced
- 2 cups low-salt chicken broth
- 3/4 cup Riesling or other fruity white wine
- 2 ounces thin prosciutto slices, cut into thin strips
- 2 teaspoons grated lemon peel
- 2 teaspoons chopped fresh thyme
- 1 teaspoon salt
- 1/2 teaspoon ground black pepper
- 3 tablespoons cornstarch mixed with 1/2 cup water
- 12 sheets fresh phyllo pastry or frozen, thawed
- 2 pounds skinless boneless chicken thighs, excess fat removed, thighs quartered
- 2 tablespoons chopped fresh Italian parsley
- 1/2 cup finely grated Parmesan cheese

Direction

- Mix 1 cup of hot water and dried porcini in a small bowl; stand for 20 minutes till porcini are soft. Drain porcini; keep liquid.
- Melt 3 tbsp. of butter in a big heavy pot on medium high heat then add garlic and fresh mushrooms; sauté for 8 minutes till mushrooms are browned. Add 1/2 tsp. of pepper, 1 tsp. of salt, thyme, lemon peel, prosciutto, wine, broth, porcini soaking liquid (leave sediment behind) and porcini. Lower heat to medium low; simmer for 20 minutes to merge flavors, uncovered. Whisk cornstarch mixture to mix. Add to skillet; mix for 1 1/2 minutes till mixture slightly thickens. Season sauce with extra salt and pepper to taste (optional). You can make this 1 day ahead; slightly cool then refrigerate, covered.
- Preheat an oven to 425°F. In a small saucepan, melt 6 tbsp. of butter; take off from heat. On a work surface, put 1 phyllo sheet; use plastic wrap sheet then damp towel to cover leftover sheet. Brush some melted butter on phyllo sheet; scrunch buttered phyllo sheet gently into a loose ball, 2 1/2-3-in. in diameter, with

both hands. Put on a work surface. Repeat using leftover melted butter and phyllo sheets.

- Boil mushroom sauce; mix in parsley and chicken. Put mixture in a 13x9x2-in. ceramic or glass baking dish; use phyllo balls to cover hot filling. Sprinkle with parmesan; bake for 15 minutes. Lower oven temperature to 350°F and bake for 20 more minutes till chicken cooks through and phyllo is golden.
- You scrunch the phyllo pastry dough to make pretty biscuits over the pot pie.

Nutrition Information

- Calories: 740
- Saturated Fat: 20 g(102%)
- Sodium: 1065 mg(44%)
- Fiber: 3 g(10%)
- Total Carbohydrate: 34 g(11%)
- Cholesterol: 207 mg(69%)
- Protein: 39 g(77%)
- Total Fat: 49 g(75%)

99. Chicken And Root Vegetable Pot Pie

Serving: 4 servings | Prep: | Cook: | Ready in:

Ingredients

- 3 cups low-sodium chicken stock
- 1 cup diced Yukon Gold potatoes
- 1 cup diced sweet potatoes
- 1 cup diced celery root
- 1 cup diced parsnip
- 1 large white onion, diced
- 1 pound boneless, skinless chicken breasts, diced
- 2/3 cup all-purpose flour
- 1 1/2 cups whole milk
- 1 cup fresh or frozen peas
- 1/4 cup chopped flat-leaf parsley
- 2 tablespoons chopped cilantro
- 1 teaspoon hot sauce

- Salt and freshly ground black pepper
- 1 sheet frozen puff pastry dough, thawed

Direction

- Preheat an oven to 400°F.
- Boil chicken stock in a big soup pot. Add onion, parsnip, celery root, sweet and Yukon Gold potatoes then cover; lower heat to medium low. Simmer for 5 minutes then add chicken; simmer till chicken is just cooked or for 10 more minutes. Use slotted spoon to remove veggies and chicken from stock; put aside.
- Put flour in a mixing bowl; add milk slowly, whisking into flour till blended well. Add this mixture into the stock; simmer till thick or for 5 minutes. Add reserved veggies and chicken, hot sauce, cilantro, parsley and peas to stock; season with pepper and salt.
- On a baking sheet, put 4 16-oz. ramekins; use veggie and chicken mixture to fill ramekins.
- Cut puff pastry to 4 pieces; lay each one on a ramekin. Press dough over ramekin edges gently.
- Bake till filling is bubbly and puff pastry is golden brown or for 20-25 minutes.
- Put hot ramekins onto serving plates.

Nutrition Information

100.   Chicken Filled Pastry (B'steeya)

Serving: Makes 10 servings | Prep: | Cook: | Ready in:

Ingredients

- 3 tablespoons extra virgin olive oil, plus more for puff pastry
- 2 pounds boneless, skinless chicken thighs
- Kosher salt and freshly ground black pepper
- 1 large onion, peeled and finely chopped

- 2 cloves garlic, peeled and minced
- 1/2 teaspoon freshly grated nutmeg
- 1/2 teaspoon ground mace
- 1 1/2 teaspoons ground cinnamon
- 1/4 teaspoon ground cloves
- 1/2 teaspoon saffron threads
- 2 to 3 cups chicken stock, or canned low-sodium broth, as needed
- 1/4 cup (1/2 stick) unsalted butter
- 1/4 cup brown sugar
- 3 tablespoons flat-leaf parsley, chopped
- 3 tablespoons cilantro, chopped
- 8 large eggs, lightly beaten
- Olive oil, as needed
- 10 sheets phyllo dough, defrosted if frozen
- 1 cup almonds, toasted and coarsely chopped
- Powdered sugar, as needed
- Ground cinnamon, as needed

Direction

- Filling: Preheat an oven to 400°F.
- Put oil in a heavy-bottom big stockpot on medium high heat. Use black pepper and salt to season chicken thighs. In batches, add chicken to hot oil; brown both sides for 5-6 minutes in total. Put browned chicken on a plate; put aside.
- Add saffron, cloves, cinnamon, mace, nutmeg, garlic and onion to same pot; sauté for 5-6 minutes till lightly golden and soft. Add 2 cups of chicken stock into the pot; scrape brown pieces up sticking to bottom of pan. Add chicken with any juices back into the pot; as needed, add extra stock to bring up liquids to chicken. Don't submerge it. Boil liquids; use tight-fitting lid to cover pot. Put in oven for 15-20 minutes till chicken is very tender and cooked through.
- When chicken is cooked, put on a plate; cool. Shred cooled chicken to bite-size, small pieces; put aside for assembly.
- Put braising liquid pot on medium heat; reduce liquids to 1 cup. Add eggs, cilantro, parsley, brown sugar and butter; cook till eggs are scrambled, constantly mixing. Take off from heat; put aside for assemble.

- Assemble: Preheat an oven to 400°F; lightly brush olive oil on paella pan or skillet.
- One by one, lay out 10 phyllo dough sheets on pan; brush each with little olive oil prior to putting next layer.
- In a layer, spread shredded chicken in middle of phyllo; leave lots of space for edges to fold up. Spread egg mixture on chicken; put almonds over.
- Fold overhanging phyllo dough over filling to enclose it in a pocket inside skillet; lightly brush olive oil on top. Bake for 10-15 minutes till pastry is golden brown and crisp.
- Use cinnamon and powdered sugar to garnish finished b'steeya. Cut into wedges; serve warm.

Nutrition Information

- Calories: 453
- Cholesterol: 246 mg(82%)
- Protein: 28 g(55%)
- Total Fat: 28 g(43%)
- Saturated Fat: 7 g(35%)
- Sodium: 606 mg(25%)
- Fiber: 3 g(13%)
- Total Carbohydrate: 23 g(8%)

101. Chickpea, Eggplant, And Tomato Tarts

Serving: Makes 4 vegetarian main-course or 8 to 10 side-dish servings | Prep: 45mins | Cook: 1.25hours | Ready in:

Ingredients

- 1 (1-lb) eggplant
- 1 3/4 teaspoons salt
- 1/2 cup extra-virgin olive oil
- 1 medium onion, halved lengthwise, then cut crosswise into 1/2-inch-thick slices
- 1 Turkish or 1/2 California bay leaf
- 3 garlic cloves, minced

- 1 (14 1/2- to 16-oz) can stewed tomatoes, drained, reserving juice, and coarsely chopped
- 1/2 teaspoon paprika (not hot)
- 1/8 teaspoon ground cumin
- 1 (15- to 19-oz) can chickpeas, rinsed and drained
- 1 teaspoon sugar
- 1 1/2 teaspoons black pepper
- 1/4 cup coarsely chopped fresh flat-leaf parsley
- 6 (17- by 12-inch) phyllo sheets (from a 1-lb package), thawed if frozen
- Garnish: fresh flat-leaf parsley leaves, torn into pieces

Direction

- Filling: peel then cut eggplant to 1/2-in. cubes; toss with 1 tsp. salt in a big bowl. Allow to stand for 15 minutes; rinse under cold water in a colander. Squeeze excess water out.
- Heat 2 tbsp. oil in a 12-in. heavy skillet on medium high heat till hot yet not smoking; cook bay leaf and onion for 5 minutes till golden, occasionally mixing. Add garlic, eggplant and 1 tbsp. oil; cook for 8-10 minutes till eggplant is tender, mixing. Add cumin, paprika and tomatoes without juice; cook for 3 minutes while mixing. Add leftover 3/4 tsp. salt, 1/2 tsp. pepper, sugar, chickpeas and reserved tomato juice; simmer for 5 minutes till most of liquid evaporates and filling is thick, occasionally mixing. Take off from heat. Mix in parsley; discard bay leaf.
- Tarts: Put oven rack in center position; preheat the oven to 425°F. Line foil on a big baking sheet.
- Unroll phyllo; use plastic wrap and a dampened kitchen towel to cover stack. Keep leftover phyllo covered. Brush some leftover oil on 1 phyllo sheet lightly; put 2 extra sheets over, brushing oil on each. Sprinkle 1/2 tsp. pepper; crosswise halve stack with sharp knife. In middle of each half, put 1 cup filling; crumple phyllo edges then shape to crescent. Leave filling exposed; use spatula to put on a

baking sheet. In same manner, make 2 more tarts; put on a baking sheet, 1/2-in. apart.
- Bake for 15-20 minutes total, rotate baking sheet after 10 minutes to 180°till tart edges are golden. Immediately serve.

Nutrition Information

- Calories: 556
- Sodium: 1008 mg(42%)
- Fiber: 14 g(56%)
- Total Carbohydrate: 57 g(19%)
- Protein: 13 g(26%)
- Total Fat: 33 g(50%)
- Saturated Fat: 5 g(23%)

---

102.   Chicks In Blankets

Serving: Makes 32 | Prep: | Cook: | Ready in:

Ingredients

- 1 17.3-ounce package frozen puff pastry (2 sheets), thawed
- 3 tablespoons (about) whole grain Dijon mustard
- 4 fully cooked chicken and apple sausages or chicken andouille sausages (about 12 ounces), each link cut crosswise into 8 rounds
- 1 large egg
- 2 teaspoons milk

Direction

- On a lightly floured work surface, unfold 1 puff pastry sheet; use fork to pierce all over. Cut pastry to 4 strips, 2 1/2-in. wide each; cut every strip to 4 squares to make 16 in total. In middle of 1 square, spread 1/4 tsp. of mustard then, put 1 sausage round over mustard; slightly press to anchor. Slightly overlapping, fold 2 opposing pastry square corners over sausage; to seal, press. Put on ungreased rimmed baking sheet, sealed side down; repeat with leftover sausage rounds, mustard and pastry then put 1/2 on 2nd baking sheet. You can make this 8 hours ahead and cover then refrigerate.

- Preheat an oven to 400°F. For glaze, whisk milk and egg in a small bowl to blend. Flip pastries right side up; brush using glaze. Bake for 10 minutes; lower oven temperature to 375°F. Bake for 12 more minutes till pastry is golden and puffed. Put on a platter; serve warm.

Nutrition Information

- Calories: 122
- Protein: 3 g(5%)
- Total Fat: 9 g(14%)
- Saturated Fat: 3 g(13%)
- Sodium: 153 mg(6%)
- Fiber: 0 g(1%)
- Total Carbohydrate: 7 g(2%)
- Cholesterol: 12 mg(4%)

103. Chocolate Raspberry Turnovers

Serving: Makes 32 small pastries | Prep: 20mins | Cook: 45mins | Ready in:

Ingredients

- 1 (17 1/4-oz) package frozen puff pastry sheets, thawed
- 1 large egg
- 1/3 cup raspberry jam
- 3 1/2 oz fine-quality milk chocolate, finely chopped
- parchment paper

Direction

- Place oven racks on lower and upper thirds of oven; preheat the oven to 425°F.
- Line parchment paper on 2 big baking sheets.

- Use a floured rolling pin to roll 1 puff pastry sheet out on a lightly floured surface to 12-in. square; brush extra flour from both sides off then cut to 16 squares.
- Whisk a pinch of salt and egg together. Put 1 tsp. chocolate and 1/2 tsp. jam in middle of each square; brush some beaten egg on square edges. Fold every square in half to make triangle; to seal, press edges. Brush some leftover egg over pastries; put on the lined baking sheet then chill on sheet while creating 16 extra pastries the same way, putting it onto 2nd baking sheet.
- Bake pastries for 20 minutes till cooked through and golden, switching sheet's positions halfway through baking; cool for 5 minutes on sheets on racks then serve warm.

Nutrition Information

104. Coconut And Pistachio Baklava

Serving: Makes 24 pieces | Prep: | Cook: | Ready in:

Ingredients

- One 1-pound box phyllo dough, thawed if frozen
- 1 1/4 cups (2 1/2 sticks) unsalted butter, melted
- 2 1/2 cups shredded unsweetened dried coconut
- 3/4 cup coarsely chopped unsalted pistachios
- 1/2 cup sugar
- 1/4 cup water
- 1 tablespoon orange flower water
- Pinch of salt
- 1 3/4 cups sugar
- 1 1/2 cups water
- Large pinch of salt
- 3 tablespoons orange flower water
- 3 tablespoons fresh lime juice

- 2 tablespoons finely chopped unsalted pistachios

Direction

- Start preheating the oven to 350°F. Rub butter on a 13-by-9-by-2-inch baking pan.
- Roll out the phyllo dough sheets; put the pile on a work surface. Use wax paper and then a wet kitchen towel to cover them so that they don't dry out. Take out 2 phyllo sheets, put them in the pan, and brush 1 tablespoon of the butter on them. Keep doing in the same way with butter and the phyllo until you finish 24 sheets of buttered phyllo.
- For the filling: In a medium-sized bowl, combine salt, orange flower water, water, sugar, pistachios, and coconut. Drizzle evenly over the phyllo in the pan with half of the filling. In the pan, put 2 sheets of phyllo and use 1 tablespoon butter to brush them. Keep doing in the same way until you finish 12 sheets of phyllo. Spread on top with the rest of the filling. Layer and butter the rest of the phyllo in the same manner. Brush bountifully butter on the top layer of the pastry and put any leftover butter on top. Slice baklava into 4 strips lengthwise and then into 6 strips crosswise using a sharp knife, be careful not to create any pressure on the phyllo.
- Put in the preheated oven and bake for 30 minutes. Decrease the heat to 300°F and bake until turning golden brown, about 1 hour and 10-15 minutes.
- For the syrup: In a medium-sized saucepan, boil salt, water, and sugar over medium-high heat, tossing until the sugar dissolves. Lower the heat and simmer until slightly thickened, about 10 minutes. Take the saucepan away from heat and mix in lime juice and orange flower water.
- Move the baklava to a wire rack to cool down for 10 minutes. Use the chopped pistachios to drizzle and top with the syrup evenly. Let it cool down entirely on the rack. (You can keep the baklava at room temperature, while covered securely, for a maximum of 2 days).

- Use a sharp knife to slice into pieces and enjoy.

Nutrition Information

- Calories: 301
- Sodium: 124 mg(5%)
- Fiber: 2 g(9%)
- Total Carbohydrate: 32 g(11%)
- Cholesterol: 25 mg(8%)
- Protein: 3 g(6%)
- Total Fat: 19 g(29%)
- Saturated Fat: 12 g(58%)

105.   Crab And Cucumber Pastries With Mustard Sauce

Serving: Serves 4 | Prep: | Cook: | Ready in:

Ingredients

- 4 sheets phyllo pastry
- 1/4 cup (1/2 stick) butter, melted
- 8 ounces flaked crabmeat
- 1/2 cup finely chopped red onion
- 1/3 cup mayonnaise
- 1/4 cup chopped fresh chives
- 1 tablespoon fresh lime juice
- 1/4 cup whipping cream
- 2 tablespoons Dijon mustard
- 2 tablespoons sour cream
- 1/2 English hothouse cucumber, cut into matchstick-size strips
- 1 tablespoon chopped fresh dill
- 1 tablespoon olive oil
- 8 teaspoons mango chutney

Direction

- Preheat the oven to 400 degrees F. On a work surface, put a sheet of phyllo; cover remaining phyllo then slather with melted butter. Add another phyllo sheet on top then slather with butter; repeat for another layer. Add the 4th sheet of phyllo on top; cut the phyllo stack into twelve squares. Place the squares on a big baking sheet. Bake for 6 minutes until golden; completely cool.

- In a big bowl, combine crabmeat and the next four ingredients; sprinkle pepper and salt to season to taste then set aside.
- In a small bowl, combine sour cream, mustard, and cream until blended; sprinkle pepper and salt to season. This can be prepared a day in advance. Place the phyllo squares in an airtight container. Separately cover the mustard sauce and crab mixture; place in the refrigerator.
- In a medium bowl, combine olive oil, dill, and cucumber; sprinkle pepper and salt then set aside for half an hour.
- In the middle of each four plates, put one square of phyllo; add a quarter cup each of crab mixture and cucumber on top. Dribble a teaspoon of chutney all over each plate. Repeat the layering process with the rest of the phyllo square, crab mixture, cucumber and chutney. Add a 3rd square of phyllo on top of each. Surround the stacks with mustard sauce.

Nutrition Information

- Calories: 477
- Saturated Fat: 14 g(70%)
- Sodium: 624 mg(26%)
- Fiber: 1 g(6%)
- Total Carbohydrate: 24 g(8%)
- Cholesterol: 113 mg(38%)
- Protein: 13 g(26%)
- Total Fat: 37 g(58%)

---

106. Cream Puffs With Lemon Cream Filling

Serving: Makes 10 servings | Prep: | Cook: |Ready in:

Ingredients

- 1/2 cup sugar
- 1 large egg
- 1/4 cup fresh lemon juice
- 1 1/2 teaspoons finely grated lemon peel
- Pinch of salt
- 3 tablespoons unsalted butter, diced
- 1 cup chilled heavy whipping cream
- 3/4 cup water
- 3/4 cup whole milk
- 3/4 cup (1 1/2 sticks) unsalted butter, diced
- 1/2 teaspoon salt
- 1 1/2 cups sifted all purpose flour (sifted, then measured)
- 6 large eggs, divided
- Robin Eggs malted milk candy (optional)
- 4 ounces high-quality white chocolate (such as Lindt or Perugina), finely chopped
- Pastry bag with 1/2-inch plain round tip

Direction

- Lemon cream filling: Whisk a pinch of salt, lemon peel, lemon juice, egg and sugar to blend in small heavy saucepan; add butter. Constantly mix on medium low heat for 4-5 minutes till thick enough to coat spoon and curd is hot; don't boil.
- Put lemon curd in medium bowl. Use electric mixer to beat cream till peaks form in another medium bowl; in 3 additions, fold whipped cream into curd. Cover; chill filling for 1 hour. You can make this 2 hours ahead, kept chilled.
- Crema puffs: Put 1 rack on bottom third and 1 rack on upper third of oven; preheat it to 425°F. Line parchment paper on 2 big rimmed baking sheets. Boil initial 4 ingredients in big heavy saucepan on medium heat till butter melts, mixing with wooden spoon. All at once, add flour; vigorously mix till dough forms and pulls away from pan sides. Mix for 1-2 more minutes till film appears on pan bottom. Put dough in big bowl; cool, occasionally mixing, for 5 minutes. Add 1 egg; beat till blended with wooden spoon. One by one, add leftover 5 eggs; beat till blended after each. Beat for 2-3 minutes till dough is shiny and smooth.
- In batches, put dough in a pastry bag with 1/2-in. plain round tip then pipe 1-1 1/4-in.

mounds on prepped baking sheets, 2-in. apart; smooth tops of mounds with wet finger.

- Bake puffs for 15 minutes then reverse baking sheets. Lower oven temperature to 350°F; bake for 30-35 more minutes till puffs are deep golden brown, firm and dry. Cool the puffs on the baking sheets.
- Assembly: Horizontally halve each puff; pull any soft dough out. Use 1 tbsp. of lemon-cream filling to fill puff bottoms. If desired, put egg-shaped candy over filling; to adhere, press on puff tops.
- Put white chocolate in a metal medium bowl; put bowl over a small saucepan with barely simmering water. Mix till chocolate is nearly melted and soft. Take from above water; mix till smooth and fully melted. Decoratively drizzle white chocolate on each cream puff with a teaspoon; put filled puffs on a platter. Refrigerate for a minimum of 15 minutes and up to 3 hours till chocolate glaze sets.

Nutrition Information

---
107.   Eggplant And Walnut Phyllo Pie

Serving: 6–8 servings | Prep: 1hours | Cook: 3hours | Ready in:

Ingredients

- 3 (1-pound) eggplants, peeled and cut into 1/2-inch-thick rounds
- About 1 1/2 cups olive oil, divided
- 3 medium leeks (white and pale green parts only)
- 2 cups coarsely grated _gravié_ra or sharp white Cheddar (5 oz)
- 3/4 cup coarsely grated Kefalotyri or Pecorino Romano (2 1/2 oz)
- 1 1/2 cups walnuts (5 1/2 ounces), chopped
- 1 1/2 teaspoons ground cumin

- 20 (12- by 7-inch) phyllo sheets, thawed if frozen

Direction

- Sprinkle 1 1/2 tsp. salt on eggplant; drain for 30 minutes in a colander then pat dry.
- Heat 3 tbsp. oil in big nonstick skillet on medium high heat till hot. In batches, fry eggplant for 5-7 minutes total per batch till golden brown and tender, adding 3 tbsp. oil per batch and flipping once. Drain on paper towels; cool down to room temperature and wipe the skillet clean.
- Preheat an oven with rack in middle to 375°F.
- Lengthwise halve leeks; slice thinly. Wash; drain.
- Cook leeks in 2 tbsp. oil in skillet on medium high heat for 7-9 minutes till golden; put in a bowl.
- Chop eggplant then add to leeks with pepper and salt to taste, cumin, nuts and cheeses.
- Trim phyllo sheets to 9-in. squares; use plastic wrap and a damp kitchen towel to cover phyllo stack. Layer 10 sheets in a 9-in. square baking dish; brush oil on each sheet lightly. Spread filling over; cover using leftover phyllo, brushing oil on each sheet.
- To vent, cut a few slits in phyllo; bake for 45-50 minutes till golden brown and puffed. Stand for 10 minutes.

Nutrition Information

- Calories: 1053
- Saturated Fat: 17 g(83%)
- Sodium: 642 mg(27%)
- Fiber: 9 g(37%)
- Total Carbohydrate: 55 g(18%)
- Cholesterol: 36 mg(12%)
- Protein: 20 g(41%)
- Total Fat: 86 g(133%)

108. Elsie's Apple Strudel With Burnt Caramel Ice Cream

Serving: Makes 8 servings | Prep: | Cook: |Ready in:

Ingredients

- 3/4 cup (1 1/2 sticks) unsalted butter, divided
- 6 Granny Smith apples (about 3 pounds), peeled, cored, chopped
- 1/2 cup plus 11 tablespoons sugar
- 1/4 teaspoon salt
- 1/2 cup raisins
- 1 1/4 cups walnuts, toasted; 1/4 cup coarsely chopped, 1 cup finely chopped
- 6 (17x13-inch) sheets phyllo pastry or twelve 14x9-inch sheets phyllo pastry, thawed if frozen
- Powdered sugar
- Burnt caramel ice cream

Direction

- Over medium heat, melt 1/4 cup of butter in a heavy large skillet. Place in apples and sauté for about 10 minutes until tender. Put in salt and half cup of sugar. Mix for about 1 minute, until the sugar is dissolved. Place in the raisins and cook for about 2 minutes until almost all of the liquid is absorbed. Mix in 1/4 cup of coarsely sliced walnuts. Smear the apple mixture into the rimmed baking sheet and let to cool.
- Line parchment paper on another rimmed baking sheet. Melt the remaining half cup of butter. Place one large phyllo sheet in the baking sheet (if you are using small phyllo, put two sheets of phyllo in the baking sheet and overlap a bit). Rub lightly with the melted butter. Drizzle with three tablespoons of finely chopped walnuts and two tablespoons of sugar. Repeat with walnuts, sugar, melted butter and four additional large phyllo sheets (or eight extra small sheets). Add the remaining phyllo sheet on top and rub with butter.
- Ladle the cooled apple mixture lengthwise down the phyllo; begin three inches in from 1 long side and leave two-inch border at the short sides. Roll up the strudel lengthwise with parchment paper as aid. Put the strudel with the seam side down onto parchment. Tuck in the ends to wrap the filling. Rub the strudel with butter. Drizzle with the remaining one tablespoon of sugar. You can make four hours ahead and refrigerate.
- Preheat an oven to 375°F. Bake the strudel for about 40 minutes, until turning golden brown. Let to cool for 15 minutes. Chop into eight slices with a serrated knife. Drizzle powdered sugar onto strudel; serve together with Burnt caramel ice cream.

Nutrition Information

109. Family Curried Beef Pot Pie

Serving: | Prep: | Cook: |Ready in:

Ingredients

- 2 tablespoons olive oil
- 1 large onion, cut into 1/4-inch dice
- 1 tablespoon minced garlic
- 1 tablespoon minced fresh ginger
- 2 tablespoons curry powder
- 3 tablespoons all-purpose flour
- 1 cup diced (1 inch) carrots
- 1 cup diced (1/2 inch) peeled potatoes
- 3 cups beef broth
- 2 cinnamon sticks, 3 inches long
- 2 tablespoons chopped mango chutney
- 1/2 cup golden raisins
- 1/2 cup frozen peas, thawed
- 1 tomato, cut into 1/2-inch dice
- 1/4 cup chopped flat-leaf parsley
- 2 cups diced (1/2 inch) leftover roast beef
- Salt and pepper, to taste

- 1 sheet frozen puff pastry, thawed

Direction

- Heat oil in a big heavy pot on low heat then add onion; cook for 8 minutes, mixing. Add flour, curry powder, ginger and garlic; cook for 2 minutes, constantly mixing.
- Add cinnamon sticks, broth, potatoes and carrots; simmer for 20 minutes, partially covered. Add pepper, salt, beef, parsley, tomato, peas, raisins and chutney; cook for 5 more minutes.
- Put mixture in a 1 1/2-qt. ovenproof round casserole dish. Roll pastry into circle 2-in. bigger than dish on a floured surface; brush some egg on dish rim. Use pastry to cover; crimp edges around rim. Cut 3 slits on top; brush leftover egg. Bake at 350°F for 40 minutes till golden.

Nutrition Information

110.   Family Size Chicken Pot Pie

Serving: Makes 6 servings | Prep: | Cook: | Ready in:

Ingredients

- 1 tablespoon each olive oil and butter
- 1 large onion, chopped
- 2 teaspoons finely minced garlic
- 2 tablespoons all-purpose flour
- 2 teaspoons dried tarragon
- 3 carrots, halved and cut into 1-inch pieces (1 1/2 cups)
- 1 cup peeled and diced (1/2-inch) russet potatoes
- 1 Granny Smith apple, cored and cut into 1/2-inch pieces
- 2 1/2 cups chicken broth
- 1/2 cup fresh or frozen peas

- 1/4 cup chopped fresh dill
- 1 medium-sized ripe tomato, seeded and cut into 1/2-inch dice
- 2 1/2 cups diced cooked chicken
- Salt and pepper, to taste
- 1 sheet prepared puff pastry (1/2 pound), thawed if frozen
- 1 egg mixed with 1 tablespoon water

Direction

- Heat butter and oil in a pot on low heat and add onion; cook for 10 minutes, mixing. Add garlic; cook for 2 more minutes. Sprinkle tarragon and flour; cook for 1-2 more minutes, constantly mixing.
- Add broth, apple, potatoes and carrots; boil. Lower heat to gently simmer; cook for 20 minutes while covered partially till veggies are tender. Add chicken, tomato, dill and peas; season with pepper and salt to taste. Cook for 5 more minutes.
- Preheat an oven to 350°F. Scoop mixture in a 2-qt. round ovenproof casserole. Roll out puff pastry to make a circle 2-in. bigger than the casserole on a lightly floured surface; brush some egg wash around the outside and inside rim of casserole. Lay pastry on top then trim overhang to 1-in. To seal, crimp edges around rim; to release steam, cut a few slits in pastry. Brush using leftover egg wash; bake for 40-45 minutes till crust is golden.

Nutrition Information

111.   Feta Puffs

Serving: Makes 21 hors d'oeuvres | Prep: | Cook: | Ready in:

Ingredients

- 1 sheet puff pastry (from a 17 1/4-ounce package), thawed

- All-purpose flour for dusting
- 3 1/2 ounce feta, crumbled (scant 1/2 cup)
- 1 tablespoon heavy cream or 1/2 tablespoon whole milk
- 1/8 teaspoon black pepper
- 1 large egg, lightly beaten
- 1 1/2 tablespoons fresh thyme leaves
- parchment paper

Direction

- Preheat an oven to 425°F.
- On a lightly floured surface, roll pastry out to 14x10-in. rectangle, around 1/8-in. thick. Preferably with pizza wheel, trim edges; cut pastry to 6 strips, 1 1/2-in. wide lengthwise. On a baking sheet, chill strips, covered with plastic wrap, for 10 minutes till cold.
- Blend 1 tbsp. of egg, pepper, cream and feta till smooth in a food processor; shape to 21 balls on a work surface.
- Brush some beaten egg on top of 1 strip keeping leftover pastry covered; space 7 cheese balls evenly down middle of strip, beginning 1/2-in. from 1 end then leave 1/2-in. at opposite end. Use another pastry strip to cover; press ends together. Press between balls of filing firmly yet gently; to seal top and bottom together, press pastry around every ball. Wipe away filling that leaks out. Brush some egg on tops of strip, not sides; sprinkle 1/2 tbsp. of thyme. Between mounds of filling, cut to make squares; put pastries on parchment-lined baking sheet, 1-in. apart. Use leftover thyme, filling and strips to create more pastries.
- In middle of oven, bake for 12 minutes till golden and puffed; serve warm.

Nutrition Information

Serving: Makes 6 servings | Prep: | Cook: | Ready in:

Ingredients

- 5 oz feta, patted dry if wet, then crumbled
- 1/4 cup walnuts, toasted and finely chopped
- 3/4 teaspoon dried Aleppo chile flakes
- 9 (17- by 12-inch) phyllo sheets (preferably spelt phyllo)
- 1 1/2 sticks (3/4 cup) unsalted butter, melted

Direction

- Preheat an oven to 350°F.
- Blend a pinch of salt, Aleppo flakes, walnuts and feta till ball starts to form in a food processor. Shape to 27 1-in. balls; roll balls to 2 1/2-in. logs.
- Leave the phyllo sheets stack; lengthwise cut to thirds. Stack thirds to 1 pile; use plastic wrap and a dampened kitchen towel to cover.
- With short end nearest you, put 1 phyllo sheet on a work surface; keep leftover sheets covered. Brush butter. Parallel to short end, put feta log in middle of phyllo sheet. Enclosing log, fold phyllo in half; brush with butter. Roll pastry up to look like a cigar, starting at log's end.
- Put on a lightly buttered baking sheet, seam side down; in same manner, create 26 extra rolls.
- Brush some butter on rolls; bake for 25 minutes till golden in center of oven. Cool on a baking sheet on rack; serve at room temperature or warm.

Nutrition Information

- Calories: 359
- Saturated Fat: 19 g(93%)
- Sodium: 358 mg(15%)
- Fiber: 1 g(3%)
- Total Carbohydrate: 16 g(5%)
- Cholesterol: 82 mg(27%)

- Protein: 6 g(12%)
- Total Fat: 31 g(47%)

113. Fuji Apple Tarte Tatin

Serving: Makes 8 servings | Prep: | Cook: | Ready in:

Ingredients

- Nonstick vegetable oil spray
- 8 medium Fuji apples
- 1 cup sugar
- 6 tablespoons water
- 1/4 cup (1/2 stick) unsalted butter
- 1 sheet frozen puff pastry (half of 17.3-ounce package), thawed

Direction

- Place rack on top third of the oven; preheat it to 425°F. Spray nonstick spray on an 8-in. diameter cake pan that has 3-in. high sides. Peel, quarter then core apples. Put in a bowl; put aside.
- Mix 6 tbsp. of water and sugar in heavy medium saucepan on medium heat till sugar melts, occasionally brushing pan sides down using wet pastry brush. Bring heat up; boil for 10 minutes without mixing till syrup is deep amber, occasionally brushing pan sides down using wet pastry brush and swirling the pan. Take the pan off the heat. Add butter; the caramel will vigorously bubble; mix to blend. Put caramel in prepped pan; cool for 5 minutes.
- In concentric circles, stand apples on end in pan, working carefully, crowding as much as you can. Cut any leftover apple quarters to thin wedges; put in empty spaces. Put pan directly on medium heat; simmer caramel for 2 minutes.
- Put pan into the oven; bake for 1 1/2 hours, lightly pressing apples with a spatula to compact occasionally, till caramel thickly bubbles and apples are tender.
- Meanwhile, on a work surface, unfold pastry sheet; cut out 9-in. round with 9-in. tart pan bottom for aid; use a fork to pierce all over. Chill till needed.
- Take pan from the oven. Put pastry over apples; tuck edges in. Put back in the oven; bake for 20 minutes till pastry is golden. Put the pan on a rack; fully cool tart for 3 hours in pan.
- Put platter over pan; hold pan and platter then invert; tart will go on platter. Slice to wedges; serve.

Nutrition Information

- Calories: 469
- Protein: 3 g(5%)
- Total Fat: 21 g(33%)
- Saturated Fat: 7 g(34%)
- Sodium: 80 mg(3%)
- Fiber: 4 g(18%)
- Total Carbohydrate: 68 g(23%)
- Cholesterol: 15 mg(5%)

114. Glazed Apricot Twists

Serving: Makes 8 pastries | Prep: 15mins | Cook: 40mins | Ready in:

Ingredients

- 1 frozen puff pastry sheet (from a 17 1/4-ounce package), thawed according to package instructions
- 1/2 cup apricot jam (6 ounces), melted
- 1/4 cup confectioners sugar
- 1 tablespoon heavy cream or milk
- 2 teaspoons fresh lemon juice
- parchment paper

Direction

- Put oven rack in center position; preheat an oven to 425°F. Line parchment paper on a baking sheet.

- Roll pastry out to 12x10-in. rectangle on lightly floured surface; then halve lengthwise. Slice each half crosswise to 4 5x3-in. strips to get a total of 8 strips.
- Spread 1/2 tbsp. of jam on each strip; lengthwise fold strips lengthwise in half to make 1 1/2-in. wide strips then twist each strip thrice; put on baking sheet.
- Bake for 15-20 minutes till golden brown; put twists on rack placed above a parchment sheet. Mix lemon juice, cream and confectioners' sugar together till smooth; brush on warm twists and serve warm.

Nutrition Information

115. Goat Cheese And Red Pepper Phyllo Triangles With Olive Frisée Salad

Serving: Makes 4 or 5 light-lunch or first-course servings | Prep: | Cook: |Ready in:

Ingredients

- 9 (17- by 12-inch) phyllo sheets, thawed if frozen
- 3/4 stick (6 tablespoons) unsalted butter, melted
- 2/3 cup rinsed and drained bottled red peppers (7-ounce jar), finely chopped and patted dry
- 5 ounces soft mild goat cheese (2/3 cup)
- 1/2 cup olive oil
- 1 tablespoon balsamic vinegar
- 1 teaspoon Dijon mustard
- 1/4 teaspoon salt
- 3 tablespoons extra-virgin olive oil
- 8 ounces frisée, torn into bite-size pieces (8 cups)
- 2 tablespoons chopped pitted Kalamata or other brine-cured black olives

Direction

- Phyllo triangles: Use 2 overlapping plastic wrap sheets to cover phyllo stack then a damp clean kitchen towel. With long side nearest you, put 1 phyllo sheet on a work surface; keep leftover sheets covered. Brush some melted butter. Put 2 extra phyllo sheets over; brush butter on each.
- Crosswise cut buttered phyllo stack to 5 12x3 1/3-in. strips.
- Near 1 corner of a strip, put 2 tsp. goat cheese and 2 tsp. red peppers; to enclose filling and make a triangle, fold phyllo corner over. Keep folding like a flag, keeping a triangular shape. Place triangle on a baking sheet, seam side down; use plastic wrap to cover. In same manner, create 14 extra triangles, using leftover filling and phyllo; you might have a bit of butter remaining.
- Heat oil in a 12-in. nonstick skillet on medium high heat till hot yet not smoking; in 2 batches, fry triangles for 1 minute per side till golden. Use tongs to put on paper towels; drain.
- Salad: Whisk salt, mustard and vinegar in a big bowl; in a slow stream, add oil, whisking till emulsified. Add olives and frisee; toss with dressing. Season with pepper. On plates, mound salad; put phyllo triangles next to it.

Nutrition Information

- Calories: 725
- Sodium: 566 mg(24%)
- Fiber: 4 g(17%)
- Total Carbohydrate: 29 g(10%)
- Cholesterol: 60 mg(20%)
- Protein: 10 g(21%)
- Total Fat: 64 g(99%)
- Saturated Fat: 21 g(106%)

116. Guava And Cream Cheese Pastry

Serving: Makes 4 to 6 servings | Prep: 20mins | Cook: 1.5hours | Ready in:

Ingredients

- 1 large egg
- 1/2 tablespoon water
- 6 ounces cream cheese, softened
- 1 tablespoon sugar
- 1/4 teaspoon pure vanilla extract
- 5 ounces guava preserves or paste (about 2/3 cup)
- 1 tablespoon fresh lemon juice
- 1 sheet frozen puff pastry (from a 17 1/4-ounce package), thawed

Direction

- Preheat an oven with rack in center to 425°F.
- Use fork to beat egg; put 1 1/2 tbsp. egg in a small bowl containing 1/2 tablespoon of water. Beat lightly to create egg wash.
- Put leftover beaten egg along with vanilla, sugar and cream cheese in a food processor; puree till smooth. Put in a small bowl.
- Puree lemon juice and guava preserves till smooth in a cleaned food processor.
- To preheat, put a baking sheet in oven for 5 minutes as you prep pastry.
- Roll pastry with a floured rolling pin to 11x9 1/2-in. rectangle on a floured work surface; crosswise halve rectangle.
- Put 1 pastry sheet on a foil sheet; leaving 1-in. borders on all sides, spread cream cheese mixture in a 3 1/2-in. wide strip down center of pastry. Over cheese mixture, dollop 2 rows of preserves lengthwise, 1-in. apart.
- Lengthwise fold leftover pastry piece in half; put folded edge nearest you. Every 1/2-in. through folded edge to the top border, cut 1 1/2-in. long slits, leaving 1-in. border on top and on sides of pastry.
- Around filling, brush some egg wash. Unfold cut pastry; lay on filling. To seal, press edges

lightly; brush some egg wash over dough. Bake for 25-30 minutes on foil on the hot baking sheet till golden brown and puffed. Put pastry on a rack; fully cool.

Nutrition Information

- Calories: 663
- Fiber: 2 g(6%)
- Total Carbohydrate: 70 g(23%)
- Cholesterol: 93 mg(31%)
- Protein: 9 g(18%)
- Total Fat: 39 g(60%)
- Saturated Fat: 15 g(73%)
- Sodium: 343 mg(14%)

117. Halvah Mille Feuilles

Serving: Makes 4 servings | Prep: 40mins | Cook: 55mins | Ready in:

Ingredients

- 8 sheets phyllo dough, defrosted if necessary
- Canola or olive oil, for brushing
- Granulated sugar, for sprinkling
- 1/3 cup honey or silan (date syrup, available at Middle Eastern markets or online)
- 1/3 cup pure tahini paste
- 2 cups non-dairy whipped topping (defrosted if necessary) or 1 cup heavy cream
- 1/2 cup crumbled halvah
- Honey or silan (date syrup), for serving
- Fresh raspberries, for serving

Direction

- Bake phyllo: preheat an oven to 350°F; line parchment paper on 2 baking sheets. Stack 8 phyllo sheets; halve crosswise. Brush oil on 1 half phyllo sheet; sprinkle sugar. Layer another half sheet over first; repeat using oil and sugar to make a stack with 4 half sheets. Complete top layer with sugar and oil. Repeat with leftover half sheets to make 3 extra stacks.

Cut every stack to 4 even pieces to create 16 stacks. Put stacks on baking sheets; bake for 8-12 minutes till golden brown. Cool for 15 minutes to room temperature.

- Halvah cream: Meanwhile, mix date or honey syrup and tahini in a small bowl. If using nondairy whipped topping, put in a big bowl; fold in honey-tahini mixture gently. Beat till soft peaks form if using cream. Incorporate into honey-tahini mixture gently; whip to stiff peaks and refrigerate till needed.
- Assemble dessert: On a dessert plate, put 1 phyllo stack; spread scant 1/4 cup of halvah cream. Repeat using 3 additional phyllo stacks and 2 extra halvah cream layers. Repeat process to create 3 extra servings. Drizzle date or honey syrup on each stack. Sprinkle halvah crumbles; garnish with raspberries.

Nutrition Information

118.   Ham And Swiss Puff Pastry Quiche

Serving: Makes 8 servings | Prep: | Cook: 40mins |Ready in:

Ingredients

- 2 sheets frozen puff pastry (one 17.3-ounce package), thawed
- 1 cup diced ham
- 2 cups coarsely grated Swiss cheese
- 2 cups sliced mushrooms
- 2 large eggs
- 1 tablespoon chopped fresh rosemary
- 1/2 teaspoon ground black pepper
- 1/2 teaspoon salt
- 1/4 teaspoon ground nutmeg
- 1 cup sour cream

Direction

- Preheat an oven to 400°F. On each of 2 baking sheets, unfold 1 pastry sheet; leaving 1/2-in. plain border, put mushrooms, cheese and ham over. Whisk nutmeg, salt, pepper, rosemary and eggs in a bowl; whisk in sour cream. On each pastry, put egg mixture on toppings; bake for 25 minutes till toppings are set and pastries are golden and puffed.

Nutrition Information

- Calories: 586
- Saturated Fat: 15 g(77%)
- Sodium: 737 mg(31%)
- Fiber: 1 g(4%)
- Total Carbohydrate: 35 g(12%)
- Cholesterol: 103 mg(34%)
- Protein: 19 g(37%)
- Total Fat: 41 g(63%)

119.   Herb And Cheese Pie

Serving: Makes 8 first-course servings | Prep: 40mins | Cook: 2.5hours |Ready in:

Ingredients

- 1 medium fennel bulb (sometimes labeled "anise"; 1 lb) with fronds
- 6 scallions (1 bunch), chopped
- 1/2 teaspoon salt
- 1 stick (1/2 cup) unsalted butter
- 1 lb 4% cottage cheese (3 cups)
- 1/2 lb feta, crumbled (2 cups)
- 4 large eggs, lightly beaten
- 2 tablespoons semolina* (sometimes labeled "semolina flour")
- 1/4 cup chopped fresh dill
- 1/4 teaspoon black pepper
- 2 tablespoons fine dry bread crumbs (not seasoned)
- 8 (17- by 12-inch) phyllo sheets, thawed if frozen
- a 9- to 9 1/2-inch (24-cm) springform pan

Direction

- In lower third of oven, put oven rack; preheat the oven to 400°F.
- Cut fennel bulb stalks off; chop sufficient fronds to get 1/4 cup. Discard stalks. Cut bulb and core to 1/4-in. dice.
- Cook 1/4 tsp. salt, scallions and fennel bulb in 2 tbsp. butter in a 10-in. heavy skillet on medium heat for 10 minutes with a cover till tender, occasionally mixing; uncover. Cook for 1-2 more minutes till liquid evaporates; put in a big bowl. Mix in leftover 1/4 tsp. salt, pepper, dill, fennel fronds, semolina, eggs and cheeses till combined.
- Melt leftover 6 tbsp. butter; brush some butter in springform pan. Sprinkle 1 tbsp. breadcrumbs on bottom. Unroll phyllo; use plastic wrap and dampened kitchen towel to cover stack. Brush some butter on 1 phyllo sheet, working quickly; keep leftover sheets covered. Fit into springform pan gently; let ends hang over. Rotate the pan a little then spread butter on another sheet of phyllo and arrange on top (sheets must not align). Sprinkle leftover 1 tbsp. breadcrumbs. Butter then fit 4 extra phyllo sheets in pan; for each sheet, rotate pan, the overhang should cover the whole rim.
- In phyllo shell, spread cheese mixture.
- Butter another phyllo sheet; fold in half crosswise. Butter once again. Fold to quarter; brush using butter. Lay over middle of filling; repeat using leftover phyllo sheet, layering over folded sheet in opposing direction. Toward middle to enclose filling and the folded phyllo, fold overhang; brush butter on top.
- Bake for 40-50 minutes till deep golden brown and puffed; cover pan loosely with foil sheet to avoid overbrowning once pie turns golden brown. Cool for 5 minutes in pan on rack. Remove pan side; cool pie on rack.
- Slice into wedges (leave base of pan underneath the pie). Serve either at room temperature or warm.

- You can bake pie 6 hours ahead; keep at room temperature, uncovered.

Nutrition Information

- Calories: 404
- Fiber: 2 g(7%)
- Total Carbohydrate: 20 g(7%)
- Cholesterol: 171 mg(57%)
- Protein: 20 g(41%)
- Total Fat: 27 g(41%)
- Saturated Fat: 15 g(77%)
- Sodium: 810 mg(34%)

---

120. Honey Roasted Onion Tart

Serving: Makes 6 appetizer servings | Prep: 1hours | Cook: 1hours40mins | Ready in:

Ingredients

- 1 sheet frozen puff pastry (half of 17.3-ounce package), thawed
- 3 bacon slices, cut crosswise into 1/2-inch pieces
- 1/4 cup honey
- 1/4 cup dry white wine
- 2 large sweet yellow onions (about 1 1/2 pounds), cut into 1/4-inch-thick rounds
- Nonstick vegetable oil spray
- 3/4 cup crème fraîche
- 1/2 teaspoon fine sea salt
- 1/8 teaspoon freshly grated nutmeg
- 1 teaspoon fresh thyme leaves

Direction

- In top third of oven, put rack; preheat it to 375°F. Roll puff pastry to 14x10-in. rectangle on lightly floured surface with lightly floured rolling pin. Toward middle on all sides, fold 1/2-in. of pastry edges to make 13x9-in. rectangle. Put pastry on big rimmed baking sheet; firmly press using fork on pastry edges to make rim then chill crust.

- Cook bacon till crisp and brown in small skillet on medium heat. Put on paper towels; drain. Keep 1 tbsp. bacon drippings from the skillet.
- Whisk reserved 1 tbsp. bacon drippings, wine and honey in big bowl then add onions; toss till coated. Use nonstick spray to coat separate big rimmed baking sheet; in even layer, spread onion mixture on sheet. Roast for 30 minutes; flip onions. Let rings separate. Roast for 30-45 minutes, turning often to evenly brown, till onions caramelize. Take out of oven; slightly cool onions.
- Put oven temperature to 400°F. Mix nutmeg, 1/4 tsp. black pepper, sea salt and crème fraiche in small bowl; spread crème fraiche with offset spatula on crust to folded edge. Put onions over crème fraiche; sprinkle bacon. Bake tart for 20-25 minutes till topping is bubbly and crust is light golden brown; sprinkle thyme. Serve.

Nutrition Information

---

121. Individual Tartes Tatin

Serving: Makes 2 individual tarts | Prep: | Cook: | Ready in:

Ingredients

- 1 Golden Delicious apple
- 1 frozen puff pastry sheet (from one 17 1/4-ounce package frozen puff pastry sheets), thawed
- 2 tablespoons unsalted butter
- 1/4 cup packed light brown sugar
- 2 tablespoons water
- Accompaniment if desired: vanilla ice cream

Direction

- Preheat an oven to 425°F.
- Peel apple then cut in half lengthwise; core. Cut 2 rounds out from pastry sheet with 1-cup 3 1/4-in. across, 2 1/4-in. deep ramekin as guide.
- Heat butter in a 7-in. heavy skillet on medium heat till foam subsides; mix in water and brown sugar. Add apple halves; cook for 3 minutes, frequently turning. Put apple halves in 2 1-cup ramekins placed on a baking sheet, cored sides up; evenly put sauce over.
- Put pastry rounds over apples; let pastry edges hang over apple sides. In middle of oven, bake tarts till pastry is golden brown and puffed or for 20 minutes; cool for 5 minutes on a rack. Invert a plate over every ramekin, 1 ramekin at a time; invert ramekin onto plate. Lift ramekins off carefully.
- Serve tarts along with ice cream

Nutrition Information

- Calories: 930
- Total Carbohydrate: 94 g(31%)
- Cholesterol: 31 mg(10%)
- Protein: 9 g(19%)
- Total Fat: 58 g(90%)
- Saturated Fat: 19 g(96%)
- Sodium: 317 mg(13%)
- Fiber: 4 g(16%)

---

122. Leek And Camembert Tart

Serving: Makes 8 first-course servings | Prep: | Cook: | Ready in:

Ingredients

- 1 17.3-ounce package frozen puff pastry (2 sheets), thawed
- 2 tablespoons (1/4 stick) butter
- 4 leeks (white and pale green parts only), sliced (about 4 cups)

- 1/4 cup water
- 2/3 cup whipping cream
- 4 ounces Camembert cheese, cut into 1/2-inch pieces
- 1 large egg
- Pinch of cayenne pepper
- Pinch of ground nutmeg
- 1/4 cup freshly grated Parmesan cheese

Direction

- Preheat an oven to 400°F. Roll each pastry sheet out to 12-in. square on a lightly floured surface; stack squares. Roll to 15-in. square. Cut stacked dough to 14-in. round with 14-in. pizza pan for guide; crimp dough edge to make 1/4-in. rim. Put on a baking sheet or a pizza pan; freeze for 10 minutes.
- Melt butter in a big heavy skillet on medium heat then add 1/4 cup water and leeks; cook for 15 minutes till leeks are tender. Season leeks using salt; put aside to cool. Simmer cream in a medium saucepan on medium heat. Lower heat to low and add camembert; mix till melted. Take off from heat; cool for 5 minutes. Whisk in nutmeg, cayenne and egg; put aside custard.
- Sprinkle crust with parmesan; spread leeks on top. Drizzle custard on top. Bake for 20 minutes till bottom is golden. Put on a rack; cool for 10 minutes. Serve at room temperature or warm.

Nutrition Information

- Calories: 499
- Protein: 10 g(20%)
- Total Fat: 37 g(58%)
- Saturated Fat: 15 g(73%)
- Sodium: 341 mg(14%)
- Fiber: 1 g(5%)
- Total Carbohydrate: 31 g(10%)
- Cholesterol: 66 mg(22%)

Serving: 8 | Prep: | Cook: 40mins | Ready in:

Ingredients

- Almond Meringue Crust
- ⅓ cup slivered or chopped blanched almonds
- ⅔ cup sugar, divided
- 1½ tablespoons cornstarch
- 3 large egg whites, at room temperature
- ¼ teaspoon cream of tartar
- ½ teaspoon vanilla extract
- Mango Topping
- 3 ripe mangoes, (¾-1 pound each)
- 1 tablespoon sugar
- ½ teaspoon freshly grated lime zest
- 1 teaspoon unflavored gelatin
- 2 tablespoons lime juice
- ¼ cup whipping cream
- ¼ cup guava jelly, or strained apricot preserves

Direction

- Almond meringue crust: Preheat an oven to 300°F; line parchment paper on baking sheet. Draw circle on paper using 10-in. cake pan or plate for guide. Flip paper over; line will show through. Otherwise, line aluminum foil on baking sheet, coat in nonstick cooking spray then dust flour; shake excess off. With your fingertip, trace the circle.
- Spread almonds in pie plate; bake till lightly toasted or for 8-15 minutes. Cool; put into food processor with cornstarch and 1/3 cup sugar. Process till nuts are ground coarsely; put aside.
- Use electric mixer on low speed to beat egg whites for 20 seconds in clean mixing bowl. Add cream of tartar; put speed on high slowly. Add leftover 1/3 cup sugar and vanilla slowly when whites start to form soft peaks; beat till stiff peaks form and meringue is glossy. Sprinkle almond-sugar mixture on meringue; use rubber spatula to fold in till just mixed.

- Put 1 cup meringue in piping bag with 1/2-in. open-star tip; spread leftover meringue inside traced circle. Pipe reserved meringue on outside edge to make rim.
- Lower oven temperature to 250°F; bake meringue crust for 50-70 minutes till firm to touch and golden. Cool on baking sheet on rack; peel foil or paper off carefully.
- Mousse: Cube 1 of the mangoes 3 hours before serving; put in blender or food processor with sugar. Process till smooth. Press puree through fine sieve above bowl to remove fibers; you should have 1/2 cup puree. Mix in lime zest; put aside.
- Sprinkle gelatin on lime juice in small heatproof bowl; stand for 1 minute till soft. Put bowl above barely simmering water till gelatin melts or microwave for 20-40 seconds on high; whisk into mango mixture. Refrigerate for 20 minutes till starting to set and slightly thick, occasionally mixing with rubber spatula. Whip cream till it just forms soft peaks in chilled bowl; fold into mango mixture gently.
- Assemble tart: Melt apricot preserves or guava jelly in small saucepan on low heat. Put meringue crust on serving plate; use 2 tbsp. guava jelly or apricot preserves to brush thin coat on crust. Put aside saucepan. Spread mango mousse inside crust; loosely cover. Refrigerate for 2 hours till mousse sets. Peel then thinly slice leftover 2 mangoes 1 hour before serving, not longer. Fan slices over mango mousse. Rewarm preserves or jelly; brush on mangoes. Refrigerate till serving time.

Nutrition Information

- Calories: 246 calories;
- Protein: 5
- Total Fat: 6
- Saturated Fat: 2
- Sodium: 26
- Fiber: 3
- Cholesterol: 8
- Total Carbohydrate: 47
- Sugar: 42

124.   Melktert

Serving: Makes 8 servings | Prep: | Cook: |Ready in:

Ingredients

- 400 g (14 ounces) puff pastry or flaky pastry (see tips, below)
- 500 ml (2 cups) full-cream milk (whole milk)
- 1 stick cinnamon
- 3 eggs, separated
- 80 ml (1/3 cup) cake flour
- 15 ml (1 tablespoon) cornflour (cornstarch)
- 80 ml (1/3 cup) castor sugar (superfine sugar — regular sugar may be substituted)
- 2 ml (1/2 teaspoon) baking powder
- 30 g (30 ml) (2 tablespoons) butter
- 15 ml (1 tablespoon) vanilla essence (vanilla extract)
- ground cinnamon

Direction

- Crust: Put oven on 400°F (200°C); grease quiche tin or 10-in. (24-cm) enamel shallow plate lightly. Roll pastry out; line tin or baking plate. Press in oiled foil piece; bake for 10 minutes then remove foil. Bake crust till golden and crisp for 5 more minutes; cool.
- Filling: Measure3/4 milk in saucepan; include in cinnamon heat right below boiling point. Put aside for 15 minutes to infuse.
- Mix baking powder, castor sugar (regular or super fine sugar), cornflour or cornstarch, flour, egg yolks and leftover milk. Strain cinnamon-flavored milk; put into a clean saucepan. Cook till custard thickens, mixing. Take off heat; whisk in vanilla essence and butter. Cool to room temperature; lower oven temperature to 350°F (180°C).
- Whisk egg white stiffly; fold into custard. Put into pastry shell; bake for 10 minutes. Lower oven temperature to 325°F (160°C); bake till

filling is set for 30 more minutes. Slide hot tart onto a plate; sprinkle ground cinnamon then serve warm.

Nutrition Information

- Calories: 184
- Fiber: 1 g(2%)
- Total Carbohydrate: 20 g(7%)
- Cholesterol: 74 mg(25%)
- Protein: 5 g(10%)
- Total Fat: 9 g(14%)
- Saturated Fat: 4 g(21%)
- Sodium: 85 mg(4%)

125.   Middle Eastern Nut Filled Multilayered Pastry (Baklava)

Serving: Makes about 36 small diamond-shaped pastries | Prep: | Cook: | Ready in:

Ingredients

- 3 cups sugar, or 2 cups sugar and 1 cup honey
- 1 1/2 cups water
- 2 tablespoons lemon juice
- 2 tablespoons light corn syrup (optional)
- 2 (3-inch) sticks cinnamon (optional)
- 4 to 6 whole cloves, or 1/2 teaspoon ground cardamom (optional)
- 1 pound blanched almonds, pistachios, walnuts, or any combination, finely chopped or coarsely ground (about 4 cups)
- 1/4 cup sugar
- 1 to 2 teaspoons ground cinnamon
- 1/4 teaspoon ground cloves or cardamom (optional)
- 1 pound (about 24 sheets) phyllo dough
- About 1 cup (2 sticks) melted butter or vegetable oil

Direction

- Syrup: Mix corn syrup, cloves, and/or cinnamon sticks (optional) with lemon juice, water and sugar on low heat for 5 minutes till sugar dissolves. Stop mixing; put heat on medium. Cook for 5 minutes till mixture is slightly syrupy; candy thermometer will read 225°. Discard whole cloves and cinnamon sticks; cool.
- Filling: Mix all filling ingredients.
- Preheat an oven to 350°. Grease a 15x10-in. jellyroll pan or a 12x9-in. or 13x9-in. baking pan.
- Put phyllo sheet in prepped pan; brush butter lightly. Repeat using 7 extra sheets; spread 1/2 filling. Put 8 more sheets over; brush butter on each. In middle layer, use torn sheets. Spread leftover nut mixture; finish with top layer of the 8 sheets, brushing butter on each. Trim overhanging edges.
- Lengthwise cut 6 even 1 3/4-in. wide strips with a sharp knife through top pastry layer; across strips, create 1 1/2-in. wide diagonal cuts to make diamond shapes.
- Sprinkle cold water lightly on top of pastry before baking to prevent pastry from curling then bake for 20 minutes. Lower heat to 300°; bake for 15 more minutes till golden brown.
- Slice through scored lines; slowly drizzle cooled syrup on hot baklava. Cool for 4 hours minimum. Cover; keep for up to 1 week at room temperature. Drizzle little extra hot syrup if baklava dries out as it is stored.

Nutrition Information

- Calories: 274
- Saturated Fat: 1 g(7%)
- Sodium: 62 mg(3%)
- Fiber: 1 g(5%)
- Total Carbohydrate: 34 g(11%)
- Protein: 3 g(6%)
- Total Fat: 15 g(23%)

126.   Millefoglie With Grappa Cream And Rhubarb

Serving: Makes 8 servings | Prep: | Cook: |Ready in:

Ingredients

- 2 1/4 cups whole milk
- 1/4 teaspoon salt
- 4 large egg yolks
- 2/3 cup sugar
- 2 tablespoons all-purpose flour
- 2 tablespoons cornstarch
- 2 tablespoons unsalted butter, cut into pieces
- 3 tablespoons grappa
- 2/3 cup chilled heavy cream
- 1 1/2 lb rhubarb stalks, cut diagonally into 1 1/4-inch pieces
- 1 cup water
- 1/3 cup sugar
- 2 tablespoons grappa
- 1 (17 1/4-oz) package frozen puff pastry sheets, thawed
- Garnish: confectioners sugar

Direction

- Custard: Boil salt and 2 cups of milk in a 3-qt. heavy saucepan. Meanwhile, whisk leftover 1/4 cup of milk, flour, cornstarch, sugar and yolks in a bowl. In slow stream, while whisking, add 1/3 of hot milk into yolk mixture; add to leftover milk in saucepan, whisking.
- Boil custard on medium heat, whisking; boil for 2 minutes, whisking. Take off from heat; mix in butter till melted. Mix in grappa. Put custard in a bowl; chill for a minimum of 1 hour till cold, surface covered in wax paper.
- As custard chills, cook rhubarb: Simmer grappa, sugar, water and rhubarb in a cleaned 3-qt. heavy saucepan for 4 minutes, gently mixing 1 or 2 times, uncovered, till rhubarb is tender yet not falling apart. Put pan in a bowl with cold water and ice; to stop cooking, stand for 2 minutes.

- Put rhubarb mixture into sieve placed above a bowl slowly. Put syrup back in saucepan, keeping rhubarb; boil for 10 minutes till reduced to 1/2 cup. Keep syrup and rhubarb at room temperature till needed, covered.
- As rhubarb cooks, prep pastry: Preheat an oven to 400°F.
- Unfold 1 puff pastry sheet; roll out gently to 14-in. square on a lightly floured surface with rolling pin. Put on buttered big baking sheet; use fork to prick all over. Repeat using leftover sheet.
- Bake in lower and upper thirds of the oven for 15 minutes total till pastry is golden and puffed, switching sheets positions halfway through baking; cool on baking sheets over racks.
- Use a big serrated knife to trim pastry edges. Cut every sheet to 12 3-in. squares; break pastry scraps to small shards.
- Making millefoglie: Use electric mixer to beat cream for custard in a bowl till it just holds soft peaks. To loosen, whisk custard; gently yet thoroughly fold in whipped cream.
- On each of 8 dessert plates, dollop 2 rounded tbsp. of grappa cream; put 1/2 of the rhubarb over. Use pastry square to cover rhubarb and cream on each plate. Create another layer using leftover pastry squares, rhubarb and grappa cream in reverse order; put pastry shards over. Evenly sift confectioners' on each serving; drizzle syrup over.

Nutrition Information

- Calories: 647
- Fiber: 3 g(10%)
- Total Carbohydrate: 64 g(21%)
- Cholesterol: 134 mg(45%)
- Protein: 9 g(19%)
- Total Fat: 38 g(59%)
- Saturated Fat: 14 g(72%)
- Sodium: 272 mg(11%)

127. Mini Shrimp Cornets

Serving: Makes 48 hors d'oeuvres | Prep: 45mins | Cook: 1.25hours | Ready in:

Ingredients

- 1 tablespoon unsalted butter
- 1/4 cup finely chopped onion
- 1 pound large shrimp (21 to 25 per pound in shell), peeled, deveined, and coarsely chopped
- 2 tablespoons medium-dry Sherry
- 1 tablespoon chopped fresh tarragon
- 1/2 teaspoon salt
- 1/4 teaspoon black pepper
- 1 (17 1/4-ounce) package frozen puff pastry sheets, thawed
- All-purpose flour for dusting
- 1 large egg
- 1 tablespoon milk
- parchment paper

Direction

- In lower and upper thirds of oven, put oven racks; preheat an oven to 400°F. Line parchment paper on 2 big baking sheets.
- Heat butter in an 8-in. skillet on medium low heat till foam subsides; cook onion for 2 minutes till soft yet not brown, occasionally mixing. Put in a bowl; cool.
- Add pepper, salt, tarragon, sherry and shrimp when onion is cool; mix till well combined.
- Roll 1 pastry sheet to 12-in. square on a lightly floured surface; in 1 direction, cut to thirds then fourths in opposing direction to create 12 3x4-in. rectangles. Diagonally halve each rectangle to make 2 triangles. On a work surface, put 1 triangle with longest edge nearest you; in middle of triangle, put 1 tsp. shrimp filling. Bring shortest side's bottom corner up to top point; wrap leftover corner around the resulting cone. To seal, pinch; put on lined baking sheet. In same manner, make more cornets; repeat with leftover pastry sheet. Chill 1st sheet of cornets while making second, loosely covered.
- Whisk milk and egg; brush some egg wash lightly over pastry tops.
- In lower and upper thirds of oven, bake for 18-20 minutes in total till golden, switching sheet positions halfway through baking.
- Cool cornets for 5 minutes on sheets on racks; use spatula to loosen from parchment gently. Serve warm.

Nutrition Information

- Calories: 69
- Protein: 2 g(4%)
- Total Fat: 4 g(7%)
- Saturated Fat: 1 g(6%)
- Sodium: 81 mg(3%)
- Fiber: 0 g(1%)
- Total Carbohydrate: 5 g(2%)
- Cholesterol: 16 mg(5%)

128. Mixed Berry Cobbler

Serving: 12 | Prep: 15mins | Cook: | Ready in:

Ingredients

- Nonstick cooking spray
- 1 14-ounce package frozen loose-pack mixed berries
- 1 (21 ounce) can blueberry pie filling
- 2 tablespoons sugar
- 1 6½-ounce package blueberry or triple-berry muffin mix
- ⅓ cup water
- 2 tablespoons cooking oil

Direction

- Use nonstick cooking spray to coat a 3 1/2-4-qt. slow cooker lightly; put aside.
- Mix sugar, pie filling and frozen mixed berries in a bowl; put berry mixture in bottom of prepped cooker.

- Cover; cook for 3 hours on low-heat setting. Put cooker on high heat setting. Mix oil, water and muffin mix till just combined in a medium bowl; put muffin mixture on berry mixture then cover. Cook till an inserted wooden toothpick in middle of muffin mixture exits clean or for 1 more hour. If possible, remove liner from cooker or turn cooker off; stand for 30-45 minutes without a cover to slightly cool before serving.
- Serve: Put warm cobbler in dessert dishes.

Nutrition Information

- Calories: 162 calories;
- Total Carbohydrate: 31
- Protein: 1
- Total Fat: 4
- Saturated Fat: 1
- Fiber: 3
- Cholesterol: 0
- Sodium: 116
- Sugar: 14

---

129. Moroccan Style Chicken Phyllo Rolls

Serving: Makes 32 hors d'oeuvres | Prep: | Cook: | Ready in:

Ingredients

- 1 small onion, finely chopped
- 1 tablespoon olive oil
- Scant teaspoon salt
- 3/4 teaspoon ground cumin
- 1/2 teaspoon ground ginger
- 1/2 teaspoon turmeric
- 1/2 teaspoon black pepper
- 1/4 teaspoon ground coriander
- 1 1/4 pound chicken thighs (with skin and bones)
- 3/4 cup low-sodium chicken broth
- 1/2 cup water

- 1 (3-inch) cinnamon stick
- 1/4 cup sliced almonds, toasted , cooled, and coarsely chopped
- 2 large eggs, lightly beaten
- 1 stick (1/2 cup) unsalted butter, melted
- 8 (17- by 12-inch) phyllo sheets, thawed if frozen
- 1 teaspoon ground cinnamon
- 2 teaspoons brown mustard seeds

Direction

- To prepare the filling: In a 3 qt. heavy saucepan, cook the coriander, pepper, turmeric, ginger, cumin and salt together with onion on medium heat for about 5 minutes, mixing until it becomes tender. Stir in cinnamon stick, water, broth and chicken, then simmer for about 45 minutes in total with cover, flip over once, until the meat becomes very tender. In a bowl, move the chicken using tongs then set aside the cooking liquid.
- Shred the chicken, get rid of the bones and skin then move to a big bowl once it's cool enough to be handled. In a 2-cup glass measure, transfer the cooking liquid (don't wipe the saucepan). Allow it to sit for a minute and remove the fat from the surface then get rid of the cinnamon stick. Put the liquid back into the saucepan and let it simmer for about 8 minutes on medium-high heat without cover until it reduces to 1/4 cup (the liquid will resemble a glaze in the pan's bottom), then stir in the almonds alongside shredded chicken.
- In a cup, set aside 2 tbsp. of beaten egg for the egg wash. Season the leftover egg lightly with pepper and salt, then cook in an 8-10-inch nonstick frypan with 1/2 tbsp. butter on medium-high heat, mixing until just set but still a bit soft. Mix the scrambled egg into the filling.
- Making rolls: In the upper and lower thirds of the oven, put the oven racks then preheat to 450 degrees F.
- On a work surface, place 1 phyllo sheet, keep the leftover phyllo sheet covered using a damp kitchen towel and overlapping sheets of

plastic wrap, then brush it liberally with some melted butter. Using a fine-mesh sieve, sift 1/4 tsp of cinnamon evenly on buttered phyllo, then put another sheet of phyllo on top and brush it liberally with butter.

- Cut the buttered phyllo stack in half crosswise then place one half with the long side nearest you. In a narrow strip along the edge nearest you, spread 1/4 cup of the chicken filling. Roll up the filling tightly in the phyllo, then leave the ends open. On a cutting board set in a baking pan, place the roll seam side facing down (it helps contain the mustard seeds when sprinkling). Use the leftover half stack to make another roll. In the same process, make 6 rolls more then move to a cutting board.
- Using the egg wash, brush the top of the rolls lightly then sprinkle mustard seeds right away; Press the seeds a bit to stick. Slice each crosswise into four portions the n place it on two baking trays, one inch apart. Bake for about 12 minutes in total, switch the positions of the baking trays halfway through the baking until the phyllo turns golden brown.
- On a rack, place the rolls and let it cool a bit.
- Note: Rolls can be prepared (not coated nor cut) a day in advance and chilled in the fridge with cover.
- Rolls can be prepared and sliced (not coated nor baked) 2 weeks in advance and frozen, wrapped tightly with a plastic wrap. Coat the frozen rolls then bake (no need to thaw) for about 20 minutes in the 350 degrees F preheated oven.

Nutrition Information

- Calories: 95
- Sodium: 98 mg(4%)
- Fiber: 0 g(1%)
- Total Carbohydrate: 3 g(1%)
- Cholesterol: 37 mg(12%)
- Protein: 4 g(8%)
- Total Fat: 7 g(11%)
- Saturated Fat: 3 g(14%)

130. Mushroom Consomme With Morels And Pastry "Hats"

Serving: Makes 6 (first course) servings | Prep: 40mins | Cook: 4.5hours | Ready in:

Ingredients

- 2 pounds white mushrooms, finely chopped (preferably in a food processor)
- 2 medium onions, chopped
- 2 quarts cold water
- 2 tablespoons 1-inch pieces fresh chives
- 1 1/2 cups boiling water
- 3/4 ounce dried morels (about 3/4 cup)
- 3/4 cup Sercial Madeira
- 1 pound frozen all-butter puff pastry, thawed
- 1 whole large egg, lightly beaten
- 1 large egg yolk
- Equipment: 6 deep (16-to 18-ounces) ovenproof bowls (4 to 4 1/2 inches across the top) such as "lion's head" bowls; a round template 1 1/2 inches larger than diameter of tops of bowls

Direction

- Preparation of mushroom consommé: In a 6-quart stockpot, simmer without cover the water, onions, white mushrooms, and 1 teaspoon of salt for 1 1/2 hours.
- Strain into a large saucepan the mushroom mixture using a large sieve lined with a damp paper towel, while slowly pressing the solids to extract liquid as much as possible; it must produce around 4 cups of consommé. (Pour in water, if less and bring consommé to boil again if too much, until it is reduced to 4 cups) Remove solids and sprinkle salt and pepper into the consommé to season.
- While consommé is simmering, prepare morels. In a small bowl add in boiling water over the morels. For about 20 minutes, immerse morels until softened.
- Using the slotted spoon, place morels into a medium-mesh sieve over a bowl. Using the

back of a spoon, press the morels to take out liquids. Add the morels liquid into the soaking liquid; reserve.

- Remove grit from morels by rinsing and place it into a small saucepan. Add in the Madeira. For 5 minutes, simmer it with cover.
- Finishing consommé: In a saucepan, add in the Madeira and morels into the consommé. When reserved soaking liquid settled, gradually add into consommé, carefully leave the last tablespoon with the sediment in the bowl.
- Add in chives into the consommé, allow to simmer with cover for 3 minutes. Let chill without cover for about 1 hour.
- Preparation for the pastry "hats": Slice in half crosswise, if the pastry comes in 1 sheet. Prepare a 13-in square on a lightly floured surface and roll out each of the pastry piece using a rolling pin that is floured lightly. On baking sheets, let rolled pastry chill for about 1 hour until it turns firm.
- On each sheet of the puff pastry, slice out 3 rounds using a template. On both sides of the pastry rounds, brush the excess flour. Brush some of whisked egg on top. For about 1 hour, chill the pastry rounds on baking sheets until it turns firm.
- Set oven to 425°F and place rack at the center; preheat.
- Distribute the cooled soup into the bowls. (Don't leave the soup to chill in bowls). Whisk yolk lightly, brushing each bowl's edges and downsides in a 1/2 inch wide strip. Work immediately, adding per piece of pastry round on top of the bowl. Slightly pull pastry to taut. Tightly seal by pressing the edge down against the side of the bowl.
- Prepare a large 4- sided sheet pan; transfer all bowls covered with pastry. Bake for 15-20 minutes until pastry turns golden brown and puffed. Serve quickly.
- Note: Consommé can be done 2 days in advance. Place in chiller and cover if it is cooled. Chill the soaked morels separately.

Nutrition Information

- Calories: 510
- Cholesterol: 64 mg(21%)
- Protein: 12 g(25%)
- Total Fat: 31 g(48%)
- Saturated Fat: 8 g(40%)
- Sodium: 229 mg(10%)
- Fiber: 4 g(14%)
- Total Carbohydrate: 45 g(15%)

131.   Mushroom Strudel

Serving: Makes 32 hors d□oeuvres | Prep: 45mins | Cook: 1.25hours | Ready in:

Ingredients

- 10 g (about 1/2 ounce) dried porcini (1/2 cup; also called cèpes)
- 1/2 cup boiling-hot water
- 1/2 pound fresh white mushrooms, trimmed and halved lengthwise
- 1/4 cup finely chopped shallots (about 2 large)
- 2 tablespoons unsalted butter
- 1/4 cup dry white wine
- 2 tablespoons finely chopped flat-leaf parsley
- 4 (17-by 12-inch) phyllo sheets, thawed if frozen
- 2 tablespoons rendered duck or goose fat or unsalted butter, melted
- Truffle oil for brushing (optional)
- Equipment: a wide-tooth serrated knife

Direction

- In boiling-hot water, soak porcini for 10 minutes in a small bowl till soft. Lift porcini out; squeeze extra liquid back into bowl. Wash porcini properly to take out any grit. Strain soaking liquid through dampened paper towel-lined sieve into another bowl; put aside.
- In a food processor, pulse white mushrooms and porcini till copped finely yet not minced.
- Cook shallots in butter in a big heavy skillet on medium heat for 1 minute till starting to soften, mixing. Add 1/4 tsp. pepper, 1/2 tsp.

salt, wine, reserved soaking liquid and mushrooms; cook for 8 minutes till liquid evaporates, occasionally mixing. Mix in parsley; spread filling on a plate. Chill for 10 minutes till cold, uncovered.

- Preheat an oven to 425°F with the rack in the center.
- As filling chills, place phyllo sheets stack on a work surface; halve crosswise. Stack halves; use plastic wrap to cover. From stack, take 1 phyllo sheet; keep leftover sheets covered. Put with long side near you; brush some duck fat lightly. Put another phyllo sheet over; brush using fat. In narrow strip along edge near you within to 1/4-in. of every end, spread 1/4 mushroom filling; roll phyllo around filling tightly and leave ends open. Put roll in baking sheet, seam side down; in same manner, create 3 more rolls, putting onto baking sheet. Bake for 12-14 minutes till golden brown; slightly cool on baking sheet on a rack. Brush very thin line of truffle oil (optional) on length of each roll using cotton swab tip; crosswise cut every roll to 8 pieces gently using serrated knife. Serve strudel at room temperature or warm.
- .

Nutrition Information

- Calories: 20
- Cholesterol: 2 mg(1%)
- Protein: 1 g(1%)
- Total Fat: 1 g(2%)
- Saturated Fat: 1 g(3%)
- Sodium: 13 mg(1%)
- Fiber: 0 g(1%)
- Total Carbohydrate: 2 g(1%)

132.   Mushroom And Goat Cheese Strudel With Balsamic Syrup

Serving: Makes 4 first-course servings | Prep: | Cook: | Ready in:

Ingredients

- 2 tablespoons plus 6 teaspoons olive oil
- 1/2 cup thinly sliced shallots
- 4 garlic cloves, minced
- 1 pound mushrooms, chopped
- 1/4 cup Sherry wine vinegar
- 1/3 cup dry Sherry
- 2 tablespoons finely chopped fresh parsley
- 3 fresh phyllo pastry sheets or frozen, thawed
- 1/2 cup crumbled soft fresh goat cheese (such as Montrachet)
- 1/2 cup balsamic vinegar
- 1 tablespoon mild-flavored (light) molasses

Direction

- Heat 2 tbsp. oil in big heavy skillet on medium heat then add garlic and shallots; sauté for 4 minutes. Put heat on high then add mushrooms; sauté for 15 minutes till golden and tender. Add sherry wine vinegar then sherry and boil for 6 minutes till nearly all liquid evaporates. Season with pepper and salt; cool. Mix in 2 tbsp. parsley.
- On work surface, put 1 phyllo sheet; brush using 2 tsp. oil. Put 2nd phyllo sheet over; brush 2 tsp. oil. Put 3rd phyllo sheet over; along 1 long phyllo side, sprinkle cheese 1-in. from edge. Put mushroom mixture on cheese; fold over short ends. Tightly roll up phyllo starting at long filled side; put on baking sheet, seam side down. Brush leftover 2 tsp. oil. Score strudel top through phyllo with long sharp knife creating 8 evenly space cuts; you can make this 4 hours ahead, chilled and covered.
- Preheat an oven to 375°F and bake strudel for 50 minutes till golden brown.

- Meanwhile, boil molasses and balsamic vinegar in a small heavy saucepan on medium heat for 10 minutes till reduced to 2 1/2 tbsp; cool.
- Cut hot strudel to 8 rounds at score marks with serrated knife; on each of 4 plates, drizzle balsamic syrup then put 2 strudel slices on syrup on each plate.

Nutrition Information

- Calories: 313
- Fiber: 2 g(9%)
- Total Carbohydrate: 25 g(8%)
- Cholesterol: 10 mg(3%)
- Protein: 10 g(19%)
- Total Fat: 20 g(30%)
- Saturated Fat: 5 g(27%)
- Sodium: 262 mg(11%)

133. Mushroom Stuffed Brie En Croûte

Serving: Serves 8 to 10 as an hors d'oeuvre | Prep: | Cook: | Ready in:

Ingredients

- 1 small onion
- 1/2 pound mushrooms
- 2 tablespoons unsalted butter
- 1 tablespoon dry Sherry
- 1/2 teaspoon freshly grated nutmeg
- a 17 1/4-ounce package frozen puff pastry sheets, thawed according to package directions
- a chilled 14- to 17-ounce wheel Brie
- 1 large egg
- Accompaniment: French bread slices or crackers

Direction

- Mince onion to get 1/2 cup. Chop mushrooms finely. Cook onion in a 9-10-in. heavy skillet on medium heat, mixing, till softened. Add nutmeg, sherry, mushrooms and pepper and salt to taste. Sauté on medium high heat, mixing, till mushroom liquid evaporates. Cool the mushroom mixture.
- Roll out 1 pastry sheet on a lightly floured surface to a 13-in. square. Use Brie as a guide to cut out a round the same size of Brie. For decoration, cut a mushroom shape out from scraps.
- Halve Brie horizontally. Roll leftover pastry sheet out to a 13-in. square. Put into a shallow baking pan. On pastry square, center the Brie's bottom half, cut side up. Spread mushroom mixture on it. Use the rest of brie half to cover mushroom mixture, cut side down.
- Wrap it snugly up on brie, without stretching pastry, to trim excess, leaving 1-in. pastry border on the brie's top. Lightly beat egg in a small bowl. Brush on the border. Put pastry round on top of Brie. Press dough edges together firmly yet gently to seal. Brush pastry's top with some egg. Put pastry mushroom on top of it. Brush mushroom lightly with some egg. Don't let egg drip over the mushroom's edge because it won't rise. Gently score pastry side, using a sharp small knife's back, with vertical marks. Don't cut through dough. Chill the brie for 30 minutes, uncovered. You can make brie 1 day ahead, loosely covered and chilled.
- Preheat the oven to 425°F.
- In center of oven, bake brie for 20 minutes till pastry is golden and puffed. In pan on rack, let brie stand for 15 minutes. Put on a serving plate using a spatula.
- Serve brie with crackers or bread.

Nutrition Information

- Calories: 394
- Total Carbohydrate: 29 g(10%)
- Cholesterol: 34 mg(11%)
- Protein: 7 g(14%)

- Total Fat: 28 g(43%)
- Saturated Fat: 9 g(43%)
- Sodium: 192 mg(8%)
- Fiber: 1 g(6%)

134. Oven Dried Tomato Tart With Goat Cheese And Black Olives

Serving: Makes 6 to 8 servings | Prep: | Cook: |Ready in:

Ingredients

- 5 tablespoons extra-virgin olive oil, divided
- 6 medium tomatoes or large romas, cored, halved crosswise, seeded
- 2 small garlic cloves, thinly slivered
- 2 tablespoons minced fresh thyme, divided
- 1 sheet frozen puff pastry (half of 17.3-ounce package), thawed
- 1 cup coarsely grated whole-milk mozzarella cheese
- 1/2 cup soft fresh goat cheese (about 4 ounces)
- 2 large eggs
- 1/4 cup whipping cream
- 1/3 cup oil-cured black olives, pitted
- 2 tablespoons freshly grated Parmesan cheese

Direction

- Preheat an oven to 300°F. Line foil on a rimmed baking sheet; brush 1 tbsp. oil on foil. Put tomato halves on baking sheet, cut side up; sprinkle 1 tbsp. thyme and garlic on tomatoes. Drizzle leftover 1/4 cup oil on top; lightly sprinkle pepper and salt. Bake for 2 hours till tomatoes start to shrink and slightly dried yet soft. Cool on sheet; you can prep this 1 day ahead; keep in a covered container in 1 layer in the fridge.
- Roll pastry to 13-in. square on a lightly floured surface. Put pastry in a 9-in. diameter tart pan that has removable bottom; firmly press pastry onto sides and bottom of pan then trim

overhang to 3/4-in. Fold in overhang; press and push crust 1/4-in. over pan. Use fork to pierce crust all over; chill for 30 minutes.
- In middle of oven, put rack; preheat to 375°F. Line foil on pastry; fill with pie weights or dried beans. Bake for 20 minutes till crust is set. Remove beans and foil; bake for 12 more minutes till crust edges are golden; if crust bubbles, pierce it with fork. Cool crust for 10 minutes. Lower oven temperature to 350°F.
- Meanwhile, mash leftover 1 tbsp. thyme, goat cheese and mozzarella cheese in medium bowl with fork. Season with pepper and salt. Add cream and eggs; mix till mixture is blended well. Evenly spread cheese filling in crust; put tomato halves, cut side up, in filling. Put olives between tomatoes; evenly sprinkle parmesan cheese over. Bake for 35 minutes till filling is set and puffed; cool for 5 minutes. Push up the pan bottom to release sides; serve the tart warm.

Nutrition Information

- Calories: 539
- Saturated Fat: 15 g(73%)
- Sodium: 469 mg(20%)
- Fiber: 3 g(11%)
- Total Carbohydrate: 26 g(9%)
- Cholesterol: 102 mg(34%)
- Protein: 16 g(32%)
- Total Fat: 42 g(65%)

135. Palmiers

Serving: Makes about 3 1/2 dozen | Prep: | Cook: |Ready in:

Ingredients

- A 17 1/4-ounce package frozen puff-pastry sheets (2 pastry sheets), thawed
- 1 cup sugar, more if needed

Direction

- Put 1 pastry sheet on work surface that's sprinkled with 1/4 cup sugar; evenly sprinkle 1/4 cup sugar over. Roll pastry sheet to 12-in. square using rolling pin; press sugar into both sides of pastry.
- Roll 1 edge up to center of pastry sheet; the same way, roll parallel edge up so 2 rolls touch. To seal roll, gently press. Tightly wrap in plastic wrap; chill for 30 minutes till firm; repeat with leftover sugar and pastry. You can make pastry rolls 2 weeks ahead, frozen.
- Heat an oven to 400°F. Use sharp knife to crosswise cut chilled pastry roll to just under 1/4-in. thick slices. You can freeze desired number of cookies and leftover frozen log again for later if using frozen roll.
- Put cookies on ungreased cooking sheet, 2-in. apart; keep leftover pastry well chilled. In batches, bake palmiers in middle of oven till tops are golden brown. Flip with offset spatula; bake for 10-12 more minutes. Put cookies on rack; cool.

Nutrition Information

- Calories: 265
- Total Fat: 12 g(18%)
- Saturated Fat: 3 g(15%)
- Sodium: 77 mg(3%)
- Fiber: 0 g(2%)
- Total Carbohydrate: 39 g(13%)
- Protein: 2 g(4%)

136. Pastry Wrapped Brie With Raspberries

Serving: Makes 8 appetizer servings | Prep: | Cook: | Ready in:

Ingredients

- 1/2 cup raspberry preserves
- 1/4 cup fresh or frozen unsweetened raspberries, thawed
- 1/2 teaspoon finely chopped fresh rosemary leaves
- 1 sheet frozen puff pastry (half of 17.3-ounce package), thawed
- 1 13.2-ounce Baby Brie cheese (about 6 to 7 inches in diameter)
- 1 large egg, beaten to blend (for glaze)
- Crackers and baguette slices
- N/A Baguette slices
- Grapes

Direction

- Preheat the oven to 400°F. In a small bowl, mix rosemary, berries and preserves to blend. Use pepper to season berry mixture. On lightly floured surface, roll pastry out to 12-in. square. Cut off top rind of cheese then throw rind. In center of pastry, put cheese, rindless side up. On cheese, spoon raspberry mixture on top. Over cheese, fold pastry on 2 opposing sides. Brush glaze on leftover 2 pastry sides. Fold it over the cheese then seal by pressing seams. Use glaze to brush pastry. Put onto baking sheet.
- Bake cheese for 30 minutes till pastry becomes deep golden brown, the pastry's top might open. Cool for 20 minutes. On a serving platter, put baked cheese. Surround with grapes, baguette slices and crackers.

Nutrition Information

137. Peach And Passion Fruit Phyllo Tarts

Serving: Serves 4 | Prep: | Cook: | Ready in:

Ingredients

- three 17- by 12-inch phyllo sheets, thawed if frozen
- 1 tablespoon unsalted butter
- 2 tablespoons crushed amaretti* (Italian almond macaroons)
- 1 1/2 cups nonfat vanilla yogurt
- 2 tablespoons sugar
- 3 firm-ripe peaches
- 1 passion fruit*
- 1 teaspoon honey
- *available at specialty foods shops and some supermarkets

Direction

- Shells: Preheat an oven to 425°F.
- Between 2 wax paper sheets, stack phyllo; use kitchen towel to cover. Melt butter in a very small saucepan. Brush 1/2 of the melted butter on 1 phyllo sheet on a work surface. Put 2nd phyllo sheet over buttered phyllo; brush using leftover butter. Evenly sprinkle amaretti crumbs on 2nd phyllo sheet; put leftover phyllo sheet over. Cut phyllo stack to quarters; fit 1 quarter in each of the 4 3-in. tart pans that have removable fluted rims. Fold in pastry overhang to make a shallow crumpled edge.
- Bake shells on a baking sheet in center of oven for 15 minutes till golden; cool in pans on rack. You can make shells 1 day ahead; keep in tart pans in a cool, dry place, loosely covered.
- Filling: Line double thickness of cheesecloth or paper towel on a sieve; put above bowl. In sieve, drain yogurt for a minimum of 1 hour, chilled and covered. Discard liquid. Put yogurt in a bowl; mix in sugar.
- Halve then pit peaches; cut to 1/2-in. thick wedges. Put wedges in a small bowl and halve passion fruit; scoop seeds and flesh into bowl. Mix in honey till well combined; you can make fruit mixture 2 hours ahead, kept covered and chilled.
- Assemble; remove shells from pans before serving. Divide yogurt between shells, smoothing tops; put fruit mixture over yogurt.

Nutrition Information

> ### 138.   Peach Raspberry Bundles With Orange Custard Sauce

Serving: Makes 8 servings | Prep: | Cook: | Ready in:

Ingredients

- 1/2 cup whipping cream
- 1/2 cup whole milk
- 1/2 teaspoon grated orange peel
- 3 large egg yolks
- 1/4 cup sugar
- Nonstick vegetable oil spray
- 1 17.3-ounce package frozen puff pastry (2 sheets), thawed
- 1 pound peaches, peeled, chopped
- 1/2 cup fresh raspberries
- 2 1/2 tablespoons plus 8 teaspoons sugar
- 2 tablespoons all purpose flour
- 1/2 teaspoon fresh lemon juice
- 1 large egg white, whisked until frothy

Direction

- Sauce: Simmer orange peel, milk and cream in small heavy saucepan; take off heat. Cover; steep for 15 minutes.
- Whisk sugar and yolks to blend in medium bowl; whisk warm milk mixture slowly into yolk mixture. Put back in the saucepan; cook for 7 minutes on medium-low heat, without boiling, constantly mixing, till mixture coats back of spoon then leaves path when a finger gets drawn across. Put in a bowl; chill for 3 hours till cold, occasionally mixing. You can make sauce 1 day ahead, kept chilled.
- Filling: Line parchment paper on a baking sheet; spray using nonstick spray. Roll 1 pastry sheet out to 14-in. square; cut out 4 circles with 5-in. diameter bowl for guide. Put circles on prepped sheet; use plastic to cover. Repeat using 2nd pastry sheet. Put pastry circles, over

- plastic wrap, on same baking sheet; freeze for 10 minutes.
- Toss lemon juice, flour, 2 1/2 tbsp. of sugar, raspberries and peaches in medium bowl.
- Roll pastry circles out to 7-in. diameter rounds on lightly floured surface; in middle of each round, put 1/4 cup of the fruit mixture. Bring dough over fruit; twist then firmly pinch to fully enclose. Put on a big baking sheet; freeze the bundles for 15 minutes at least. You can make this 1 day ahead, kept frozen.
- Preheat an oven to 400°F; brush egg white all over bundles. Sprinkle 1 tsp. of sugar on each; bake for 22 minutes till golden. Cool for a minimum of 10 minutes on a baking sheet on a rack.
- In middle of each of the 8 plates, put 2 tbsp. of sauce; put 1 bundle in middle of every plate. Serve warm.

Nutrition Information

- Calories: 524
- Cholesterol: 87 mg(29%)
- Protein: 8 g(15%)
- Total Fat: 33 g(51%)
- Saturated Fat: 10 g(49%)
- Sodium: 174 mg(7%)
- Fiber: 2 g(9%)
- Total Carbohydrate: 51 g(17%)

139.   Pear Clafoutis With Phyllo Crisps, Cider Sauce, And Quince Sorbet

Serving: Makes 6 servings | Prep: | Cook: | Ready in:

Ingredients

- 3 (17- by 12-inch) phyllo sheets, stacked and covered with 2 sheets of plastic wrap and a dampened kitchen towel
- 2 tablespoons unsalted butter, melted
- 3 tablespoons sugar
- 6 large egg yolks
- 1/4 cup sugar
- 2 tablespoons all-purpose flour
- 2 tablespoons cornstarch
- 2 vanilla beans, halved lengthwise
- 2 cups whole milk
- 1 tablespoon unsalted butter
- 5 tablespoons unsalted butter, softened
- 1/3 cup sugar
- 1/4 cup plus 2 tablespoons almond flour
- 2 tablespoons all-purpose flour
- 1/4 teaspoon salt
- 1 large egg
- 6 firm-ripe small Bosc pears (2 pounds total)
- 3 tablespoons unsalted butter plus additional for ramekins
- 3 tablespoons sugar plus additional for coating ramekins
- Accompaniments: cider sauce and quince sorbet
- 6 (8-ounce) ramekins (3 3/4 inches in diameter and 1 3/4 inches deep)

Direction

- Phyllo crisps: On a work surface, put 1 phyllo sheet; keep leftover sheets covered. Brush using some butter; sprinkle 1 tbsp. sugar. Halve sheet crosswise to make 2 rectangles; crumple each to around 4-in. diameter peaked free-form round. Put on a baking sheet using a metal spatula; in same manner, make 4 more crisps with leftover sugar, butter and phyllo. Dry for a minimum of 8 hours without a cover at room temperature.
- In center of oven, put oven rack; preheat oven to 500°F.
- Bake crisps for 2-4 minutes till golden; they burn easily so watch closely. Use spatula to put on rack; cool.
- Pastry cream: Whisk 2 tbsp. sugar and yolks in a metal bowl. Sift cornstarch and flour into a bowl; whisk till well combined.
- Use a sharp knife to scrape vanilla bean seeds into a small heavy saucepan; keep pods for another time. Add leftover 2 tbsp. sugar and milk; boil.

- In a stream, add hot milk into egg mixture, whisking; put into saucepan. Simmer for 3 minutes, whisking; take pan off from heat then whisk in butter.
- Through a fine-mesh sieve, force pastry cream into a bowl; chill for 1 hour, surface covered with wax paper.
- Almond cream: Use an electric mixer on medium speed to beat salt, flours, sugar and butter for 1-2 minutes in a bowl till fluffy and pale. Add egg; beat well.
- Pears: In center of oven, put oven rack; preheat the oven to 300°F.
- Peel pears; slice into quarter lengthwise then core. Melt butter in a 12-in. ovenproof heavy skillet on medium high heat till foam subsides; sauté pears for 2 minutes, occasionally turning. Sprinkle sugar on pears; cook for 5 minutes till pears start to be pale golden and sugar melts, occasionally turning.
- Put skillet in oven; roast pears for 5-7 minutes till very tender. Cool down to room temperature.
- Baking: Put oven temperature on 350°F. Generously butter ramekins. Coat in sugar; knock excess out.
- Beat pastry cream into almond cream till well combined; evenly spread 1/4 cup cream in bottom of a ramekin. Put 2 pear pieces over. Spread 1/4 cup more cream on pears; put 2 more pear pieces over. Repeat in leftover 5 ramekins. Put ramekins on a baking sheet; bake clafoutis for 30-35 minutes till golden and puffed; cool in ramekins for 1 hour on a rack.
- On each of 6 big plates, put 1 clafoutis in ramekin; put phyllo crisp over each. Serve quince sorbet and cider sauce on the side.

Nutrition Information

- Calories: 637
- Sodium: 203 mg(8%)
- Fiber: 6 g(24%)
- Total Carbohydrate: 75 g(25%)
- Cholesterol: 280 mg(93%)
- Protein: 10 g(20%)

- Total Fat: 33 g(51%)
- Saturated Fat: 17 g(86%)

140.   Pear Tarte Tatin With Vanilla And Ginger

Serving: Makes 6 to 8 servings | Prep: | Cook: | Ready in:

Ingredients

- 1 sheet frozen puff pastry (half of 17.3-ounce package), thawed
- 1/2 cup sugar
- 1/4 cup water
- 1 teaspoon light corn syrup
- 2 tablespoons (1/4 stick) unsalted butter
- 1/2 vanilla bean, split lengthwise, seeds scraped into small bowl
- 1 tablespoon grated peeled fresh ginger
- 5 medium-size firm Anjou pears (about 2 1/4 pounds), peeled, halved, cored, each half cut into 4 wedges
- Whipped cream

Direction

- Roll pastry to 10-in. square on lightly floured surface; trim edges to create 10-in. diameter round. Use fork to pierce round all over; slide onto rimless baking sheet then cover. Chill pastry for up to 1 day or while prepping pears.
- Use water and ice to fill big skillet; put aside. Mix corn syrup, 1/4 cup water and sugar till sugar dissolves in 10-in. diameter heavy nonstick ovenproof skillet on low heat. Increase heat; boil till syrup is dark amber color, swirling occasionally and using wet pastry brush to brush skillet sides down for 5 minutes. Take off heat; whisk in butter then ginger and vanilla-bean seeds. The caramel will bubble up. Put pears in circle in skillet, overlapping and cut side down; if needed, put a few around edge. Put skillet on medium heat; cook for 23 minutes till syrup thickens so it coats spoon and pears are tender. Put hot

skillet over ice in big skillet to quickly cool pear mixture; you can make this 4 hours ahead, stand at room temperature.

- Preheat an oven to 375°F. Put puff pastry round over pear mixture in skillet; around pears, tuck edges in. Bake tart for 35 minutes till pastry is golden and puffed; fully cool tart for 1 hour minimum and up to 6 hours in pan.
- Preheat an oven to 375°F; in oven, rewarm tart for 8 minutes. Put platter over skillet; hold platter and skillet together using oven mitts. Flip over to release tart; serve the tart with whipped cream.

Nutrition Information

141.   Pear And Fig Strudels With Ginger Cream

Serving: Makes 8 servings | Prep: | Cook: | Ready in:

Ingredients

- 1 1/2 pounds fresh figs, stemmed, each cut into 6 wedges (about 5 cups)
- 1 1/2 pounds firm but ripe pears
- 1/2 cup sugar
- 1/2 cup frozen cranberry-raspberry concentrate, thawed
- 1 1/2 teaspoons grated lemon peel
- 6 tablespoons dry breadcrumbs
- 4 tablespoons sugar
- 1 1/2 teaspoons ground cinnamon
- 10 frozen phyllo sheets, thawed
- 3/4 cup (1 1/2 sticks) unsalted butter, melted
- Ginger Cream

Direction

- Filling: Preheat an oven to 450°F. Butter a big baking sheet generously; in 1 layer, put pear and fig pieces on prepped sheet. Sprinkle sugar. Roast for 20 minutes till starting to

brown around edges and tender. Put fruit and juices from sheet to a medium bowl; cool. Mix in lemon and cranberry-raspberry concentrate; chill till cold.

- Strudels: Butter a separate big baking sheet. Mix 1 tsp. cinnamon, 3 tbsp. sugar and breadcrumbs in a small bowl. On a work surface, put kitchen towel; with short end toward work surface edge, put 1 phyllo sheet over towel. Use plastic wrap then a damp kitchen towel to cover leftover phyllo. Brush some melted butter on phyllo sheet; sprinkle 1/8 of the breadcrumb mixture. Put 2nd phyllo sheet over; brush using some melted butter then sprinkle 1/8 breadcrumb mixture. Repeat using 2 extra phyllo sheets, brushing melted butter on each then sprinkling 1/8 breadcrumb mixture on each. Put 5th phyllo sheet over; brush some melted butter but don't sprinkle breadcrumb mixture.
- Along 1 short side of the phyllo stack, put 1/2 fig mixture using a slotted spoon; leaving 1-in. plain border on the long sides, spread in 3-in. wide strip. Sprinkle 1/4 tsp. cinnamon and 1/2 tbsp. sugar on fig mixture. Fold phyllo's long sides in over filling; brush melted butter on folded sides. Roll phyllo up beginning at filled short side, fully enclosing filling. Brush melted butter all over. Put strudel on baking sheet, seam side down; repeat assembly process to create 2nd strudel. You can make it 1 day ahead. Use plastic wrap to cover; chill.
- In middle of oven, put rack; preheat to 375°F. Lightly brush melted butter on strudels; bake for 20 minutes till golden brown. Cool for 10 minutes; you can make this 6 hours ahead, standing at room temperature. On diagonal, cut each strudel to 4 pieces with a serrated knife; discard ends. On each of 8 plates, put 1 piece; put ginger cream next to it. Serve either at room temperature or warm.

Nutrition Information

- Calories: 432
- Fiber: 6 g(26%)

- Total Carbohydrate: 66 g(22%)
- Cholesterol: 46 mg(15%)
- Protein: 4 g(7%)
- Total Fat: 19 g(30%)
- Saturated Fat: 11 g(57%)
- Sodium: 156 mg(7%)

142. Pear, Cherry, And Pine Nut Tartlets

Serving: Makes 9 | Prep: | Cook: | Ready in:

Ingredients

- 1/2 cup apricot jam
- 1/2 teaspoon almond extract
- 1 large Bartlett pear (about 8 ounces), peeled, halved, cored, cut into 1/4-inch cubes
- 3/4 cup dried Bing cherries (about 4 ounces), coarsely chopped
- 1 sheet frozen puff pastry (half of 17.3-ounce package), thawed but still very cold
- 1 large egg yolk, beaten to blend
- 2 tablespoons pine nuts, toasted

Direction

- Preheat an oven to 400°F; line parchment paper on a baking sheet. Mix almond extract and jam in small saucepan. Put 3 tbsp. jam mixture in medium bowl. Add cherries and pears; toss.
- Cut 9 rounds from puff pastry with 3-in. diameter cookie cutter; discard trimmings. Evenly spacing, put rounds over baking sheet. Use fork to pierce center of pastries; leave 1/4-in. edge unpierced. Brush beaten egg yolk on edges. Mound fruit mixture in middle of pastries; press to compact. Bake for 25 minutes till golden brown.
- Heat leftover jam mixture till just starting to boil in saucepan on medium high heat; brush jam mixture on pastry edges and filling. Sprinkle pine nuts. Put tarts on rack; fully cool.

You can make it 8 hours ahead, kept at room temperature.

Nutrition Information

- Calories: 235
- Saturated Fat: 3 g(15%)
- Sodium: 76 mg(3%)
- Fiber: 1 g(6%)
- Total Carbohydrate: 29 g(10%)
- Cholesterol: 20 mg(7%)
- Protein: 3 g(6%)
- Total Fat: 12 g(19%)

143. Pecan Orange Baklava Pie

Serving: 16–20 servings | Prep: 1hours | Cook: 1hours45mins | Ready in:

Ingredients

- 2/3 cup honey
- 2 (3") cinnamon sticks
- 1 1 /2 cups sugar, divided
- 3 tablespoons bourbon
- 3 cups raw pecans (about 12 ounces)
- 1/2 teaspoon ground cinnamon
- 1 teaspoon finely grated orange zest, plus 1 teaspoon orange curls
- 20 (17x12") sheets fresh phyllo pastry or frozen, thawed
- 1 cup (2 stick) unsalted butter, melted
- A 9-inch springform pan

Direction

- Preheat an oven to 350°F. Boil 1 cup of water, 1 cup of sugar, cinnamon sticks and honey in a heavy medium saucepan on medium high heat, mixing till sugar melts. Lower heat to medium; boil for 15-18 minutes till syrup reduces to 1 1/2 cups. Put in a medium bowl and mix in bourbon; cool.

- Meanwhile, on big rimmed baking sheet, spread pecans; toast for 13-15 minutes till golden brown. Cool. Put nuts in food processor and add the leftover 1/2 cup of sugar, 1 tsp. of orange zest and ground cinnamon; pulse till chopped coarsely.
- Put phyllo sheet stacks on a work surface; use plastic wrap to cover then a damp kitchen towel. Cut to 9-in. circles carefully, leaving as much phyllo leftover as you can, using a springform pan's bottom as guide and beginning at phyllo edge. Cover phyllo circles. Cut leftover phyllo to 4 1/2-in. half-circles using pan's bottom as a guide.
- Put bottom in pan; brush butter on bottom. Put 1 phyllo circle in pan; generously brush using butter. Repeat using 2 extra phyllo circles. Put 2 halves over to make a full circle; brush using butter. Put full circle over; brush using butter. Spread 1/5, (around 1 cup) of nut mixture on phyllo. Repeat the layers 4 more times; as needed, layer half circles in between full circles. Put leftover phyllo sheets over; brush butter on top.
- Cut through top layer with sharp knife to divide to 8 equal wedges; don't cut through to pan bottom. Inside 1 wedge, create 2 straight cuts, parallel to 1 wedge side, 1-in. apart. In adjacent eighth to mirror first cuts, create 2 extra cuts, making 3 V-shapes; repeat with leftover 3 quadrants. To make 6 diamond shapes within every eighth, create 2 extra cuts per eighth. Put pan to a rimmed baking sheet; bake pie for 45 minutes till phyllo is golden brown.
- In 4 additions, put cooled syrup on hot baklava; put orange curls over. Cool; cut baklava to thin slices.
- You can make syrup 1 day ahead, chill and cover. You can make baklava 3 days ahead, covered and kept in room temperature.

Nutrition Information

- Calories: 394
- Sodium: 104 mg(4%)
- Fiber: 2 g(10%)
- Total Carbohydrate: 41 g(14%)
- Cholesterol: 27 mg(9%)
- Protein: 3 g(7%)
- Total Fat: 25 g(39%)
- Saturated Fat: 8 g(40%)

144. Pepperoni And Asiago Pinwheels

Serving: Makes about 60 pinwheels | Prep: | Cook: | Ready in:

Ingredients

- 1/2 cup grated Asiago cheese*
- 3/4 teaspoon dried thyme
- 3/4 teaspoon dried oregano
- 1/4 teaspoon ground black pepper
- 1 sheet frozen puff pastry (half of 17.3-ounce package), thawed
- 2 tablespoons honey-Dijon mustard
- 2 ounces packaged sliced pepperoni (about twenty-four 1 1/2-inch-diameter slices)
- 1 large egg, beaten to blend
- Nonstick vegetable oil cooking spray

Direction

- In a medium bowl, mix initial 4 ingredients. Halve puff pastry crosswise to create 2 rectangles. Leaving 1-in. plain border on 1 long edge, spread 1 tbsp. of mustard on 1 puff pastry rectangle; in 1 layer, put 1/2 of pepperoni over mustard. Put 1/2 of cheese mixture over pepperoni; brush egg on plain border. Roll pastry up beginning at side opposing plain border; seal at egg-coated edge. Put pastry roll on medium baking sheet, seam side down. Repeat with leftover egg, cheese mixture, pepperoni, mustard and pastry rectangle; chill rolls for 30 minutes till firm or wrap then chill for up to a day. Preheat an oven to 400°F. Line foil on 2 baking sheets; spray vegetable oil spray lightly. Cut every pastry roll to 30 1/4-in. thick rounds; put pinwheels on prepped sheets. Bake for 15 minutes till golden. Put on a platter; serve.

Nutrition Information

- Calories: 33
- Fiber: 0 g(0%)
- Total Carbohydrate: 2 g(1%)
- Cholesterol: 5 mg(2%)
- Protein: 1 g(2%)
- Total Fat: 2 g(4%)
- Saturated Fat: 1 g(4%)
- Sodium: 46 mg(2%)

145.   Philadelphia Clam Pies

Serving: Makes 6 main-course servings | Prep: 45mins | Cook: 114hours | Ready in:

Ingredients

- 1 1/2 lb boiling potatoes
- 1/2 stick (1/4 cup) unsalted butter
- 1 bacon slice, chopped
- 1 large onion, chopped
- 1 garlic clove, finely chopped
- 1/2 teaspoon salt
- 1 Turkish or 1/2 California bay leaf
- 1 sprig fresh thyme
- 1 whole clove
- 3 medium carrots, cut into 1/4-inch dice
- 2 celery ribs, cut into 1/4-inch dice
- 2 tablespoons dry white wine
- 1 (8-oz) bottle clam juice
- 2 teaspoons cornstarch
- 24 small clams (1 1/2 to 2 inches across), shucked, reserving their liquor, and chopped if desired
- 1 (17 1/2-oz) package frozen puff pastry, thawed
- 1 large egg, lightly beaten
- 6 (12- to 14-oz) deep ovenproof soup bowls

Direction

- Peel potatoes; cut to 1/4-in. dice.
- Heat bacon and butter in a 12-in. heavy skillet on medium high heat till foam subsides then add salt, garlic and onion; cook for 5 minutes till onion is pale golden, occasionally mixing. Add potatoes, celery, carrots, clove, thyme and bay leaf then lower heat to medium; cook for 15 minutes till veggies are nearly tender and golden, occasionally mixing, don't burn. Add wine; scrape up brown bits.
- Mix cornstarch and clam juices. Add to veggies in skillet; simmer. Cover the skillet; simmer for 5 minutes till veggies are tender. Uncover; mix in clams with their liquor. Simmer; cook for 1 minute. Take off from heat; cool, uncovered, to warm. Discard clove and bay leaf.
- Place oven rack in center position; preheat the oven to 425°F.
- Roll 1 pastry sheet out on a lightly floured surface with lightly floured rolling pin to 12-in. square; cut 3 pastry squares at least 1-in. bigger all around than soup bowl's tops. Repeat with leftover pastry sheet.
- Leaving at least 3/4-in. space between filling surface and bowl tops, divide clam filling to soup bowls. Brush egg on 1 pastry square; use it to cover 1 bowl, egg side down, firmly pressing pastry edges on outside of bowl. Repeat with leftover bowls and pastry squares; brush leftover egg over pastry tops.
- Bake the pies in bowls for 20 minutes in a big shallow baking pan till pastry is puffed and golden.

Nutrition Information

- Calories: 1819
- Saturated Fat: 14 g(69%)
- Sodium: 5165 mg(215%)
- Fiber: 23 g(92%)
- Total Carbohydrate: 303 g(101%)
- Cholesterol: 65 mg(22%)
- Protein: 45 g(90%)

103

- Total Fat: 49 g(75%)

146.　Phyllo Nests With Strawberries And Honey

Serving: Makes 4 servings | Prep: | Cook: | Ready in:

Ingredients

- 1 (1-pound) package frozen phyllo (not thawed)
- 2 tablespoons unsalted butter, melted
- 4 teaspoons confectioners sugar
- 1/2 cup chilled heavy cream
- 1/2 tablespoon granulated sugar
- 2 teaspoons honey
- 8 strawberries, cut into 1/4-inch slices

Direction

- Crosswise cut 2 3/8-in. thick slices from 1 end of phyllo log; don't unroll. Thaw slices for 5 minutes; keep leftover frozen phyllo for another time.
- Preheat an oven to 375°F.
- Brush some melted butter on baking sheet lightly.
- Unfurl phyllo roll slices on work surface carefully; discard paper or plastic rolled within. Separate strands gently; keep parallel. Gather to 4 groups, 14 strands each. Use plastic wrap to cover 3 groups. Hold 1 end of leftover uncovered group of strands gently; brush some melted butter. Use fine-mesh sieve to dust 1/2 tsp. confectioners' sugar; flip. Brush butter on other side; in same manner, dust confectioners' sugar. Coil up coated strands loosely to make small nest; put on baking sheet. Repeat to make 3 extra nests with leftover cluster.
- In middle of oven, bake nests for 8-10 minutes till golden. Cool nests for 8-10 minutes on sheet on rack.
- Use electric mixer to beat granulated sugar and cream till it just holds soft peaks in bowl.

Drizzle 1/4 tsp. honey over each phyllo nest; put 1 tbsp. whipped cream in middle. Put strawberries and leftover cream over; drizzle 1/4 tsp. extra honey on each.

Nutrition Information

- Calories: 528
- Saturated Fat: 12 g(61%)
- Sodium: 560 mg(23%)
- Fiber: 3 g(11%)
- Total Carbohydrate: 70 g(23%)
- Cholesterol: 56 mg(19%)
- Protein: 9 g(18%)
- Total Fat: 24 g(36%)

147.　Phyllo Pizza With Smoked Mozzarella And Cherry Tomatoes

Serving: Makes 6 appetizer servings | Prep: | Cook: | Ready in:

Ingredients

- 12 to 13 ounces cherry tomatoes and/or pear tomatoes
- 1 tablespoon extra-virgin olive oil
- 3/4 teaspoon coarse kosher salt
- 1/2 teaspoon dried oregano
- 12 12x9-inch sheets fresh phyllo pastry or frozen, thawed
- 6 tablespoons (3/4 stick) unsalted butter, melted
- 4 tablespoons finely grated Parmesan cheese, divided
- 3/4 cup (packed) coarsely grated smoked mozzarella cheese* (about 3 ounces)
- 1/2 yellow bell pepper, cut into thin strips
- 1/4 cup quartered pitted Kalamata olives
- 2 teaspoons coarsely chopped fresh oregano

Direction

- Preheat an oven to 400°F. Toss oregano, salt, olive oil and tomatoes in medium bowl. On a big rimmed baking sheet, scatter tomatoes; roast for 22 minutes till starting to collapse and soft. Take out of oven; cool tomato mixture. Maintain the oven temperature.
- Put phyllo sheet stack on work surface; use plastic wrap to cover then a damp kitchen towel to avoid drying.
- Brush some melted butter on another big rimmed baking sheet; on baking sheet, put 1 phyllo sheet. Lightly brush melted butter; put 2nd phyllo sheet over. Brush using butter; put 3rd sheet over then brush using butter. Sprinkle 1 tbsp. parmesan; for a total of 4 tbsp. parmesan and 12 phyllo sheets, repeat thrice. Sprinkle grated mozzarella on stacked phyllo sheets; leave 1/2-in. plain border. Put olives, pepper strips and roasted tomatoes over.
- Bake pizza for 25-27 minutes till phyllo is crisp; sprinkle with 2 tsp. fresh oregano. Use a big metal spatula to loosen pizza from sheet; slide onto cutting board.

Nutrition Information

---

148. Phyllo Triangles Stuffed With Fresh Cheese (briouats Bil Jben)

Serving: Makes about 16 stuffed triangles | Prep: | Cook: | Ready in:

Ingredients

- 1/2 lb/225 g ricotta, fresh semisoft farmer's cheese, or Mexican queso fresco
- 1 large egg
- Heaped 1 Tbsp finely chopped fresh cilantro
- 4 sheets phyllo dough or warqa, plus more in case of breakage
- Olive oil for brushing
- 1 egg yolk, whisked

- Honey
- Light olive oil or vegetable oil for frying
- 1 Tbsp toasted sesame seeds

Direction

- Use fork to blend cilantro, egg and cheese in a medium mixing bowl.
- Unroll phyllo sheets on flat clean work surface; cut to at least 9-in./23 cm long, 3-in./7.5 cm wide strips. Put a few strips facing away from you; use plastic wrap to cover leftover strips to avoid drying out. Brush olive oil on strips lightly.
- On end of every strip nearest you, put 1 tbsp. cheese filling; fold over to make triangle. Fold to make another triangle then so on to the end. Brush egg yolk on end of triangle; fold loose end over brushed yolk. Put triangles on a plate without touching each other; repeat with leftover cheese filling and phyllo strips.
- In middle of each of the 6 dessert plates, put generous dollop of honey.
- Heat at least 1/2-in./1.25 cm. oil in big skillet or sauté pan till surface shimmers; lower heat to medium. In small batches, put phyllo triangles in oil gently; fry for 30-60 seconds till golden brown and firm, turning once. Use slotted spoon to put on paper towels; drain.
- On each plate, put 2 or 3 rolls; drizzle honey over. Sprinkle sesame seeds then serve hot.

Nutrition Information

---

149. Phyllo Wrapped Figs With Prosciutto And Stilton

Serving: Makes 8 servings | Prep: | Cook: | Ready in:

Ingredients

- 16 teaspoons Stilton cheese (about 4 ounces)
- 32 dried black Mission figs

- 4 6x4-inch thin prosciutto slices, cut lengthwise in half
- 8 sheets fresh phyllo pastry or frozen, thawed
- 3/4 cup (1 1/2 sticks) unsalted butter, melted
- 2 cups ruby Port
- 1/4 cup balsamic vinegar
- 2 tablespoons sugar
- 1 1/2 cups whipping cream
- 4 1/2 tablespoons pine nuts, toasted

Direction

- Shape 2 tsp. cheese to 1-in. long log. Put 4 dried figs around the cheese; gently press to adhere. Around fig bundle, wrap 1 prosciutto strip; repeat with leftover prosciutto, figs and cheese.
- On a work surface, put 1 phyllo sheet. Keep leftover phyllo covered using plastic wrap and a damp towel. Lightly brush melted butter on phyllo. Put 2nd phyllo sheet over; brush using butter. Repeat using 2 extra phyllo sheets. Slice stacked phyllo sheets to 4 6-in. squares; discard the phyllo trimmings. In middle of 1 phyllo square stack, put 1 fig bundle. Toward middle, bring up all phyllo square edges; firmly squeeze at top, making a pouch and fully enclosing fig bundle then put on a baking sheet. Repeat using leftover fig bundles, melted butter and phyllo sheets to make 8 pouches total. Brush leftover melted butter on outside of phyllo pouches. You can make this 6 hours ahead, refrigerated and covered. Preheat an oven to 375°F; bake the pouches for 17 minutes till golden.
- Meanwhile, boil sugar, balsamic vinegar and port in a medium saucepan for 15 minutes till reduced to 1/4 cup.
- Boil pine nuts and cream in another medium saucepan as port mixture is reducing for 8 minutes till reduced to 1 cup; take cream sauce off from heat. Season sauce with pepper and salt to taste.
- On each of 8 plates, scoop 2 tbsp. cream sauce; put 1 phyllo pouch over sauce. Lightly drizzle port sauce on each; serve.

Nutrition Information

- Calories: 1089
- Fiber: 24 g(95%)
- Total Carbohydrate: 172 g(57%)
- Cholesterol: 111 mg(37%)
- Protein: 14 g(29%)
- Total Fat: 43 g(66%)
- Saturated Fat: 23 g(115%)
- Sodium: 486 mg(20%)

150. Phyllo Wrapped Salmon With Leeks And Red Bell Pepper

Serving: Serves 6 | Prep: | Cook: | Ready in:

Ingredients

- 8 tablespoons (1 stick) butter
- 4 cups matchstick-size strips red bell peppers (about 2 large)
- 2 cups matchstick-size strips leek (white and pale green parts only; about 1 large)
- 1/2 cup dry white wine
- 1 teaspoon dried crushed red pepper
- 1/2 cup thinly sliced fresh basil
- 1 teaspoon salt
- 12 sheets fresh phyllo pastry or frozen, thawed
- 6 5-ounce 6x2x1-inch skinless salmon fillets

Direction

- Melt 2 tbsp. butter in a big heavy skillet on medium high heat then add leek and bell peppers; sauté for 6 minutes till leek is tender. Add crushed red pepper and wine into skillet; simmer for 4 minutes till liquid evaporates. Take off heat; cool veggie mixture. Mix in salt and basil.
- Preheat an oven to 400°F. In a small saucepan, melt leftover 6 tbsp. butter. On a work surface, put 1 pastry sheet; cover leftover phyllo sheets. Brush some melted butter; put 2nd pastry sheet over then brush using melted butter. 5-

in. in from 1 short end, put 1 salmon fillet on pastry sheet crosswise. Put 1/4 cup veggie mixture over salmon fillet; fold 5-in. pastry section over salmon then fold in the sides. Roll up to make rectangular packet; put, veggie side up, in a big heavy baking sheet. Brush melted butter all over packet; repeat with leftover veggies, salmon fillets, melted butter and pastry sheets. You can make this 6 hours ahead, refrigerated and covered with plastic wrap.

- Bake salmon for 35 minutes till salmon is cooked through and pastry is pale golden.

Nutrition Information

- Calories: 605
- Fiber: 3 g(14%)
- Total Carbohydrate: 31 g(10%)
- Cholesterol: 119 mg(40%)
- Protein: 33 g(67%)
- Total Fat: 37 g(57%)
- Saturated Fat: 15 g(73%)
- Sodium: 668 mg(28%)

151.   Pigs In Sleeping Bags

Serving: Makes 36 (9 to 12 servings) | Prep: | Cook: | Ready in:

Ingredients

- 1 tablespoon unsalted butter
- 1/4 cup minced shallot
- 2 large garlic cloves, minced
- 3 tablespoons panko (Japanese breadcrumbs)
- 3 tablespoons whole milk
- 3/4 cup drained sauerkraut
- 1 tablespoon Dijon mustard plus more for serving
- 3/4 teaspoon caraway seeds, toasted, lightly crushed
- Kosher salt and freshly ground black pepper
- 8 ounces ground pork

- 1 14-ounce package Dufour Pastry Kitchens frozen puff pastry, thawed
- All-purpose flour (for dusting)
- 1 large egg, beaten to blend

Direction

- Melt butter in small skillet on medium heat then add shallot; cook for 4-5 minutes till soft, occasionally mixing and if needed, reducing heat to avoid burning. Add garlic; cook for 1 minute till aromatic, occasionally mixing. Put shallot mixture in big bowl; cool.
- Mix milk and panko in small bowl; stand for 2-3 minutes till milk is absorbed. Put in bowl with shallot mixture. Squeeze extra liquid from sauerkraut. Chop coarsely; add to bowl. Mix in caraway seeds and 1 tbsp. Dijon mustard; season with pepper and salt. Stir well. Add pork; mix gently with hands or fork till just combined; don't overmix.
- Line parchment paper on baking sheet. Roll pastry to 14x10-in. rectangle on lightly floured surface; lengthwise cut to 3 14x3 1/3-in. strips. Put strips on prepped baking sheet. Pat sausage to make thin log of filling down middle of 1 pastry strip with 1/3 sausage filling; leave 1-in. border at each end. To enclose, fold pastry over sausage mixture; to seal, press pastry together. To ensure that sausage is wrapped tightly, fold seam under; repeat with leftover sausage mixture and pastry.
- To release steam, cut diagonal small slits along top of pastries at 1-in. intervals; brush beaten egg on sides and top of pastry. Chill for 30 minutes in freezer; you can make pastries 2 weeks ahead, covered with plastic wrap tightly then foil; keep frozen.
- Preheat an oven to 425°F; if frozen, no need to thaw, bake pastries for 15 minutes till light brown and puffed. Lower heat to 350°F; bake for 25 minutes till pastry is fully puffed and golden and sausage is cooked through; slightly cool. Crosswise cut sausage rolls to 1-in. pieces; serve with bowl of Dijon mustard for a dip.

Nutrition Information

- Calories: 314
- Cholesterol: 38 mg(13%)
- Protein: 8 g(16%)
- Total Fat: 22 g(34%)
- Saturated Fat: 7 g(33%)
- Sodium: 216 mg(9%)
- Fiber: 1 g(5%)
- Total Carbohydrate: 21 g(7%)

---

152.   Pigs In A Blanket

Serving: 6 | Prep: 10mins | Cook: 20mins | Ready in:

Ingredients

- 8 frankfurters
- 8 slices American processed cheese
- 1 (10 ounce) package refrigerated biscuit dough

Direction

- Set the oven to preheat at 350°F (175°C).
- Wrap each frankfurter with cheese. Follow that with biscuit wrapping. Place them on a cookie tray. The biscuit overlap should face down, so toothpicks won't be needed.
- Bake in the oven for 10-15 minutes, until they become brown.

Nutrition Information

- Calories: 458 calories;
- Total Carbohydrate: 24.8
- Cholesterol: 57
- Protein: 17.1
- Total Fat: 31.8
- Sodium: 1760

---

153.   Pigs In A Blanket With Hoisin And Scallion

Serving: Makes 32 pieces | Prep: 30mins | Cook: 1hours10mins | Ready in:

Ingredients

- 1 large egg
- One 14- to 17-ounce box of puff pastry (preferably all-butter puff), thawed according to package directions
- Chinese five-spice powder, for sprinkling
- 2 pounds fully cooked pork breakfast sausage (preferably unflavored), halved lengthwise if thick, and cut into 32 pieces (about 2 1/2 inches each)
- 3 tablespoons hoisin sauce
- 2 scallions, thinly sliced
- Sesame seeds, for sprinkling

Direction

- Preheat oven to 400 degrees F. Place the racks in the lower and upper thirds of oven. Put parchment paper on two 13-in x 18-in cookie sheets. Whisk a tablespoon water and egg in a bowl. Get the filling ingredients ready, set aside.
- Roll each sheet of 17oz. puff pastry package in a 9-in x 12-in rectangle. Sprinkle the 5-spice powder on the surface of both pastry sheets. Slice lengthwise each sheet in eight strips measuring 1 1/2-in. wide. Slice the strips across in two 4 1/2 inch long pieces. You should end up with 32 pastry pieces.
- Slather a quarter teaspoon hoisin in the middle of each pastry; add a sprinkle of scallion on top. Spread egg wash on one of the narrow ends of pastry, place a piece of sausage on, and roll the pastry to seal. With its seam down, arrange the pastry on the prepared cookie sheets. Spread egg wash on top of every pastry; top with sesame seeds. Let them chill in the refrigerator for 15 minutes. Bake for 23-27 minutes until the pastries are puffed and golden.

- If using Dufour or any all-butter puff pastry, roll the sheets on a floured surface in 12-in x 18-in rectangles. Sprinkle 5-spice powder on lightly and slice lengthwise in eight strips measuring 1 1/2-in. wide. Slice the strips across in four 4 1/2 inch long pieces until you have 32 pastry pieces. Continue with recipe.

Nutrition Information

---

154.   Pineapple Tart

Serving: Serves 8 | Prep: | Cook: |Ready in:

Ingredients

- vegetable-oil cooking spray
- three 2 1/2-inch-square graham crackers
- 1 1/2 tablespoons granulated sugar
- four 17- by 12-inch phyllo sheets, thawed if frozen, stacked between 2 sheets wax paper and covered with a kitchen towel
- 2 tablespoons unsalted butter, melted
- 1 large ripe pineapple (about 41/4 pounds), peeled, halved lengthwise, cored, and cut crosswise into 1/4-inch-thick slices
- 1/4 cup packed light brown sugar
- 1/4 cup granulated sugar
- seeds scraped from 1/2 vanilla bean, halved lengthwise, and pod reserved

Direction

- Shell: Preheat an oven to 375°F; coat vegetable-oil cooking spray on 11-in. tart pan with removable fluted rim lightly.
- Grind sugar and graham crackers to fine crumbs in a food processor. Line 1 phyllo sheet on tart pan quickly; let edges overhang evenly. Dot butter on phyllo bottom of tart pan in 4 or 5 places with pastry brush. Evenly sprinkle 1/3 crumb mixture on phyllo in bottom of tart pan; put another phyllo sheet over, putting it at right angles to the 1st phyllo sheet so the overhang is even all around. Use butter to dot phyllo; in same manner, sprinkle 1/3 crumb mixture. Repeat layering process with leftover butter, 1/3 crumb mixture and 2 phyllo sheets the same way, finishing with phyllo. Use scissors to trim phyllo overhang to 1-in. beyond tart pan rim; roll toward middle, making shallow edge just inside the tart pan. Brush leftover butter on shell; bake for 12 minutes or till crisp and golden in middle of oven. Cool shell in the tart pan on the rack; you can make shell 1 day ahead, kept in tart pan, covered loosely, in dry cool place.
- Filling: Simmer reserved vanilla pod, vanilla seeds, sugars and pineapple in heavy 12-in. skillet on medium heat for 25 minutes till pineapple is slightly translucent and most liquid evaporates, flipping pineapple occasionally and carefully, keep pieces whole, lower heat as liquid evaporates. Slightly cool mixture; discard vanilla pod.
- In overlapping concentric circles, put pineapple in shell; put leftover syrup in skillet over. You can make tart 1 day ahead; keep at room temperature, loosely covered.

Nutrition Information

---

155.   Pistachio Phyllo Crisps

Serving: Makes 2 crisps | Prep: 30mins | Cook: 30mins |Ready in:

Ingredients

- 2 tablespoons shelled salted pistachios
- 2 tablespoons sugar
- 1 (17- by 12-inch) phyllo sheet, thawed if frozen
- 2 tablespoons unsalted butter, melted

Direction

- Preheat an oven to 350°F.

- Grind pistachios finely in spice or electric coffee grinder; mix in sugar.
- Crosswise cut phyllo sheet to 3 even pieces; stack pieces between wax paper. Use lightly dampened kitchen towel to cover stack. Put 1 phyllo piece on parchment paper-lined baking sheet; brush some butter. Sprinkle 1/2 pistachio sugar; put another phyllo piece over. Brush some butter on phyllo; sprinkle leftover pistachio sugar. Put leftover phyllo piece over; gently press down. Brush some butter then chill stack for 10 minutes.
- Cut 2 4-in. rounds out with sharp paring knife, using ramekin's rim as a guide; discard scraps. Use parchment piece to cover rounds; bake in center of oven for 10 minutes till golden. Cool crisps on a baking sheet on rack.

Nutrition Information

- Calories: 259
- Saturated Fat: 8 g(41%)
- Sodium: 48 mg(2%)
- Fiber: 2 g(7%)
- Total Carbohydrate: 22 g(7%)
- Cholesterol: 31 mg(10%)
- Protein: 4 g(7%)
- Total Fat: 19 g(29%)

156. Plum Tarte Tatin

Serving: Makes 6 servings | Prep: | Cook: | Ready in:

Ingredients

- 1 cup crème fraîche*
- 1 teaspoon grated orange peel
- 1 sheet frozen puff pastry (half of 17.3-ounce package), thawed
- 2 1/4 pounds sweet firm red plums (such as Burgundies or Satsumas), halved, pitted
- 2 tablespoons plus 2/3 cup sugar, divided
- 1 tablespoon fresh lemon juice
- 1 1/2 teaspoons finely grated lemon peel
- 1/8 teaspoon ground nutmeg
- 1/2 vanilla bean, split lengthwise
- 6 tablespoons (3/4 stick) unsalted butter

Direction

- Whisk orange peel and crème fraiche in small bowl then cover; chill. On lightly floured surface, roll pastry; to make circle, trim corners. Put on plate; you can prep crust and crème fraiche 1 day ahead; chill, separately covered.
- Preheat an oven to 400°F. Mix vanilla bean seeds, nutmeg, lemon peel, lemon juice, 2 tbsp. sugar and plums in big bowl; stand for 30 minutes.
- Melt butter in 9-in. diameter heavy ovenproof skillet on medium heat; evenly sprinkle leftover 2/3 cup sugar on melted butter. Put plums tightly in concentric circles, cut side up in skillet; at first, plums will look slightly uneven, it'll soften while cooking to make even layer. Drizzle juices from bowl on top; cook on medium heat, gently shaking skillet to avoid sticking. Cook for 35 minutes till syrup is deep red, slightly pressing plums to make compact layer. Take off heat; cool for 10 minutes.
- Slice crust over plums in skillet; around plums at skillet edge, press down crust edges. To let steam escape, cut a few slits; bake for 30 minutes till golden brown. Fully cool tart in skillet.
- Rewarm in skillet on high heat for 3 minutes to loosen. Put big platter on skillet; hold skillet and platter together with oven mitts. Invert; let tart settle onto platter. Lift skillet off carefully; stand at room temperature for 30 minutes minimum and up to 4 hours; serve it with orange crème fraiche.

Nutrition Information

- Calories: 582
- Saturated Fat: 16 g(78%)
- Sodium: 121 mg(5%)
- Fiber: 3 g(12%)

- Total Carbohydrate: 66 g(22%)
- Cholesterol: 50 mg(17%)
- Protein: 5 g(10%)
- Total Fat: 35 g(54%)

---

157.   Poppy Seed And Pecan Strudel

Serving: 8–10 servings | Prep: 1hours | Cook: 2hours | Ready in:

Ingredients

- 3 cups pecans (about 10 oz.)
- 1 cup whole milk
- 3/4 cup poppy seeds
- 10 Tbsp. unsalted butter, divided
- 3/4 cup (packed) light brown sugar
- 1 1/2 tsp. kosher salt
- 1 tsp. vanilla extract
- 6 (17x12") sheets fresh phyllo pastry or frozen, thawed
- 1 large egg, beaten to blend
- Powdered sugar (for serving)

Direction

- Preheat an oven to 325°F; spread pecans out on a big rimmed baking sheet. Toast for 13-15 minutes till fragrant and slightly darkened in color; cool.
- Boil poppy seeds and milk in a medium saucepan. Lower heat to medium low; simmer for 13-15 minutes till milk is nearly fully evaporated, occasionally mixing; cool.
- Scrape into food processor then cut 6 tbsp. butter to pieces; add to food processor with vanilla, salt, brown sugar and pecans. Process till paste forms.
- Melt leftover 4 tbsp. butter in small saucepan or microwave on medium heat. Line parchment on rimmed baking sheet; brush some melted butter on it.
- On work surface, put stack of 6 phyllo sheets; use plastic wrap then a damp kitchen towel to cover.
- With long side facing you, put prepped baking sheet; stack 2 phyllo sheets over. Lightly brush with butter. Put another phyllo sheet over; lightly brush with butter. Repeat with 2 extra sheets then put final sheet over; don't brush with butter.
- In an even layer, spread poppy seed mixture on pastry with offset or rubber spatula; on all sides, leave 1-in. border. Roll pastry up gently beginning at long side nearest you; turn it seam side down. Tuck the exposed ends underneath. Cut horizontal slits with sharp knife halfway through roll, spacing it every 1-in. along the length then brush egg.
- Bake strudel for 40-45 minutes till crisp and golden. Put baking sheet on wire rack; cool strudel.
- Dust powdered sugar over then slice before serving.
- You can bake strudel 1 day ahead; fully cool. Cover with plastic wrap; keep at room temperature.

Nutrition Information

- Calories: 591
- Saturated Fat: 13 g(64%)
- Sodium: 322 mg(13%)
- Fiber: 6 g(25%)
- Total Carbohydrate: 38 g(13%)
- Cholesterol: 64 mg(21%)
- Protein: 9 g(17%)
- Total Fat: 48 g(74%)

---

158.   Potato And Tuna Turnovers

Serving: Makes 6 | Prep: | Cook: | Ready in:

Ingredients

- 12 ounces potatoes, peeled, quartered
- 2 large eggs
- 1 3/4 teaspoons salt
- 1 6-ounce can tuna packed in oil, drained, 2 tablespoons oil reserved
- 3/4 cup chopped green onions
- 1 tablespoon drained capers
- 18 sheets frozen phyllo pastry, thawed
- 1/4 cup chopped fresh Italian parsley
- 1/4 cup vegetable oil plus additional vegetable oil (for frying)

Direction

- Cover 1 tsp. salt, whole eggs (don't crack) and potatoes with enough cold water in a big heavy pot; cover pot partially. Simmer for 10 minutes on medium heat. Remove eggs; simmer for 15 more minutes till potatoes are tender. Drain; put potatoes in a big bowl. Crack eggs and remove shells. Put eggs in a bowl with potatoes; mash eggs and potatoes coarsely with fork. Mix in leftover 3/4 tsp. salt, 1/4 tsp. pepper, capers, green onions, reserved tuna oil and tuna; put aside.
- Line plastic wrap on 2 baking sheets. On a work surface, stack phyllo sheets; cut phyllo to 18 rounds with 9-in. plate for guide and shears. On a work surface, stack 3 phyllo rounds quickly. Use plastic and damp kitchen towel to cover leftover phyllo sheets to avoid drying. In middle of phyllo, put generous 1/4 cup of filling. Sprinkle 1/6 parsley; brush oil on edge. To make half-moon, fold phyllo, slightly pressing. Fold edge over; to seal, press. Put turnover on baking sheet; repeat with leftover oil, parsley, filling and phyllo.
- Line 3 paper towels on baking sheet. Put oil in a big skillet to 1/2 deep, heating it to 350°F. Into oil, slide 1 turnover; fry for 1 minute till bottom is golden. Put turnover on a plate with slotted spatula; flip. Slide into oil; fry for1 minute till bottom is golden. On baking sheet, drain; repeat with leftover turnovers.

Nutrition Information

- Calories: 382
- Saturated Fat: 2 g(12%)
- Sodium: 457 mg(19%)
- Fiber: 3 g(11%)
- Total Carbohydrate: 41 g(14%)
- Cholesterol: 67 mg(22%)
- Protein: 16 g(32%)
- Total Fat: 17 g(26%)

159. Prosciutto And Gruyère Pastry Pinwheels

Serving: Makes about 30 | Prep: | Cook: |Ready in:

Ingredients

- 1 sheet frozen puff pastry (half of 17.3-ounce package), thawed
- 4 ounces thinly sliced prosciutto
- 2 tablespoons chopped fresh basil
- 3/4 cup (packed) finely grated Gruyère cheese (about 2 1/2 ounces)
- 1 egg, beaten to blend

Direction

- On work surface, put pastry sheet; halve to make 2 9 1/2 x 4 3/4-in. rectangles. On 1 rectangle, put 1/2 prosciutto; along 1 side, leave 1/2-in. border. Sprinkle 1/2 basil on prosciutto then 1/2 cheese; brush egg glaze on plain border. Roll pastry up like a jellyroll, beginning at long side opposing border, gently pressing to seal long edges; use plastic to wrap. Repeat with leftover egg, cheese, basil, prosciutto and pastry to make 2nd log. Refrigerate for 3 hours minimum and up to 2 days till firm.
- In middle of oven, put rack; preheat to 400°F. Line parchment paper on 2 big baking sheets. Crosswise cut logs to 1/2-in. thick rounds; put rounds on prepped sheets, 1-in. apart. 1 sheet at a time, bake for 16 minutes till pastries are golden brown. Put pastries on racks using metal spatula; slightly cool. Serve warm.

Nutrition Information

- Calories: 64
- Cholesterol: 11 mg(4%)
- Protein: 3 g(5%)
- Total Fat: 4 g(7%)
- Saturated Fat: 1 g(7%)
- Sodium: 141 mg(6%)
- Fiber: 0 g(1%)
- Total Carbohydrate: 4 g(1%)

160.   Quick Apple Tart

Serving: Makes 6 servings | Prep: | Cook: | Ready in:

Ingredients

- 1 sheet frozen puff pastry (half of 17.3-ounce package), thawed
- 3 medium Golden Delicious apples, peeled, cored, very thinly sliced
- 2 tablespoons (1/4 stick) unsalted butter, melted
- 3 tablespoons cinnamon sugar (or 3 tablespoons sugar mixed with scant 1/2 teaspoon ground cinnamon)
- 1/4 cup apricot jam, melted

Direction

- Preheat an oven to 400°F; line parchment paper on a baking sheet. On parchment paper, unfold pastry. Pierce 1/2-in. border around pastry edge with tines of fork; pierce middle all over. In 4 rows, put apples over pastry, leaving border clear and overlapping apple slices. Brush melted butter on apples; sprinkle cinnamon sugar over. Bake for 30 minutes; on apples, brush melted jam. Bake tart for 8 more minutes till golden; serve at room temperature or warm.

Nutrition Information

- Calories: 364
- Saturated Fat: 6 g(32%)
- Sodium: 109 mg(5%)
- Fiber: 3 g(11%)
- Total Carbohydrate: 45 g(15%)
- Cholesterol: 10 mg(3%)
- Protein: 3 g(7%)
- Total Fat: 20 g(30%)

161.   Quick Puff Pastry

Serving: Makes 2 1/2 pounds | Prep: | Cook: | Ready in:

Ingredients

- 4 cups all-purpose flour
- 1 1/2 teaspoons salt
- 6 1/2 sticks (3 1/4 cups) unsalted butter, cut into 1/2-inch cubes, chilled
- 1 cup cold water

Direction

- Sift salt and flour in a food processor bowl with blade attachment.
- Add diced, chilled butter; pulse 3-5 times till butter pieces are lima bean sized. Add water to mixture; pulse 3 times. On a lightly floured work surface, invert crumbly mass.
- Shape mass to long rectangle with bench scraper and rolling pin. Flip 1/3 rectangle toward center using bench scraper; flip other end to middle like a business letter. Rotate dough 90°.
- Reshape then roll dough to rectangle; repeat folding and rotating procedure thrice for 4 turns total. Immediately refrigerate till firm if dough is sticky or soft during the process.
- Wrap dough in plastic wrap after 4 turns; create 4 indentations in dough with a finger, one for each time dough was turned. Refrigerate dough till firm or for 45 minutes minimum.
- Unwrap and discard plastic when dough was refrigerated for 45 minutes; keep rolling pin

and work surface well-floured. To seal the shape, press down on each of 4 dough sides.

- Roll away from you, stating with rolling pin at middle; return to middle then roll toward you. Repeat folding and rotating dough process twice for 6 times total.
- Wrap finished dough in plastic wrap after 6th turn; refrigerate before baking till well-chilled. Quick puff pastry keeps for up to 3 days or for a few months frozen.

Nutrition Information

- Calories: 323
- Protein: 3 g(5%)
- Total Fat: 27 g(42%)
- Saturated Fat: 17 g(86%)
- Sodium: 156 mg(6%)
- Fiber: 1 g(2%)
- Total Carbohydrate: 17 g(6%)
- Cholesterol: 72 mg(24%)

162. Raspberry Crème Fraîche Puff

Serving: Makes 1 serving | Prep: 10mins | Cook: 1hours | Ready in:

Ingredients

- 1 sheet puff pastry (from a 17 1/4-oz package), thawed
- 3 tablespoons crème fraîche
- 2 teaspoons granulated sugar
- 3 oz raspberries (1/2 cup)
- Confectioners sugar for dusting

Direction

- Place oven rack on upper third of oven; preheat oven to 400°F.
- Unfold a pastry sheet; use sharp knife to cut 3-in. square from pastry; keep leftover pastry for a different use.

- On ungreased baking sheet, bake pastry square for 15-20 minutes till golden brown. Put pastry on a rack; fully cool. Horizontally cut pastry to 2 layers. Mix granulated sugar and crème fraiche together till sugar dissolves.
- Put bottom pastry half on a plate before serving; put raspberries and crème fraiche over. Let some berries spill out on plate. Use top pastry half to cover; dust confectioners' sugar over.
- Thawed pastry keeps for 2 days, chilled, wrapped in wax paper first then in plastic wrap.

Nutrition Information

- Calories: 1512
- Total Fat: 102 g(157%)
- Saturated Fat: 28 g(142%)
- Sodium: 631 mg(26%)
- Fiber: 8 g(31%)
- Total Carbohydrate: 132 g(44%)
- Cholesterol: 22 mg(7%)
- Protein: 19 g(39%)

163. Rhubarb Tart With Orange Glaze

Serving: Makes 8 servings | Prep: 20mins | Cook: 50mins | Ready in:

Ingredients

- 1 cup fresh orange juice
- 1 tablespoon fresh lime juice
- 1/2 cup sugar
- 3/4 pound rhubarb stalks, thinly sliced diagonally (1/8 inch)
- 1 sheet frozen puff pastry (from a 17 1/4-ounces package), thawed
- 1/2 teaspoon grated orange zest
- Accompaniment: vanilla ice cream

Direction

- Preheat an oven to 400°F with the rack in the center.
- Mix sugar, lime juice and orange juice in bowl; add rhubarb. Stand for 10 minutes, occasionally mixing.
- Meanwhile, halve pastry lengthwise; roll each piece out on lightly floured surface with floured rolling pin to 11x7-in. rectangle. Side by side, put pastry rectangles on ungreased big baking sheet.
- Score a line parallel to every edge lightly to create 1/2-in. border around every pastry rectangle; don't cut all the way through. Use fork to prick pastry inside border all over.
- Through sieve above a bowl, strain rhubarb mixture; keep liquid. Within border, put 1/2 rhubarb, slightly overlapping slices over 1 pastry rectangle. Repeat with leftover rhubarb and pastry.
- Bake for 30 minutes till pastry is golden and puffed and bottom of pastry is golden.
- Meanwhile, boil saved rhubarb liquid in small saucepan for 15-18 minutes till reduced to 1/4 cup, skimming foam if needed.
- Put tarts on rack. Brush glaze on pastry and rhubarb; sprinkle zest over.

Nutrition Information

- Calories: 241
- Sodium: 78 mg(3%)
- Fiber: 1 g(5%)
- Total Carbohydrate: 32 g(11%)
- Protein: 3 g(6%)
- Total Fat: 12 g(18%)
- Saturated Fat: 3 g(15%)

164.   Rhubarb And Ricotta Cheese Puff Pastry Tartlets

Serving: Makes 8 servings | Prep: | Cook: | Ready in:

Ingredients

- 2 pounds rhubarb, sliced 1/2 inch thick
- 2 1/2 cups plus 3 tablespoons (packed) golden brown sugar
- 1 17.3-ounce package frozen puff pastry (2 sheets), thawed
- 2 cups whole-milk ricotta cheese
- 2/3 cup powdered sugar
- 1 egg, beaten to blend (for glaze)

Direction

- Cook 2 1/2 cups of brown sugar and rhubarb in a big pot on low heat for 35 minutes, occasionally mixing, till rhubarb is tender yet not falling apart and syrup forms. Put rhubarb mixture in sieve placed above a big bowl; cover the sieve. Chill juices and rhubarb overnight.
- Preheat an oven to 400°F. On a floured surface, roll 1 pastry sheet out to 12-in. square; cut to 4 6-in. squares. Cut 6-in. round from each with a small plate as guide. On ungreased baking sheet, put rounds; use fork to pierce. Bake for 5 minutes; use spatula to flatten. Bake for 10 more minutes till golden; repeat using 2nd pastry sheet to create 8 crusts. Maintain the oven temperature.
- Blend powdered sugar and ricotta in a bowl; brush egg glaze on each crust. Leave 1/2-in. plain border then spread 1/8, around 1/4 cup of cheese mixture on every crust. Bake tartlets for 10 minutes till topping is set; you can make this 1 hour ahead, allow to stand at room temperature.
- Preheat a broiler. Put rhubarb juices in a small saucepan; boil for 8 minutes till reduced to thick syrup, occasionally mixing. Spread rhubarb 3/4-in. thick on a rimmed baking sheet then sprinkle 3 tbsp. of brown sugar; broil for 4 minutes till dark brown in spots and top is crisp.
- Scoop rhubarb on tartlets; drizzle rhubarb syrup over. Serve.

Nutrition Information

- Calories: 708

- Fiber: 3 g(12%)
- Total Carbohydrate: 94 g(31%)
- Cholesterol: 52 mg(17%)
- Protein: 13 g(26%)
- Total Fat: 32 g(49%)
- Saturated Fat: 11 g(56%)
- Sodium: 231 mg(10%)

165.   Rhubarb Raspberry Jalousie

Serving: Makes 6 servings | Prep: | Cook: |Ready in:

Ingredients

- 2 tablespoons (1/4 stick) unsalted butter
- 4 cups 1/2-inch-thick slices fresh rhubarb (from about 2 pounds)
- 1 cup raspberry preserves with seeds
- 1/4 cup plus 2 tablespoons sugar
- 1 sheet frozen puff pastry (half of 17.3-ounce package), thawed
- 1 large egg, beaten to blend (for glaze)
- Vanilla ice cream

Direction

- Melt butter in a medium heavy saucepan on medium heat then add rhubarb; cover. Simmer for 10 minutes till rhubarb falls apart and is tender. Add 1/4 cup sugar and preserves; cook for 35 minutes without a cover till reduced to 2 cups and very thick, frequently mixing. Refrigerate filling for 1 hour minimum without a cover till cold. You can make this 2 days ahead, covered and refrigerated.
- Preheat an oven to 400°F; line parchment paper on a big baking sheet. On a lightly floured surface, roll out pastry to 16x12-in. rectangle. Halve pastry lengthwise to make 2 16x6-in. rectangles. Put 1 rectangle on prepped baking sheet; scoop filling on pastry, leaving 1-in. plain border. Brush glaze on border. Put 2nd rectangle over; to seal, firmly press edges. Brush glaze on edges; fold over the edges to

make 1/2-in. border. Use fork tines to seal by pressing border. Brush glaze over pastry; sprinkle 2 tbsp. sugar over. Slice 1 1/2-in. slits crosswise with a sharp knife down middle of pastry, exposing filling, at 2-in. intervals.
- Bake pastry for 25 minutes till golden brown; cool pastry for 45 minutes on sheet to lukewarm. Slice to 6 pieces crosswise then serve with ice cream.

Nutrition Information

166.   Roasted Pear Tarte Tatin With Brown Sugar Balsamic Swirl Ice Cream

Serving: Makes 8 servings | Prep: | Cook: |Ready in:

Ingredients

- 1/2 cup sugar
- 1/4 cup (1/2 stick) unsalted butter, cut into small cubes
- 2 tablespoons light corn syrup
- 4 large Bosc pears (2 1/4 to 2 1/2 pounds), peeled, halved, cored
- 1 sheet frozen puff pastry (half of 17.3-ounce package), thawed
- 1 1/2 tablespoons pear nectar
- Brown Sugar-Balsamic Swirl Ice Cream

Direction

- Put 1 rack in top third and 1 rack in middle of the oven; preheat to 375°F. Evenly sprinkle sugar on bottom of 9-in. diameter heavy cake pan with 2-in. high sides. On sugar, scatter butter cubes; drizzle light corn syrup. Put pear halves snugly in cake pan, cut side up, narrow end pointing toward middle. Pears might not lie flat but they will fit evenly and shrink while cooking.

- Put the pan on middle rack in oven; bake pears for 2 3/4 hours till dark brown in spots and tender.
- Meanwhile, line parchment paper on a big baking sheet. On a work surface, unfold thawed puff pastry sheet; cut 9-in. round from pastry sheet using a separate 9-in. diameter cake pan for guide. Put pastry round on prepped baking sheet; put baking sheet in oven on upper rack. Bake pastry round for 20 minutes till golden brown and puffed; fully cool pastry round.
- Lift pears from syrup carefully in cake pan using a slotted spoon to put on big plate; cool. You can make pastry round and pears 4 hours ahead. Keep cake pan with syrup. Stand syrup, pastry and pears at room temperature. Put pastry round on a platter, flat side up, before serving. Put pears over pastry round carefully, cut side down, narrow end in middle. Set the pan with the syrup on medium-high heat. Boil for 2-3 minutes till syrup is dark amber color, occasionally whisking. Take off heat then add pear nectar; it'll bubble up. Whisk till caramel is smooth; scoop on pears.

Nutrition Information

---
167.   Roasted Pineapple Tartlets

Serving: Makes 8 | Prep: | Cook: | Ready in:

Ingredients

- 1 (17.3-ounce) package frozen puff pastry (2 sheets), thawed
- 1 2/3 cups sugar
- 1 1/2 cups (or more) water
- 2 vanilla beans, split lengthwise
- 1/4 cup dark rum
- 1 large banana
- 2 tablespoons chopped peeled fresh ginger
- 2 dried chiles de árbol*
- 1 large (4 1/2-pound) pineapple, trimmed, peeled, left whole
- 1 large egg yolk blended with 1 tablespoon milk (for glaze)
- Vanilla ice cream

Direction

- Roll pastry out to 11-in. squares on a floured surface; from each square, cut 4 5-5 1/2-in. rounds with small plate as guide. Put rounds on 2 heavy baking sheets then cover; chill. You can make this 1 day ahead, chilled.
- Mix 1/2 cup water and sugar in a heavy medium saucepan; scrape in vanilla bean seeds. Mix on medium low heat till sugar dissolves, using wet pastry brush to brush pan sides down occasionally. Increase heat; boil for 10 minutes till syrup is deep amber color, occasionally swirling pan. Take off heat. Add 1 cup water; it will vigorously bubble then add rum. Mix on very low heat till caramel bits dissolve; simmer for 2 minutes. Cool syrup for 15 minutes; put in blender. Add chiles de arbol, ginger and banana; puree till sauce is smooth.
- Preheat an oven to 350°F. Put pineapple on 13x9x2-in. glass baking dish then put sauce on top; flip pineapple to coat. Roast for 1 hour 15 minutes till tender, if sauce becomes thick, add extra water by tablespoonfuls and basting often with sauce. This can be prepared 1 day in advance. Chill till cold; cover. Keep chilled.
- Preheat an oven to 375°F. Put pineapple on a work surface; scrape sauce into dish. Crosswise cut pineapple to 1/4-in. thick rounds; from each round, cut core out. In middle of every pastry round, put 1 pineapple round. Brush sauce on pineapple; brush egg glaze on pastry edges.
- Bake tartlets for 25 minutes till pastry is brown; rewarm sauce. Put scoop of vanilla ice cream over each tartlet. Drizzle warm sauce; serve.

Nutrition Information

- Calories: 599
- Total Carbohydrate: 89 g(30%)
- Cholesterol: 23 mg(8%)
- Protein: 6 g(11%)
- Total Fat: 24 g(37%)
- Saturated Fat: 6 g(31%)
- Sodium: 158 mg(7%)
- Fiber: 3 g(12%)

---

168. Roasted Tomato And Herb Tart

Serving: Makes 4 to 6 appetizer servings | Prep: | Cook: | Ready in:

Ingredients

- 12 large garlic cloves, peeled
- 1 teaspoon plus 2 tablespoons olive oil
- 4 red heirloom plum tomatoes, halved lengthwise
- 4 yellow heirloom plum tomatoes, halved lengthwise
- 1/2 teaspoon coarse kosher salt
- 1/2 teaspoon ground black pepper
- 1 sheet frozen puff pastry (half of 17.3-ounce package), thawed
- 1 1/4 cups grated Gruyère cheese (about 4 ounces), divided
- 2 teaspoons chopped fresh thyme
- 2 teaspoons chopped fresh rosemary

Direction

- Preheat an oven to 375°F. Put garlic on a 6-in. foil square; drizzle 1 tsp. oil on garlic. Seal foil packet. Toss 2 tbsp. oil, pepper, salt and tomatoes in bowl. Put tomatoes on rimmed baking sheet, cut side up. Drizzle juices in bowl on tomatoes. On same sheet, put garlic packet; bake for 50 minutes till garlic is soft. Take out of oven; put temperature to 400°F.

- Meanwhile, line parchment paper on a baking sheet. Roll puff pastry to 10-in. square on floured surface; put on prepped sheet. Pierce pastry all over with fork; chill for 20 minutes.
- Sprinkle 3/4 cup of cheese on pastry; leave 1-in. plain border. In alternating colors, put tomatoes on cheese in 4 rows, cut side up; put garlic cloves between tomatoes. Sprinkle 1/2 cup cheese, rosemary and thyme. Bake tart for 25 minutes till golden; serve either at room temperature or warm.

Nutrition Information

- Calories: 570
- Sodium: 552 mg(23%)
- Fiber: 3 g(12%)
- Total Carbohydrate: 38 g(13%)
- Cholesterol: 31 mg(10%)
- Protein: 15 g(30%)
- Total Fat: 41 g(63%)
- Saturated Fat: 12 g(62%)

---

169. Roasted Winter Vegetable Baklava

Serving: 6 servings | Prep: 45mins | Cook: 1.75hours | Ready in:

Ingredients

- 1/2 cup walnuts (2 ounces), toasted
- 1/4 cup fine dry plain bread crumbs
- 1 pound Yukon Gold potatoes
- 2 medium fennel bulbs, trimmed, reserving fronds, bulbs halved and sliced lengthwise 1/4 inch thick
- 3/4 pound parsnips (3 medium), sliced diagonally 1/3 inch thick
- 1/2 pound carrots (3 medium), sliced diagonally 1/3 inch thick
- 1 large onion, halved and sliced
- 3/4 cup olive oil, divided
- 2/3 cup water

- 1/3 cup chopped dill
- 8 (17-by 12-inch) phyllo sheets, thawed if frozen
- Equipment: a shallow 3-quart oval or rectangular baking dish

Direction

- Preheat an oven with racks in lower and upper thirds to 425°F.
- Pulse breadcrumbs and walnuts till nuts are chopped finely, not ground, in a food processor.
- Peel potatoes; cut 1/4-in. thick. Divide all veggies among 2 big 4-sided sheet pans; toss each pan of veggies with 1/2 tsp. pepper, 1/2 tsp. salt and 3 tbsp. oil.
- Roast veggies for 35-40 minutes till golden brown in spots and soft, mixing and switching pan positions halfway through; with 1 rack in center, leave oven on.
- To each pan of veggies, add 1/3 cup water; mix and scrape brown bits from bottom. Chop 1/4 cup of fennel fronds; mix all veggies in 1 pan. Toss with dill and fennel fronds.
- Brush some leftover olive oil on baking dish. Use plastic wrap and a damp kitchen towel to cover phyllo sheet stack; keep leftover phyllo covered. Put 1 sheet on a work surface, working quickly. Brush with some oil gently; sprinkle 2 rounded tbsp. walnut mixture. Put another phyllo sheet over; repeat brushing then sprinkling. Put 3rd sheet over; brush using oil.
- In 1/2 of baking dish, drape phyllo stack; press up the side and into bottom gently, leaving an overhang. Create another stack using leftover walnut mixture, extra oil and 3 extra phyllo sheets. Drape into other 1/2 of dish; the phyllo will overlap in middle of dish.
- Put veggies in phyllo shell and fold overhang toward middle over the filling, it won't cover veggies; brush oil on edge. Brush leftover oil on leftover 2 phyllo sheets; tear in half and crumple. Put over filling.

- Bake for 20-25 minutes till phyllo is deep golden brown in middle of oven; before serving, cool for 5 minutes.

Nutrition Information

- Calories: 545
- Sodium: 235 mg(10%)
- Fiber: 10 g(39%)
- Total Carbohydrate: 53 g(18%)
- Protein: 8 g(15%)
- Total Fat: 35 g(55%)
- Saturated Fat: 5 g(24%)

---

170.   Rustic Apple Tarts With Calvados Whipped Cream

Serving: Makes 4 servings | Prep: 30mins | Cook: 50mins | Ready in:

Ingredients

- 1/3 cup plus 1/2 tablespoon sugar
- 1/2 cup apple cider or apple juice
- 1 tablespoon cider vinegar
- 1 lb small Gala apples (about 4; left unpeeled)
- 1 frozen puff pastry sheet (from a 17 1/4-oz package), thawed
- 3 tablespoons unsalted butter
- 1 tablespoon Calvados
- 1/2 cup chilled heavy cream
- 1 teaspoon sugar
- 1 teaspoon Calvados
- an adjustable-blade slicer

Direction

- Tart: Place oven rack on lower third of oven; preheat the oven to 425°F.
- In a dry 10-in. heavy skillet, cook 1/3 cup sugar, undisturbed, on medium heat till it starts to melt. Cook till sugar melts to pale golden caramel, occasionally mixing with a fork. Tilt skillet; add vinegar and cider slowly;

caramel will vigorously steam and harden. Simmer on medium low heat till caramel dissolves, occasionally mixing.

- Use slicer to cut apples to 1/8-in. thick slices as syrup simmers, rotating around each core; discard cores. Put apples slices in hot syrup in skillet; toss gently to coat. Take off from heat; stand for 5-10 minutes till apples are wilted by syrup, occasionally mixing.
- Roll puff pastry sheet out to 12-in. square on a lightly floured surface using floured rolling pin as apples stand. Cut to quarters to make 4 6-in. squares; brush excess flour off from both sides.
- Overlapping if needed, put squares in a big shallow baking pan; after edges get folded in later, squares will fit without touching.
- In a sieve above bowl, drain apples; keep syrup. Decoratively mound slices on every square; all around, leave 3/4-in. border. Fold border on apples along edges; as needed, pinch edges together. Use total of 1 tbsp. butter to dot tops of apples; sprinkle leftover 1/2 tbsp. sugar.
- Bake tarts for 25-30 minutes till bottoms and edges are golden brown, pastry is puffed and apples are tender.
- Boil saved syrup, Calvados and leftover 2 tbsp. butter in skillet as tart bakes till reduced to 1/3 cup and thick; drizzle or brush hot syrup on tarts.
- Cream: Use electric mixer or a whisk to beat sugar, calvados and cream in a chilled bowl till cream holds soft peaks then serve with tarts.

Nutrition Information

- Calories: 680
- Protein: 5 g(11%)
- Total Fat: 43 g(66%)
- Saturated Fat: 18 g(91%)
- Sodium: 168 mg(7%)
- Fiber: 4 g(14%)
- Total Carbohydrate: 67 g(22%)
- Cholesterol: 64 mg(21%)

---

171.   Salmon And Spinach Roll In A Puff Pastry

Serving: Makes 8 to 10 servings | Prep: | Cook: |Ready in:

Ingredients

- 1 package puff pastry (2 sheets)
- 1 tablespoon fresh parsley, chopped
- 1 tablespoon fresh thyme, chopped
- 4 tablespoons butter
- 1/2 shallot, chopped
- 1 1/2 cups frozen chopped spinach, thawed and drained
- 3 8-ounce salmon filets, diced
- salt and pepper
- olive oil
- Dill Hollandaise

Direction

- Preheat an oven to 350°.
- Put 2 puff pastry sheets over each other. On a lightly floured surface, roll puff pastry out to 12x15-in. rectangle; sprinkle pepper, salt, thyme and parsley.
- Melt 2 tbsp. butter in a sauté pan; sauté shallots till translucent. Add spinach; sauté for 3 minutes. Take off heat; cool the mixture.
- On pastry, spread spinach; put diced salmon over. Use pepper and salt for seasoning.
- Roll pastry up, tucking in ends while rolling. Use parchment paper buttered with 2 tbsp. butter to wrap pastry; to hold roll together, tie up with kitchen string. Rub olive oil on outside of paper; put on baking sheet. Bake for 45 minutes.
- Unwrap, then slice the roll; serve with dill hollandaise.

Nutrition Information

- Calories: 591
- Saturated Fat: 12 g(62%)

- Sodium: 388 mg(16%)
- Fiber: 1 g(6%)
- Total Carbohydrate: 29 g(10%)
- Cholesterol: 62 mg(21%)
- Protein: 22 g(45%)
- Total Fat: 43 g(66%)

172. Savory Mushroom And Parmesan Palmiers

Serving: 48 palmiers | Prep: 45mins | Cook: 2.5hours | Ready in:

Ingredients

- 1/4 cup olive oil, plus more for brushing
- 1 pound cremini mushrooms, trimmed and thinly sliced (5 cups)
- 3 large shallots, thinly sliced
- 6 large garlic cloves, chopped
- 2 bay leaves
- 1 sprig rosemary
- 2 sprigs thyme
- 3 sprigs tarragon
- 2/3 cup dry white wine
- 1/4 cup Marsala wine
- 6 tablespoons unsalted butter
- 1/2 cup panko (Japanese breadcrumbs) or plain coarse breadcrumbs
- 1/2 cup grated Parmesan (2 ounces)
- 2 teaspoons kosher salt
- 1 1/2 teaspoons freshly ground black pepper
- All-purpose flour, for rolling
- 12 ounces all-butter puff pastry, frozen and thawed
- Flaky sea salt, for sprinkling
- Two large rimmed baking sheets; parchment paper

Direction

- In a big and deep pan, heat oil; add in garlic, shallots, and mushrooms. On medium-high heat, cook and stir frequently for 15mins until they start to brown. Using a kitchen string, bind tarragon, bay leaves, thyme, and rosemary together then put in the pan. Pour in a quarter cup and two tablespoon water, Marsala, and wine. Cook for half an hour until the liquid evaporates, stir from time to time. Take out the bundle of herbs; mix pepper, panko, salt, and Parmesan in the mixture. Puree the mixture on a food processor until smooth; allow the mixture to cool down to room temperature.
- Spread the puff pastry to a rectangle measuring 9-in x 15-in on a floured workspace. Put the rectangle on a rimmed baking sheet lined with parchment paper; freeze for 5mins until firm. Evenly slather mushroom purée over the puff pastry. Firmly roll the pastry from one long side up until the middle. Repeat the motion on the other side. Softly stretch the roll until 18 inches long. Freeze for an hour until firm.
- Preheat the oven to 400 degrees F; position the rack on the upper and lower thirds of the oven. Place parchment paper on another rimmed baking sheet. With a big sharp knife, halve the roll crosswise and slice into quarter-inch portions. Place the slices an inch apart on the baking sheet. Slather oil and add flaky salt. Bake for half an hour until palmiers are crisp and golden, turn the sheets from up to down and back to front after 15mins of cooking time. Allow the ears to cool on baking sheets.
- You can make the logs a week in advance. Wrap them in plastic and freeze. The palmiers can be cooked a week in advance; place in a lidded container and store at room temperature. Crisp them again in a 325 degrees F oven for 8-10mins. Serve.

Nutrition Information

- Calories: 82
- Total Carbohydrate: 6 g(2%)
- Cholesterol: 5 mg(2%)
- Protein: 2 g(3%)
- Total Fat: 6 g(9%)
- Saturated Fat: 2 g(10%)

- Sodium: 72 mg(3%)
- Fiber: 0 g(2%)

---

173.   Savory Palmiers

Serving: Makes about 64 palmiers | Prep: | Cook: |Ready in:

Ingredients

- frozen puff pastry sheets, thawed but kept chilled
- 2 cups Parmigiano-Reggiano, finely grated
- Silpat (available at cookware stores) or parchment paper

Direction

- Preheat an oven to 400°F' line parchment or Silpat on baking sheets.
- On a work surface, sprinkle some cheese; use puff pastry sheet to cover it. Evenly sprinkle extra cheese on pastry sheet; roll out with rolling pin into a 10-in. square. Fold in 2 opposing square corners so sides meet in the middle; fold in same sides of pastry again to meet in the middle.
- Fold half of the pastry on top of the other; slice into 1/2-in. thick slices crosswise. In cheese, dip cut sides of every piece; put on the lined baking sheet, cut side down. Repeat using 3 leftover pastry sheets.
- In batches, bake palmiers in center of the oven for 12 minutes till golden on bottom. Flip; bake for 5-7 more minutes till golden on bottom. Put on a rack; fully cool.

Nutrition Information

---

174.   Skillet Phyllo Pie With Butternut Squash, Kale, And Goat Cheese

Serving: 4 servings | Prep: | Cook: |Ready in:

Ingredients

- 3 tablespoons olive oil, plus more for brushing
- 2 medium red onions, finely chopped
- 1/2 small butternut squash (about 1 pound), peeled, cut into 3/4-inch pieces
- 1 1/2 teaspoons chopped thyme
- 1/2 teaspoon crushed red pepper flakes
- 1 bunch Tuscan kale, ribs and stems removed, thinly sliced crosswise
- 2 large eggs, beaten to blend
- 3 ounces Parmesan, grated
- 1 teaspoon finely grated lemon zest
- Kosher salt, freshly ground pepper
- 8 ounces frozen phyllo pastry, thawed (half a 1-pound package)
- 4 ounces fresh goat cheese or feta, crumbled

Direction

- Put rack on lower third of oven then preheat to 400°F. In a big ovenproof skillet, heat 3 tbsp. oil on medium heat. Add onions; cook for 6-8 minutes till soft yet not browned, occasionally mixing. Add squash; cook for 8-10 minutes till nearly tender, occasionally mixing. Mix in red pepper flakes and thyme; put in a medium bowl and cool. Wipe out then reserve skillet.
- Add lemon zest, parmesan, eggs and kale to squash mixture; to combine, mix gently. Season with pepper and salt. Inside reserved skillet, layer phyllo sheets. Put squash-and-kale mixture in phyllo; dot goat cheese on top. Lightly brush oil on phyllo edges; fold over filling, slightly overlapping, leaving center exposed.
- Cook pie on medium heat for 3 minutes till pastry bottom is just golden; to check, use heatproof rubber spatula to lift up one side carefully. Put skillet in oven; bake pie for 20-25 minutes till phyllo is crisp and golden brown

and kale is tender and wilted. Cool pie for at least 15 minutes in skillet; slice to wedges.
- You can bake pie 6 hours ahead; cool. Keep at room temperature, uncovered.

Nutrition Information

- Calories: 544
- Saturated Fat: 11 g(54%)
- Sodium: 840 mg(35%)
- Fiber: 6 g(24%)
- Total Carbohydrate: 52 g(17%)
- Cholesterol: 120 mg(40%)
- Protein: 24 g(48%)
- Total Fat: 28 g(43%)

175.   Smoked Salmon Barquettes

Serving: Makes 24 tartlets | Prep: 30mins | Cook: 2hours | Ready in:

Ingredients

- 1 1/2 cups all-purpose flour
- 1 1/4 sticks (10 tablespoons) cold unsalted butter, cut into 1/2-inch cubes
- 1/2 teaspoon salt
- 3 to 5 tablespoons ice water
- 1/4 cup finely diced red onion
- 2 teaspoons fresh lemon juice
- 3 1/2 oz sliced fine-quality smoked salmon, finely chopped (1 1/4 cups)
- 1 tablespoon sour cream at room temperature
- 1/2 tablespoon unsalted butter, melted
- 1 teaspoon finely grated fresh lemon zest
- 1/4 teaspoon black pepper
- 1 oz salmon roe (caviar)
- Garnish: fresh dill sprigs
- a pastry or bench scraper; 24 (3 1/2-inch) barquette molds; parchment paper; pie weights or raw rice

Direction

- Dough: In a bowl, use pastry blender or your fingertips (or pulse in food processor), to blend salt, butter and flour till most of mixture looks like coarse meal with roughly pea-size small butter lumps. Evenly drizzle 3 tbsp. of ice water over; use fork to gently mi or /pulse in a processor till incorporated.
- Squeeze a small handful; 1/2 tbsp. at a time, add leftover ice water, pulsing or mixing till just incorporated if it doesn't hold together then test again. Don't overwork the mixture, or pastry will become tough.
- Turn mixture out on a lightly floured surface; divide to 4 portions. In forward motion, distribute fat by smearing each portion 1 or 2 times with heel of your hand. Use scarper to gather dough; divide to 2 pieces. Flatten every piece to 4-in. square; chill squares for a minimum of 1 hour till firm, wrapped in plastic wrap.
- Barquette shells: Roll 1 dough piece out to 13-in. square on a lightly floured surface; keep leftover dough chilled. Put 12 barquette molds close together on a work surface; drape rolled-out dough on top of molds. Roll lightly floured rolling pin on molds to cut dough; press into molds lightly. Repeat with leftover dough; use fork to prick every shell a few times. Chill all shells for 30 minutes till firm in a shallow baking pan.
- Preheat an oven to 375°F.
- In a shallow pan, put barquette molds close together; use parchment to cover. On top of parchment over molds, put pie weights; bake in center of oven for 15 minutes till shell edges are pale golden. Remove weights and parchment carefully; bake shells for 7-10 more minutes till golden. Cool shells for 10 minutes in molds on a rack. Remove from molds; fully cool.
- As shells bake and cool, prep filling: Mix a pinch of salt, lemon juice and onion in a bowl; stand for 30 minutes at room temperature. Mix in pepper, zest, butter, sour cream and salmon.
- Assemble barquettes: Use scant tsp. of salmon mixture to fill each barquette shell; put scant 1/4 tsp. of caviar over.

Nutrition Information

- Calories: 96
- Sodium: 68 mg(3%)
- Fiber: 0 g(1%)
- Total Carbohydrate: 7 g(2%)
- Cholesterol: 20 mg(7%)
- Protein: 3 g(5%)
- Total Fat: 6 g(10%)
- Saturated Fat: 4 g(18%)

176. Smoked Salmon Napoleans With Greens

Serving: Serves 4 | Prep: | Cook: | Ready in:

Ingredients

- 1/2 cup white wine vinegar
- 1/4 cup minced shallots
- 1 cup bottled clam juice
- 1/2 cup corn oil
- 4 large egg yolks
- 1/4 cup minced fresh dill
- 6 fresh phyllo pastry sheets or frozen, thawed
- 7 tablespoons butter, melted
- 1 1/2 tablespoon sesame seeds
- 8 ounces (about) thinly sliced smoked salmon
- 4 teaspoons minced onion
- 1/4 cup olive oil
- 1 1/2 tablespoons white wine vinegar
- 8 cups torn curly endive

Direction

- Sauce: Boil shallots and vinegar in a heavy medium saucepan for 6 minutes till nearly no liquid remains. Add oil and clam juice; simmer for 10 minutes till reduced to 1 cup. In a medium bowl, whisk yolks; whisk in simmering sauce slowly. Put sauce back in pan; mix on medium low heat for 3 minutes, don't boil, till thermometer reads 140°F. Strain

into a bowl; stir in dill. You can make this 8 hours ahead then chill.

- Napoleons: Preheat an oven to 425°F. Line waxed paper on cooling rack; butter 2 baking sheets. On a work surface, put 1 phyllo sheet; brush using melted butter. Put 2nd sheet over the top; brush with butter. Keep layering and buttering using leftover sheets. Cut phyllo to 12 4 1/2 x 2-in. rectangles; arrange on prepped sheets, spacing apart from each other. Sprinkle sesame seeds; bake for 8 minutes till phyllo is golden, closely watching to avoid burning. Put phyllo on waxed paper-lined rack using a metal spatula; cool.
- Rewarm sauce on low heat, constantly mixing; don't boil. On a work surface, put 4 phyllo rectangles; use salmon to cover each. Season with pepper; sprinkle 1/2 tsp. of onion on each. Scoop 1 tsp. of sauce on top; put another phyllo rectangle over each then salmon. Use pepper to season. Sprinkle 1/2 tsp. of onion on each then scoop 1 tsp. of sauce on top; put leftover phyllo rectangles over.
- Whisk vinegar and oil in big bowl. Add curly endive; toss to coat then season with pepper and salt. Divide salad between 4 plates; put 1 napoleon over each. Serve with leftover sauce separately.

Nutrition Information

- Calories: 812
- Saturated Fat: 21 g(105%)
- Sodium: 936 mg(39%)
- Fiber: 4 g(15%)
- Total Carbohydrate: 21 g(7%)
- Cholesterol: 251 mg(84%)
- Protein: 21 g(42%)
- Total Fat: 71 g(110%)

177. Spiced Palmiers

Serving: Makes about 64 | Prep: | Cook: | Ready in:

Ingredients

- 1/2 cup sugar
- 4 teaspoons ground cinnamon
- 1 tablespoon ground cardamom
- 2 teaspoons ground allspice
- 1 teaspoon ground cloves
- 1 14-ounce package frozen puff pastry (such as Dufour), thawed
- All-purpose flour (for dusting)
- 3 tablespoons unsalted butter, melted, divided

Direction

- Line parchment paper on baking sheet. Mix spices and sugar in small bowl. Unfold pastry to 14x10-in. rectangle on lightly floured work surface; if needed, roll out. Lightly brush butter; sprinkle on 1/4 cup spiced sugar. Halve lengthwise.
- Fold both long sides of 1 strip of pastry so outer edges meet in middle of strip; brush extra butter. Sprinkle 2 tbsp. spiced sugar; lengthwise fold in half to make 14-in. long, 1-in. wide log. Repeat with leftover pastry strip.
- Put logs on prepped baking sheet; use plastic wrap to cover. Chill for 30 minutes till firm; you can prep palmier dough 2 weeks ahead; keep in freezer airtight. Before continuing, thaw overnight in fridge.
- Preheat an oven to 425°F; line parchment paper on 2 baking sheets. Crosswise cut each log to 1/4-in. slices then lay slices flat on prepped baking sheets, 1-in. apart.
- Bake palmiers for 8 minutes till golden on bottom. Flip palmiers with thin metal spatula; lightly brush butter. Sprinkle extra spiced sugar; bake for 15 more minutes till pastry is golden brown and sugar is bubbly. Put palmiers on wire rack; cool. You can make palmiers 2 days ahead; keep at room temperature, airtight.

Nutrition Information

- Calories: 46
- Protein: 0 g(1%)

- Total Fat: 3 g(4%)
- Saturated Fat: 1 g(5%)
- Sodium: 16 mg(1%)
- Fiber: 0 g(1%)
- Total Carbohydrate: 5 g(2%)
- Cholesterol: 1 mg(0%)

178. Spicy Cumin Cheese Straws

Serving: Makes about 24 cheese straws | Prep: | Cook: | Ready in:

Ingredients

- 4 ounces extra-sharp Cheddar cheese, shredded fine (about 1 1/4 cups)
- 1/2 teaspoon ground cumin
- 1/4 teaspoon cayenne, or to taste
- 1 sheet (about 1/2 pound) frozen puff pastry, thawed
- an egg wash made by beating 1 large egg with 2 teaspoons water
- 1 tablespoon cumin seed
- coarse sea salt to taste

Direction

- Toss cayenne, ground cumin and cheese in a small bowl.
- Roll pastry to 14x12-in. rectangle on a lightly floured surface; brush some egg wash. Crosswise halve pastry to make 2 12x7-in. rectangles. On 1 rectangle, sprinkle cheese. Put 2nd rectangle, egg-wash side down, over; firmly press it to force any air pockets out. Slightly roll pastry out to adhere layers to make rectangle around 12 1/2 x 7 1/2-in. Brush some leftover egg wash on pastry; evenly sprinkle sea salt and cumin seed.
- Cut pastry to 7 1/2-in. long, 1/2-in. wide strips with a sharp knife or pastry wheel. Twist strips; put on baking sheets. To keep strips twisted, press ends onto sheet. You can prep cheese straws 2 weeks ahead at this

point; freeze cheese straws for 1 hour or till frozen on baking sheet then put in resealable freezer bag. Before proceeding, don't thaw cheese straws.

- Preheat an oven to 425°F then grease 2 baking sheets.
- Put 1/2 cheese straws on 1 baking sheet, 1-in. apart; bake for 10-12 minutes or till pale golden in center of oven. In same manner, bake leftover cheese straws.
- Serve them warm at room temperature.

Nutrition Information

- Calories: 80
- Protein: 2 g(5%)
- Total Fat: 6 g(9%)
- Saturated Fat: 2 g(11%)
- Sodium: 65 mg(3%)
- Fiber: 0 g(1%)
- Total Carbohydrate: 4 g(1%)
- Cholesterol: 14 mg(5%)

179. Spinach And Sorrel Spanakopita

Serving: | Prep: | Cook: | Ready in:

Ingredients

- 1 (10-oz) package frozen chopped spinach
- 1 cup chopped scallions
- Salt
- 1 tablespoon olive oil
- 1/4 pound fresh sorrel leaves, chopped (2 packed cups)
- 1 egg yolk, lightly beaten
- 8 ounces feta, crumbled (1 cup)
- 1/4 teaspoon ground nutmeg
- 3 tablespoons chopped fresh dill, or to taste
- Freshly ground black pepper
- 10 (17- by 12-inch) sheets phyllo, thawed if frozen
- 1 1/2 sticks (3/4 cup) unsalted butter, melted

Direction

- Prepare the filling. Cook the spinach following the package directions; use a colander to drain. Run to refresh under cold water to stop cooking then drain again thoroughly. Move the spinach on a clean kitchen towel, do not use terry cloth. Twist the ends of the towel together to release as much liquid from the spinach as possible; move spinach to a big bowl.
- On medium heat, cook scallions with a quarter teaspoon salt for 2-3 minutes in a 9 to 10-in non-stick pan with olive oil, stir until soft; add sorrel. Cook and stir for a minute until wilted. If too dry, add a tablespoon of water. When heated, the sorrel with immediately become khaki gray in color. Combine the spinach and sorrel mixture; stir well.
- Mix in yolk, then feta, pepper and salt to taste, dill, and nutmeg until well blended.
- Prepare the Phyllo Triangles. Preheat the oven to 375 degrees F. Put parchment paper on a big rimmed baking sheet.
- Put two overlapping plastic wrap sheets and a damp kitchen towel to cover the phyllo stack.
- On a work surface, arrange one phyllo sheet from the stack with the long side closest to you then slather butter all over. Cover the remaining phyllo sheets. Slice the buttered stack lengthwise into four strips, each about 3x17 inches long.
- Place a heaping teaspoonful of filling close to one corner of the strip closest to you. Fold the corner of phyllo over the filling to enclose and make a triangle. Continue to fold strip like a flag while keeping a triangle shape. Slather butter all over the triangle; place triangle in a parchment-lined sheet with the seam-side down. Make more triangles in the same way with the rest of the phyllo.
- Place the spanakopita in the freezer for 20 minutes until firm for best results.
- Bake triangles for 20-25 minutes until golden brown in the middle of the oven; slightly cool on a rack.

- The triangles can be formed three days in advance without baking. Place on a rimmed baking sheet then freeze until firm. Arrange in a single layer in a heavy-duty sealed plastic bag; freeze more. Do not thaw, bake the frozen pastries in the same way as above.

Nutrition Information

- Calories: 255
- Total Carbohydrate: 14 g(5%)
- Cholesterol: 65 mg(22%)
- Protein: 5 g(11%)
- Total Fat: 20 g(31%)
- Saturated Fat: 12 g(58%)
- Sodium: 262 mg(11%)
- Fiber: 2 g(8%)

180. Spinach, Feta, And Phyllo Purses

Serving: Makes 30 hors d'oeuvres | Prep: | Cook: |Ready in:

Ingredients

- 1 1/2 cups finely chopped onion
- 1/2 cup olive oil
- two 10-ounce packages frozen spinach, cooked, drained, squeezed dry by handfulls, and chopped
- 2 cups grated Feta (about 1/2 pound)
- 2 teaspoons dried dill
- four 16- x 12-inch sheets of phyllo, stacked between 2 sheets of wax paper and covered with a dampened kitchen towel

Direction

- Cook onion in 1/4 cup oil in a heavy skillet on medium low heat till golden, occasionally mixing. Add spinach; cook mixture till well combined while mixing. Take skillet off from heat; mix in dill and feta. Cool filling.

- Lay 1 phyllo sheet with long side facing you on a work surface; lightly brush some leftover 1/4 cup oil then layer another sheet. Lightly brush it with some leftover oil. Cut sheets to thirds lengthwise with a sharp knife; cut each length to fifths crosswise to make 15 4x3 1/2-in. sections. Put level tsp. of the filling in middle of every phyllo section. 1 section at a time, gather phyllo corners over filling; gently twist phyllo. Put pastries in an oiled jellyroll pan; create pasties the same way with leftover filling, oil and phyllo. Bake pastries for 25 minutes or till golden in the lower third of the preheated 375°F oven. You can bake pastries 1 day ahead; keep chilled, loosely covered with plastic wrap. Reheat pastries for 10 minutes or till heated through in 375°F oven.

Nutrition Information

- Calories: 67
- Saturated Fat: 2 g(8%)
- Sodium: 97 mg(4%)
- Fiber: 1 g(2%)
- Total Carbohydrate: 3 g(1%)
- Cholesterol: 7 mg(2%)
- Protein: 2 g(4%)
- Total Fat: 5 g(8%)

181. Spinach, Feta, And Pine Nut Phyllo Tart

Serving: Serves 6 as a main course | Prep: | Cook: |Ready in:

Ingredients

- 1/2 cup pine nuts (about 3 ounces)
- 1 medium onion
- 1/3 cup olive oil
- two 10-ounce packages frozen chopped spinach, thawed
- 1/2 teaspoon salt
- 2 large eggs

- 1/2 cup crumbled feta (about 3 ounces)
- 1 tablespoon fine dry bread crumbs
- seven 17- by 12-inch phyllo sheets
- 5 tablespoons unsalted butter
- 6 tablespoons plus 1/4 cup freshly grated Parmesan

Direction

- Preheat an oven to 375°F.
- Filling: Toast pine nuts in a shallow baking pan in middle of oven for 4 minutes till golden; cool. Chop onion finely; cook in oil in a big heavy skillet on medium low heat till soft, mixing. To remove as much liquid as you can, squeeze spinach; mix with salt into onion. On medium heat, cook spinach mixture for 1-2 minutes till liquid evaporates, occasionally mixing; slightly cool. Whisk eggs till combined in a big bowl; mix in breadcrumbs, feta, pine nuts and spinach mixture till well combined. You can make filling 1 day ahead, covered and chilled; before proceeding, bring filling down to room temperature.
- Stack phyllo sheets; use 2 overlapping plastic wrap sheets then a dampened kitchen towel to cover. Melt butter in a small saucepan; slightly cool. Brush butter lightly on 10 1/2 x 7 1/2 x 1-in. rectangular tart pan with removable fluted rim lightly.
- Lightly brush butter on 1 phyllo sheet on a work surface; evenly sprinkle 1 tbsp. parmesan on buttered phyllo. Repeat layers with 5 tbsp. parmesan, butter and 5 extra phyllo sheet; put last phyllo sheet on stack. Brush with butter lightly. Put phyllo in tart pan; let excess hang over edge. Put filling on phyllo, evenly spreading. Fold pastry edges over filling; leave middle uncovered. Brush butter over phyllo lightly; sprinkle leftover 1/4 cup parmesan on exposed filling. Bake tart for 25-30 minutes in middle of oven till golden; serve tart at room temperature or warm.

Nutrition Information

- Calories: 535
- Total Carbohydrate: 21 g(7%)
- Cholesterol: 113 mg(38%)
- Protein: 18 g(36%)
- Total Fat: 42 g(65%)
- Saturated Fat: 15 g(73%)
- Sodium: 596 mg(25%)
- Fiber: 4 g(17%)

---

182. Strawberry Blueberry Napoleons

Serving: Makes 12 | Prep: | Cook: | Ready in:

Ingredients

- 24 9x14-inch sheets fresh or thawed frozen phyllo pastry (about 3/4 pound)
- 6 tablespoons (3/4 stick) unsalted butter, melted
- 16 teaspoons plus 1/2 cup sugar
- 2/3 cup balsamic vinegar
- 1 pound mascarpone cheese,* whisked to loosen
- 1 cup chilled heavy whipping cream
- 2 teaspoons vanilla extract
- 3 1-pint baskets fresh strawberries, hulled, thinly sliced
- 4 1/2-pint baskets fresh blueberries
- Powdered sugar

Direction

- Preheat an oven to 350°F; line parchment paper on 2 big baking sheets. On a work surface, put 1 phyllo sheet; use plastic wrap and damp kitchen towel to cover leftover phyllo. Brush some melted butter on phyllo sheet; sprinkle 1/2 tsp. sugar. Put 2nd phyllo sheet over. Brush using some melted butter; sprinkle 1/2 tsp. sugar. Repeat using 2 extra phyllo sheets, brush melted butter on each then sprinkle 1/2 tsp. sugar on each. Lengthwise halve phyllo stack; crosswise cut into thirds to make 6 4 1/4-in. squares. Put squares on 1 prepped baking sheet, evenly spacing apart. To make 6 more squares, repeat with 4 extra phyllo sheets; put on 2nd baking sheet, evenly spacing apart. Bake phyllo for 7 minutes till light golden. Put phyllo stacks on rack with a spatula; fully cool. Repeat with leftover sugar, butter and phyllo sheets to create 36 squares in total. You can make phyllo squares 2 days ahead; keep between waxed paper layers at room temperature in airtight container.

- Boil 4 tsp. sugar and vinegar in a small saucepan on medium high heat. Lower heat to low; simmer for 25 minutes till reduced to 1/4 cup and syrupy. Refrigerate for 1 hour till cold; you can make this 1 day ahead, refrigerated.
- Beat leftover 1/2 cup sugar, vanilla extract, cream and mascarpone till stiff peaks form in a big mixing bowl; you can make mascarpone filling 1 day ahead, refrigerated, covered.
- Put 1/4 blueberries and strawberries aside for garnish. On a work surface, put 12 phyllo squares; spread 1 tbsp. mascarpone filling on each. Use leftover sliced strawberries to cover; spread 1 tbsp. filling on strawberries. With corners slightly askew to the bottom square, put 12 more phyllo squares over filling. Spread 1 tbsp. filling on each square; use leftover blueberries to cover. Spread 1 more tbsp. filling on blueberries. With corners slightly askew to the center square, put final 12 phyllo squares over. You can make this 3 hours ahead. On 2 big baking sheets, put napoleons; covered, refrigerated.
- Over each napoleon, scoop a dollop of filling; use saved blueberries and strawberry slices as garnish. Dust powdered sugar over. In middle of each plate, put 1 napoleon; around edge of plates, drizzle balsamic reduction.

Nutrition Information

- Calories: 586
- Cholesterol: 117 mg(39%)
- Protein: 7 g(14%)
- Total Fat: 37 g(57%)

- Saturated Fat: 21 g(104%)
- Sodium: 295 mg(12%)
- Fiber: 5 g(20%)
- Total Carbohydrate: 61 g(20%)

---

183. Sugar Glazed Prune Tartlets

Serving: Makes 9 small pastries | Prep: | Cook: | Ready in:

Ingredients

- Butter for greasing baking sheet
- 1 frozen puff pastry sheet (from a 17 1/4-oz package), thawed
- 1 egg white, lightly beaten
- 27 pitted prunes (sometimes called dried plums; 1/2 lb)
- 1 tablespoon sugar
- 1/4 teaspoon cinnamon

Direction

- In upper third of oven, put oven rack; preheat the oven to 425°F then butter a baking sheet.
- Unfold pastry sheet; cut to 9 3-in. squares. Put squares on baking sheet; brush some egg white on squares lightly. In leftover egg white, toss prunes. Put 3 prunes in middle of every square; let extra egg drip off. Leave 1/2-in. border around the edge. Mix cinnamon and sugar; sprinkle on tartlets.
- Bake for 10-15 minutes till pastry is golden brown and puffed. Put tartlets on a rack; cool for 10 minutes to warm.

Nutrition Information

184. Swiss Chard And Herb Tart

Serving: Makes 8 appetizer or 4 first course servings | Prep: | Cook: | Ready in:

Ingredients

- 1 pound Swiss chard, stems and ribs removed
- 1 1/2 tablespoons extra-virgin olive oil
- 1 garlic clove, minced
- 1 15-ounce container whole-milk ricotta cheese
- 1/2 cup freshly grated Parmesan cheese
- 2 large eggs
- 1/2 teaspoon salt
- 1/4 teaspoon ground black pepper
- 1/4 teaspoon minced fresh thyme
- 1/4 teaspoon minced fresh oregano
- 1/8 teaspoon grated nutmeg
- 1 17.3-ounce package frozen puff pastry (2 sheets), thawed

Direction

- Cook chard for 2 minutes in a big pot of boiling salted water till just wilted; drain. Squeeze liquid out; chop chard.
- Heat oil in a big heavy skillet on medium heat and add garlic; sauté for 1 minute. Add chard; sauté for 5 minutes till excess liquid evaporates. Put chard mixture in a big bowl; slightly cool. Mix in ricotta and following 7 ingredients.
- Put rack into bottom third of oven and preheat to 375°F. On a lightly floured surface, roll 1 pastry sheet out to 14-in. square; put pastry on a 9-in. diameter tart pan that has removable bottom. Trim the edges; leave 1-in. overhang. Use chard mixture to fill pastry; brush pastry brush dipped into water lightly on pastry overhang. Roll 2nd pastry sheet out to 13-in. square. Trim pastry square to 10-in. round using tart pan for a guide then drape on filling; seal edges then fold in.
- Bake for 45 minutes till pastry is golden brown; cool for 10 minutes.

- Take out sides of pan from tart; put on a platter then cut to wedges. Serve.

Nutrition Information

- Calories: 510
- Cholesterol: 78 mg(26%)
- Protein: 16 g(31%)
- Total Fat: 36 g(55%)
- Saturated Fat: 12 g(61%)
- Sodium: 451 mg(19%)
- Fiber: 2 g(8%)
- Total Carbohydrate: 32 g(11%)

185. Swiss Honey Walnut Tart

Serving: Serves 10 to 12 | Prep: | Cook: | Ready in:

Ingredients

- 1/3 cup plus 1 tablespoon whipping cream
- 1/4 cup honey
- 1 tablespoon unsalted butter
- 2/3 cup sugar
- 3 tablespoons water
- 1 tablespoon fresh lemon juice
- 1 teaspoon vanilla extract
- 1 17 1/4-ounce package frozen puff pastry (2 sheets), thawed
- 2 cups coarsely chopped walnuts
- 1 large egg, beaten to blend
- 1 large egg yolk

Direction

- Mix butter, honey and 1/3 cup of cream till butter melts in small saucepan on medium heat. Mix lemon juice, water and sugar till sugar dissolves in heavy medium saucepan on low heat. Increase heat; boil but don't stir for 12 minutes till syrup is golden, swirling pan occasionally and brushing sides down using a wet pastry brush. Take off from heat. Add warm cream mixture; it'll bubble up. Mix till smooth on very low heat; add vanilla. Chill for 1 hour till cold, uncovered; you can make this 1 day ahead, kept chilled and covered.

- Roll 1 pastry sheet out to 11-in. square on a floured surface; trim to 10-in. round with a 10-in. diameter cake pan bottom for guide. Put on ungreased baking sheet. Roll 2nd pastry sheet out to 11-in. square; trim to 11-in. round with an 11-in. diameter tart pan bottom for guide. Score design on 11-in. round with fork; from center, cut small hole.
- Stir nuts into cold caramel. In 1-in. pastry border on baking sheet, brush beaten egg. Spread filling on pastry; mounding in middle and leaving a 1-in. border then cover using the 11-in. round. To seal, press. Fold bottom pastry edge over the top pastry; tightly seal the edge. Mix yolk and 1 tbsp. of cream into leftover beaten egg; brush egg mixture over tart. Chill tart for 1 hour on the baking sheet.
- Preheat an oven to 400°F; bake tart for 25 minutes till golden. Cool; you can make this 8 hours ahead.

Nutrition Information

- Calories: 502
- Total Carbohydrate: 49 g(16%)
- Cholesterol: 51 mg(17%)
- Protein: 5 g(11%)
- Total Fat: 27 g(42%)
- Saturated Fat: 11 g(53%)
- Sodium: 143 mg(6%)
- Fiber: 2 g(8%)

186. Thin Apple Tarts

Serving: Makes 4 servings | Prep: | Cook: | Ready in:

Ingredients

- 2 small Granny Smith apples, peeled, cored, and halved
- 1/2 cup water

- 1/2 cup sugar
- 2 tablespoons fresh lemon juice
- 2 tablespoons unsalted butter
- 1 frozen puff pastry sheet (from a 17 1/4-oz package), thawed

Direction

- Slice apple halves to 1/16-in. thick slices crosswise; put in a bowl.
- Boil butter, lemon juice, sugar and water in small saucepan, mixing till sugar dissolves; put on apples. Flip apples till slightly wilted; drain in a colander placed above a bowl, keeping liquid.
- Preheat an oven to 425°F.
- Roll pastry sheet out to 12 1/2-in. square on a lightly floured surface; cut out 4 6-in. rounds. Put rounds on a lightly buttered baking sheet; put overlapping apple slices over. Bake for 25 minutes in the center of the oven till golden brown.
- Boil reserved liquid till reduced to 1/3 cup in a saucepan; brush over baked tarts.

Nutrition Information

- Calories: 528
- Saturated Fat: 10 g(48%)
- Sodium: 156 mg(6%)
- Fiber: 3 g(12%)
- Total Carbohydrate: 63 g(21%)
- Cholesterol: 15 mg(5%)
- Protein: 5 g(10%)
- Total Fat: 29 g(45%)

187. Three Cheese Phyllo Triangles With Onions And Yogurt

Serving: Makes about 36 triangles | Prep: | Cook: | Ready in:

Ingredients

- 1/3 cup extra virgin olive oil, plus more for brushing pastries
- 2 large onions, finely chopped (about 2 cups)
- 1 1/2 cups (about 12 ounces) fresh Greek myzithra, whole milk ricotta, or farmer's cheese, crumbled
- 3/4 cup (about 3 ounces) Greek feta, crumbled
- 3/4 cup (about 2 ounces) grated Greek kefalotyri cheese or other hard sheep's milk cheese, such as pecorino
- 1/2 cup thick Greek or Mediterranean-style yogurt or drained plain yogurt
- 1/3 cup finely chopped fresh dill
- 2 large eggs
- Salt and freshly ground black pepper to taste
- 1 pound (about 18 sheets) commercial phyllo, defrosted and at room temperature

Direction

- Heat 3 tbsp. olive oil on medium heat in a big, nonstick is best, skillet; cook onions for 10-12 minutes or till onions are lightly golden and soft; mix while cooking. Take off from heat; put aside.
- Mix dill, cooked onions, leftover olive oil, yogurt and cheeses. Lightly beat eggs; add to mixture, stirring well. Season with pepper and salt.
- Have phyllo ready. Put sheets in front of you; lengthwise cut to 4 even columns with sharp knife. Stack them; use dry kitchen towel and then a damp kitchen towel over to keep stack covered. Preheat oven to 350°F; oil 2 baking sheets lightly.
- Remove 1 phyllo strip; lightly brush olive oil. Put another strip over; brush oil. Put 1 tsp. filling in lower right hand phyllo corner, 1/2-in. from edge. Fold right corner up to make a right triangle; keep folding like a flag. Put on the baking sheet, seam side down. Continue till you use all filling and phyllo; bake for 12-15 minutes in middle of oven or till golden and puffed; serve warm.

Nutrition Information

- Calories: 95
- Sodium: 119 mg(5%)
- Fiber: 0 g(2%)
- Total Carbohydrate: 8 g(3%)
- Cholesterol: 19 mg(6%)
- Protein: 3 g(7%)
- Total Fat: 5 g(8%)
- Saturated Fat: 2 g(10%)

188. Tofu, Greens And Sun Dried Tomato Strudel With Red Pepper Sauce

Serving: Makes 6 servings | Prep: | Cook: | Ready in:

Ingredients

- 1 bunch kale, stems and ribs cut away and discarded, leaves finely chopped (about 4 cups)
- 1 tablespoon olive oil
- 1 1/2 cups chopped onion
- 3 garlic cloves, minced
- 7 ounces firm tofu (half of one 14-ounce package), drained, cut into 1/2-inch pieces
- 4 ounces grated reduced-fat provolone cheese
- 1/2 cup grated Asiago cheese
- 2 tablespoons chopped fresh dill
- 1 1/2 teaspoons all purpose flour
- 6 oil-packed sun-dried tomato halves, patted dry, chopped
- Nonstick olive oil spray
- 6 frozen phyllo pastry sheets, thawed
- Red Pepper Sauce

Direction

- Cook kale for 5 minutes in a big pot of boiling salted water till tender. Drain and cool; squeeze dry. In a big heavy skillet, heat oil on medium heat. Add garlic and onion; sauté for 7 minutes till tender. Cool.
- Chop flour, dill, cheeses and tofu finely in a processor; put in a bowl. Mix in sun-dried

tomatoes, kale and onion mixture; season with pepper and salt.

- Preheat an oven to 350°F; spray oil spray on a big baking sheet. One above the other, stack 2 phyllo sheets on a work surface; spray oil spray on phyllo. Put 2 extra phyllo sheets over; spray using oil spray. Repeat with leftover 2 phyllo sheets. Lengthwise spread tofu mixture down middle of phyllo in 3-in. wide strip; on each short side, leave 1 1/2-in. border. Fold short phyllo sides in over filling; fully enclosing filling, roll up into a log. Spray oil spray on phyllo log; put strudel on the prepped baking sheet.
- Bake strudel for 40 minutes till golden brown; you can make this 2 hours ahead, allowing to stand at room temperature. Rewarm for 15 minutes till heated through in 350°F oven; cool for 10 minutes. Slice strudel to 6 pierces crosswise then put on plates; scoop red pepper sauce next to it.

Nutrition Information

┌─────────────────────────────────────┐
│ **189.   Tomato And Tapenade**   │
│   **Tartlets**   │
└─────────────────────────────────────┘

Serving: Makes 6 | Prep: | Cook: | Ready in:

Ingredients

- 1 17.3-ounce package frozen puff pastry (2 sheets), thawed
- 1/2 cup (about) green- or black-olive tapenade*
- 5 to 6 ripe medium tomatoes, preferably assorted colors, cut into 1/4-inch slices
- 12 ounces fresh mozzarella cheese, thinly sliced
- Fleur de sel or coarse kosher salt
- Extra-virgin olive oil
- Balsamic vinegar
- 18 small fresh basil leaves

- 6 green or black olives, pitted, sliced
- A thick paste or spread made from brine-cured olives, capers, anchovies, and various seasonings; available at some supermarkets and at specialty foods stores and Italian markets.

Direction

- Put racks in bottom and top third of oven; preheat the oven to 400°F. Line parchment paper on 2 baking sheets. One by one, roll pastry to 13-in. square on a floured surface; cut 4 rounds out from 1 sheet then 2 rounds from 2nd sheet using 6-in. diameter plate; keep leftover pastry for another use. Put 3 rounds on each baking sheet; use fork to pierce each round. Put another parchment sheet over rounds; put another baking sheet over parchment on every sheet.
- On each oven rack, put 1 baking sheet stack; bake for 10 minutes. Rotate the baking sheets; bake for 10 more minutes till rounds are golden. Remove top parchment sheets and top baking sheets carefully using oven mitts; bake for 3 more minutes till deep golden. Put sheets on rack; cool. You can make it 1 day ahead, keep at room temperature, airtight.
- Put oven temperature to 450°F. On each pastry round, spread generous tbsp. tapenade; leave 1/2-in. border around edges. In pinwheel pattern, alternate 4 mozzarella slices and 4 tomato slices over each pastry; bake for 2 minutes till cheese just starts to melt. Sprinkle pepper and fleur de sel; drizzle balsamic vinegar and olive oil. Put olive slices and few basil slices over each tartlet; immediately serve.

Nutrition Information

- Calories: 703
- Cholesterol: 50 mg(17%)
- Protein: 19 g(39%)
- Total Fat: 51 g(78%)
- Saturated Fat: 18 g(88%)
- Sodium: 791 mg(33%)

- Fiber: 3 g(12%)
- Total Carbohydrate: 44 g(15%)

190. Turkey And Broccoli Pot Pies

Serving: Makes 2 servings; can be doubled | Prep: | Cook: | Ready in:

Ingredients

- 1 frozen puff pastry sheet (half of 17.3-ounce package), thawed
- 1 14- to 16-ounce turkey thigh, skinned, boned, diced
- 1 teaspoon poultry seasoning
- 2 tablespoons (1/4 stick) butter
- 1 cup small broccoli florets
- 3/4 cup chopped red bell pepper
- 2 tablespoons all purpose flour
- 1 1/4 cups canned low-salt chicken broth

Direction

- Preheat an oven to 400°F. On a work surface, unroll pastry sheet; cut 2 3 1/2-in. squares out. Keep leftover sheet for another time. On a small baking sheet, put squares; use fork to pierce squares a few times. Bake for 15 minutes till golden and puffed.
- Meanwhile, sprinkle pepper, salt and poultry seasoning on turkey. Melt butter in a big skillet on medium high heat then add turkey; sauté for 5 minutes till brown. Add bell pepper and broccoli; sauté for 2 minutes till broccoli is crisp yet tender. Sprinkle flour on broccoli and turkey; mix for 1 minute. Add broth and boil, mixing browned bits up. Simmer for 10 minutes till turkey cooks through and sauce thickens. Season with pepper and salt.
- Divide turkey mixture to 2 1 1/4-2-cup soufflé dishes or custard cups; put pastry square over each.

Nutrition Information

- Calories: 1110
- Saturated Fat: 23 g(115%)
- Sodium: 492 mg(20%)
- Fiber: 3 g(13%)
- Total Carbohydrate: 68 g(23%)
- Cholesterol: 156 mg(52%)
- Protein: 49 g(98%)
- Total Fat: 71 g(110%)

191. Upside Down Caramelized Apricot Tart

Serving: Makes 8 servings | Prep: | Cook: | Ready in:

Ingredients

- 1/2 to 3/4 cup sugar
- 2 tablespoons water
- 3 tablespoons unsalted butter
- 2 tablespoons whipping cream
- 9 fresh apricots
- 1 sheet frozen puff pastry (half of 17.3-ounce package), thawed

Direction

- Put rack in middle of oven; preheat it to 425°F. Mix 3/4 cup sugar for fresh apricots or 1/2 cup sugar for canned apricots and 2 tbsp. water in small heavy saucepan on medium low heat till sugar dissolves. Increase heat; boil without mixing for 8 minutes, occasionally using pastry brushed dipped into water to brush pan sides down and swirling pan, till syrup is deep amber. Add cream and butter; it will vigorously bubble. Mix on low heat till caramel bits melt. Put caramel into 10-in. diameter nonstick ovenproof skillet immediately; swirl to cover skillet's bottom. Put apricot halves carefully and tightly together over caramel, rounded side down.
- Roll puff pastry sheet to 12 1/2-in. square on lightly floured surface; cut pastry to 12-in.

round with 12-in. tart pan bottom or platter for guide. Put puff pastry round over apricots in skillet; press down pastry gently around apricots at skillet's edge. Bake tart for 25 minutes till pastry is deep golden and puffed. Take out of oven; cool for 1 minute. To loosen, cut around pastry edge. Put big rimmed platter over skillet; tightly hold platter and skillet together wearing oven mitts. Invert; let syrup and tart fall onto platter. Lift skillet off carefully; rearrange apricots that get dislodged then serve warm.

Nutrition Information

- Calories: 297
- Fiber: 1 g(5%)
- Total Carbohydrate: 34 g(11%)
- Cholesterol: 16 mg(5%)
- Protein: 3 g(6%)
- Total Fat: 17 g(27%)
- Saturated Fat: 6 g(32%)
- Sodium: 79 mg(3%)

192.　　Vegetable Tortes

Serving: Makes 2 tortes (each serving 8) | Prep: 2hours | Cook: 5hours | Ready in:

Ingredients

- 2 1/2 lb boiling potatoes such as Yukon Gold
- 2 lb cremini mushrooms, trimmed and halved
- 2 shallots, coarsely chopped
- 1/2 teaspoon dried thyme, crumbled
- 1 stick (1/2 cup) unsalted butter
- 1/2 cup dry white wine
- 1/4 cup whole milk, heated
- 1 large garlic clove, minced
- 1/2 cup chopped scallion greens
- 1 1/2 (15-oz) boxes frozen peas, thawed
- 2 lb eggplants
- 1/4 cup olive oil
- 7 red bell peppers

- 5 frozen puff pastry sheets (from three 17 1/4-oz packages), thawed
- 6 tablespoons fine dry bread crumbs
- 3/4 lb smoked Gouda or mozzarella, coarsely grated (2 cups)
- 1 large egg, lightly beaten
- a food mill fitted with fine disk and 2 (10-inch) springform pans

Direction

- Cook potatoes: Use cold salted water to cover potatoes by 1-in.; simmer for 20 minutes till just tender.
- As potatoes cook, prep mushrooms: In 2 batches, chop thyme, shallots and mushrooms finely in a food processor. Sauté 1/2 the mixture with pepper and salt to taste in 2 tbsp. butter in a 12-in. heavy skillet on medium high heat for 5 minutes till the released mushroom liquid evaporates, occasionally mixing. Add 1/4 cup wine; simmer for 2 minutes till wine evaporates, mixing. Put into a bowl; cool. In same manner, cook leftover mushroom mixture; as needed, season.
- Potato filling: In a colander, drain potatoes; peel when cool to handle. Through a food mill, force warm potatoes into a big bowl. Mix in pepper and salt to taste, peas (don't crust), leftover 4 tbsp. butter, scallions, garlic and hot milk; cool down to room temperature.
- Broiling eggplants: Preheat a broiler.
- From opposing sides of every eggplant, lengthwise cut 2 thin slices; discard. Lengthwise cut eggplants to 1/4-in. thick slices; brush oil on both sides. Season with pepper and salt. In 1 layer, put some eggplant slices on broiler pan rack; broil 2-3-in. from heat, in batches, for 5 minutes total till both sides are golden brown and tender, turning once. On broiler rack, cool cooked eggplant for 5 minutes; put on a plate. In same manner, broil the leftovers.
- Roast peppers: On their sides, lay bell peppers on gas burner racks; put flames on high. Alternatively, put peppers on broiler pan rack 2-in. from heat. Roast the peppers for 5-8

minutes till skins blackened, turning with tongs. Put peppers in a big bowl; stand for 15 minutes, covered. Peel peppers; discard skins. Lengthwise slit peppers. Open peppers flat; discard ribs and seeds. Pat dry peppers.

- Pastry shells: Oil the springform pans. Use a floured rolling pin to roll 1 puff pastry sheet to 16x10 1/2-in. rectangle on a lightly floured surface. Trim edges; lengthwise halve pastry. Line 1 pastry half on 1/2 of side of a pan; leave 1-in. bottom edge on pan's bottom and 1 1/2-in. overhang at top. Press pastry gently into bottom of pan. Repeat using leftover half dough sheet so pan side is fully lined. Press together pastry edges where they meet gently. Roll another pastry sheet to 14-in. square; use bottom of springform pan for guide to cut into 10-in. round. Keep pastry scraps for another time. In bottom of pan, put round; to seal, press edges. While repeating process with 2 extra pastry sheets and leftover pan, chill pastry-lined pan.

- Tortes: Evenly sprinkle breadcrumbs on bottoms of pastry shells. In following manner, divide filling ingredients among pastry shells, seasoning every layer using salt and evenly and firmly pressing each layer in pans: potato mixture, a cup of cheese so half a cup each per pan, eggplant, the mushroom mixture (firmly press down on mushrooms using paper towels to remove extra moisture, repeating process till towels are nearly dry), roasted peppers, then leftover cup of cheese.

- Use a floured rolling pin to roll leftover pastry sheet to 16x12-in. rectangle on a lightly floured surface; crosswise cut to 1/2-in. wide strips with a sharp knife or pizza wheel. Brush egg on pastry overhang; in lattice pattern, put 1/2 strips over filling in every torte. Trim strips at pan edge. Press strip ends into pastry on pan sides gently; roll overhang into the inside pan edge. Brush egg on rolled edges and lattice; chill tortes for 45 minutes.

- Bake tortes: In bottom of third oven, put oven rack; cover with big foil sheet. Preheat the oven to 425°F.

- In oven, bake tortes on foil for 45-50 minutes till well browned, rotating pans halfway through baking. Tent edges with foil if tortes are too brown. Put tortes in pans to a rack. Around inside pan edges, run a sharp knife; remove pan sides carefully. Cool tortes for a minimum of 1 hour (to enjoy warm) and up to 3 hours (to enjoy at room temperature)

Nutrition Information

- Calories: 1354
- Total Carbohydrate: 117 g(39%)
- Cholesterol: 85 mg(28%)
- Protein: 31 g(61%)
- Total Fat: 86 g(133%)
- Saturated Fat: 28 g(142%)
- Sodium: 760 mg(32%)
- Fiber: 14 g(58%)

---

193. **Vermont Cheddar Cheese And Herbed Twists**

Serving: Makes about 36 | Prep: | Cook: | Ready in:

Ingredients

- 1 3/4 cups finely grated sharp white cheddar cheese (about 6 ounces)
- 3/4 teaspoon dried thyme
- 3/4 teaspoon dried rubbed sage
- 1/2 teaspoon coarsely ground black pepper
- 1 sheet frozen puff pastry (half of 17.3-ounce package), thawed

Direction

- In small bowl, mix initial 4 ingredients.
- Roll puff pastry to 18x10-in. rectangle on lightly floured work surface; it'll be thin. Evenly sprinkle 1/3 cheese mixture on 1/2 pastry; fold plain pastry half on cheese to make 10x9-in. rectangle then press to adhere. Repeat twice, rolling to 18x10-in. rectangle,

sprinkle 1/3 cheese mixture then folding. Roll pastry again to 18x10-in. rectangle. Put on unlined baking sheet; chill for 30 minutes.

- Put 1 rack in bottom third and 1 rack in top third of oven then preheat to 425°F; line parchment paper on 2 big baking sheets. Crosswise halve pastry to make 2 10x9-in. rectangles. Trim then discard uneven pastry edges. Crosswise cut every rectangle to scant 1/2-in. wide strips; twist every strip several times. Put on prepped baking sheets, 1/2-3/4-in. apart. Lightly dab ends with water; press to adhere to the parchment.
- Bake twists for 10 minutes in total till golden brown, reversing sheets positions halfway through baking; on sheets, cool twists. You can make this 1 day ahead; tightly cover twists tightly on sheets with foil and keep at room temperature. Rewarm in 350°F oven, uncovered, for 5 minutes till heated through (optional).
- Serve at room temperature or warm.

Nutrition Information

- Calories: 57
- Saturated Fat: 2 g(8%)
- Sodium: 47 mg(2%)
- Fiber: 0 g(1%)
- Total Carbohydrate: 3 g(1%)
- Cholesterol: 5 mg(2%)
- Protein: 2 g(3%)
- Total Fat: 4 g(6%)

194.   Walnut Frangipane And Banana Tartlets

Serving: Makes 8 servings | Prep: | Cook: | Ready in:

Ingredients

- 2/3 cup walnuts, toasted, cooled
- 1/3 cup all purpose flour
- 1/4 teaspoon baking powder
- 1/8 teaspoon salt
- 1/2 cup (1 stick) unsalted butter, room temperature
- 5 tablespoons plus 8 teaspoons sugar
- 1/4 cup plus 1 teaspoon (packed) golden brown sugar
- 2 large eggs
- 1 17.3-ounce package frozen puff pastry (2 sheets), thawed
- 3 small bananas, cut on diagonal into 3x1/3-inch ovals
- 1/4 cup apricot jam, heated
- Powdered sugar

Direction

- Blend initial 4 ingredients till nuts are finely ground in a processor. Beat brown sugar, 5 tbsp. of sugar and butter with electric mixer till blended in a bowl. Beat in eggs then ground walnut mixture; you can make this 1 day ahead, covered and chilled.
- On a lightly floured surface, roll each pastry sheet out to 10-in. square. Cut 4 rounds out from every square with 5-in. diameter plate for a guide. In middle of every 5-inch round, score 4-inch diameter circle with the tip of a small knife; don't cut through pastry completely. Use fork to pierce 4-in. centers. On a big baking sheet, put pastry rounds; chill for a minimum of 1 hour and up to 1 day till very cold.
- Preheat an oven to 375°F. Over 4-in. middle of every pastry round, spread 2 1/2 tbsp. of frangipane; keep leftover frangipane for another time. Decoratively put banana ovals over frangipane; sprinkle 1 tsp. of sugar on bananas on every tart. Bake for 25 minutes till bananas start to brown and pastry is deep golden.
- Brush warm apricot jam on bananas; sift powdered sugar on tartlets. Serve at room temperature or warm.

Nutrition Information

- Calories: 623

- Fiber: 2 g(9%)
- Total Carbohydrate: 66 g(22%)
- Cholesterol: 77 mg(26%)
- Protein: 8 g(15%)
- Total Fat: 38 g(58%)
- Saturated Fat: 14 g(69%)
- Sodium: 226 mg(9%)

195. Walnut And Pistachio Baklava

Serving: Makes 32 pieces | Prep: 1hours | Cook: 4hours | Ready in:

Ingredients

- 2 cups sugar
- 2/3 cup honey (preferably Greek)
- 2 cinnamon sticks
- 2 tablespoons fresh lemon juice
- 3 cups walnuts (10 to 11 ounces)
- 3 cups natural raw unsalted pistachios (13 to 14 ounces)
- 3/4 cup sugar
- 2 teaspoons finely grated lemon peel
- 1 1/2 teaspoons ground cinnamon
- 1/2 cup finely diced dried apple rings (1 1/2 ounces)
- 20 17 x 12-inch sheets fresh phyllo pastry or frozen, thawed
- 1 1/2 cups (3 sticks) unsalted butter, melted

Direction

- Syrup: Boil 1 cup water and all ingredients in a heavy medium saucepan on medium high heat, mixing till sugar dissolves. Lower heat to medium; boil for 15 minutes till syrup reduces to generous 2 cups. Put in bowl; fully cool. You can make this 1 day ahead, covered and chilled.
- Baklava: Place 1 rack in bottom third and 1 rack in top third of oven; preheat it to 350°F. On a big rimmed baking sheet, spread walnuts; on another big rimmed baking sheet, spread pistachios. Put nuts in oven; toast for 5 minutes then cool nuts. Put nuts to processor; add ground cinnamon, lemon peel and 3/4 cup sugar. Blend with on/off turns till nuts get ground to medium-fine texture. Put nut mixture in a big bowl; mix in dried apples.
- On a work surface, put a phyllo sheet stack; use plastic wrap sheet then damp kitchen towel to cover. Brush some melted butter on 13x9x2-in. metal baking pan; with half phyllo sheet hanging on 1 long side, put 1 phyllo sheet in pan. Brush some melted butter on phyllo in pan; fold over overhang to create 2 12x8 1/2-in. layers. Brush some melted butter; repeat buttering and stacking to make 10 layers total using 4 extra phyllo sheets. Spread 1/3, generous 2 cups, of nut mixture to within 1/2-in. of edge on phyllo in pan. Repeat layering twice more using 5 sheets of phyllo and 1/3 of the remaining nut mixture per time. Put 5 extra folded phyllo sheets over; lengthwise cut through top phyllo layers with sharp knife to make 4 strips without cutting through to bottom of pan. Crosswise cut phyllo to create 16 rectangles; bake for 45 minutes till phyllo is golden.
- Scoop cold syrup on hot baklava slowly; cool to room temperature. You can make this 1 day ahead then cover; allow to stand at room temperature.
- Crosswise halve each baklava rectangle to get 32 pieces total. Put baklava on platter; serve.

Nutrition Information

- Calories: 332
- Cholesterol: 23 mg(8%)
- Protein: 5 g(10%)
- Total Fat: 21 g(32%)
- Saturated Fat: 7 g(34%)
- Sodium: 60 mg(3%)
- Fiber: 2 g(10%)
- Total Carbohydrate: 35 g(12%)

196. Warm Banana Tartlets With Peanut Crunch Ice Cream

Serving: Makes 8 servings | Prep: | Cook: | Ready in:

Ingredients

- 1 1/2 cups whipping cream
- 1 1/2 cups half and half
- 1 1/4 cups chopped lightly salted roasted peanuts (about 6 ounces)
- 1/2 cup sugar
- 7 large egg yolks
- 2/3 cup chopped peanut brittle
- 2/3 cup plus 2 tablespoons sugar
- 6 tablespoons (3/4 stick) unsalted butter, room temperature
- 2 large egg yolks
- 2 tablespoons all purpose flour
- 2/3 cup finely chopped lightly salted roasted peanuts (about 3 ounces)
- 1 17.3-ounce package frozen puff pastry (2 sheets), thawed
- 1 egg, beaten to blend (for glaze)
- 4 bananas, peeled, thinly sliced into rounds

Direction

- Ice Cream: Simmer half and half and cream in heavy medium saucepan then add peanuts. Cover; take off heat. Let stand for half an hour. Through sieve above big bowl, strain cream mixture, pressing on solids to extract a lot of liquid. Whisk yolks and sugar in; put in saucepan. Mix on medium low heat for 4 minutes, don't boil, till leaves path on back of a spoon when you draw a finger across and custard is thick. Strain in medium bowl. Chill till cold, uncovered. Put custard in ice cream maker; follow manufacturer's instructions to process. Put ice cream in a container; mix brittle in then cover. Freeze till firm. You can make this 3 days ahead, kept frozen.
- Tartlets: Preheat an oven to 350°F. Beat butter and 2/3 cup sugar using electric mixer till blended well in medium bowl. Beat yolks in.

Mix flour in then nuts. Put aside peanut cream.

- On work surface, unfold pastry. Cut every pastry sheet to 4 squares; use fork to pierce all over. Put 4 parties squares onto each of the 2 baking sheets and space them apart. Brush pastry with egg glaze. Spread 2 tbsp. peanut cream on every pastry; leave 1/2-in. plain border. Put bananas over peanut cream in overlapping slices. Sprinkle 2 tbsp. sugar; bake for 30 minutes till crusts are golden brown. Put on plates; serve it warm with ice cream.

Nutrition Information

- Calories: 1106
- Fiber: 6 g(22%)
- Total Carbohydrate: 94 g(31%)
- Cholesterol: 319 mg(106%)
- Protein: 21 g(41%)
- Total Fat: 75 g(116%)
- Saturated Fat: 28 g(140%)
- Sodium: 274 mg(11%)

197. Warm Onion Tart With Thyme

Serving: Serves 6 | Prep: | Cook: | Ready in:

Ingredients

- 1 Spanish onion
- 1 tablespoon unsalted butter
- 1 tablespoon fresh thyme leaves
- Salt and freshly ground black pepper
- 1 sheet frozen puff pastry, thawed according to package directions

Direction

- Peel onion; halve through the root. Trim ends; lengthwise julienne onion.
- Melt butter in a small sauté pan on medium heat then add thyme and onion; cook for 10-15

minutes or till onion is deep golden brown, occasionally mixing. Season with pepper and salt to taste; keep warm till serving.

- Meanwhile, preheat an oven to 400°F.
- Unfold puff pastry sheet on lightly floured work surface; flip to keep creases from splitting. To flatten sheet, gently pat down.
- Stamp 6 rounds out with 1-in. round fluted cookie cutter; put on an ungreased baking sheet then bake till golden brown and puffed or for 8-10 minutes.

Nutrition Information

198.   Zeppole With Chocolate Sauce

Serving: Makes about 50 | Prep: | Cook: |Ready in:

Ingredients

- 8 ounces 70% bittersweet chocolate, chopped
- 1 cup heavy whipping cream
- 1/4 cup honey
- 2 cups plus 1/2 tablespoon bread flour
- 1/2 cup plus 1/2 tablespoon whole milk
- 3 tablespoons sugar
- 1 1/2 teaspoons lemon zest
- 3/4 teaspoon active dry yeast (from 1 envelope)
- 3/4 teaspoon fine sea salt
- 2 large eggs
- 3/4 cup (1 1/2 stick) unsalted butter, room temperature, cut into cubes
- Vegetable oil (for deep-frying)
- Powdered sugar

Direction

- Sauce: In a medium bowl, put chocolate. Mix honey and cream till it starts to bubble in a small saucepan on medium heat. Put on chocolate; whisk till smooth and keep warm.

You can make it 3 hours ahead, chilled, covered. Before using, rewarm.

- Zeppole: Beat flour and following 6 ingredients in a stand mixer bowl fitted with paddle till dough forms on low speed. Add butter slowly; beat till absorbed between additions, scraping down bowl sides occasionally. Put speed on medium; beat for 3 minutes till glossy and smooth. Scrape dough from bowl sides and paddle. Use plastic wrap to cover; allow to rise for 2 hours. Put sufficient oil in a heavy, deep 5-qt. pot to reach 1 1/2 inch deep; attach deep-fry thermometer on pot's side. Heat oil till it reaches 325°F on medium heat; by heaping teaspoonfuls, 1-in. diameter rounds, drop dough into oil in batches. Cook for 4 minutes per batch till zeppole are cooked and golden, occasionally turning. Put zeppole on paper towels with a slotted spoon; drain. Over zeppole, sift powdered sugar. Or, place sugar in a paper bag then add zeppole; gently shake to coat. Serve it with sauce to dip.

Nutrition Information

- Calories: 119
- Fiber: 0 g(2%)
- Total Carbohydrate: 10 g(3%)
- Cholesterol: 29 mg(10%)
- Protein: 2 g(3%)
- Total Fat: 9 g(13%)
- Saturated Fat: 5 g(25%)
- Sodium: 43 mg(2%)

Chapter 5: Awesome Puff Pastry Recipes

***

199.   Air Fryer Breakfast Toad In The Hole Tarts

Serving: 4 | Prep: 5mins | Cook: 25mins | Ready in:

Ingredients

- 1 sheet frozen puff pastry, thawed
- 4 tablespoons shredded Cheddar cheese
- 4 tablespoons diced cooked ham
- 4 eggs
- chopped fresh chives (optional)

Direction

- Preheat air fryer to 200°C/400°F.
- On flat surface, unfold pastry sheet; cut to 4 squares.
- In air fryer basket, put 2 pastry squares; cook for 6-8 minutes.
- Remove basket from the air fryer. Gently press every square with metal tablespoon to make an indentation. In each hole, put 1 tablespoon ham and 1 tablespoon cheddar cheese. Put 1 egg over each.
- Put basket back in air fryer; cook for 6 more minutes to desired doneness. Take tarts out of basket; cool for 5 minutes. Repeat with leftover eggs, ham, cheese and pastry squares.
- Use chives to garnish tarts.

Nutrition Information

- Calories: 446 calories;
- Total Carbohydrate: 27.9
- Cholesterol: 199
- Total Fat: 31
- Protein: 14.2
- Sodium: 377

200.   Aisha's Apple Puff Pastries

Serving: 8 | Prep: 10mins | Cook: 40mins | Ready in:

Ingredients

- 2 apples, peeled and diced
- 2 tablespoons honey
- 1 tablespoon brown sugar
- 1/2 teaspoon ground cinnamon
- 1 sheet puff pastry, cut into 8 squares

Direction

- Set the oven to preheat at 175°C (350°F).
- Place a steamer insert into a saucepan and pour in water to just below the steamer's bottom. Heat water to the boiling point. Put in the apples, cover and steam until tender, about 15 minutes.
- Mix together cinnamon, brown sugar, honey, and softened apples in a bowl.
- On a flat work surface, spread the squares of puff pastry. Add 1 tablespoon apple mixture to each square's middle. Fold each square's corners upward and seal the edges together by pinching to keep the filling in place. Transfer the squares onto a baking sheet.
- In preheated oven, bake for 20 to 25 minutes till the pastry becomes golden brown and rises.

Nutrition Information

- Calories: 207 calories;
- Total Fat: 11.5
- Sodium: 76
- Total Carbohydrate: 24.5
- Cholesterol: 0
- Protein: 2.3

201.   Allie's Delicious Baked Dumplings

Serving: 8 | Prep: 15mins | Cook: 45mins | Ready in:

Ingredients

- 1 (17.5 ounce) package frozen puff pastry, thawed
- 1 cup white sugar
- 3/8 cup dry bread crumbs
- 3 tablespoons ground cinnamon
- 1 pinch ground nutmeg
- 1 egg, beaten
- 4 Granny Smith apples - peeled, cored and halved
- 1 cup confectioners' sugar
- 1 teaspoon vanilla extract
- 3 tablespoons milk

Direction

- Preheat an oven to 220 ° C or 425 ° F. Oil a baking sheet lightly.
- Unroll every pastry sheet into 12x12-inches. Slice into quarters, making 8 to 6-inches squares.
- Mix nutmeg, cinnamon, bread crumbs and sugar in small bowl. Brush beaten egg on one pastry square. Put a tablespoon mixture of bread crumb in middle. Put an apple half on top of bread crumbs, core side facing down. Put one more tablespoon of the mixture. Bring four pastry corners up and press sides together to enclose seams fully. Redo with the rest of the apples.
- Brush beaten egg on every dumpling. Put in prepped oven for 15 minutes, then lower heat to 175 ° C or 350 ° F and keep baking for an additional of 25 minutes, till slightly browned. Cool fully at room temperature.
- To prepare frosting, mix vanilla and confectioners' sugar and sufficient milk to create a pourable consistency. Sprinkle on top of cooled dumplings. Serve in the same day.

Nutrition Information

- Calories: 563 calories;
- Total Fat: 24.4
- Sodium: 202
- Total Carbohydrate: 82.3
- Cholesterol: 24

- Protein: 6.4

202.   Almond Bear Claws

Serving: 24 | Prep: 2hours | Cook: 25mins |Ready in:

Ingredients

- 1/3 cup almond paste
- 2 3/4 cups ground almonds
- 1/2 cup white sugar
- 1 pinch salt
- 2 tablespoons butter
- 2 egg whites
- 1/2 teaspoon almond extract
- 2 teaspoons amaretto liqueur
- 3 pounds puff pastry
- 1 egg
- 1 tablespoon water
- 3 tablespoons sliced almonds, for garnish
- 3 tablespoons confectioners' sugar for dusting

Direction

- Using an electric mixer, whisk and break the almond paste apart in a big bowl; add in salt, sugar, and almonds. Keep on mixing until the paste is not lumpy. On high speed, mix in amaretto liqueur, butter, almond extract, and egg whites until very fluffy; set aside.
- On a lightly floured surface, roll half of the dough at a time in 8-in wide and quarter inch thick rectangle; cut the edges. Make 2 four-inch wide strips by slicing it in half along the length.
- Preheat oven to 200°C or 400°F. Place parchment paper on baking sheets.
- Pour almond filling in the pastry bag until half full; tube filling in the middle of every strip. Beat water and egg together; brush mixture on one end of every strip. Bring the end of each strip together to cover the filling; gently press to seal. Graze egg wash on each piece and add top with sliced almonds. Slice into 3-4-inch portions; form "claws" by making half inch

cuts on the sealed side. Arrange bear claws 2-in apart in baking pan. Place in the refrigerator and repeat the process with the leftover dough half.

- Bake for 25-30 mins until the pastry is golden and the almonds are toasted; cool. Sprinkle confectioners' sugar. Serve.

Nutrition Information

- Calories: 419 calories;
- Sodium: 157
- Total Carbohydrate: 36.3
- Cholesterol: 10
- Protein: 10.3
- Total Fat: 26.4

203.   Apple Brie Bites

Serving: 24 | Prep: 20mins | Cook: 15mins |Ready in:

Ingredients

- 1 sheet frozen puff pastry, thawed
- 5 ounces Brie cheese
- 1/2 cup MUSSELMAN'S® Apple Butter
- 1/4 cup chopped pecans

Direction

- Start preheating the oven to 400°F.
- Press the seams of puff pastry together. Slice the sheet into 4 parts equally and then slice each part into 6 pieces. Use a rolling pin to roll each pastry piece into a square shape. In 24 oiled mini muffin cups, put the squares.
- Put 1/2 teaspoon of chopped pecans, 1 teaspoon of apple butter, and 1/2 teaspoon of Brie in each muffin cups.
- Put in the preheated oven and bake for 13-15 minutes. Enjoy warm.

Nutrition Information

- Calories: 93 calories;
- Protein: 2.1
- Total Fat: 6.3
- Sodium: 62
- Total Carbohydrate: 7.4
- Cholesterol: 6

204.   Apple Cheese Danish

Serving: 18 | Prep: 55mins | Cook: 20mins |Ready in:

Ingredients

- 1 (24 ounce) carton cottage cheese
- 3 apples - peeled, cored and thinly sliced
- 1 teaspoon lemon juice
- 1 (8 ounce) package cream cheese, at room temperature
- 1/2 cup white sugar
- 1 egg
- 1 teaspoon vanilla extract
- 1 (17.5 ounce) package frozen puff pastry, thawed
- 3 tablespoons white sugar for decoration

Direction

- Use cheesecloth or heavy duty paper towels to line strainer and place the cottage cheese in it. Use paper towels to pat dry and reserve for 5 to 10 minutes.
- Put apples in a bowl, and drizzle with lemon juice to avoid Browning.
- Mix together the vanilla extract, egg, 1/2 cup sugar, drained cottage cheese and cream cheese in the bowl of an electric mixer, and blend for 1 to 2 minutes until near smooth on high speed.
- Prepare the oven by preheating to 400° F (200°C). Get a two baking sheets and use parchment paper to line.
- Slice into nine pieces each of the puff pastry sheets; 18 in total. One at a time, roll the portions out to make squares that is 5 x 5 inch. Avoid using too much pressure or rolling over

the edges of the dough to make sure the pastries puff up.

- Put a square in front of you so that it would look like a diamond. Spoon a generous amount of cheese filling down to the Center of each square, leave 1/4 inch of space at the bottom edges and top. Spread out 4 to 5 slices of apple down the middle of each cheese-filled square. Take the right and left corners together to meet in the middle and secure by pinching.
- Send the Danish to a baking sheet and re-do with the left pastries.
- Drizzle sugar on top of each bundle and place inside the preheated oven and bake for about 20 minutes until pastry is golden brown in color.

Nutrition Information

- Calories: 279 calories;
- Sodium: 262
- Total Carbohydrate: 24.5
- Cholesterol: 30
- Protein: 8.1
- Total Fat: 16.7

205.   Apple Chicken Sausage Brunch Braid

Serving: 12 | Prep: 30mins | Cook: 45mins | Ready in:

Ingredients

- olive oil
- 4 links apple-chicken sausage, diced
- 2 cups diced sweet potatoes
- 2 stalks celery, diced
- 1/2 cup diced red onion
- 1/2 cup diced red bell pepper
- 2 cloves garlic, chopped
- salt and ground black pepper to taste
- 1 cup seedless green grapes, halved
- 1 (3 ounce) package cream cheese, softened
- 1/2 cup crumbled blue cheese, or more to taste

- 1 teaspoon dried rosemary, crushed
- 2 sheets frozen puff pastry, thawed
- 1 tablespoon sliced almonds, or as needed (optional)

Direction

- Preheat the oven to 400°F (200°C).
- In a skillet, put in the olive oil and let it heat up; put in the red bell pepper, apple-chicken sausage, celery, garlic, sweet potatoes and red onion and let it cook in hot oil for about 15 minutes while stirring it until the vegetables are well-cooked but are not yet soft. Place the cooked mixture in a big bowl and sprinkle it with black pepper and salt to taste. Add in the grape halves and mix everything together.
- In a bowl, combine the blue cheese, rosemary and cream cheese together.
- Put the puff pastry sheets at the bottom of a big baking sheet. Flatten out the puff pastry sheets using a rolling pin and connect the long edges of the puff pastries together to form 1 big pastry sheet. Use a sharp knife to cut strips that are about 1 1/2 inches away from each other and are 3 inches deep, beginning at the long edge. Do the whole cutting process again on the other long edge of the puff pastry; you'll end up with a pastry sheet that has pastry strips hanging on opposite long edges with a wide uncut part in the middle.
- Fill the uncut part in the middle of the pastry sheet evenly with the prepared sausage filling then top it off with spoonfuls of the prepared blue cheese mixture.
- Braid the pastry strips hanging on the edges by lifting and crossing two opposite strips on top of the filling and twisting it once to keep the two strips in place. Do the whole crossing and twisting process again for the rest of the strips. Scatter sliced almonds evenly on top of the braided stuffed pastry.
- Put it in the preheated oven and let it bake for about 30 minutes until the puff pastry turns golden brown in color and the filling is already hot.

Nutrition Information

- Calories: 364 calories;
- Sodium: 341
- Total Carbohydrate: 27
- Cholesterol: 47
- Protein: 9.5
- Total Fat: 24.6

206. Apple Crumble Tart

Serving: 8 | Prep: 30mins | Cook: 45mins | Ready in:

Ingredients

- 1/2 (17.5 ounce) package frozen puff pastry, thawed
- 1 tablespoon butter, melted
- 3 apple - peeled, cored, and chopped
- 3/8 cup all-purpose flour
- 3/8 cup chopped blanched almonds
- 1/2 cup white sugar
- 1/4 teaspoon ground cinnamon
- 3 tablespoons butter, chilled
- 1/4 teaspoon vanilla extract
- 3 egg yolks
- 3 tablespoons white sugar
- 1/3 cup dry Marsala wine

Direction

- Set oven to 175°C (350°F) and start preheating.
- Combine cinnamon, 1/2 cup sugar, almonds and flour in a small bowl. Put in vanilla extract and chilled butter. Using a pastry blender, cut mixture until fine and crumbly. Put aside.
- Unroll pastry dough and cut out one circle of 10 inches. Transfer to a big baking sheet without grease. Brush melted butter on top. Spread apples on the dough's center, leaving a border of about 1/2 inch width. Spread almond topping evenly onto apples; make sure not to make it touch the pastry border.
- Bake at 175°C (350°F) for 30 minutes until golden browned.

- To make sabayon: combine egg yolks and 3 tablespoons sugar in a heatproof bowl or a top of a double boiler. Over simmering water, heat the mixture while beating constantly with a handheld electric mixer. Once frothy, put in marsala; continue to beat until the mixture starts to thicken. Be careful not to overcook or the mixture will curdle. Remove from heat. Serve while still warm and over apple tart.

Nutrition Information

- Calories: 401 calories;
- Total Carbohydrate: 45.4
- Cholesterol: 92
- Protein: 5.2
- Total Fat: 21.8
- Sodium: 123

207. Apple Lattice Fruit Bake

Serving: 10 | Prep: 25mins | Cook: 40mins | Ready in:

Ingredients

- 3/4 cup brown sugar
- 1/3 cup water
- 2 tablespoons all-purpose flour
- 6 Granny Smith apples - peeled, cored and sliced
- 1/2 cup chopped pecans
- 1/2 cup chopped dried mixed fruit
- 1 sheet frozen puff pastry, thawed
- 1 tablespoon white sugar
- 1/4 teaspoon ground cinnamon

Direction

- Set the oven to 375°F (190°C), and start preheating.
- In a large bowl, mix flour, water and brown sugar until smooth. Put in dried fruit, pecans and apples; toss into the brown sugar mixture until coated well. Pour the mixture into a 9x13

inch baking dish. Using a pizza cutter, slice the puff pastry into ten strips of 1-inch. Place 5 strips over the apples lengthwise, and cut the rest of strips in half. Lay the 10 smaller strips over the apples widthwise to make the lattice. Combine cinnamon and white sugar, then sprinkle on top of the lattice.

- Bake in the preheated oven for 40-45 minutes until the mixture is bubbly, and the lattice turns golden brown.

Nutrition Information

- Calories: 303 calories;
- Protein: 2.9
- Total Fat: 13.5
- Sodium: 67
- Total Carbohydrate: 45.6
- Cholesterol: 0

---

208.   Apple Marzipan Puff Pastry Tart

Serving: 12 | Prep: 25mins | Cook: 35mins | Ready in:

Ingredients

- 1 sheet frozen puff pastry, thawed
- 1 (4 ounce) package marzipan
- 3 large McIntosh apples - peeled, cored, and sliced
- 3 tablespoons cornstarch
- 2 tablespoons cold butter, cut into small cubes
- 2 tablespoons all-purpose flour
- 1 teaspoon ground cinnamon, or more to taste
- 1/8 teaspoon ground nutmeg
- 3/4 cup brown sugar, or to taste
- 1/4 cup chopped lightly toasted pecans
- 1 egg, beaten

Direction

- Set oven to preheat at 450°F (230°C). Use aluminum foil or parchment paper to line a baking sheet.
- Roll out the puff pastry into a circle, 14- to 15-inch in size, on a floured surface. Transfer onto the lined baking sheet.
- Put marzipan between 2 pieces of plastic wrap and roll into a circle about 11 inches in diameter. Take off the plastic wrap and put marzipan in the middle of the puff pastry.
- Toss together nutmeg, cinnamon, cornstarch, flour, butter, and apples in a large bowl. Put in the brown sugar and quickly toss.
- Place the apple slices onto the marzipan in concentric circles, and leave out about 3 inches of pastry at the edges. Add the apple filling in layers, pile them high up and put in all the remaining dry bits in the bowl. Sprinkle pecans on top.
- Fold up the puff pastry's edges around the filling, leave the center open and pinch the overlapping edges. Gently press the pastry around the filling to squeeze out any in between excess air. Brush around the top with a little egg.
- In the preheated oven, bake until apples are fork-tender and puff pastry is golden brown, for 35 to 40 minutes.

Nutrition Information

- Calories: 276 calories;
- Total Fat: 13.2
- Sodium: 75
- Total Carbohydrate: 38.3
- Cholesterol: 21
- Protein: 3.1

---

209.   Apple Tartlets

Serving: 12 | Prep: 10mins | Cook: 15mins | Ready in:

Ingredients

- 1 (17.5 ounce) package frozen puff pastry, thawed
- 6 red apples, thinly sliced
- 1/2 cup lemonade
- 12 pats unsalted butter
- 1/2 cup superfine sugar
- 1/2 cup apricot preserves
- 1 pinch coarse sugar crystals, or as needed

Direction

- Start preheating oven to 350°F (175°C).
- Divide the puff pastry into 12 equal squares then place on the baking sheet.
- Dip the apple slices in the lemonade. Arrange onto each puff pastry square diagonally; sprinkle one pat butter over each. Top each square with superfine sugar.
- Bake in prepared oven for 12 minutes or until the tartlet edges turn golden.
- Boil the apricot jam in a saucepan; cook while stirring for 1-2 minutes until the jam is thinned. Brush the warm tartlets with jam; top each with the sugar crystals.

Nutrition Information

- Calories: 357 calories;
- Sodium: 109
- Total Carbohydrate: 43.8
- Cholesterol: 11
- Protein: 3.3
- Total Fat: 19.7

210.   Apple Turnovers

Serving: 8 | Prep: 30mins | Cook: 25mins | Ready in:

Ingredients

- 2 tablespoons lemon juice
- 4 cups water
- 4 Granny Smith apples - peeled, cored and sliced

- 2 tablespoons butter
- 1 cup brown sugar
- 1 teaspoon ground cinnamon
- 1 tablespoon cornstarch
- 1 tablespoon water
- 1 (17.25 ounce) package frozen puff pastry sheets, thawed
- 1 cup confectioners' sugar
- 1 tablespoon milk
- 1 teaspoon vanilla extract

Direction

- Mix 4 cups of water and lemon in a big bowl. To keep from browning, put sliced apples in water.
- Melt butter in big skillet on medium heat then drain water from apples; put in hot skillet. Mix and cook for 2 minutes. Add cinnamon and brown sugar; cook for 2 minutes more while mixing. Mix 1 tbsp. of water and cornstarch together; put in the skillet then stir well. Cook till sauce is thick or for 1 minute. Take off from heat; slightly cool.
- Preheat an oven to 200°C (400°F).
- Unfold puff pastry sheets; press back together to repair any cracks. Trim every sheet to a square; cut each bigger square to 4 smaller squares. Scoop apples onto the middle of every square; from corner to corner, fold over to a triangle shape. To seal, press edges together. Put turnovers on a baking sheet, 1-in. apart from each other.
- In the preheated oven, bake for 25 minutes till turnovers are lightly browned and puffed; fully cool prior to glazing.
- Glaze: Mix vanilla, milk and confectioners' sugar in a small bowl; if needed, add more milk or sugar to adjust thickness. Drizzle glaze on cooled turnovers.

Nutrition Information

- Calories: 562 calories;
- Cholesterol: 8
- Protein: 4.8
- Total Fat: 25.9

- Sodium: 184
- Total Carbohydrate: 80

---

211. Apple Cranberry Crostada

Serving: 8 | Prep: | Cook: | Ready in:

Ingredients

- 3 tablespoons butter
- 2 pounds Granny Smith apples (or other firm, crisp apples), peeled, quartered, cored and sliced 1/4-inch thick
- 1 pound Macintosh apples (or other soft-textured apples that fall apart when cooked), peeled, quartered, cored, and sliced 1/4-inch thick
- 1/2 cup sugar
- 1/2 cup dried cranberries
- 1 sheet frozen puff pastry, thawed but still cold (follow package directions)
- 1 egg white, lightly beaten
- 1 tablespoon sugar
- Optional: Ice cream or lightly sweetened whipped cream (optional)

Direction

- In a large skillet, heat the butter over medium-high. Add in cranberries, 1/2 cup sugar and apples; cover up and cook for around 5 minutes, until apples release the liquid. Discard the lid and keep cooking, stir often for approximately 5 more minutes, until soft apples fall apart and the juice turns into a thin-syrup consistency. Pour it onto a jellyroll pan or large-lipped cookie sheet. Let it cool down to room temperature or store in an airtight container in the fridge up to 5 days.
- Set the oven rack to the low position and set the oven to 400°. On a slightly floured work surface, open the puff pastry sheet. Roll it into approximately a 10x16-inch rectangle. Place to a large cookie sheet. (Recommend lining the sheet with parchment paper to ensure that the crostada doesn't stick and help clean up easier).
- Spread cooker apples on top of the pastry, making a border of 2 inch. Fold up pastry borders over apples. Unfold the corners and create ruffled creases so the dough don't overlap. Use a brush to brush pastry borders with egg white and sprinkle the remaining 1 tablespoon sugar on top. Bake in the oven for 25-30 minutes, until the pastry turns golden brown. Serve warm or at room temperature with desired ice cream or whipped cream.

Nutrition Information

- Calories: 396 calories;
- Total Fat: 17.7
- Sodium: 128
- Total Carbohydrate: 59.7
- Cholesterol: 19
- Protein: 3.8

---

212. Argentine Meat Empanadas

Serving: 10 | Prep: | Cook: | Ready in:

Ingredients

- 1/2 cup shortening
- 2 onions, chopped
- 1 pound lean ground beef
- 2 teaspoons Hungarian sweet paprika
- 3/4 teaspoon hot paprika
- 1/2 teaspoon crushed red pepper flakes
- 1 teaspoon ground cumin
- 1 tablespoon distilled white vinegar
- 1/4 cup raisins
- 1/2 cup pitted green olives, chopped
- 2 hard-cooked eggs, chopped
- salt to taste
- 1 (17.5 ounce) package frozen puff pastry sheets, thawed

Direction

- Melt shortening in a sauté pan, add chopped onions. Cook the onions just until they start to turn golden. Take away from heat and mix in salt to taste, crushed red pepper flakes, hot paprika, and sweet paprika.
- To slightly cook the meat, on a sieve, spread the meat and add boiling water. Let the meat cool. In a plate, put the meat and season with vinegar, cumin, and salt to taste. Stir and put the meat into the onion mixture. Stir thoroughly and put on a flat plate to harden and cool.
- Slice puff pastry dough into 10 round shells. Put on each round with the meat mixture by 1 spoonful; add some of the hard-boiled egg, olives, and raisins. Make sure the filling not touch the edges of the pastry because its greasiness will prevent good sealing. Wet the edge of the pastry a little, fold in half and attach the edges together. The shape should look like a semicircle. There should have 2/3-1/2-in. flat edge of pastry for you to work with. To seal, twist the edges, step by step, between index finger and thumb, ensuring that you press it before releasing the pinch and proceeding on to the next curl. Other ways of sealing like using 1 fork or pinching without curling cannot avoid juice leaking when baking, and the empanadas must be juicy.
- Start preheating the oven to 350°F (180°C). On a cookie sheet lined with a parchment paper, put the empanadas. Make sure to use a fork to prick the empanada close to the curl to release steam while baking. Use egg to glaze for shine, and bake for 20-30 minutes until turning golden.

Nutrition Information

- Calories: 498 calories;
- Protein: 14.7
- Total Fat: 36.8
- Sodium: 326
- Total Carbohydrate: 27.7
- Cholesterol: 73

213.   Asparagus And Mushroom Puff Pastry Pie

Serving: 8 | Prep: 15mins | Cook: 45mins | Ready in:

Ingredients

- 1/2 cup butter
- 2 bunches fresh asparagus, trimmed and cut into 1 inch pieces
- 6 cloves garlic, diced
- 1 pound sliced fresh mushrooms
- 1 cup prepared hollandaise sauce
- 1 (17.25 ounce) package frozen puff pastry, thawed

Direction

- Prepare the oven by preheating it to 400° F (200° C).
- Place a big pan over medium heat and melt the butter in it. Mix in the asparagus and cook for another 10 minutes. Add the garlic and mushrooms, stirring them in; keep on cooking and stirring until the mushrooms are already tender then set it aside.
- Follow the package directions when preparing the hollandaise sauce. Add it to the asparagus and mushrooms, stirring it in.
- In the bottom of a 9x13 baking dish, lay a sheet of puff pastry out flat, letting extra dough if there's any, to go up the sides. Place the asparagus mixture over the dough, spreading it evenly. Put the other sheet of pastry on top of it and then pinch the edges together to seal it.
- Bake until the pastry is golden brown, about 25 to 30 minutes. Leave it to cool for a few minutes before you slice and serve.

Nutrition Information

- Calories: 558 calories;

- Total Carbohydrate: 34.5
- Cholesterol: 120
- Protein: 9.9
- Total Fat: 43.9
- Sodium: 315

214. Australian Meat Pies

Serving: 12 | Prep: 30mins | Cook: 35mins | Ready in:

Ingredients

- 1 pound ground beef
- 1 onion, chopped
- 3/4 cup water
- 1/4 cup ketchup
- 2 teaspoons Worcestershire sauce
- 2 cubes beef bouillon
- 1/2 teaspoon dried oregano
- 1/4 teaspoon ground pepper, or to taste
- 1/4 cup cornstarch
- 1/4 cup cold water
- 1 (15 ounce) package refrigerated pie crusts for a double-crust pie
- 1 sheet frozen puff pastry, thawed
- 1 egg, beaten

Direction

- Set the oven to 200°C or 400°F to preheat. Coat a 12-cup muffin tin with grease.
- Heat a big skillet on moderately high heat. Cook and stir in the hot skillet with onion and ground beef for 5-7 minutes, until meat is crumbly and browned. Drain and get rid of grease. Put in black pepper, oregano, bouillon cubes, Worcestershire sauce, ketchup and 3/4 cup of water. Bring to a boil and lower heat to simmer for 10 minutes, until mixed.
- In a bowl, combine together cornstarch and 1/4 cup of cold water to make a paste, then stir into the meat mixture. Cook for 5 minutes longer, until thickened. Take away from the heat.

- Cut the pie crusts into twelve circles with a 4-in. biscuit cutter, then use a circle to line each muffin cup, pressing into bottom and sides. Fill meat mixture into each cup. Cut puff pastry dough into twelve circles with a 3-in. biscuit cutter. Put a circle on top of each filled muffin cup and seal edges together. Use beaten egg to brush tops of pastry.
- In the preheated oven, bake for 15-20 minutes, until crusts are flaky and browned. Allow to cool in pan for 10 minutes prior to taking out of pies.

Nutrition Information

- Calories: 377 calories;
- Total Fat: 24.8
- Sodium: 359
- Total Carbohydrate: 27.6
- Cholesterol: 39
- Protein: 10.4

215. B'stilla

Serving: 4 | Prep: 30mins | Cook: 1hours | Ready in:

Ingredients

- 2 skinless, boneless chicken breast halves
- 2 tablespoons chicken bouillon granules
- 2 cups hot water
- 3 eggs
- 2 tablespoons chopped fresh parsley
- 1 teaspoon ground cinnamon
- 2 teaspoons white sugar
- 1 (17.5 ounce) package frozen puff pastry, thawed
- salt and pepper to taste
- 1/4 cup butter, melted

Direction

- Preheat the oven to 360°F (180°C).

- In a small saucepan, put in the chicken breasts and pour in the water and bouillon so that the chicken breasts are soaked. Poach the chicken breasts on medium-low heat until it reaches near below boiling point. Let the chicken breasts cook for 8-10 minutes until the chicken is not pink inside. Slice the chicken into cubes. Keep the bouillon aside.
- Mix 1/2 cup of the reserved bouillon, chopped parsley and eggs together in a small bowl. Combine the sugar and cinnamon together in another bowl.
- Roll 1 sheet of pastry out to a square that is 12 inches in size. Halve the other sheet of pastry and roll each halved pastry out to a square that is 8 inches in size. In a 9-inch pie pan, put in the 12-inch square pastry so that it fits inside.
- Put an even layer of half of the diced chicken on top of the bottom square pastry. Layer 1/2 of the egg mixture evenly on top of the chicken layer. Dust it off with 1/2 of the sugar-and-cinnamon mixture then put in the salt and pepper. Place one of the two 8 inch square pastries on top of the sugar-and-cinnamon mixture. Put another layer of the diced chicken, egg mixture and sugar-and-cinnamon mixture over the first 8-inch square pastry. Season it with extra pepper and salt. Put the other 8 inch square pastry on top. Fold the hanging edges of the bottom 12-inch square pastry over the topmost square pastry. Use a brush to grease the top with melted margarine or butter.
- Put it in the preheated oven and let it bake for 40 minutes until it turns golden brown in color. Serve it either cold or lukewarm.

Nutrition Information

- Calories: 908 calories;
- Cholesterol: 201
- Protein: 25.8
- Total Fat: 63.5
- Sodium: 1028
- Total Carbohydrate: 58.8

---

216.   BBQ Chicken Puffs

Serving: 24 | Prep: 15mins | Cook: 20mins | Ready in:

Ingredients

- 1 tablespoon vegetable oil, or as needed
- 1 sheet frozen puff pastry, thawed
- 1 (4 ounce) package cream cheese, cut into 1/2-inch squares
- 1 cup shredded cooked chicken
- 1/4 cup barbeque sauce
- 1/2 teaspoon red pepper flakes, or to taste (optional)
- 1/2 cup shredded Cheddar cheese

Direction

- Preheat an oven to 175 °C or 350 °F. Oil a mini muffin tin.
- Into 3 individual rectangles, slice puff pastry on the creases. Put onto a slightly floured surface. With a slightly floured rolling pin, roll out a rectangle to 1/8-inch thickness. Cut pastry into 8 rounds approximately 2 1/2-inches across. Redo with another 2 rectangles.
- Into the oiled muffin cups, force the pastry rounds. In the base of every cup, put a square of cream cheese.
- In a bowl, combine red pepper flakes, barbeque sauce and shredded chicken together. Into every cup, scoop approximately 2 teaspoons of mixture till even with top of cup.
- In the prepped oven, bake for 20 to 25 minutes till filling is heated through and pastry is golden brown. Over of every pastry, scoop a teaspoon Cheddar cheese 3 minutes prior taking off from oven.

Nutrition Information

- Calories: 101 calories;
- Total Fat: 7.3

- Sodium: 86
- Total Carbohydrate: 5.7
- Cholesterol: 12
- Protein: 3.3

217.   Baked Apple Roses

Serving: 2 | Prep: 25mins | Cook: 45mins | Ready in:

Ingredients

- 1 large red apple, cored and very thinly sliced
- 1/4 cup white sugar
- 1 teaspoon ground cinnamon
- 1 sheet frozen puff pastry, thawed
- 1/4 cup melted butter
- 1 egg
- 2 teaspoons water
- 1 teaspoon confectioners' sugar (optional)

Direction

- Prepare the oven by preheating to 400 degrees F (200 degrees C). Get 2 small ramekins and butter (6 to 8 ounce) and sprinkle with white sugar.
- On a plate, slightly overlap the apple slices if needed. Place inside the microwave for about 45 minutes on high temperature until apples become a little soft. Use plastic wrap to cover and a kitchen towel.
- In a bowl, mix together the cinnamon and sugar.
- Spin puff pastry to less than 1/8 inch thick. Cut two 3x12-inches rectangle using a pizza cutter. Set aside the left portions for later use.
- Scatter on top of dough the melted butter; put an ample amount of cinnamon-sugar.
- Along 1 long edge of dough, put in the apple slices, about 1/4 inch far from edge of dough, slightly overlap the slices. Turn the underside of dough on top of apple slices to make a long "folder" of dough surrounded with apple slices revealing.

- In a bowl, beat together the water and egg. Sweep with egg wash the surface of dough.
- To taste, drizzle with more cinnamon-sugar.
- Beginning from one end, turn dough not that tight to make a rose-shaped pastry.
- Use end of dough strip to seal roll.
- Put roses in prepared ramekins. Drizzle with a bit more of cinnamon-sugar. Put ramekins on the center of wire rack of preheated oven.
- Bake for about 45 minutes or until brown well in color. Get ramekins using a tongs and let it cool for 5 to 10 minutes on a baking sheet. Separate from ramekins the apple roses and completely cool on rack. Sprinkle with confectioner's sugar prior to serving.

Nutrition Information

- Calories: 1058 calories;
- Total Fat: 71.3
- Sodium: 496
- Total Carbohydrate: 96.3
- Cholesterol: 143
- Protein: 12.1

218.   Baked Brie En Croute

Serving: 10 | Prep: 10mins | Cook: 20mins | Ready in:

Ingredients

- 1 egg
- 1 tablespoon water
- 1 (17.3 ounce) package frozen puff pastry (such as Pepperidge Farm®), thawed
- 1/2 cup apricot preserves
- 3/4 cup dried cranberries
- 1/2 cup sliced almonds
- 1 (7 inch) wheel Brie cheese

Direction

- Heat oven to 200°C (400°F) beforehand. Use parchment paper to line a baking sheet.

- For making the egg wash, whisking together water and egg.
- Gently rolling puff pastry out to a 14-inch square shape. To create a circle, use pizza cutter/knife to cut corners off. Spread over the pastry with apricot preserves, leave a 1-inch border around the edge. Use almonds and cranberries to dredge over the pastry, in the center, lay Brie cheese.
- Brushing some of the egg wash onto the edges of the pastry. Folding bottom and top of pastry over the dough; cut off 2 inches every edge. To completely cover the Brie cheese, folding remaining pastry on top. For sealing, use your fingers to press the seams. Removing leaked out apricot preserves.
- Remove wrapped cheese to baking sheet, seam-side down. Use egg wash to brush top.
- In the preheated oven, allow to bake for about 20 minutes till top gets golden brown. Allow to rest for approximately 30 minutes before serving.

Nutrition Information

- Calories: 497 calories;
- Protein: 13.1
- Total Fat: 32
- Sodium: 371
- Total Carbohydrate: 40.9
- Cholesterol: 56

219.   Baked Brie In Puff Pastry

Serving: 8 | Prep: 5mins | Cook: 20mins | Ready in:

Ingredients

- 1/2 (17.5 ounce) package frozen puff pastry, thawed
- 1 (8 ounce) wheel Brie cheese
- 1/4 cup sliced almonds

Direction

- Preheat oven to 175°C/350°F. Prepare a 9-inch pie pan with grease.
- Divide the wheel of Brie into two flatter wheels by slicing down in half, horizontally. Place puff pastry onto the pie pan and place one half of the brie on the pastry dough, rind-side down.
- Sprinkle top evenly with almonds. Place the other brie half on top of the almonds, rind-side up. Bundle around the brie with the pastry dough.
- Bake in for 15 to 20 minutes. Before serving, allow to cool for at least 5 minutes.

Nutrition Information

- Calories: 281 calories;
- Total Fat: 21
- Sodium: 255
- Total Carbohydrate: 14.5
- Cholesterol: 28
- Protein: 8.7

220.   Baked Brie With Caramelized Onions

Serving: 8 | Prep: 15mins | Cook: 45mins | Ready in:

Ingredients

- 1 head garlic
- 1/4 cup butter
- 1 yellow onion, sliced
- 1 Granny Smith apple - peeled, cored and sliced
- 1 (8 ounce) wedge Brie cheese
- 1 sheet frozen puff pastry, thawed
- 1 tablespoon melted butter

Direction

- Preheat oven to 205°C/400°F. On a baking sheet, add garlic and drizzle olive oil over it.

Roast garlic until soft, about 15 to 20 minutes. Set aside.

- While roasting, place a skillet over medium heat and melt 1/4 cup of butter. Add apples and onions in the hot butter; cook and stir until browned and tender. Set aside.
- On thawed puff pastry, arrange brie over the top. Top the onion and apple mixture over the brie. Fold the pastry over the brie and pinch to seal. Brush melted butter over the pastry.
- Bake until golden brown, for 20 to 25 minutes. Add whole cloves of roasted garlic to garnish, serve hot.

Nutrition Information

- Calories: 348 calories;
- Sodium: 306
- Total Carbohydrate: 19.5
- Cholesterol: 47
- Protein: 8.8
- Total Fat: 26.6

221.   Baked Curry Triangles

Serving: 12 | Prep: 20mins | Cook: 20mins | Ready in:

Ingredients

- 1/2 pound ground beef
- 1/4 onion, chopped
- 5 tablespoons curry powder, or more to taste
- 1 sheet puff pastry, cut into 6 squares
- 1 egg, beaten

Direction

- Preheat an oven to 190 °C or 375 °F.
- In a nonstick skillet, cook and mix onion and beef for 5 minutes till beef is browned. Mix in curry powder for 1 to 2 minutes till heated through and aromatic.
- Diagonally slice puff pastry squares to form 12 triangles. Fold every triangle in 1/2, patting

edges of 1 side together, and retaining a gap for filling. With curried beef, stuff every triangle and press edges to close.

- With a pastry brush, glaze every triangle with beaten egg. On a baking sheet, put the triangles.
- In the prepped oven, bake for 15 to 20 minutes till golden brown and they puffed up.

Nutrition Information

- Calories: 161 calories;
- Total Fat: 10.7
- Sodium: 68
- Total Carbohydrate: 11.1
- Cholesterol: 27
- Protein: 5.5

222.   Baked Stuffed Brie With Cranberries & Walnuts

Serving: 8 | Prep: 20mins | Cook: | Ready in:

Ingredients

- 1 small wheel of brie (about 6 to 8 inches), chilled
- 1/4 cup dried cranberries
- 1/4 cup chopped walnuts
- 1 sheet frozen puff pastry, thawed, plus extra for (optional) design
- 1 egg, beaten with
- 1 teaspoon water

Direction

- Using a sharp paring knife to score all the way around the side of a wheel of brie. Directly cut on the "equator" through the rind. Wrap a dental floss/a long piece of string on the newly made cut around the brie. Loop one end of the string over the other end (a half knot). Then pull the string's ends in opposite ways, cutting the brie in half.

- On one cut side of the brie, press the dried cranberries; on the other side, press walnut. Put the 2 sides back together quickly with the cranberries over the walnuts. Press together and stuff any walnuts or cranberries that fell out back in.
- On a floured surface, roll a thawed sheet of puff pastry out into an approximately 1/8-inch thick sheet. In center of pastry, lay brie. Pull up edges gently to make sure there is enough dough to wrap the brie entirely. If there is too much dough, trim the corners off. Brush egg wash on dough. Fold one of the dough's edge over the brie, then the other side. Fold the remaining edges over and encase the brie complexly. If necessary, trim excess pieces of dough. Turn the brie in order for the seam to be at the bottom; to snug the dough against the brie, press the sides in gently. Brush egg wash on the sides and top of the wrapped brie.
- If you want to decorate the brie using cut-out shapes of extra puff pastry, use dough that is extremely cold (almost still frozen) to guarantee the sharp lines. Use egg wash to brush decorative pieces lightly. Let the brie sit for an hour in the freezer (this step is crucial; see note below).
- Heat oven to 220°C (425°F) beforehand. Use parchment paper to line a rimmed baking sheet.
- On the prepared baking sheet, lay the brie. In preheated oven, allow to bake on the center rack for approximately 20 minutes till browned and the cheese is leaking. (It is rare if the brie does not leak through, but it takes 20-25 minutes for the cheese to melt and the pastry to get browned.)

Nutrition Information

- Calories: 304 calories;
- Total Fat: 22.3
- Sodium: 261
- Total Carbohydrate: 17.4
- Cholesterol: 49
- Protein: 9.3

223.   Banana Nutella® Bites

Serving: 48 | Prep: 25mins | Cook: 15mins | Ready in:

Ingredients

- cooking spray
- 3 (10x15-inch) sheets of frozen puff pastry, thawed
- 1 cup chocolate-hazelnut spread (such as Nutella®), divided
- 3 bananas, sliced
- Frosting:
- 1/2 (8 ounce) package cream cheese, softened
- 2 1/4 cups heavy whipping cream
- 1/4 cup white sugar
- 1 teaspoon vanilla extract

Direction

- Preheat the oven to 190 ° C or 375 ° F. Using cooking spray, coat 2 24-count mini-muffin tins.
- Slice every sheet of puff pastry into 4. Slice every quarter making 4 square portions. Fill every mini-muffin cup with a square of puff pastry.
- On top of every pastry square, scatter a teaspoon of chocolate-hazelnut spread. Put 3 slices of banana over.
- In the prepped oven, bake for 15 to 18 minutes, till golden brown. Turn onto wire rack to fully cool.
- In bowl, whip cream cheese for 2 minutes using electric mixer till smooth. Put in vanilla extract, sugar and heavy cream; whip till icing is creamy and thick.
- Spoon or pipe cream cheese icing over the banana slices top.

Nutrition Information

- Calories: 148 calories;

- Sodium: 52
- Total Carbohydrate: 12.9
- Cholesterol: 10
- Protein: 1.8
- Total Fat: 10.2

224.   Beef Vino Puff

Serving: 4 | Prep: 20mins | Cook: 35mins | Ready in:

Ingredients

- 4 (4 ounce) beef tenderloin filets
- 2 tablespoons olive oil
- 1 shallot, minced
- 1 teaspoon minced garlic, or to taste
- 1 cup Pinot Noir (or other semi-dry red wine)
- 1 pinch garlic salt, or to taste
- 1 pinch Italian seasoning, or to taste
- 1 (8 ounce) package cream cheese, softened
- 2 sheets frozen puff pastry, thawed
- 1 egg white (optional)
- 1/4 cup water (optional)

Direction

- Preheat the oven's broiler and place oven rack approximately 6-inch away from heat source.
- In pan of a broiler, put the beef tenderloin filets and broil for 2 minutes on each side, till browned slightly yet remain very rare. Take off the filets and reserve to rest; lower the heat to 190 ° C or 375 ° F.
- In skillet, heat the olive oil on moderate heat and cook and mix garlic and shallot for 5 minutes, till shallot is clear.
- Add in Pinot Noir, boil, and cook for 10 minutes till sauce is cooked down by 1/2, mixing frequently. Mix in Italian seasoning and garlic salt. Lower the heat to low.
- Into sauce, gently mix cream cheese till you have creamy purple sauce. Take sauce off heat.
- On work area, place sheets of puff pastry and halve every sheet widthwise.

- Onto a half sheet of puff pastry, scoop a liberal amount of sauce, and place one tenderloin filet onto the middle of sauce.
- Fold sheet of puff pastry on top of sauce and steak, and force the along edges surrounding to enclose. Redo with the rest of the steaks. Onto one baking sheet, put the steaks covered with pastry.
- In bowl, whip water and egg white and brush mixture over the pastry tops.
- In oven, bake for 25 minutes, till pastry turn puffed and browned and steaks are the preferred doneness. An inserted instant-read meat thermometer into the middle of meat must register at minimum of 65 ° C or 145 ° F.

Nutrition Information

- Calories: 1231 calories;
- Total Carbohydrate: 59.9
- Cholesterol: 157
- Protein: 45.6
- Total Fat: 84.8
- Sodium: 630

225.   Beef, Mushroom And Guinness® Pie

Serving: 6 | Prep: 25mins | Cook: 2hours35mins | Ready in:

Ingredients

- 3 tablespoons olive oil, divided
- 1 pound cubed beef stew meat
- 2 slices bacon, chopped
- 1 white onion, chopped
- 1 carrot, sliced
- 1/3 pound crimini mushrooms, sliced
- 1 clove garlic, crushed
- 1 teaspoon white sugar
- 1 1/2 tablespoons all-purpose flour
- 1 cup Irish stout beer (such as Guinness®)
- 1 1/4 cups beef stock

- 1/2 teaspoon ground thyme
- 2 bay leaves
- 1/2 teaspoon cornstarch, or as needed
- 1 teaspoon water
- 1 sheet frozen puff pastry, thawed
- 1 egg, beaten

Direction

- In a big pot over medium heat, heat 2 tablespoons olive oil, brown all sides of the beef stew meat for 10 minutes; reserve. Heat the leftover 1 tablespoon olive oil, then cook bacon just till it starts to brown; Mix in the sugar, garlic, mushrooms, carrot and onion. Cook the vegetables for additional of 10 to 15 minutes till browned and soft.
- Mix in the flour till smoothly combined, then slowly add in the beef stock and Irish stout beer. Add in the bay leaves, thyme and the reserved cooked beef. Cover, boil; lower heat to a simmer for an hour and 15 minutes till the meat is tender; mixing from time to time. Uncover, increase heat to medium, and let the stew boil for 15 minutes longer till slightly thickened. Combine water and cornstarch together, then mix into the stew; allow to simmer to incorporate flavors for additional of 30 minutes. Take off heat; Throw bay leaves away.
- Preheat oven to 175°C or 350°F.
- In a 9-inch pie dish, scatter the filling; cut the puff pastry into a 10-inch round, then put over the filling. Using a fork, crimp and pinch pastry edges, securing it to the dish; using a sharp knife, slice 2 steam vents into the pastry. Glaze top of the pie with beaten egg.
- In the preheated oven, bake 30 to 40 minutes till crust is browned.

Nutrition Information

- Calories: 500 calories;
- Total Fat: 31.7
- Sodium: 259
- Total Carbohydrate: 28.6
- Cholesterol: 77

- Protein: 21.8

226.   Beefburger Parcels

Serving: 4 | Prep: 30mins | Cook: 30mins | Ready in:

Ingredients

- 1 pound ground beef
- 1 onion, finely chopped
- 1 clove garlic
- 1 tablespoon olive oil
- 1 tablespoon Worcestershire sauce
- 1 teaspoon Italian seasoning
- salt and pepper to taste
- 1 egg
- 1 tablespoon olive oil
- 1 onion, chopped
- 1/2 pound fresh mushrooms, finely chopped
- 1 (17.25 ounce) package frozen puff pastry
- 1 egg, beaten
- 1 cup red grape juice
- 1 cube beef bouillon
- 1 tablespoon Worcestershire sauce
- 1 tablespoon cornstarch, mixed with equal parts water

Direction

- Set an outdoor grill to preheat to high heat and oil the grate lightly. Set an oven to preheat to 200°C (400°F).
- Mix together 1 tbsp olive oil, garlic, 1 chopped onion and ground beef in a big bowl. Season it with pepper, salt, Italian seasoning and Worcestershire sauce, then add the egg and stir well. Form it into four thick patties that are not too big in diameter. Cook the burgers on the grill until it turns brown.
- In a frypan, heat 1 tbsp of olive oil over medium heat. Sauté the chopped mushrooms and one chopped onion until caramelized and brown.
- Slice the puff pastry into four squares and roll the pieces big enough to wrap the burgers.

Distribute the mushroom mixture in the middle of each pastry, then put the burgers on top. Wrap the pastry surrounding the burgers and seal the edges. Put the parcels on the baking trays, seam side down, then brush it using beaten egg.

- Bake for 25-30 minutes in the preheated oven or until the pastry turns golden brown and puffed. Serve together with red grape sauce.
- In the meantime, prepare the red grape sauce: Mix together the bouillon, Worcestershire sauce and grape juice in a saucepan over medium heat. Combine the water and cornstarch and mix into the sauce. Slowly bring to a boil, mixing continuously, until it becomes thick.

Nutrition Information

- Calories: 1203 calories;
- Total Fat: 85.8
- Sodium: 1009
- Total Carbohydrate: 75.6
- Cholesterol: 190
- Protein: 33.1

227.   Boeuf En Croute

Serving: 2 | Prep: 35mins | Cook: 20mins | Ready in:

Ingredients

- 1 teaspoon olive oil
- 2 (6 ounce) beef tenderloin filets
- 1 tablespoon butter
- 8 ounces fresh white mushrooms, minced
- 1/3 cup minced shallot
- 2 cloves garlic, minced
- 2 tablespoons red wine
- 4 6-inch squares of frozen puff pastry, thawed but still cold
- 1 1/2 cups red wine
- salt and pepper to taste
- 1 egg (optional)
- 2 tablespoons milk (optional)

Direction

- In a heavy skillet, heat olive oil over high heat until very hot. Sear the filets for 1-2 minutes each side until both sides are evenly brown in color. Take the filets from the skillet and keep it in the fridge for at least 1 hour to chill. The filets need to be cold.
- Melt the butter in the same skillet over medium heat. Cook and stir the garlic, mushrooms and shallot for 6-8 minutes until the mushrooms have released its juices and the shallots are translucent and soft. Mix in 2 tablespoons of red wine and scrape off any browned bits on the pan. Give it a stir to dissolve the browned bits in wine. Put the mushroom mixture in a bowl and keep it in the fridge for about 45 minutes.
- On a clean work surface, put 2 pieces of puff pastry and place the chilled filet on top of each pastry. Distribute the mushroom mixture evenly on top of the chilled filet and add another piece of puff pastry on top. Fold the puff pastry and pinch the edges together to seal the stuffing inside, cut off any excess pastry for a clean finish. Cut a little slit on top of each stuffed pastry.
- Let a saucepan with 1 1/2 cups of red wine simmer over medium heat for about 15 minutes until the wine has reduced in half. Put in pepper and salt to taste. While the wine sauce is simmering, beat milk and eggs in a bowl and coat the top of the stuffed pastries with the egg mixture for a browner crust, if desired. Keep the stuffed pastries in the fridge to keep it chilled.
- Preheat the oven to 450°F (230°C). Cover the bottom of a baking sheet with parchment paper.
- Put the chilled stuffed puff pastries on the prepared baking sheet. Put in the preheated oven and bake for about 15 minutes until the pastry is crispy and golden brown in color and the filets are of the desired doneness (for medium-rare. cook it for about 15 minutes).

Check the temperature of the filet using an instant-read thermometer inserted in the middle, it should be at 130°F (54°C). To serve, keep each filet in the pastry shell and spoonfuls of wine sauce on top.

Nutrition Information

- Calories: 3274 calories;
- Total Fat: 215.3
- Sodium: 1359
- Total Carbohydrate: 232.4
- Cholesterol: 196
- Protein: 68.7

228. Brie Cheese Appetizer

Serving: 8 | Prep: 10mins | Cook: 30mins | Ready in:

Ingredients

- 1 (8 ounce) wheel Brie cheese
- 3 tablespoons apricot preserves
- 1/2 (17.5 ounce) package frozen puff pastry, thawed
- 1 egg white

Direction

- Preheat the oven to 175 °C or 350 °F. Slightly oil a cookie sheet.
- Halve one Brie cheese wheel to have 2 rounds of cheese. Scatter peach or apricot preserves on the cut side of one circle brie half. Form a sandwich from two Brie halves, preserves should be in the middle of each halve. With a sheet of puffed pastry, wrap the whole Brie wheel and onto the prepped cooking sheet, turn the whole creation so seam side is facing down. With egg white, glaze puffed pastry.
- Let bake for half an hour till pastry in golden brown. Serve right away.

Nutrition Information

- Calories: 286 calories;
- Sodium: 264
- Total Carbohydrate: 19.1
- Cholesterol: 28
- Protein: 8.6
- Total Fat: 19.5

229. Brie, Cranberries, And Pistachio Wreath

Serving: 6 | Prep: 15mins | Cook: 15mins | Ready in:

Ingredients

- 1 (8 ounce) round puff pastry sheet
- 3 tablespoons cranberry sauce
- 6 ounces Brie cheese, sliced
- 2 tablespoons chopped pistachio nuts
- 1 egg, beaten
- 1 teaspoon dried rosemary

Direction

- Preheat the oven to 200 ° C or 400 ° F. Line parchment paper on a baking sheet.
- On prepped baking sheet, spread puff pastry. Put one 4-inches bowl upside facing down in the middle; using paring knife, mark a round and from the middle to edge of marked round, create 4 cuts, creating a shape like star. Take bowl off. Scatter cranberry sauce on dough center surrounding; put pistachios and Brie slices on top.
- Put pastry outer edge and a point of star inwards on top of filling; pinch together. Redo with the other dough pieces, till it looks much like a wreath. Brush with the beaten egg and scatter rosemary over.
- In the prepped oven, bake for 15 minutes, till golden brown and Brie cheese has melted partially. Take out of oven and rest for 5 minutes prior to serving.

Nutrition Information

- Calories: 341 calories;
- Total Fat: 24.2
- Sodium: 296
- Total Carbohydrate: 21.3
- Cholesterol: 56
- Protein: 10.1

230.   Brunch Omelet Torte

Serving: 8 | Prep: 1hours | Cook: 30mins | Ready in:

Ingredients

- 1 (17.5 ounce) package frozen puff pastry sheets, thawed
- Potatoes:
- 1/4 cup butter
- 6 red potatoes, peeled and sliced 1/8 inch thick
- 1 onion, thinly sliced into rings
- 1/4 teaspoon salt
- 1/4 teaspoon black pepper
- Omelet:
- 2 tablespoons butter, divided
- 6 eggs
- 1/4 cup chopped fresh parsley
- 1 pinch salt
- 1 pinch black pepper
- 2 tablespoons water
- Filling:
- 8 ounces cooked ham, thinly sliced
- 2 cups shredded Cheddar cheese, divided
- 1 egg
- 1 tablespoon water

Direction

- On a surface lightly covered with flour, gently roll each sheet of puff pastry into a 12-inch square. In a deep-dish springform pan or pie plate, place a sheet of puff pastry and set aside.
- In a large frying pan, melt a quarter cup butter until butter sizzles. Put a quarter teaspoon pepper, a quarter teaspoon salt, onion and potatoes in. Cook over medium-high heat with the lid on, 12-15 minutes, turning occasionally, up to when potatoes lightly turn browned, crisp and soft. Remove from heat and set aside.
- In a bowl, whisk 2 tablespoons water, a pinch of salt and pepper, parsley and eggs until well combined. Over medium heat in a clean skillet, melt a tablespoon of butter until sizzling.
- Pour half (3/4 cup) of omelet mixture in the heated skillet. Over medium heat, cook and use a spatula to slightly lift edges when omelet mixture sets, allowing raw mixture to flow to the bottom. Keep cooking for about 2-3 minutes until set. Onto cookie sheet, slide cooked omelet. Do again with the rest of omelet mixture and tablespoon of butter.
- Preheat oven to 375°F (190°C).
- In a pie plate, place puff pastry and top with layers of ingredients in below order: 1 of the omelets, 4 ounces of ham, 1/2 of the fried potatoes and a cup of shredded cheese. Add the rest of omelet, cheese, ham and potatoes on top. Put the remaining puff pastry sheet over the torte to cover. Press edges of both puff pastry sheets together to shape a rim and trim off excess. Flute or crimp edges. Now the torte can be stored overnight in the refrigerator.
- Whisk 1 tablespoon water and 1 egg together in a small bowl; brush over puff pastry.
- In preheated oven, bake for 30-35 minutes, until the pastry turns golden brown rich. Let sit for at least 5 minutes; cut into wedges. The torte can be served warm or at the room temperature.

Nutrition Information

- Calories: 781 calories;
- Sodium: 927
- Total Carbohydrate: 55.3
- Cholesterol: 231
- Protein: 25.5
- Total Fat: 51.1

231. Brussels Sprouts And Feta Pastry Roll

Serving: 6 | Prep: 20mins | Cook: 25mins | Ready in:

Ingredients

- 15 Brussels sprouts, trimmed and cut in half
- 2 tablespoons fresh lemon juice
- 3 tablespoons balsamic vinegar, or to taste
- 1 teaspoon honey, or to taste
- 1/4 cup olive oil
- salt and ground black pepper to taste
- 1/4 cup chopped fresh basil
- 1 small white onion, chopped
- 1/4 cup walnuts
- 1/4 cup almonds
- 1 (6 ounce) container sheep-milk feta cheese, crumbled
- 2 (8 inch) square sheets of frozen puff pastry, thawed

Direction

- Preheat the oven to 190°C or 375°Fahrenheit. Line a sheet of parchment paper in the baking pan.
- In a pot with an inch-deep water; boil Brussels sprouts. Cover and let it simmer on medium-low heat for 5-7mins until tender and bright green. Take off heat, drain, and let it cool.
- In a bowl, combine black pepper, lemon juice, salt, balsamic vinegar, olive oil, and honey; set aside.
- In a food processor work bowl, put in the cooled Brussels sprouts, almonds, basil, walnuts, and onion; process for 15 seconds until finely chopped. Transfer Brussels sprouts mixture in a bowl; stir in lemon juice mixture and feta cheese until it forms into a moist filling.
- On a work surface, spread two sheet of puff pastry. Split the filling in half; scoop and press 1/2 of the filling on each pastry. Keep a 3/4in

of puff pastry in one end of the pastry square. Roll each square up into a roll and pink the unfilled end of the pastry sheet closed. Arrange the filled rolls with the seam-side down in the prepared pan.
- Bake for about 20mins in the preheated oven until golden brown. Serve hot.

Nutrition Information

- Calories: 511 calories;
- Total Fat: 39.1
- Sodium: 445
- Total Carbohydrate: 31.7
- Cholesterol: 25
- Protein: 11.2

232. Caramel Pecan Kringle

Serving: 8 | Prep: 15mins | Cook: 20mins | Ready in:

Ingredients

- 3/4 cup Marzetti's® Old Fashioned Caramel Dip, or more if needed
- 1 cup pecans, divided
- 1 sheet puff pastry, divided
- For Icing:
- 1/2 cup confectioners' sugar
- 1 tablespoon cream or milk
- 1/4 teaspoon vanilla extract
- Pinch of salt

Direction

- Preparing the Kringle: Preheat the oven to 350°F. On a sheet pan, put in all of the pecans and let it toast for 8 minutes. Let the toasted pecans cool down then slice it to smaller pieces and put it aside.
- Switch the temperature of the oven to 400°F. Use a parchment paper to line a baking pan.
- Spread out the folded puff pastry in the middle of the prepared baking pan. Distribute

1/2 of the Marzetti Old Fashioned Caramel Dip evenly in the middle section of the puff pastry. Top it off with 1/3 cup of pecans.

- Fold 1/3 of the puff pastry over the filled middle section where the pecans and caramel are.
- Spread the remaining Marzetti Old Fashioned Caramel Dip and 1/3 cup of pecans evenly onto the dough layer. Fold the remaining 1/3 of the puff pastry over the layer of pecans and caramel to fully cover it.
- Put it in the preheated oven and let it bake for 15-20 minutes or until the puff pastry turns golden brown in color.
- Preparing the icing: Mix all of the icing ingredients together and add in extra cream if need be.
- Allow the baked Kringle to cool down a bit then drizzle the prepared icing on top. Top it off with the remaining pecans.
- Let the Kringle fully cool down then cut it into slices and serve.

Nutrition Information

- Calories: 411 calories;
- Cholesterol: 6
- Protein: 3.6
- Total Fat: 27.4
- Sodium: 151
- Total Carbohydrate: 40

233.   Caramelized Onion And Mushroom Tarte Tatin

Serving: 8 | Prep: 20mins | Cook: 50mins | Ready in:

Ingredients

- 1/4 cup unsalted butter
- 1 large sweet onion (such as Vidalia®), sliced
- 2 tablespoons olive oil
- 1 (8 ounce) package crimini mushrooms, sliced
- 1 pinch salt and ground black pepper to taste

- 1 (17.5 ounce) package frozen puff pastry, thawed
- 1 (11 ounce) log goat cheese
- 1 egg, beaten
- 1 pinch thyme, or to taste

Direction

- In a saucepan, melt butter over medium-low heat; cook and stir onion in hot butter for about 30 to 60 minutes until caramelized and soft.
- In a skillet, heat olive oil over medium-high heat; cook and mix mushrooms for approximately 10 minutes until browned and soften yet crisp. Add pepper and salt to season.
- Preheat oven to 400 °F (200 °C).
- On a lightly-floured work surface, roll puff pastry out. Use a round cutter to cut out circles of 5-inch and arrange on a baking sheet.
- In the preheated oven, bake for around 12 minutes until puffed and lightly browned. Onto a wire rack, place puffs to fully cool.
- Whip egg and goat cheese together until smooth in a bowl. Add thyme to season. Smear mixture of goat cheese on cooled pastry puffs; put mushrooms and caramelized onions on top of each. Return pastries onto baking sheet.
- Bake for nearly 5 minutes in oven until warmed through.

Nutrition Information

- Calories: 584 calories;
- Sodium: 391
- Total Carbohydrate: 31.4
- Cholesterol: 69
- Protein: 15.1
- Total Fat: 44.6

234. Cheater's Apple Strudel

Serving: 8 | Prep: 20mins | Cook: 30mins | Ready in:

Ingredients

- flour for dusting
- 1 (17.5 ounce) package frozen puff pastry sheets (2 sheets), thawed
- water, as needed
- 6 small tart apples - peeled, cored, and sliced thinly
- 1 1/2 teaspoons ground cinnamon
- 1 tablespoon brown sugar
- 1/4 cup toasted slivered almonds
- 1/4 cup butterscotch chips
- 1 tablespoon butter, melted
- 1/2 teaspoon white sugar

Direction

- Preheat the oven to 190°C/375°F. Dust the working surface using flour lightly. Line parchment paper on a baking sheet.
- Join 2 puff pastry sheets by the short edges to create a long rectangle on the prepped work surface. Along the edges, brush water; gently press down to seal with fingertips.
- Mix butterscotch chips, almonds, brown sugar, cinnamon and apple slices together till evenly combined in a bowl; put mixture on 1 of the pastry's long edges. Fold 1 pastry side on the mixture; roll into a long strudel. Be sure to seal both ends. Brush melted butter on pastry; create 2-in. diagonal slits on strudel's length using a sharp knife. Put onto the prepped baking sheet.
- In the preheated oven, bake for 15 minutes. Sprinkle sugar over the top of strudel; put back in oven for 15-20 minutes more till pastry is flaky and golden brown.

Nutrition Information

- Calories: 474 calories;
- Total Carbohydrate: 50
- Cholesterol: 4
- Protein: 5.8
- Total Fat: 28.4
- Sodium: 169

235. Cheese Bourekas

Serving: 12 | Prep: 30mins | Cook: 30mins | Ready in:

Ingredients

- 2 eggs
- 2 cups shredded mozzarella cheese
- 1 teaspoon dried parsley
- 1 pinch garlic powder
- 1 pinch onion powder
- 1 pinch salt
- 1 pinch black pepper
- 1 (17.5 ounce) package frozen puff pastry
- 2 teaspoons water
- 2 tablespoons sesame seeds

Direction

- Preheat an oven to 175 °C or 350 °F. Oil a baking sheet.
- In a medium bowl, whisk an egg, and add in cheese. Put pepper, salt, onion powder, garlic powder and parsley to season.
- Cut every puff pastry sheet on a slightly floured surface into 6 even squares to yield 12 squares in all. In small bowl, whisk the rest of the egg with water. With egg wash, lightly glaze edges of every square. In the middle of every square, put a heaping tablespoon of cheese mixture. Fold the pastry on top of filling, and using a fork, seal the edges. Put to prepped baking sheet, glaze with the rest of egg wash and scatter sesame seeds on top.
- In the prepped oven, let bake till golden brown for half an hour. Serve right away.

Nutrition Information

- Calories: 294 calories;

- Total Carbohydrate: 19.6
- Cholesterol: 43
- Protein: 8.9
- Total Fat: 20.1
- Sodium: 230

236. Cheese Ramkin

Serving: 12 | Prep: | Cook: | Ready in:

Ingredients

- 1 (17.25 ounce) package frozen puff pastry, thawed
- 1 egg
- 1 cup milk
- 1 tablespoon all-purpose flour
- 1/8 teaspoon ground black pepper
- 1 pinch ground nutmeg
- 2 cups shredded Gruyere cheese

Direction

- Preheat an oven to 200 °C or 400 °F.
- On a slightly floured area, unroll puff pastry sheets to quarter-inch thickness. Slice into squares, 3-inch in size. Into the cups of two dozen cup muffin tins, force the squares to create pastry cups.
- Beat together the nutmeg, pepper, flour, milk and egg in a medium bowl. Mix in cheese till equally combined. Divide the mixture equally between pastry cups.
- In the prepped oven, let bake for 12 to 15 minutes, till the filling has puffed up and pastry is golden brown. Allow to cool in pans till can easily be touched prior taking off. Serve while warm or at room temperature.

Nutrition Information

- Calories: 315 calories;
- Cholesterol: 37
- Protein: 9.6

- Total Fat: 22
- Sodium: 175
- Total Carbohydrate: 19.8

237. Chef John's Asparagus Tart

Serving: 1 | Prep: 15mins | Cook: 25mins | Ready in:

Ingredients

- 1 6x9-inch sheet frozen puff pastry, thawed
- 6 spears fresh asparagus, trimmed
- 1 tablespoon Dijon mustard
- 1 1/2 teaspoons creme fraiche
- 1 pinch ground black pepper
- 1 pinch cayenne pepper
- 2 teaspoons butter, melted
- 2 tablespoons freshly grated Parmigiano-Reggiano cheese, or to taste

Direction

- Preheat the oven to 200 °C or 400 °F. Line a silicone baking mat on a baking sheet.
- On the prepped baking sheet, lay out puff pastry. To form a half-inch wide border, fold edges up. Puncture inner base of dough fully using a fork.
- In the prepped oven, bake for 10 minutes till puffed and golden. To deflate, push puffed middle down using back of a fork.
- Boil a big pot of slightly salted water. Put asparagus and allow to cook without cover for a minute till bright green. Let drain in colander and quickly dunk in ice water for few minutes till cold to end the cooking process. Allow to drain.
- In a small bowl, mix cayenne pepper, black pepper, creme fraiche and mustard together; scatter into the base of cooled tart shell. Put the asparagus spears, clipping as needed to suit the tart shell, in the middle of tart over the mustard spread. Glaze top of asparagus and

crust with melted butter and over the top, scatter Parmigiano-Reggiano cheese.

- In the oven, bake for 10 to 12 minutes till asparagus is soft and pastry is browned.

Nutrition Information

- Calories: 795 calories;
- Sodium: 869
- Total Carbohydrate: 58.8
- Cholesterol: 40
- Protein: 14.6
- Total Fat: 56.6

238. Chef John's Sausage Rolls

Serving: 8 | Prep: 30mins | Cook: 30mins | Ready in:

Ingredients

- 1 pound ground pork
- 2 tablespoons finely minced onion
- 1 clove crushed garlic
- 1 tablespoon minced fresh sage
- 1 tablespoon dry bread crumbs
- 1 1/4 teaspoons kosher salt, or to taste
- 1/2 teaspoon freshly ground black pepper
- 1/4 teaspoon ground coriander
- 1/4 teaspoon dried thyme
- 1/8 teaspoon cayenne pepper
- 1/8 teaspoon freshly grated nutmeg
- 1 egg
- 1 teaspoon water
- 1 sheet frozen puff pastry, partially thawed
- Sesame seeds for garnish (optional)

Direction

- In a mixing bowl, add nutmeg, cayenne pepper, thyme, coriander, pepper, salt, bread crumbs, sage, garlic, onions, and ground pork. Mix thoroughly and evenly distribute ingredients using a fork for 2 to 3 minutes. Half the mixture and transfer each half on a

plastic wrap. Dampen fingers and shape each half into a cylinder with the same length of the puff pastry. Roll up the plastic wrap into a round roll. Transfer to refrigerator until ready to use.

- Make an egg wash by whisking water and eggs together.
- Separate the semi-frozen puff pastry dough into thirds. Halve one of the thirds lengthwise. Bring the pastry to room temperature.
- On the long edge of the 2 larger pastry pieces, brush a 2 inch strip of egg wash. Place the narrower pieces on the egg wash strip, overlapping about 1 inch, to make a wider piece of pastry dough. Press lightly to form 2 wide lengths of pastry dough.
- Transfer the 2 sheets of dough on lightly floured parchment paper. Lightly dust the top of the dough with flour. Place another sheet of parchment paper over the dough to cover. Gently roll over until dough has even thickness. Remove the top sheet of parchment.
- Flatten the long edges of the dough slightly, about 1 inch wide. When the roll-up is completed, the seam side won't be thicker than the rest of the dough. Place a sausage log at the end of a pastry sheet. Begin to roll the sausage log in the pastry, brushing the far edge with egg wash before sealing the edges together. . Place on parchment paper seam side down, then place on a dish. Repeat process with 2nd sausage roll. Freeze for 10 minutes until dough is firm.
- Preheat oven to 375 degrees F (190 degrees C). Line a silicone mat on a baking sheet. Lightly flour a surface and transfer rolls to it. Brush sides and top with egg wash lightly. Divide into 8 pieces and sprinkle sesame seeds. Transfer to the prepared baking sheet standing up, or seam side down. Gently press each roll down to slightly flatten, preventing it from tipping over while baking. Bake in preheated oven for 30 minutes, or until nicely browned, pastry is cooked through and bottoms are browned.

Nutrition Information

- Calories: 300 calories;
- Sodium: 418
- Total Carbohydrate: 15
- Cholesterol: 57
- Protein: 13.3
- Total Fat: 20.6

239.   Chickaritos

Serving: 3 dozen. | Prep: 30mins | Cook: 20mins | Ready in:

Ingredients

- 3 cups finely chopped cooked chicken
- 1-1/2 cups shredded sharp cheddar cheese
- 1 can (4 ounces) chopped green chilies
- 4 green onions, finely chopped
- 1 teaspoon hot pepper sauce
- 1 teaspoon garlic salt
- 1/4 teaspoon paprika
- 1/4 teaspoon ground cumin
- 1/4 teaspoon pepper
- 2 packages (17.3 ounces each) frozen puff pastry, thawed
- 1 large egg, beaten
- Salsa and guacamole

Direction

- Preheat oven to 425 degrees F. Mix the chilies, pepper sauce, cheese, onions, seasonings, and chicken in a large bowl.
- In a lightly floured surface unfold a sheet of puff pastry. Roll the sheet into a rectangle with a dimension of the 12x9 inch. Slice into nine rectangles.
- Scoop across the middle of each rectangle 2 tablespoons of the filling. Brush the pastry edges with water and roll the pastry over the filling. Using a fork, press the edges to seal. Do the same procedure with the rest of the filling

and pastries. Keep in the refrigerator with cover until its ready for baking.
- Prepare a lightly greased baking sheet then place pastries, seam side down. Brush tops with egg. Bake for 20 to 25 minutes until golden brown. Serve while warm alongside guacamole and salsa.

Nutrition Information

- Calories: 213 calories
- Fiber: 2g fiber)
- Total Carbohydrate: 16g carbohydrate (0 sugars
- Cholesterol: 31mg cholesterol
- Protein: 11g protein.
- Total Fat: 12g fat (4g saturated fat)
- Sodium: 294mg sodium

240.   Chicken Curry Puffs

Serving: 9 | Prep: 30mins | Cook: 50mins | Ready in:

Ingredients

- 1 tablespoon vegetable oil
- 1/2 teaspoon ground coriander
- 1/2 teaspoon ground turmeric
- 1/2 teaspoon ground cumin
- 2 teaspoons curry powder
- 1/2 cup coconut milk, or more as needed
- 2 red onions, chopped
- 1 stalk lemon grass, thinly sliced
- 1 red chile pepper, roughly chopped
- 1 large russet potato, diced
- 3/4 pound skinless, boneless chicken breast, cut in bite-sized pieces
- 1 teaspoon salt
- 1 (17.25 ounce) package frozen puff pastry, thawed

Direction

- Place a saucepan over medium-low heat and heat the vegetable oil. Stir in curry powder, cumin, turmeric, and coriander. Cook until fragrant, just a few seconds. Add red pepper, lemon grass, onions, and coconut milk. Cook for 7 minutes, or until the vegetables are tender. Stir in potatoes, cook for another 12 minutes. Add additional coconut milk if the mixture appears too dry. Stir chicken in and add salt to season. Continue to cook and stir, allow the potatoes and chicken to absorb most of the liquid. Spread the mixture on a plate, allow to cool.
- Preheat oven to 190°C/375°F. Line parchment paper on two baking sheets. Cut 9 squares out of each sheet of puff pastry. Spoon a heaping amount of filling on the center of each square. Form a small pouch by pinching the four corners of the square together at the top. Arrange each pastry pouch 1 inch apart on the prepared baking sheet.
- Bake for 22 to 27 minutes, or until golden brown. Allow to cool for 10 minutes, then transfer to a wire rack to continue cooling. Serve at room temperature, or warm.

Nutrition Information

- Calories: 424 calories;
- Total Fat: 25.3
- Sodium: 423
- Total Carbohydrate: 35.5
- Cholesterol: 22
- Protein: 14.2

---

241. Chicken Plum Pie

Serving: 6 | Prep: 25mins | Cook: 50mins | Ready in:

Ingredients

- 1 sheet frozen puff pastry, thawed
- 1 pound cooked chicken meat, shredded
- 4 purple plums - pitted, peeled and chopped

- 3 tablespoons chicken broth
- 1/2 teaspoon ground mace
- 1/4 teaspoon ground cinnamon
- 1 pinch ground cloves
- salt and freshly ground black pepper to taste
- 2 purple plums, pitted and sliced
- 2 tablespoons melted butter
- 1 tablespoon light brown sugar

Direction

- Preheat the oven to 190 °C or 375 °F. Force sheet of puff pastry into a square or round pan, 8-inch in size.
- In the prepped oven, let bake for 10 minutes till base of pastry is really browned lightly.
- In a bowl, combine together the cloves, cinnamon, mace, chicken broth, 4 chopped plums and chicken, and season with pepper and salt to taste. Top the partially-baked crust with scoop of mixture, and over the top, set 2 plums slices. Sprinkle melted butter on pie, and scatter brown sugar over.
- Let the pie bake for 40 minutes in oven till slices of plum have caramelized and crust turn golden brown.

Nutrition Information

- Calories: 461 calories;
- Sodium: 179
- Total Carbohydrate: 28.1
- Cholesterol: 69
- Protein: 22.1
- Total Fat: 28.9

---

242. Chicken Pot Pies With Puff Pastry

Serving: 4 | Prep: 20mins | Cook: 40mins | Ready in:

Ingredients

- 1/2 cup unsalted butter

- 4 cups chicken broth, divided
- 1/2 cup all-purpose flour
- 1/4 cup dried onion flakes
- 1 dash hot pepper sauce
- 1 teaspoon ground black pepper
- 1/2 teaspoon dried thyme
- 1 bay leaf
- 1 (8 ounce) can carrots, drained
- 1 (8 ounce) can white potatoes
- 2 cups diced cooked chicken
- 4 slices Swiss cheese
- 1 sheet frozen puff pastry, cut into four squares
- 1 egg, beaten with
- 1 tablespoon water

Direction

- Start preheating the oven to 400°. Spray cooking spray over four small oven-proof bowls.
- In a saucepan, melt the butter over medium heat. Mix in two cups of the chicken broth, stir in all flour, pour in remaining chicken broth gradually until it becomes a smooth and slightly thick base. Stir in carrots, bay leaf, thyme, pepper, hot pepper sauce and onion flakes. Cook for 5 mins. Mix in the chicken and potatoes, cook for 5 more mins.
- Put a slice of Swiss cheese into bottom of each prepared bowl. Equally portion chicken mixture into 4 bowls, over cheese. Arrange the puff pastry square over the top of each bowl, lightly press around rim. Brush egg and water mixture over the pastry. Put 4 bowls on the baking sheet.
- Bake for 25 mins or until the pastry is golden brown and puffed. Allow to rest at least 5 mins. Enjoy!

Nutrition Information

- Calories: 948 calories;
- Cholesterol: 193
- Protein: 35.3
- Total Fat: 64.8

- Sodium: 1501
- Total Carbohydrate: 55.9

243. Chicken Spinach Feta Puff Pastry Pockets

Serving: 8 | Prep: 10mins | Cook: 48mins | Ready in:

Ingredients

- 2 skinless, boneless chicken breasts, cut into 1-inch cubes
- 2 teaspoons minced garlic
- 1 teaspoon dried parsley
- 1/2 teaspoon lemon juice
- 1/4 teaspoon ground black pepper
- 2 slices bacon, cut into bite-size pieces
- 1 small onion, diced
- 1 (10 ounce) package fresh spinach
- 1/2 cup crumbled feta cheese
- 1 (17.25 ounce) package frozen puff pastry sheets, thawed

Direction

- Preheat an oven to 200 °C or 400 °F. With parchment paper, line a baking sheet.
- In a bowl, put the chicken with pepper, lemon juice, parsley and garlic.
- In a big skillet, put the bacon and allow to cook over medium-high heat for 5 minutes, flipping from time to time, till crispy and equally browned. Let bacon slices drain on paper towels, setting aside grease in skillet.
- In bacon grease, sauté chicken for 5 to 7 minutes till not pink on the outside anymore. Put the onion; cook and mix for 5 minutes till onion is translucent. To pan, put the spinach, a handful at a time, for 3 minutes till it starts to wilt. Take off from heat.
- Halve every pastry sheet. On a floured surface, stretch out the pastry. On top of every piece. Layer a portion of bacon-spinach mixture, chicken and feta cheese. Fold the pastry on top of filling and flute edges using fingers. On the

prepped baking sheet, put the pockets seam-side facing down.

- In the prepped oven, bake for half an hour till golden brown.

Nutrition Information

- Calories: 415 calories;
- Total Fat: 26.8
- Sodium: 350
- Total Carbohydrate: 30.1
- Cholesterol: 28
- Protein: 13.9

244. Chicken Wellington

Serving: 8 | Prep: 45mins | Cook: 33mins | Ready in:

Ingredients

- 2 tablespoons olive oil
- 2 tablespoons butter
- 8 small boneless, skinless chicken breasts
- salt and ground black pepper to taste
- 1 large onion, finely chopped
- 1/2 pound baby bella mushrooms, sliced, or more to taste
- 1 tablespoon minced garlic
- 2 tablespoons chopped fresh parsley
- 2 sheets frozen puff pastry, thawed
- 1 (8 ounce) package cream cheese, softened
- 2 tablespoons Dijon mustard
- egg, slightly beaten

Direction

- Heat butter and olive oil on medium heat in a big skillet. Season chicken breasts with black pepper and salt; cook chicken in hot oil for 4 minutes per side till nearly cooked through and golden. Put onto plate.
- In same skillet, put garlic, mushrooms and onion; mix and cook for 5 minutes till onions

are tender and mushrooms lose their moisture. Mix in parsley.

- Preheat an oven to 190°C/375°F; line parchment paper on a baking sheet.
- Roll each puffy pastry sheet out on floured work surface to 14-in. square; cut every sheet to 4 even squares. Put a chicken breast in middle of every square.
- In a small bowl, mix Dijon mustard and cream cheese; spread some cream cheese mixture on every chicken breast. Put 2 tbsp. mushroom mixture over each. Brush water on edges of each square; wrap around chicken. Put on a baking sheet, seam side down; brush beaten egg on tops.
- In the preheated oven, bake for 20 minutes till golden brown and puffed. Remove from oven; before serving, halve.

Nutrition Information

- Calories: 607 calories;
- Total Carbohydrate: 31.8
- Cholesterol: 110
- Protein: 26.1
- Total Fat: 41.8
- Sodium: 420

245. Chicken And Broccoli Cups

Serving: 1 dozen. | Prep: 15mins | Cook: 25mins | Ready in:

Ingredients

- 2-1/2 cups diced cooked chicken breast
- 1 can (10-3/4 ounces) reduced-fat reduced-sodium condensed cream of chicken soup, undiluted
- 1 cup frozen chopped broccoli, thawed and drained
- 2 small plum tomatoes, seeded and chopped
- 1 small carrot, grated

- 1 tablespoon Dijon mustard
- 1 garlic clove, minced
- 1/4 teaspoon pepper
- 1 sheet frozen puff pastry, thawed
- 1/4 cup grated Parmesan cheese

Direction

- Mix the first eight ingredients together in a big bowl. Lay to one side. Spread out puff pastry on a lightly floured work area. Roll into a rectangle with 12-inch by 9-inch dimensions. Slice rectangle into 4 strips along its length and 3 strips widthwise. Push puff pastry squares carefully into muffin cups greased with cooking spray.
- Put a dollop of chicken mixture in each of the pastry cups. Top with Parmesan cheese. Bake for 25 to 30 minutes at 375 °F until golden brown. Serve while it's still warm.

Nutrition Information

- Calories: 182 calories
- Sodium: 310mg sodium
- Fiber: 1g fiber)
- Total Carbohydrate: 13g carbohydrate (0 sugars
- Cholesterol: 23mg cholesterol
- Protein: 10g protein.
- Total Fat: 10g fat (3g saturated fat)

246. Chocolate Clouds

Serving: 24 | Prep: 55mins | Cook: 15mins | Ready in:

Ingredients

- 1 (17.3 ounce) package frozen puff pastry (such as Pepperidge Farm®), thawed
- 1 (3.9 ounce) package instant chocolate pudding mix
- 1 cup low-fat milk

- 1/2 (8 ounce) container frozen whipped topping, thawed
- 1 tablespoon confectioners' sugar for dusting, or to taste

Direction

- Preheat the oven to 200 ° C or 400 ° F.
- Unfold 2 puff pastry sheets and spread onto a slightly floured work area. Slice every sheet, making 3 strips through fold marks, then slice every strip making 4 squares to create a dozen pastry squares on every sheet. Put the squares onto baking sheet.
- In the prepped oven, bake for 15 minutes, till puff pastry turn golden brown. Cool squares fully.
- In bowl, mix milk and pudding mix for a minute, till smooth and thick; rest for 3 minutes to end thickening. Into pudding, fold whipped topping gently. Into pastry bag fastened with medium tip, turn the mixture of chocolate mousse.
- Slowly open one pastry square corner with a butter knife or a finger. Using knife, create one small pocket in pastry. Into the opening, pipe approximately a tablespoon of chocolate mousse; once pastry pocket is full, a bit of mousse will show at opening area. Redo with the rest of mousse mixture and pastry squares. Lightly sprinkle confectioners' sugar on pastries.

Nutrition Information

- Calories: 150 calories;
- Sodium: 122
- Total Carbohydrate: 15.1
- Cholesterol: < 1
- Protein: 2
- Total Fat: 9.2

247.   Clinton's Special Vegetarian Quiche

Serving: 7 | Prep: 40mins | Cook: 1hours | Ready in:

Ingredients

- 1 (17.5 ounce) package frozen puff pastry, thawed
- 1 cup fresh spinach, cleaned and stemmed
- 4 tablespoons water
- 1/4 teaspoon ground nutmeg
- 1 onion, chopped
- 2 tablespoons butter
- 5 eggs
- 1 cup cottage cheese
- 1 cup shredded Cheddar cheese
- salt and pepper to taste
- 2 tomatoes, thinly sliced

Direction

- Turn on the oven at 400°F (200°C) to preheat. Spray non-sticking cooling oil on a quiche dish.
- Line puff pastry on the quiche dish, press firmly to make the pastry in place and trim away the excess. Blind bake about 10 minutes.
- Put spinach and 4 tablespoons of water in a large skillet. Boil the mixture over medium heat and cover the skillet. Cook until the spinach is already, about 2 minutes and let drain. Put nutmeg into the spinach and purée the mixture.
- Sauté the onion with butter (or margarine) in a skillet to taste. Sauté until the onions are tender and transparent.
- Beat eggs in a medium mixing bowl. Whisk in 1/2 cup of cheese, spinach, and the cottage cheese. Flavor with salt and pepper. At the base of the pastry-lined quiche dish, place in the onions. Put the tomatoes over the onions. Transfer the egg-mixture to the onions and tomatoes; on the top, sprinkle with the cheese left.

- Bake at 350°F (175°C) until firm in the middle, 45-50 minutes. You can enjoy it hot or cold, whatever you like.

Nutrition Information

- Calories: 574 calories;
- Total Carbohydrate: 36.3
- Cholesterol: 161
- Protein: 18.7
- Total Fat: 39.6
- Sodium: 485

248.   Contest Winning Curried Chicken Turnovers

Serving: 2 dozen. | Prep: 40mins | Cook: 20mins | Ready in:

Ingredients

- 1/2 cup finely chopped celery
- 1/4 cup finely chopped onion
- 1/4 cup finely chopped carrot
- 2 teaspoons butter
- 1 tablespoon all-purpose flour
- 1-1/2 teaspoons curry powder
- 1/4 teaspoon salt
- 1/2 cup chicken broth
- 1-1/2 cups diced cooked chicken
- 1/4 cup sour cream
- 1/4 cup plain yogurt
- 1 package (17.3 ounces) frozen puff pastry, thawed
- 1 egg yolk
- 1 teaspoon water

Direction

- In a big pan, sauté onion, carrot and celery in butter until tender, about 4 to 6 minutes. Add in the flour, salt and curry powder. Mix to blend well. Pour broth and cook to a boil. Continue cooking and stirring for another minute until sauce thickens. Take the pan from heat then mix in sour cream, yogurt and the chicken.

- Spread out pastry sheet on a lightly floured work area. Roll into a rectangle, creating a 12-in. by 10-in. dimension. Using a floured 3-inch round cookie cutter, carve out 12 rounds from each rectangle pastry sheet. Scoop 2 teaspoons of the chicken mixture and place on one side of each round. Use water to dampen the edges then fold dough over filling. Seal edges by pressing with a fork.
- On a greased baking sheet, arrange the rounds 1 in. apart. Beat water and egg yolk together in a small bowl. Brush pastry with the egg wash. Bake for 17 to 20 minutes at 400°F or until golden brown. Serve while it's still warm.

Nutrition Information

- Calories: 132 calories
- Sodium: 127mg sodium
- Fiber: 2g fiber)
- Total Carbohydrate: 12g carbohydrate (0 sugars
- Cholesterol: 19mg cholesterol
- Protein: 4g protein.
- Total Fat: 7g fat (2g saturated fat)

---

249. Corned Beef Hash & Egg Pastry Squares

Serving: 4 | Prep: 30mins | Cook: 40mins | Ready in:

Ingredients

- 1 sheet frozen puff pastry
- 1 (15 ounce) can HORMEL® Mary Kitchen® Corned Beef Hash
- 1 cup shredded Swiss cheese, divided
- 4 large eggs
- salt and pepper to taste
- 2 chopped green onions
- Sriracha hot chili sauce (optional)

Direction

- Thaw the puff pastry sheet for 30 minutes at room temperature, or until it is workable yet still cold.
- Set the oven to 400°F (200°C) for preheating. Use the parchment paper to line the baking sheet.
- Set the large skillet over medium-high heat. Add the corned beef hash. Cook and stir the mixture for 15 minutes, breaking the larger pieces down, or until the hash starts to crisp up and the fat is rendered. Spread the mixture out, and then transfer them onto a paper towel-lined plate.
- Unroll the puff pastry onto the second sheet of parchment paper dusted lightly with flour. Roll out it to form an 11x11-inches square. Cut it into four 5 1/2 x 5 1/2-inches square pieces.
- Arrange the squares onto the prepared baking sheet. Make sure that the squares are not touching to each other. Use a fork to prick the middle of each square a few times. Let them bake inside the preheated oven for 10 minutes until the pastry has puffed in the center. Press the center of each pastry down gently, leave some small puffed border around its edges.
- Distribute the corned beef between the pastry squares, making sure that you leave a 1/2-inch border. Top each with 1/4 cup of Swiss cheese. Form a slight well in the center of the toppings for the eggs.
- Crack the egg carefully into the square's center, and then sprinkle it with pepper and salt.
- Bake for 12-15 minutes, or until the eggs are cooked according to your desired doneness.
- Sprinkle chopped green onions on top. Before serving, drizzle them with siracha sauce.

Nutrition Information

- Calories: 676 calories;
- Total Fat: 45.4
- Sodium: 765
- Total Carbohydrate: 41

- Cholesterol: 236
- Protein: 25.8

- Cholesterol: 15
- Protein: 4.9
- Total Fat: 14.3
- Sodium: 119
- Total Carbohydrate: 13.2

250. Crabby Cliff's Mushroom Puffs

Serving: 18 | Prep: 20mins | Cook: 20mins | Ready in:

Ingredients

- 2 tablespoons olive oil
- 3 cups fresh chopped mushrooms
- 2 green onions, chopped
- 1 clove garlic, crushed
- 1/2 teaspoon ground cayenne pepper
- 4 ounces cream cheese, softened
- 1 (6 ounce) can crabmeat, drained and flaked
- 1 (17.5 ounce) package frozen puff pastry sheets, thawed

Direction

- Prepare the oven by preheating to 400°F (200°C).
- Heat olive oil in a medium saucepan set over medium heat. Place in the cayenne pepper, garlic, green onions, and mushrooms then stir. Cook for 10 minutes, or until softened. Place the mushroom mixture into a medium bowl. Mix in the crabmeat and cream cheese.
- Roll each pastry sheet into a 12x12-inch square on a lightly floured flat surface. Slice each sheet into nine 4x4-inch squares. Put 1 tablespoon of the mushroom mixture onto each pastry square. Then fold the squares by bringing the corners to the middle, making an X. Transfer the squares to a medium baking sheet.
- Bake in the preheated oven for 20 minutes, or until golden brown.

Nutrition Information

- Calories: 199 calories;

251. Cranberry Brie Bites

Serving: 24 | Prep: 15mins | Cook: 18mins | Ready in:

Ingredients

- 1 (8 ounce) round Brie cheese, rind removed
- cooking spray
- 1 sheet frozen puff pastry, thawed
- 1/2 cup cranberry sauce
- 1/3 cup finely chopped walnuts
- sea salt to taste

Direction

- Freeze Brie cheese for 20 minutes. With cooking spray, coat a miniature muffin pan.
- Unroll a puff pastry sheet into a rectangle, 10x14-inch in size. Slice sheet lengthwise into four equal strips and crosswise into six equal strips; it should yield 24 squares. Distribute and gently press them into muffin cups.
- Slice chilled Brie cheese into 3/4-inch 2 dozen portions. To every muffin cup lined with pastry, put a teaspoon cranberry sauce; push in a piece of Brie and put a teaspoon of chopped walnuts on top. Scatter sea salt over bites. Refrigerate for a minimum of half an hour up to 3 days.
- Preheat an oven to 200 °C or 400 °F.
- In the prepped oven, bake the bites for 18 to 20 minutes till golden brown.

Nutrition Information

- Calories: 106 calories;
- Total Fat: 7.5
- Sodium: 99

- Total Carbohydrate: 7
- Cholesterol: 9
- Protein: 2.9

252. Cranberry Grapefruit Cheese Tarts With Zesty Thyme And Pink Peppercorn Sprinkles

Serving: 6 | Prep: 20mins | Cook: 1hours5mins | Ready in:

Ingredients

- Jam:
- 1 cup Ocean Spray® Craisins® Dried Cranberries
- 1 cup finely chopped fresh grapefruit
- 3/4 cup Ocean Spray® 100% Ruby Red Grapefruit Juice
- 1 cup granulated sugar
- 1/2 teaspoon roughly chopped fresh thyme leaves
- 1/2 teaspoon coarsely ground pink peppercorns
- 1/2 teaspoon ground ginger
- For Assembling:
- 2 sheets frozen puff pastry, thawed
- 3 1/2 ounces crumbled goat cheese
- Glaze:
- 2 ounces mascarpone cheese
- 1 cup powdered sugar
- 3 tablespoons heavy cream
- 1/2 teaspoon vanilla extract
- Garnishes:
- Grapefruit zest
- Chopped fresh thyme leaves
- Coarsely ground pink peppercorns

Direction

- Whisk together all jam ingredients in a medium saucepan over medium heat. Bring to a simmer, then lower the heat in order to keep at a gently simmer. Cook for 35 to 40 minutes or until mixture reaches the consistency of a thin jam. The jam will be more thick when cooling. Set aside for 20 to 25 minutes until completely cooled.
- Set the oven to 375°F and start preheating. Line parchment paper on a large baking sheet. Unroll 1 puff pastry sheet and cut into 3 sections along the lines. Cut each segments in half in order to form 6 rectangles. Spread cooled jam on top of each rectangle to about 1/2 inch from the edges. Add goat cheese on top. Lightly brush water on edges.
- Cut the remaining puff pastry sheet in the same manner and arrange one on top of each filled rectangle. Use the side of a fork to seal the pastry by pressing down the edges gently and crimping edges with tines.
- It's fine if some jam spilled out, but try to avoid it if possible. Bake for 25 to 30 minutes in preheated oven or until the bottoms of pastry is no longer doughy and pastry is golden brown in color. Cool for 5 minutes on the baking sheet, then transfer to a wire rack, allow to rest on wire rack for about 35 minutes until completely cooled.
- Whisk all glaze ingredients together. Spread on each pastry a thin layer. Add couple pinches of peppercorns, thyme, and grapefruit zest on top.

Nutrition Information

- Calories: 894 calories;
- Sodium: 296
- Total Carbohydrate: 115.1
- Cholesterol: 35
- Protein: 10.5
- Total Fat: 42.7

253. Cream Cheese Puff Pastry

Serving: 12 | Prep: 20mins | Cook: 20mins | Ready in:

Ingredients

- cooking spray
- 1 sheet frozen puff pastry, thawed
- 1 (8 ounce) package cream cheese, softened
- 1 egg, beaten

Direction

- Preheat the oven to 175 degrees C (350 degrees F). Gently grease the baking sheet using cooking spray.
- Halve the thawed puff pastry sheet. Chop each half into six small square pieces. Add one spoonful of the cream cheese onto one side of each square piece. Fold over diagonally to have the triangular shape. Use the water to brush the edges and press to seal up.
- Move the pastries into prepped baking sheet. Brush the beaten egg on the top of pastries to add shine.
- Bake in preheated oven for roughly 20 minutes or till the top turns golden.

Nutrition Information

- Calories: 181 calories;
- Protein: 3.3
- Total Fat: 14.5
- Sodium: 110
- Total Carbohydrate: 9.6
- Cholesterol: 34

254.   Crispy Bacon Twists With Gouda And Apricot Preserves

Serving: 15 | Prep: 20mins | Cook: 45mins | Ready in:

Ingredients

- 2 sheets frozen puff pastry dough, thawed
- 1 egg, beaten
- 1 cup apricot preserves or your favorite flavor
- 2 cups shredded Gouda cheese
- 2 tablespoons chopped fresh rosemary leaves

- 2 pounds Smithfield® Hometown Original Bacon
- Flour for dusting
- Nonstick cooking spray

Direction

- Preheat the oven to 375 ° F. Line foil on 2 rimmed baking pans, in the pans, place the baking racks, and with nonstick spray, slightly coat racks.
- Unroll a sheet of puff pastry on slightly floured area into about 8 by 12-inch. Lightly brush beaten egg on top and thinly scatter top of dough with half-cup of preserves. Evenly sprinkle with a tablespoon of rosemary and a cup shredded cheese, slightly forcing mixture of cheese into the dough. Fold dough short end on top to seal the mixture of cheese and slightly roll to enclose. Slice short-wise into about 15 half-inch strips. Redo with the rest of ingredients and puff pastry.
- Spread out a bacon slice on diagonal. Hold a strip of prepped dough by ends and put a dough strip end horizontally on top of bacon end and with dough downward, roll the bacon, expanding strip of dough as you roll. On prepped rack, put finished spiral-wrapped bacon twist and redo.
- Let twists bake for 35 to 45 minutes or till bacon crisp and pastry turn browned, turning pans as necessary for equal cooking. Cool for 5 minutes and take twists off racks gently with spatula. Serve at room temperature or while warm.

Nutrition Information

- Calories: 640 calories;
- Sodium: 1261
- Total Carbohydrate: 29.5
- Cholesterol: 94
- Protein: 24.2
- Total Fat: 47.2

255.　　Crispy Cheese Twists

Serving: 24 | Prep: | Cook: | Ready in:

Ingredients

- 1/2 cup Parmesan cheese
- 3/4 teaspoon ground black pepper
- 1/2 teaspoon garlic powder
- 1 (17.5 ounce) package frozen puff pastry, thawed
- 1 egg white

Direction

- Mix the garlic powder, pepper and parmesan cheese. Unfold the pastry sheets on the cutting board. Use the egg white to brush them slightly; drizzle each sheet with a quarter of cheese mixture. Gently press into the pastry, flip; repeat the process. Chop each sheet into 12 (1-in.) strips; twist them.
- Add onto the ungreased cookie sheet and bake in 175 degrees C (350 degrees F) oven till turning golden brown or for 15 minutes.

Nutrition Information

- Calories: 121 calories;
- Total Fat: 8.3
- Sodium: 79
- Total Carbohydrate: 9.4
- Cholesterol: 1
- Protein: 2.3

256.　　Curry Chicken Pot Pie With Puff Pastry Crust

Serving: 8 | Prep: 10mins | Cook: 50mins | Ready in:

Ingredients

- 1 (17.25 ounce) package frozen puff pastry, thawed
- 4 cups frozen mixed vegetables
- 1 tablespoon canola oil, or more as needed
- 1 1/2 cups low-sodium chicken broth
- 1/2 cup milk
- 3 tablespoons butter, divided
- 1 cup chopped onion, or to taste
- 1 cup chopped celery
- 3 tablespoons all-purpose flour
- 1 teaspoon curry powder
- 2 tablespoons dried parsley
- 1 teaspoon salt
- 1/2 teaspoon ground black pepper
- 2 cups cubed cooked chicken

Direction

- Start preheating the oven to 200°C (400°F).
- Unroll the puff pastry onto a flat work surface and slice it into 6-8 circles.
- In a bowl, toss the canola oil and the frozen vegetables and evenly spread onto a rimmed baking sheet.
- Bake for about 15-20 minutes in the preheated oven until the vegetables become golden brown. Take it out of the oven. Do not turn off the oven. Line the aluminum foil onto a shallow baking pan.
- In a saucepan, heat the milk and broth on medium heat.
- In a saucepan, melt 1 tbsp. of butter on medium heat. Put in celery and onion, cook while stirring for about 5 minutes until it becomes translucent.
- Whisk the remaining 2 tbsp. of butter into the celery mixture; cook while stirring for about 3-5 minutes until the water is evaporated. Put in curry and flour, stir for about 1-2 minutes until combined. Pour in the hot milk mixture, stir for about 6-8 minutes until thickened. Put in pepper, salt, and parsley. Toss in the chicken and the browned vegetables. Add the mixture to the prepared baking pan. Add the puff pastry circles on top.
- Bake for about 25 minutes in the preheated oven until the mixture is hot and bubbly and the puff pastry is browned.

Nutrition Information

- Calories: 516 calories;
- Total Fat: 32.4
- Sodium: 558
- Total Carbohydrate: 39.4
- Cholesterol: 40
- Protein: 17.5

257. Curry Root Vegetable Pot Pie

Serving: 8 | Prep: 20mins | Cook: 40mins | Ready in:

Ingredients

- 1 3/4 cups sweet potato, peeled and cut into 2-inch chunks
- 1 3/4 cups red potatoes, peeled and cut into 2-inch chunks
- 1 3/4 cups parsnips, peeled and cut into 2-inch chunks
- 1 3/4 cups carrots, peeled and cut into 2-inch chunks
- 2 tablespoons olive oil
- sea salt and ground black pepper to taste
- 1 tablespoon butter
- 1 cup chopped onion
- 2 tablespoons butter
- 1 1/2 cups vegetable broth
- 1/2 cup whole milk
- 3 tablespoons all-purpose flour
- 1 1/2 teaspoons curry powder, or more to taste
- 1 (17.25 ounce) package frozen puff pastry, thawed and cut into four 5-inch squares

Direction

- Preheat an oven to 200°C or 400°F.
- In roasting pan, put carrots, parsnips, red potatoes and sweet potato. Toss along with the olive oil; add black pepper and sea salt to season.
- In the preheated oven, roast sweet potato mixture for 20 minutes to half an hour till vegetables are softened slightly.
- In a pot, heat a tablespoon of butter over moderate heat; cook and mix onion for 3 to 5 minutes till softened slightly. Put 2 additional tablespoons of butter and sweet potato mixture; add black pepper and salt to season. Cook and mix for 2 to 3 minutes till butter is liquified.
- In another saucepan over moderate heat, heat milk and vegetable broth together till mixture is nearly at a boil.
- Mix curry powder and flour into the sweet potato mixture till equally coated. Slowly add broth mixture into the sweet potato mixture; mix for 3 minutes till liquid thickens. Distribute the mixture to 4 pot pie dishes. Put a puff pastry square on top of each.
- Bake in the preheated oven until pastry is golden brown and puffed, 17 to 20 minutes.

Nutrition Information

- Calories: 518 calories;
- Total Carbohydrate: 52.5
- Cholesterol: 13
- Protein: 7.4
- Total Fat: 31.6
- Sodium: 356

258. Deconstructed French Onion Soup Tartlet

Serving: 4 | Prep: 10mins | Cook: 30mins | Ready in:

Ingredients

- 2 tablespoons olive oil
- 2 tablespoons butter
- 1 large white onion, sliced
- 1 clove garlic, minced
- 1/4 cup white wine
- 1/2 cup beef broth

- 1 teaspoon dried thyme
- 1/2 teaspoon kosher salt (such as Diamond Crystal®)
- 1/4 teaspoon ground black pepper
- 1 sheet puff pastry
- 1/2 cup grated Parmesan cheese
- 1 cup shredded mozzarella cheese

Direction

- Preheat the oven to 200 ° C or 400 ° F.
- In skillet on moderately-high heat, heat together the butter and olive oil for 2 to 3 minutes till butter melts. In hot oil mixture, sauté garlic and onion for 15 to 20 minutes, till onion starts to caramelize.
- Add white wine on top of onion mixture; simmer and cook for 2 minutes, till aromatic. Put in the thyme and beef broth; cook till liquid cooks down by half. Add black pepper and kosher salt in mixture to season.
- Clip puff pastry and suit into one tart pan. Score rim through the pastry edge. Using fork, prick the middle of pastry. Scatter the mixture of onion on top of pastry; put mozzarella cheese and Parmesan cheese on top.
- In prepped oven, bake for 15 to 20 minutes, till crust turn golden brown.

Nutrition Information

- Calories: 590 calories;
- Protein: 16
- Total Fat: 43
- Sodium: 860
- Total Carbohydrate: 32.8
- Cholesterol: 42

259.   Easy 3 Ingredient Cheese Pinwheels

Serving: 24 | Prep: 15mins | Cook: 15mins | Ready in:

Ingredients

- 1/2 (17.5 ounce) package frozen puff pastry, thawed
- 1 (8 ounce) container cream cheese with herbs
- 6 ounces sliced Swiss cheese

Direction

- Preheat oven to 190°C/375°F. Line parchment paper on a baking sheet.
- On a lightly floured flat work surface, roll out the puff pastry into a rectangle. Thinly spread herbed cream cheese over the pastry. Top with slices of Swiss cheese; leave a margin of 1-inch. Tightly roll up the pastry.
- Slice 1/4-inch-thick slices from the roll. Place slices on the prepared baking sheet.
- Bake for 15 to 20 minutes on the center rack of the oven, or until puffed and lightly browned.

Nutrition Information

- Calories: 116 calories;
- Total Fat: 8.9
- Sodium: 93
- Total Carbohydrate: 5.6
- Cholesterol: 16
- Protein: 3

260.   Easy Apple Strudel

Serving: 6 | Prep: 30mins | Cook: 40mins | Ready in:

Ingredients

- 1 Granny Smith apple - peeled, cored and coarsely shredded
- 3 Granny Smith apples - peeled, cored and sliced
- 1 cup brown sugar
- 1 cup golden raisins
- 1 sheet frozen puff pastry, thawed
- 1 egg
- 1/4 cup milk

Direction

- Preheat an oven to 200°C/400°F; line parchment paper on a baking sheet.
- Put apples in a big bowl. Mix in golden raisins and brown sugar and put aside. Put puff pastry onto baking sheet then lightly roll using a rolling pin. Put apple filling lengthwise down center of pastry; lengthwise fold pastry around mixture. Use a little water on your fingers to seal pastry edges then rub pastry edges together. Whisk milk and egg, brushing over pastry.
- In preheated oven, bake till golden brown for 35-40 minutes.

Nutrition Information

- Calories: 501 calories;
- Sodium: 130
- Total Carbohydrate: 87.9
- Cholesterol: 32
- Protein: 5.6
- Total Fat: 16.5

261.   Easy As Chicken Pot Pie

Serving: 6 | Prep: 20mins | Cook: 50mins | Ready in:

Ingredients

- 1 sheet frozen puff pastry, thawed
- 1 1/3 cups frozen peas and carrots
- 2/3 cup frozen corn kernels
- 2 tablespoons butter
- 1/4 cup all-purpose flour
- 2 cups milk
- 1 teaspoon crumbled dried thyme, or to taste
- 2 cups diced cooked chicken
- salt and ground black pepper to taste

Direction

- Preheat the oven to 190 ° C or 375 ° F.

- Cut puff pastry with pizza cutter to 8 even-sized strips. Make square lattice by weaving strips and put on an oiled baking sheet.
- In prepped oven, bake for 10 to 15 minutes, till it barely begins to brown. Take out of oven and reserve.
- In a microwavable bowl, put corn, carrots and frozen peas and in microwave, cook for 5 to 10 minutes, till cooked yet remain firm.
- In skillet, liquify butter on moderate heat. Mix in flour and let cook for a minute. Add in milk and stir while cooking, mix till mixture become smooth. Put in thyme and keep cooking till mixture thickens. Mix in chicken and cooked vegetables. Add pepper and salt to season. Cook for 5 to 7 minutes, till heated completely, mixing often.
- Into one 2-quarts baking dish, add the mixture of chicken. Lay pastry lattice over. In the prepped oven, bake for 10 to 15 minutes, till crust turn golden brown.

Nutrition Information

- Calories: 435 calories;
- Total Carbohydrate: 33.6
- Cholesterol: 52
- Protein: 20.7
- Total Fat: 24.6
- Sodium: 217

262.   Easy Chicken Quiche

Serving: 8 | Prep: 15mins | Cook: 35mins | Ready in:

Ingredients

- cooking spray
- 1 frozen puff pastry - thawed, unfolded, and lightly rolled
- 1 tablespoon Dijon mustard
- 1 tablespoon butter
- 1 cup chopped green onions
- 2 cloves garlic, chopped

- 1 1/2 cups chopped cooked chicken
- 3 eggs
- 1 1/2 cups heavy cream
- 1 teaspoon salt
- 1/2 teaspoon nutmeg
- 1/2 teaspoon ground black pepper
- 1/2 teaspoon Italian seasoning
- 2 cups shredded Gouda cheese

Direction

- Preheat oven to 375°F (190°C). Coat a 9-inch pie dish using cooking spray.
- Line puff pastry all over the sides and bottom of the prepared pie dish. Cut off any excess pastry. Brush Dijon mustard over the bottom of the crust.
- In a saucepan, melt butter over medium heat. Put chopped green onion in melted butter and cook for about 5 minutes until tender. Add garlic; cook for 1 minute more. Stir in chicken; cook for another minute.
- In a bowl, stir together Italian seasoning, ground black pepper, nutmeg, salt, heavy cream, and eggs.
- Sprinkle half of the Gouda cheese in a layer over the pastry and place chicken mixture over. Stream in egg mixture. Sprinkle top with the remainder of Gouda cheese.
- Bake quiche for about 25 minutes in the preheated oven until firm and golden.

Nutrition Information

- Calories: 520 calories;
- Total Carbohydrate: 17.4
- Cholesterol: 180
- Protein: 20.2
- Total Fat: 41.4
- Sodium: 727

263. Easy English Quiche Lorraine

Serving: 4 | Prep: 10mins | Cook: 50mins |Ready in:

Ingredients

- 1 sheet frozen puff pastry, thawed
- 1 cup milk
- 3 eggs
- 1/4 cup frozen chopped spinach, thawed and drained
- salt and ground black pepper to taste
- 1 cup shredded Swiss cheese
- 3/4 cup chopped cooked ham
- 1 small tomato, sliced (optional)

Direction

- Preheat the oven at 230°C (450°F). Press down puff pastry sheet to the sides and the bottom of an 8-inch pie plate or a shallow casserole dish.
- In a bowl, whisk pepper, salt, spinach, eggs, and milk. For the pastry crust in the plate, spread cheese lightly; scatter the surface with ham. Add egg mixture on top of the ham and top with the remaining cheese. Place tomato slices on the cheese.
- Bake in the prepared oven for 20 minutes. Lower the temperature to 175°C (350°F) and keep on baking for 30 minutes more or when the crust is browned.

Nutrition Information

- Calories: 611 calories;
- Sodium: 663
- Total Carbohydrate: 33.4
- Cholesterol: 189
- Protein: 25.3
- Total Fat: 41.8

264. Easy Pumpkin Turnovers

Serving: 18 | Prep: 30mins | Cook: 15mins | Ready in:

Ingredients

- 1 cup canned pumpkin
- 1/4 cup brown sugar
- 2 teaspoons ground cinnamon
- 2 teaspoons pumpkin pie spice
- 2 sheets frozen puff pastry, thawed

Direction

- Set the oven to 175°C or 350°F. Take 2 baking sheets and line them with parchment paper.
- In a bowl, combine pumpkin pie spice, pumpkin, cinnamon, and brown sugar.
- Roll the puff pastry out into a 12-in by 12-in square and cut nine 4-in squares out of each sheet.
- Using a spoon to proportion and place the pumpkin mixture in the middle of the pastry squares; dab water on the square's edges then fold from corner to cover. Secure by pinching the edges together; arrange on the parchment-lined baking sheets.
- Bake for 15mins in the preheated oven until the pastry is golden brown and puffed. Let cool for 10mins on the pans then move to a wire rack; completely cool.

Nutrition Information

- Calories: 165 calories;
- Total Fat: 10.3
- Sodium: 100
- Total Carbohydrate: 16.5
- Cholesterol: 0
- Protein: 2.1

265. Easy Spinach And Gouda Cheese Quiche

Serving: 8 | Prep: 15mins | Cook: 35mins | Ready in:

Ingredients

- cooking spray
- 1 (17.5 ounce) package frozen puff pastry, thawed
- 1 tablespoon Dijon mustard
- 1 tablespoon butter
- 1 cup chopped green onions
- 2 cloves garlic, chopped
- 4 cups fresh spinach
- 1 1/2 cups heavy cream
- 3 eggs
- 1 teaspoon salt
- 1/2 teaspoon nutmeg
- 1/2 teaspoon ground black pepper
- 1/2 teaspoon Italian seasoning
- 2 cups shredded Gouda cheese

Direction

- Preheat oven to 375°F (190°C). Coat a 9-inch pie dish using cooking spray.
- Line the sides and base of the prepared pie dish with puff pastry. Cut off any excess pastry. Brush Dijon mustard all over the bottom.
- In a saucepan, melt butter over medium heat. Put chopped onions in melted butter, and cook for about 5 minutes until tender. Add garlic; cook for 1 more minute. Stir in spinach; cook for another minute longer.
- In a bowl, combine Italian seasoning, black pepper, nutmeg, salt, eggs, and heavy cream.
- Place half of the Gouda cheese over the puff pastry in a layer; arrange spinach mixture over the cheese. Stream in egg mixture. Sprinkle top with the remainder of Gouda cheese.
- Bake for about 25 minutes in the preheated oven until quiche is set and turns golden.

Nutrition Information

- Calories: 647 calories;
- Total Fat: 51.3
- Sodium: 801
- Total Carbohydrate: 32
- Cholesterol: 161
- Protein: 15.7

- Calories: 280 calories;
- Total Carbohydrate: 41.5
- Cholesterol: 5
- Protein: 2.5
- Total Fat: 11
- Sodium: 199

266.   Eccles Cakes

Serving: 12 | Prep: 20mins | Cook: 15mins | Ready in:

Ingredients

- 1 pound shortdough pastry
- 1/3 cup white sugar
- 2 tablespoons butter
- 3/4 cup currants
- 1 ounce candied mixed citrus peel
- 1/2 teaspoon ground nutmeg
- 1/2 teaspoon ground allspice
- 1 egg white, beaten
- 1/8 cup white sugar

Direction

- Cook 2 tbsp. of butter and 1/3 cup of sugar in a medium saucepan on medium heat till melted. Add allspice, nutmeg, candied peel and currant; keep cooking till heated through. Take off from heat; cool.
- Preheat an oven to 220°C (425°F).
- Roll pastry out to 1/8-in. thick on a lightly floured surface; cut to 4-in. rounds. On middle of every pastry circle, put a small spoonful of filling; draw edges together over fruit then pinch to seal. Flip over; gently press to flatten cakes with a rolling pin.
- In middle of every pastry, create 2 small slash marks or small hole; brush beaten egg white. Sprinkle sugar over; put on a cookie sheet.
- In the preheated oven, bake for 15 minutes or till lightly browned around edges.

Nutrition Information

267.   Elegant Mushroom Pie Recipe

Serving: 8 | Prep: 25mins | Cook: 40mins | Ready in:

Ingredients

- 6 tablespoons butter, divided
- 1 1/2 pounds baby bella (crimini) mushrooms, sliced
- 1/4 cup chopped sweet onion
- 1/2 lemon, juiced
- 1/2 teaspoon dried thyme
- 5 tablespoons all-purpose flour
- 1 1/4 cups Swanson® Chicken Broth
- 1/3 cup Marsala wine
- 2 tablespoons half-and-half
- salt and pepper to taste
- 1 (17.3 ounce) package frozen puff pastry, thawed
- 1 egg, beaten

Direction

- Preheat the oven to 190 ° C or 375 ° F. Using non-fat cooking spray, coat a pie plate, 9-inch in size.
- In a big skillet, liquify 3 tablespoons of butter on moderate heat. Put in onions and mushrooms for 10 minutes, mixing from time to time, till liquid from mushrooms has reduced. Mix in thyme and lemon juice and let simmer for 2 minutes.
- In another saucepan, liquify 3 tablespoons of butter. Mix in flour and mix continuously for a minute. Slowly put in the half-and-half, Swanson(R) Chicken Broth and Marsala, mixing till sauce thickens and become smooth,

for 3 minutes. Sauce must be extremely thick. Season with pepper and salt to taste.

- To sauce broth/Marsala mixture, turn the mixture of mushroom; mix thoroughly.
- Unroll a puff pastry sheet to suit pie plate. Force equally into the pie plate base and sides; clip the extra pastry. Into pastry shell, scoop mixture of mushroom.
- Unroll another puff pastry sheet, and put over. Clip extra, and flute edge to enclose. Make several slits in top for vent. Brush beaten egg on pie top.
- In the prepped oven, bake for 40 minutes, till golden brown and mushroom mixture bubbles. Slightly cool the pie prior to serving.

Nutrition Information

- Calories: 496 calories;
- Total Fat: 33.2
- Sodium: 428
- Total Carbohydrate: 37.2
- Cholesterol: 48
- Protein: 10

268. English Quiche Lorraine

Serving: 4 | Prep: 10mins | Cook: 50mins | Ready in:

Ingredients

- 1 sheet frozen puff pastry, thawed
- 4 slices bacon - cooked and crumbled
- 2 eggs
- 1 cup milk
- 2 cups shredded Swiss cheese
- salt and black pepper to taste
- 1 small tomato, thinly sliced

Direction

- Set oven to 450°F (220°C) to preheat. Fit the puff pastry into the side and bottom of an 8-inch pie plate or shallow casserole dish.

- Beat milk and eggs in a small bowl, using a fork, until incorporated. Season mixture with pepper and salt. Sprinkle Swiss cheese in a thin layer into the bottom of the pastry crust. Top the cheese with crumbled bacon. Stream the egg mixture into the crust and sprinkle top with the remainder of cheese. Place tomato slices all over the top of the quiche.
- Bake for 20 minutes in the preheated oven. Lower temperature to 350°F (175°C). Keep baking until the crust is browned, for 30 minutes longer.

Nutrition Information

- Calories: 761 calories;
- Protein: 34.8
- Total Fat: 53.6
- Sodium: 971
- Total Carbohydrate: 34.4
- Cholesterol: 179

269. Fancy Sammich

Serving: 6 | Prep: 20mins | Cook: 50mins | Ready in:

Ingredients

- 1 1/2 pounds pork tenderloin
- 1/8 cup soy sauce
- 1/4 cup Worcestershire sauce
- 1 lemon, juiced
- salt and pepper to taste
- 1 (17.5 ounce) package frozen puff pastry, thawed

Direction

- Mix well the lemon juice, Worcestershire sauce, and soy sauce in a medium nonporous bowl. Add the pork to the bowl. Flip so that all sides are coated well. Cover and put into the refrigerator for a minimum of 2 hours to marinate.

- Set the oven at 190°C (375°F) to preheat. Arrange the tenderloin in a 9x13 in. baking dish.
- Bake for 20-30 minutes without covering in the preheated oven, until the temperature inside the pork reaches 60°C (140°F).
- Take the pork out of the oven. Drain the liquid from the baking dish and keep to make gravy if you want. Unroll 2 puff pastry sheets and wrap the dough over each tenderloin piece. Seal the edges to completely cover the meat. Put back into the baking dish.
- Bake for 20 minutes in the preheated oven until the pastry becomes golden brown.

Nutrition Information

- Calories: 564 calories;
- Total Carbohydrate: 41.4
- Cholesterol: 49
- Protein: 24
- Total Fat: 33.8
- Sodium: 654

270.   Fish Fillet En Croute

Serving: 4 | Prep: 20mins | Cook: 30mins | Ready in:

Ingredients

- 1 (8 ounce) fillet cod, cut into 2 pieces
- 1 sheet frozen puff pastry, thawed and cut into 2 rectangles
- salt and ground black pepper to taste
- 1/4 cup crumbled feta cheese
- 1/2 (4 ounce) jar roasted red bell peppers, drained and sliced
- 1 sprig fresh thyme, leaves removed
- 1 egg, lightly beaten

Direction

- Preheat the oven to 220 degrees C (425 degrees F). Line a baking sheet using parchment paper.

- Ad each cod fillet piece on one of the puff pastry rectangles and use pepper and salt to season well. Drizzle thyme leaves, roasted red peppers, and half of the feta cheese to each fish fillet. Fold pastry over the fish and pinch edges together to form a pouch. Use beaten egg to brush top and place in the prepped baking sheet.
- Bake in the preheated oven for roughly half an hour till fish could be easily flaked using a fork and puff pastry becomes golden brown.

Nutrition Information

- Calories: 442 calories;
- Total Fat: 28
- Sodium: 473
- Total Carbohydrate: 28.7
- Cholesterol: 81
- Protein: 18.4

271.   Fish Wellington

Serving: 4 | Prep: 30mins | Cook: 25mins | Ready in:

Ingredients

- 1 (1 pound) fillet cod
- 1/4 cup butter
- 2 tablespoons chopped onion
- 2 3/4 cups fresh mushrooms, chopped
- salt and black pepper to taste
- 4 1/2 ounces smoked salmon pate
- 2 tablespoons heavy cream
- 1 sheet frozen puff pastry, thawed
- 1 egg, beaten

Direction

- Preheat oven to 220 degrees C (425 degrees F). Halve cod fillet horizontally to yield two thin slices; put aside.
- Melt butter on medium heat in a skillet. Mix in mushrooms and onion and cook for 3 to 5

minutes till tender. Use pepper and salt to season; put aside to cool down a bit.

- Blend the cream and pate in a medium-sized bowl. Stir in mushrooms and onions.
- Roll out the pastry to have 12x14 in. rectangle on a surface that is floured a bit. Put 1 cod fillet slice in the middle of the rectangle. Spread with half of the pate mixture and layer with the other piece of fillet. Spread leftover pate mixture over. Fold pastry edges over the filling towards the middle, and use egg to seal. Brush pastry on every side using egg.
- Bake till becomes golden brown for 25 minutes in the preheated oven. Serve while still warm.

Nutrition Information

- Calories: 602 calories;
- Protein: 29.6
- Total Fat: 40.6
- Sodium: 382
- Total Carbohydrate: 30.3
- Cholesterol: 138

272. Flaky Cinnamon Cookies

Serving: 18 | Prep: | Cook: | Ready in:

Ingredients

- 1 (17.5 ounce) package frozen puff pastry, thawed
- 1/4 cup ground cinnamon
- 1/4 cup packed brown sugar

Direction

- Start preheating the oven at 400°F (200°C).
- In a small bowl, mix sugar and cinnamon. Roll out each pastry sheet and dust the sugar mixture evenly over the surface. Roll up the sheet the long way, and cut into 15 slices. Arrange on a cookie sheet and bake in the prepared oven in 15 minutes.

Nutrition Information

- Calories: 165 calories;
- Total Carbohydrate: 16.5
- Cholesterol: 0
- Protein: 2.1
- Total Fat: 10.4
- Sodium: 69

273. French Vanilla Slices (Mille Feuilles)

Serving: 8 | Prep: 30mins | Cook: | Ready in:

Ingredients

- 2 cups milk
- 7 1/2 tablespoons all-purpose flour
- 1 whole vanilla bean
- 3/4 cup castor sugar or superfine sugar
- 1 pinch salt
- 6 egg yolks
- 1 1/2 (17.5 ounce) packages frozen puff pastry
- 1/2 cup apricot preserves (optional)
- confectioners' sugar for dusting

Direction

- In the small-sized saucepan, heat the milk till forming the small bubbles. Drop in the vanilla pod, take the saucepan out of the heat, and put aside to let it cool down till just warm. In the medium-sized saucepan, mix egg yolks, salt, and sugar and flour together. Whip for a while, and then slowly stir in the warm milk. Let it simmer on medium low heat till the custard becomes thick, mixing continuously using a wooden spoon to avoid sticking. Move the custard into the bowl, and let it cool down, mixing from time to time.
- Preheat the oven to 200 degrees C (400 degrees F). Roll out the puff pastry into one sheet that is roughly half an in. in thickness; this should be the same size as the 17x14 in. baking sheet.

- Add pastry on the baking sheet, and prick all over using a fork.
- Bake in the preheated oven for 28 minutes. Take out of the oven, and let the pastry cool down on the baking sheet.
- Once the pastry has cooled down totally, move it out of the baking sheet to the hard surface, and chop in lengthwise into three 4-5 in. in width strips. Spread 1 strip thickly along with custard. Add the second strip directly on top of the first strip; spread top equally with the jam. Use third strip to cover, and dust with the confectioners' sugar. Using a very sharp knife, chop into 8 rectangle pieces.

Nutrition Information

- Calories: 753 calories;
- Cholesterol: 159
- Protein: 11.5
- Total Fat: 39.6
- Sodium: 266
- Total Carbohydrate: 88.4

---

274. Fresh Fruit Frangipane Tart

Serving: 8 | Prep: 30mins | Cook: 45mins | Ready in:

Ingredients

- For the Tart:
- 3 puff pastry rectangles
- For the Filling:
- 1 1/2 tablespoons butter, softened
- 1/3 cup white sugar
- 1 tablespoon white sugar
- 1 large egg
- 3/4 cup almond flour
- 1/4 teaspoon fine salt
- 1/8 teaspoon vanilla extract
- 1/4 teaspoon almond extract (optional)
- 3 pluots, or to taste
- For the Glaze:

- 3 tablespoons apricot jam (optional)
- 2 teaspoons water (optional)

Direction

- Preheat an oven to 200 °C or 400 °F.
- On a silicone mat-lined-baking-sheet or parchment paper, put a puff pastry piece. Slightly dampen using water one of short edges. Connect moistened edge to the end of other puff pastry. Press pieces together to create a long rectangle, clipping off loose ends using dough scraper as necessary.
- Slice the 3rd piece of puff pastry lengthwise to make an-inch strips. Using finger, dampen outer edges of the long rectangle; stick pastry strips over. Poke shallow holes on the entire bottom of dough with a fork. Avoid pricking the lifted border.
- In the prepped oven, let the pastry shell bake for 15 minutes till it begins to become golden brown. Take out of oven. Lower oven heat to 190 °C or 375 °F. Reset the borders and using flat side of fork, force the bottom down. Allow to cool fully while making the filling.
- In a bowl, put 1/3 cup plus a tablespoon of sugar and butter; with spatula, smear together till incorporated. Beat in egg till mixture becomes creamy. Put in almond extract, vanilla extract, salt and almond flour. Combine well. Slice every pluot to make 6 wedges. With almond paste, fill pastry shell. Snugly stick pluots into the filling but not too deeply.
- In the prepped oven, bake for 30 to 40 minutes till browned and almond filling is firm. Turn tart out onto a wire rack and allow to cool fully for a minimum of 40 minutes.
- In a microwave-safe bowl, mix together water and apricot jam. Boil in microwave. Allow to cool till warm. Brush cooled tart with glaze.

Nutrition Information

- Calories: 329 calories;
- Sodium: 204
- Total Carbohydrate: 36.7

- Cholesterol: 29
- Protein: 4.1
- Total Fat: 18.8

---

275.   Greek Pumpkin Pie

Serving: 6 | Prep: 30mins | Cook: 30mins | Ready in:

Ingredients

- 2 (15 ounce) cans pumpkin puree
- 3/4 cup white sugar
- 1 cup raisins
- 1 cup fine semolina
- 1/2 teaspoon ground cinnamon
- 1/4 teaspoon ground cloves
- 1/8 teaspoon ground nutmeg
- 2 sheets frozen puff pastry, thawed
- 1 egg, slightly beaten

Direction

- Preheat the oven to 175 °C or 350 °F.
- Oil a rimmed baking sheet.
- In a skillet over medium heat, heat pumpkin puree, mixing from time to time till puree is thick and most of liquid has vaporized. Mix in nutmeg, cloves, cinnamon, semolina, raisins and sugar. Take off from heat.
- Line the prepared baking sheet with one puff pastry sheet. Scatter pumpkin mixture on top of pastry and cover with the rest of the pastry sheet. With beaten egg, brush the top of puff pastry.
- In the prepped oven, bake for 30 to 40 minutes till golden brown.

Nutrition Information

- Calories: 773 calories;
- Sodium: 557
- Total Carbohydrate: 112.4
- Cholesterol: 31
- Protein: 12.8

- Total Fat: 32.3

---

276.   Guinness® Steak Pie

Serving: 4 | Prep: 25mins | Cook: 45mins | Ready in:

Ingredients

- 1 tablespoon butter
- 1/2 pound beef shoulder steak, cubed
- 1 small sweet potato, diced
- 2 carrots, sliced
- 2 red potatoes, diced
- 1/2 yellow onion, diced
- 1/2 teaspoon garlic powder
- ground black pepper to taste
- 1 cup Irish stout beer (such as Guinness®)
- 1 (.75 ounce) packet dry brown gravy mix
- 1/2 teaspoon garlic powder
- 1/4 teaspoon dried thyme
- 1/2 (17.5 ounce) package frozen puff pastry, thawed

Direction

- Set the oven to 190°C or 375°F to preheat.
- On high heat, heat a big skillet then put yellow onion, red potatoes, carrots, sweet potato, beef cubes and butter into hot skillet. Sprinkle 1/2 tsp. of garlic powder and black pepper over meat and vegetables. Cook and stir for 10 minutes, until all sides of meat turn brown. Remove meat and vegetables to a 1-qt. baking dish.
- In a saucepan, whisk together black pepper, thyme, 1/2 tsp. of garlic powder, brown gravy mix and beer on moderate heat. Bring mixture to a simmer, then turn heat to low and cook for 5 minutes while whisking continuously, until sauce thickens. Drizzle vegetables and meat with sauce.
- Trim puff pastry to fit the top of baking dish and use pastry to cover the dish.
- In the preheated oven, bake for 45-50 minutes

until the filling is bubbly and puff pastry turns deep golden brown.

Nutrition Information

- Calories: 562 calories;
- Total Fat: 33.2
- Sodium: 486
- Total Carbohydrate: 48.8
- Cholesterol: 34
- Protein: 13.6

277.   Hasselback Pear Tart

Serving: 8 | Prep: 20mins | Cook: 35mins | Ready in:

Ingredients

- 1 sheet frozen puff pastry - thawed, unfolded, and lightly rolled
- 2 Bartlett pears, halved and cored
- 2 d'Anjou pears, halved and cored
- 1 red pear, halved and cored
- 2 tablespoons white sugar
- 1/2 lemon, juiced
- 1/2 (8 ounce) package cream cheese, softened
- 1/2 cup confectioners' sugar
- 1/2 teaspoon vanilla extract
- 1 tablespoon turbinado sugar

Direction

- Preheat the oven to 200 degrees C (400 degrees F). Fit the puff pastry into one 10-in. square tart pan with the removable sides.
- Add one pear half, with the cut-side facing downward, onto the working surface. Add one chopstick above and one below pear half, so pear is framed on top and bottom. Thinly chop pear half lengthwise, stopping when knife hits chopstick and leaving bottom a quarter in. of pear intact. Repeat the process with the rest of pear halves.

- Add the hasselbacked pears into the bowl; put in the lemon juice and white sugar and coat by lightly tossing. Allow the hasselbacked pears to rest for 5 minutes.
- Combine together vanilla extract, confectioners' sugar, and cream cheese in the bowl; spread on the puff pastry. Arrange the hasselbacked pears on the cream cheese layer, chopping some of the halves into quarters if necessary to fit in. Fan out each pear a bit and sprinkle any accumulated juices from pear bowl on the pears. Drizzle the turbinado sugar on the tart.
- Bake in preheated oven for roughly 35 minutes or till the juices become bubbly and the crust becomes puffed and brown a bit. Let the tart cool down for 15 minutes prior to slicing.

Nutrition Information

- Calories: 326 calories;
- Sodium: 118
- Total Carbohydrate: 43.2
- Cholesterol: 15
- Protein: 3.7
- Total Fat: 16.5

278.   Herbed Brie In Puff Pastry

Serving: 32 | Prep: 15mins | Cook: 30mins | Ready in:

Ingredients

- 3/4 teaspoon chopped fresh parsley
- 1 clove garlic, minced
- 1 teaspoon dried rosemary
- 1 teaspoon dried thyme
- 1 teaspoon dried marjoram
- 2 ounces thinly sliced salami, chopped
- 1 (2.2 pound) wheel Brie cheese
- 1 sheet frozen puff pastry, thawed
- water
- 1 egg, beaten

Direction

- Preheat the oven to 175 °C or 350 °F.
- Combine together salami, marjoram, thyme, rosemary, garlic and parsley. Halve the Brie crosswise, to make 2 wheels. On one of cut sides, scatter herb mixture and salami and put the other half of Brie wheel over. In the middle of puff pastry sheet, put the Brie. Fold up puff pastry and on top of the Brie, press to seal the pastry with a small amount of water if needed. Glaze pastry with beaten egg.
- In the prepped oven, let the pastry bake for half an hour till golden brown. Take off from oven and let rest for 15 minutes prior serving.

Nutrition Information

- Calories: 155 calories;
- Protein: 7.7
- Total Fat: 12.2
- Sodium: 253
- Total Carbohydrate: 3.7
- Cholesterol: 39

---

279. Homemade Chicken Pot Pies

Serving: 24 | Prep: 15mins | Cook: 1hours15mins | Ready in:

Ingredients

- 2 pounds skinless, boneless chicken breast halves
- 2 (32 ounce) cartons low-sodium chicken broth
- 5 tablespoons butter, divided
- 2 tablespoons olive oil
- 2 cups diced Yukon Gold potatoes
- 3 large carrots, diced
- 1 cup frozen sweet corn
- 2 large stalks celery, diced
- 1/2 cup frozen peas
- 3 teaspoons minced garlic
- 3 teaspoons salt
- 2 teaspoons ground black pepper
- 1 teaspoon dried rosemary
- 1/2 teaspoon ground nutmeg
- 1/2 teaspoon ground thyme
- 1/2 teaspoon ground sage
- 1/2 cup all-purpose flour
- 4 cups heavy whipping cream
- salt and cracked black pepper to taste (optional)
- 2 (17.5 ounce) packages frozen puff pastry, thawed
- 1 egg, whipped, or more to taste

Direction

- Into a big pot, put the chicken breasts and submerge in chicken broth; boil. Lower heat to moderately-low and let simmer for 20 to 25 minutes, till juices run clear and not pink anymore in the middle. Remove chicken from broth; chop or shred as wished. Retain broth hot.
- In a big stockpot or Dutch oven, liquify 3 tablespoons of butter with olive oil on moderately-high heat. Put in garlic, peas, celery, corn, carrots and potatoes. Sauté for 15 minutes till onions soften and become clear. Put in sage, thyme, nutmeg, rosemary, 2 teaspoons of black pepper and 3 teaspoons of salt. Cook and mix till blended into the mixture of vegetable, for a minute.
- In vegetable mixture, liquify leftover 2 tablespoons of butter. Dust top with flour. Cook for a minute, mixing continuously, till vegetables are covered. Scoop in hot chicken broth, a cup at one time, mixing continuously, till pot is filled sufficiently; you might not be needing the entire broth.
- Into pot, mix heavy cream; slightly increase heat. Put in the shredded chicken. Add pepper and salt to season. Cook for 5 minutes, mixing from time to time and scratching the base, till flavors meld. Lower the heat and simmer with no cover for 20 minutes, till filling is thick. Cool for 5 minutes.

- Preheat an oven to 190 ° C or 375 ° F. Oil 2 12-cup muffin tins. Line aluminum foil on 2 baking sheets and place muffin tins over.
- Into the muffin cups, put the filling.
- Onto a work area, roll the puff pastry and even it out a little. Slice into 2 dozen portions, a bit bigger than muffin cups. Put pieces of pastry over the filling in muffin cups, allowing approximately quarter-inch pastry to hang over edges. Brush whipped egg on top of pot pies. Add pepper and salt to season. Make a few slits for venting.
- In prepped oven, bake for 15 to 25 minutes, till golden brown. Rest for a minimum of 5 minutes prior to serving.

Nutrition Information

- Calories: 478 calories;
- Cholesterol: 91
- Protein: 14
- Total Fat: 35.2
- Sodium: 503
- Total Carbohydrate: 27.3

280.   How To Make Cheese Sticks

Serving: 9 | Prep: 25mins | Cook: 20mins | Ready in:

Ingredients

- 1/2 (17.5 ounce) package frozen puff pastry
- 2 teaspoons olive oil (preferably drained from a tin of anchovies)
- 1 pinch salt and freshly ground black pepper to taste
- 1 pinch cayenne pepper, or to taste
- 1/4 cup shredded sharp white Cheddar cheese
- 5 tablespoons freshly shredded Parmigiano-Reggiano cheese, divided

Direction

- Preheat an oven to 200 °C or 400 °F. Line parchment paper or a silicone baking mat on a baking sheet.
- Onto a floured work area, put 1 sheet of frozen puff pastry dough and let the dough thaw just till it can be unfolded. Into a flat sheet, roll dough out; with olive oil, glaze puff pastry dough top. Put cayenne pepper, black pepper and salt to season.
- Onto the dough, scatter 1/4 cup Parmigiano-Reggiano cheese and white Cheddar cheese, coating the top. Put a piece of plastic wrap on top; firmly push seasonings and cheese into dough using fingers or by putting a sheet pan onto dough on top of plastic and forcing it down.
- Take off the plastic and cut dough down to the seam lines into 3 pieces with a sharp knife or pizza cutter; slice every third lengthwise into 3 for 9 breadsticks total.
- Get a dough strip, put on the work surface, it seasoned side facing down and to create a dough rolled tube with seasoned side out, twirl from each end 8 or 9 times. Onto prepped baking sheet, put the breadsticks.
- On top of the sticks scatter leftover 1 tablespoon Parmigiano-Reggiano cheese. Gently roll the sticks to even up their forms and collect and push any dropped cheese onto surfaces.
- In the prepped oven, bake for approximately 10 minutes; turn over and keep baking for 10 to 20 minutes longer till breadsticks are crisp and browned. Once a picked-up stick ends droops, bake for few minutes more. Allow to cool on a wire rack prior serving.

Nutrition Information

- Calories: 184 calories;
- Cholesterol: 5
- Protein: 3.8
- Total Fat: 13.2
- Sodium: 134
- Total Carbohydrate: 12.4

281. Individual Turkey Pot Pies

Serving: 4 | Prep: 20mins | Cook: 25mins | Ready in:

Ingredients

- 3 tablespoons butter
- 1/2 cup diced onion
- 1/2 cup sliced celery
- 1/4 cup flour
- 1 tablespoon minced fresh rosemary
- 1 teaspoon chopped fresh thyme
- 1/4 teaspoon black pepper
- 2 cups College Inn® Chicken Broth
- 2 cups cubed cooked turkey
- 1 cup frozen peas and carrots
- 1 1/2 cups chopped cooked green beans
- 1 (17.3 ounce) package frozen puff pastry sheets, thawed according to package directions
- 1 egg
- 1 tablespoon water

Direction

- Preheat the oven to 400°F. Melt the butter on medium heat in the big saucepan. Cook the pepper, thyme, rosemary, flour, celery and onion for 3 minutes, whisking continuously.
- Gradually pour in the broth, whisk till becoming smooth. Cook, whisking continuously till becoming thick.
- Whisk in the green beans, carrots, peas, and turkey. Scoop into 4 10-ounce ramekins.
- Chop 4 circles out of the puff pastry sheet, using the outer edge of the ramekin as a guide. Add the pastry on the turkey mixture in each ramekin. Blend the water and egg; brush on the pastry. Add the ramekins onto the rimmed baking sheet.
- Bake till turning puffed and golden brown or for 25 minutes. Allow it to rest for 10 minutes prior to serving.

Nutrition Information

- Calories: 994 calories;
- Cholesterol: 127
- Protein: 33.8
- Total Fat: 64.3
- Sodium: 1072
- Total Carbohydrate: 70.3

282. Jambalaya Pot Pie

Serving: 6 | Prep: 45mins | Cook: 1hours | Ready in:

Ingredients

- 1/2 cup uncooked white rice
- 3/4 cup water
- 2 Italian sausage links
- 2 tablespoons butter
- 2 tablespoons all-purpose flour
- 2 cups whole milk
- 3 tablespoons Cajun seasoning, or to taste
- 1 cup cooked chicken meat, shredded
- 3 drops liquid smoke flavoring, or to taste
- 1/2 cup finely chopped onion
- 1/2 cup chopped red bell pepper
- 2 cloves garlic, minced, or more to taste
- 1/2 cup uncooked shrimp - peeled, deveined, and tails removed
- 2 sheets frozen puff pastry, thawed
- 1 beaten egg

Direction

- In saucepan, boil water and rice on high heat. Lower the heat to moderately-low, put cover, and simmer for 15 minutes, till liquid has been soaked in and rice become chewy. Rest the rice for 5 minutes with cover. Remove cover, and cool.
- Preheat the oven to 200 ° C or 400 ° F. Oil a pie dish, 9-inch in size.
- Into big skillet, put sausage links on moderately-high heat, and cook for 3 to 4 minutes on each side, till browned on each

side. Take off from heat, and slice into quarter-inch pieces; reserve. In big saucepan, liquify butter on moderate heat, and mix in flour. Cook flour for a minute, till foamy-looking; mix in milk. Reduce heat to moderately-low, and let the sauce simmer while you complete the rest of the steps; mix frequently. To taste, mix in Cajun seasoning. Once sauce is thick enough to cover back of spoon, take off from heat.

- Toss liquid smoke flavoring and chicken meat in bowl. Stir in shrimp, garlic, red bell pepper, onion, cooked sausage and cooked rice till well blended. To moisten the filling, add in approximately 3/4 the white sauce.
- To assemble pie, clip puff pastry sheets into 10x10-inch; in prepped pie dish, lay one sheet. The square corners will stay out. Fill the base crust with mixture of rice, and add in leftover quarter the white sauce. Put the leftover puff pastry on sheet; press edges to enclose. Brush beaten egg on pie top.
- In the prepped oven, bake for 20 minutes to half an hour, till crust turn flaky in the middle and golden brown.

Nutrition Information

- Calories: 753 calories;
- Sodium: 1326
- Total Carbohydrate: 60.1
- Cholesterol: 92
- Protein: 22.1
- Total Fat: 46.9

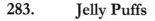

283.   Jelly Puffs

Serving: 30 | Prep: 20mins | Cook: 10mins | Ready in:

Ingredients

- 1 cup marshmallow fluff
- 1 cup strawberry jelly
- 1 sheet frozen puff pastry, thawed

Direction

- Preheat the oven to 200 ° C or 400 ° F.
- In bowl, whip together the strawberry jelly and marshmallow fluff till well-blended. Slice the dough of puff pastry into 3-inch portions.
- Drop spoonful of marshmallow fluff mixture onto the middle half of puff pastry portions; put one more puff pastry piece on top of each and press edges to enclose. Onto baking sheet, put the enclosed pieces.
- In the prepped oven, bake for 10 to 15 minutes, till golden brown and puffed.

Nutrition Information

- Calories: 84 calories;
- Total Carbohydrate: 13.7
- Cholesterol: 0
- Protein: 0.6
- Total Fat: 3.1
- Sodium: 23

284.   Koulibiaka

Serving: 6 | Prep: 30mins | Cook: 55mins | Ready in:

Ingredients

- For the Pilaf:
- 2 tablespoons butter
- 2 1/2 tablespoons finely chopped onion
- 1/2 cup uncooked long-grain white rice
- 1 cup chicken broth
- salt and pepper to taste
- Sauce:
- 1/4 cup butter
- 1/2 cup all-purpose flour
- 2 cups chicken broth
- 1/4 cup butter
- 4 ounces button mushrooms, quartered
- 1 1/2 cups finely chopped onion
- 1 teaspoon fresh-squeezed lemon juice
- 2 hard-cooked eggs, chopped

- 1/4 cup chopped fresh dill
- 12 cabbage leaves
- 6 (4 ounce) salmon fillets, skin removed
- salt and ground black pepper to taste
- 2 (17.25 ounce) packages frozen puff pastry, thawed
- 1 egg
- 1 tablespoon water

Direction

- Make the rice pilaf. In a pot on medium heat, melt 2 tablespoons of butter. Mix 2 1/2 tablespoons of onion in; stir and cook until it becomes soft and translucent, 5 minutes. Pour the rice in and mix well to coat rice with butter. Empty 1 cup of chicken broth into the pan and continue cooking until mixture starts to boil. Turn heat to low. Cover the pan let it simmer for 20 minutes until all the broth has been absorbed and rice is fluffy. Add pepper and salt and pepper to taste then set aside.
- Put pot on medium and melt 1/4 cup butter. Sprinkle a little flour in the butter, when it starts bubbling then butter is ready. Add flour and whisk until it is consistency of frosting for cake. Continue to cook and whisk continually, until flour turns golden and starts smelling like toasted bread, 20 minutes. Stir 2 cups of chicken broth in the pan and let it simmer for 5 minutes until thick and bubbly. If desired, reserved 1/4 cup of the sauce for serving, pour the rest in rice pilaf.
- In another skillet, heat 1/4 cup butter on medium. Toss mushrooms in and cook for 5 minutes until softened. Add 1 1/2 cups of onion and continue to sauté and stir for 8 minutes, until the onion is tender and becomes translucent. Mix together, the onions, mushrooms and rice mixture. Let the mixture cool a light; then mix in lemon juice, fresh dill and chopped hard-boiled eggs.
- Set an oven to 400°F or 200°C to preheat. Apply butter on a parchment paper lining a cookie sheet.
- Lightly salt a big pot of water and bring it to a boil. Drop cabbage leaves in and, without covering the pot, let it cook for 2 minutes until the leaves soften. Scoop cabbage leaves into a colander, then submerge them in ice water straightaway. Leave the leaves for several minutes to stop cooking. Drain well once the leaves have turned cold and pat dry with a clean kitchen towel or paper towels.
- Take out the puff pastry and roll it on a lightly floured surface to about 1/4-inch thick. Create 6 rectangular shapes by cutting the pastry about 2 inches longer and 3x wider than salmon fillets. For each rectangle layer the following ingredients in this order - 2 cabbage leaves, scoop of rice mixture, fillet skin-side up, sprinkle salt and black pepper to taste, and another spoonful of rice over the fillet. Encase the fillets by folding the cabbage leaves over them. The folded leaves should be in the center of puff pastry.
- Create a packet from the pastry by folding the short ends in, and the sides together. Squeeze the seams together to seal. Do this for all the pastry rectangles and arrange them seam down on the cookie sheet lined with parchment paper. In the center of each pastry, gently make a small slit where steam will escape from. Meanwhile, create an egg wash by beating together 1 tablespoon of water and egg in a small bowl. Brush each pastry with it.
- Bake pastries for about 15 minutes until they turn a deep golden brown. To confirm if the dish is done, insert a thermometer in the pastry and the salmon's temperature should read 135°Fahrenheit or 57°Celsius.

Nutrition Information

- Calories: 1384 calories;
- Cholesterol: 205
- Protein: 40.6
- Total Fat: 90.7
- Sodium: 631
- Total Carbohydrate: 101.9

285. Lamb Patties

Serving: 18 | Prep: 15mins | Cook: 30mins | Ready in:

Ingredients

- 1 pound ground lamb
- 5 green chile peppers, diced
- 3 onions, peeled and chopped
- 1 tablespoon dark soy sauce
- 1 tablespoon Worcestershire sauce
- 2 tablespoons ginger paste
- 2 tablespoons garlic paste
- 1/2 teaspoon ground white pepper
- 1/2 teaspoon ground cinnamon
- 1/2 teaspoon ground cardamom
- 1/2 teaspoon ground cloves
- 2 tablespoons chopped fresh cilantro
- 1 (17.5 ounce) package frozen puff pastry sheets, thawed
- 1 egg, beaten

Direction

- Combine ground lamb with Worcestershire sauce, soy sauce, chilies, and onion in a large pot. Season lamb mixture with cloves, cardamom, cinnamon, white pepper, garlic and ginger pastes. Cook for about 15 minutes over medium heat, stirring sometimes, until onions are soft and meat is evenly browned. Stir in cilantro, cover the pot and put to one side.
- Turn oven to 375°F (190°C) to preheat. Flatten sheets of puff pastry on a work surface lightly coated with flour. Divide each pastry into 9 squares and roll out to a thickness of 1/4 inch. Place about 1 1/2 tablespoons of meat mixture into the middle of each square. Brush water around the edges, fold corner over filling to make a triangle, and press edges to seal. (Avoid overstuffing because triangles will burst in the oven when baking). Arrange patties about 1 inch apart on a baking sheet lined with foil. Lightly brush beaten egg over tops.

- Bake patties in the preheated oven until all sides are golden brown, for 12 to 15 minutes. Serve right away for the best flavor.

Nutrition Information

- Calories: 222 calories;
- Total Fat: 14.1
- Sodium: 247
- Total Carbohydrate: 15.7
- Cholesterol: 27
- Protein: 7.2

286. Lamb Puff Pastry Bite Appetizer

Serving: 10 | Prep: 30mins | Cook: 20mins | Ready in:

Ingredients

- 1 tablespoon diced garlic
- 1/2 teaspoon salt
- 1/2 teaspoon ground black pepper
- 1/4 teaspoon ground cumin
- 1/4 teaspoon ground coriander
- 1/4 teaspoon ground allspice
- 1 pound ground lamb
- 1 egg
- 2 teaspoons water
- 2 (10x15-inch) sheets of frozen puff pastry, thawed
- 1/2 cup tzatziki sauce

Direction

- In a bowl, mix allspice, coriander, cumin, pepper, salt and garlic; add lamb. Shape lamb mixture to 10-in. logs, thick as hotdogs.
- Whisk water and egg to make egg wash in a small bowl.
- Lay puff pastry sheets onto slightly floured work surface; gently roll to smooth creases. Cut pastry to 10x4-in. strips; brush pastry with egg wash. On each pastry strip, put 1 lamb log;

wrap dough around lamb. To seal, pinch edges. Wrap in plastic wrap; chill for 1 hour.

- Preheat an oven to 220°C/425°F; line parchment paper on a baking sheet.
- Remove plastic wrap; use a sharp knife to cut each pastry piece to 8 pieces. Put onto lined baking sheet in 1 layer; brush egg wash on each piece.
- In preheated oven, bake for 20 minutes till golden brown. Serve with tzatziki sauce.

Nutrition Information

- Calories: 375 calories;
- Total Fat: 35
- Sodium: 279
- Total Carbohydrate: 23
- Cholesterol: 49
- Protein: 12.4

287. Lobster Pot Pie

Serving: 8 | Prep: 1hours | Cook: 1hours27mins |Ready in:

Ingredients

- 1/2 cup clarified butter, divided
- 1 cup minced onion
- 1 tablespoon thinly sliced shallots
- 1 tablespoon minced garlic
- 1 tablespoon thinly sliced leeks
- 1 cup diced acorn squash
- 1 cup minced parsnips
- 1 cup diced carrots
- 1 cup minced celery
- 1/2 cup diced celery root (celeriac)
- 1/2 cup all-purpose flour
- 4 cups lobster stock
- 1 cup minced crimini mushrooms
- 6 tablespoons sherry wine
- 1/2 cup chopped fresh tarragon
- 1/2 cup chopped fresh parsley

- 1/4 teaspoon hot pepper sauce (such as Tabasco®)
- salt and ground black pepper to taste
- 2 bay leaves
- 2 tablespoons sherry vinegar
- 1 cup cooked and coarsely chopped lobster meat
- 1 cup sweet baby peas
- 1 (17.5 ounce) package frozen puff pastry, thawed

Direction

- In a frying pan over medium heat, heat 1/4 cup of butter, mix in onion. Stir and cook for 5 minutes until the onion is tender and begins to turn opaque. Mix in leeks, garlic, and shallots, cook for 2-3 minutes until tender. Add celery roots, celery, carrots, parsnips, and acorn squash. Lower the heat to low and cook the vegetables for 10 minutes until tender. Move the vegetables to a bowl.
- Start preheating the oven to 450°F (232°C)
- In the same frying pan over medium heat, heat the rest of the butter until bubbly when drizzling with a pinch of flour into the oil. Mix in the flour to create a thick paste with the consistency as of cake frosting. Keep cooking the roux, mixing nonstop for 20 minutes until the flour begins to smell like toast and turns golden.
- Mix pepper, salt, pepper sauce, parsley, tarragon, sherry wine, mushrooms, lobster stock, and vegetable mixture into the roux. Stir and cook for 12-15 minutes until firm. Mix in sherry vinegar. Add peas and lobster meat. Put the roux mixture on a ramekin or a casserole plate. Put a cover on and put above or close to the hot oven until ready to use.
- Spread the puff pastry. Slice the sheets into crusts slightly bigger than the pie plate. Push 1 layer on the bottom of a 9-inch pie dish.
- Put in the preheated oven and bake for 8 minutes until slightly brown. Take out and use the roux mixture to fill. Put top crust on the filling; seal it by pushing its edge onto the bottom crust.

- Keeping baking for 30-35 minutes until the top crust is golden brown.

Nutrition Information

- Calories: 583 calories;
- Cholesterol: 47
- Protein: 14.1
- Total Fat: 37.4
- Sodium: 565
- Total Carbohydrate: 47.4

288.   Macapuno Bars

Serving: 18 | Prep: 15mins | Cook: 30mins | Ready in:

Ingredients

- cooking spray
- 1 (17.5 ounce) package frozen puff pastry, thawed
- 6 egg yolks
- 2 (12 ounce) jars macapuno strings
- 1/4 cup butter, softened
- 1/2 teaspoon vanilla extract

Direction

- Prepare the oven by preheating to 400°F (200°C). Use cooking spray to coat a 9x13-inch baking dish.
- On the bottom of the prepared baking dish, scatter one puff pastry, extending so it touches the edges.
- Place the pastry in the preheated and bake for approximately 5 minutes until browned lightly.
- In a stainless-steel bowl, whisk egg yolks until smooth. Add vanilla, softened butter, and macapuno strings to egg yolks; mix.
- Set the stainless-steel bowl on a pot full of boiling water; put the macapuno mixture and cook for approximately 5 minutes, whisking frequently, until it thickens. Place on the baked

puff pastry and scatter in an equal layer. Then stretch the unbaked puff pastry on the top of macapuno layer.
- Place in the preheated oven and bake for approximately 18 minutes until the top layer turns golden brown. Let it cool at room temperature.

Nutrition Information

- Calories: 296 calories;
- Protein: 2.9
- Total Fat: 15
- Sodium: 78
- Total Carbohydrate: 37
- Cholesterol: 75

289.   Maple Pear Tarte Tatin

Serving: 8 | Prep: 15mins | Cook: 30mins | Ready in:

Ingredients

- 1/2 (17.3 ounce) package frozen puff pastry, thawed
- 1/4 cup butter
- 1/3 cup brown sugar
- 1/4 teaspoon ground cinnamon
- 1 pinch ground nutmeg
- 1/4 cup maple syrup
- 4 firm pears - peeled, cored, and halved, or more as needed

Direction

- Preheat the oven to 190°C or 375°F.
- On a slightly floured area, unroll puff pastry making quarter-inch thickness; refrigerate.
- In a cast iron skillet, 9-inch in size, liquify the butter on moderate heat; mix in nutmeg, cinnamon and brown sugar, and cook while mixing for 5 minutes, till sugar melts. Mix into mixture of brown sugar with maple syrup;

cook and mix till mixture starts to become bubbly. Take skillet off heat.

- Put a pear half in the middle of skillet, cut side facing up. Halve the rest of pear halves once more; surround the middle pear with pear quarters, cut sides facing up.
- Set the skillet on moderately-low heat; let pears cook for 5 minutes, use syrup mixture to baste them, till they start to become tender. Take skillet off heat.
- Take puff pastry out of fridge; top pears with pastry, tuck pastry edges in pears surrounding inside the skillet.
- In the prepped oven, bake for 20 minutes, till pastry turn golden and puffed; cool for five minutes. Top skillet with a serving plate; flip over to take out the tart, skillet is still hot. Serve while warm.

Nutrition Information

- Calories: 329 calories;
- Total Carbohydrate: 42.4
- Cholesterol: 15
- Protein: 2.6
- Total Fat: 17.6
- Sodium: 122

290.   Marjolaine

Serving: 10 | Prep: 35mins | Cook: 10mins | Ready in:

Ingredients

- 1/2 (17.5 ounce) package frozen puff pastry, thawed
- 1/4 cup finely chopped hazelnuts
- 1 cup chopped semisweet chocolate
- 4 ounces light cream cheese, softened
- 1/2 cup brown sugar
- 3 tablespoons strong brewed coffee, cold
- 1/2 cup ground hazelnuts
- 1/2 cup ground almonds
- 2 cups heavy cream

Direction

- Preheat the oven to 230 ° C or 450 ° F. Line parchment paper on a baking sheet.
- Roll puff pastry on a slightly floured area into square, 13x13-inch in size. Clip into 12x12-inch using sharp knife. Slice into 3 4x12-inch even strips. Puncture every strip a few times using fork. Place on prepped baking sheet. Scatter hazelnuts over.
- In prepped oven, bake till golden and puffed for 8-10 minutes. Cool. In case not even in size, clip using serrated knife, with a gentle sawing movement.
- In bowl on just simmering water, liquify the chocolate, mixing continuously, till smooth. Let come to room temperature. Whip coffee, brown sugar and cream cheese together in a big bowl till smooth. Mix in liquified chocolate. Fold in the ground hazelnuts and almonds. Beat cream in big bowl till peaks create. Into mixture of cheese, fold a third of whipped cream, then immediately fold in the rest of whipped cream till no streaks left.
- Over a puff pastry strip, scatter a third of filling. Redo the layers. Chill till set, for 3 hours. Slice into 10 pieces using serrated knife, with a gentle sawing movement.

Nutrition Information

- Calories: 545 calories;
- Sodium: 116
- Total Carbohydrate: 36.4
- Cholesterol: 72
- Protein: 8.1
- Total Fat: 43

291.   Mark's English Sausage Rolls

Serving: 12 | Prep: 15mins | Cook: 20mins | Ready in:

Ingredients

- 1 (16 ounce) package pork sausagemeat
- 1 (17.25 ounce) package frozen puff pastry sheets, thawed
- 1/4 cup Dijon mustard
- 1 beaten egg

Direction

- Preheat oven to 200 degrees C (400 degrees F).
- Unfold puff pastry sheets, and chop along fold lines of each of the sheets to shape 6 same-sized squares for the total number of 12 square pieces. Use the mustard to brush each square. Separate the sausage into 12 pieces, and roll to the small-sized logs. Place one log on every square. Roll the dough round sausage, and seal it using the small amount of the beaten egg. Add the rolls to the ungreased baking sheet, and use the remaining egg to brush the tops.
- Bake in preheated oven till rolls become puffed and golden or for 20 minutes. Watch after every 10 minutes or so to avoid burning. These can freeze (unbaked) very good.

Nutrition Information

- Calories: 329 calories;
- Total Fat: 23.9
- Sodium: 569
- Total Carbohydrate: 19.5
- Cholesterol: 37
- Protein: 8.6

292. Meat Pie, Southern Version

Serving: 10 | Prep: 40mins | Cook: 50mins | Ready in:

Ingredients

- 1 pound ground beef
- 1/2 pound ground pork
- 1 large onion, chopped
- 1 green bell pepper, chopped
- 2 stalks celery, finely diced
- 3 cloves garlic, minced
- 1 small carrot, finely chopped
- 1 large baking potato, peeled and finely chopped
- 1 bay leaf
- 1 teaspoon dried thyme leaves
- 2 tablespoons chopped fresh parsley
- 1 teaspoon Worcestershire sauce
- salt-free seasoning blend to taste
- salt and pepper to taste
- 2 beef bouillon cubes
- 1 cup hot water
- 2 cups shredded mild Cheddar cheese
- 2 sheets frozen puff pastry, thawed
- 1 egg yolk
- 1 tablespoon water

Direction

- Preheat the oven to 175 ° C or 350 ° F. Using cooking spray, coat a dish, 9x13-inch in size.
- On moderately-high heat, heat a nonstick big skillet and mix in ground pork and ground beef. Cook and mix till meat turns crumbly, equally browned, and not pink anymore. Let drain and throw any extra grease. Mix in celery, bell pepper and onion. Put cover and lower heat to moderate; cook for 5 minutes, mixing often, till vegetables soften and onion is clear.
- In the middle of skillet, create a well and add minced garlic right on pan base. Cook till aromatic, for 30 seconds to a minute, and then mix garlic with mixture of meat. Put in pepper and salt, seasoning blend, Worcestershire sauce, parsley, thyme, bay leaf, potato and carrot.
- In hot water, melt bouillon cubes in bowl, and add it to mixture of meat; combine thoroughly. Boil, lower heat to low, put cover, and simmer for 10 to 15 minutes, till carrots are tender.
- In the prepped baking dish, lay a sheet puff pastry. Force pastry gently into corners and up sides of dish. Turn the meat in the crust using

slotted spoon and scatter equally. Do not add liquid to pie. Put Cheddar cheese over.

- Whip a tablespoon of water and egg yolk together. Brush the bottom puff pastry sheet's edges. Lay another puff pastry sheet on top of baking dish, forcing using fork to enclose edges. Brush egg wash on top and to vent crust, prick using fork a few times.

- In the prepped oven, bake for 50 minutes, till filling is bubbling and pastry turn golden brown. Monitor 15 minutes after to avoid excessive-browning, tent in aluminum foil, if needed. Take pie out of oven and rest for 10 minutes prior to serving.

Nutrition Information

- Calories: 530 calories;
- Sodium: 491
- Total Carbohydrate: 31.4
- Cholesterol: 86
- Protein: 22.2
- Total Fat: 35

---

293.   Meatless Mushroom Tart

Serving: 8 | Prep: 25mins | Cook: 1hours2mins |Ready in:

Ingredients

- 1 (17.25 ounce) package frozen puff pastry, thawed according to package instructions
- 3 tablespoons butter, melted
- 2 1/2 cups chopped yellow onion
- 8 cups portobello mushrooms, coarsely chopped
- 2 tablespoons fresh thyme leaves, finely chopped
- 1 (8 ounce) package cream cheese, cut into cubes, at room temperature
- salt and ground black pepper to taste
- 1 large egg yolk
- 1 tablespoon milk

Direction

- Preheat the oven to 200 ° C or 400 ° F. Oil one baking sheet slightly.
- Line a puff pastry sheet on one pie dish, 10-inch in size. Clip the edge so an-inch overhangs dish rim.
- In prepped oven, bake for 5 to 10 minutes, barely long enough to set pastry.
- Slice another puff pastry sheet into an-inch-wide strips. Put strips on prepped baking sheet. Chill baked pie shell and strips for a minimum of 30 minutes to a day.
- Meantime, in skillet, liquify the butter on moderately-high heat. Mix in onions, and cook for 6 minutes, till transparent and soft. Mix in thyme and mushrooms, and cook for 6 minutes, till mushrooms are soft and render their juices. Into mixture of mushroom, stir cream cheese, mixing till liquified. Season with pepper and salt to taste.
- Into the pie shell, scoop the mixture of mushroom. In lattice pattern, place the pastry strips along the filling. Fold and flute strips end together with pie shell edge clipping any needed pastry to create a smooth edge.
- In small bowl, whip together milk and egg yolk, and use to brush pie top.
- In prepped oven, bake for 45 minutes, till filling is heated completely and crust turn golden brown. Test for doneness after half an hour. Cool for 30 minutes more prior to serving.

Nutrition Information

- Calories: 523 calories;
- Protein: 10
- Total Fat: 37.9
- Sodium: 274
- Total Carbohydrate: 38
- Cholesterol: 68

294. Mediterranean Meat Pies (Sfeeha)

Serving: 18 | Prep: 20mins | Cook: 15mins | Ready in:

Ingredients

- 1 pound ground beef
- 1/2 pound ground lamb
- 1 white onion, finely chopped
- 3/4 cup pine nuts
- 1/8 teaspoon ground cinnamon
- salt and ground black pepper to taste
- 1/3 cup lemon juice
- 1 egg, beaten
- 2 (17.3 ounce) packages frozen puff pastry, thawed

Direction

- Place the large skillet over medium-high heat. Stir in chopped onion, ground beef and ground lamb, salt, black pepper, pine nuts, and cinnamon. Cook until the meat is browned all over, crumbly, and no longer pink. Let it drain and remove any excess grease.
- Mix in lemon juice. Taste the mixture to adjust the seasonings. Allow the meat mixture to cool.
- Set the oven to 350°F (175°C) for preheating. Grease the baking sheet lightly, or you can line it with a parchment paper.
- Roll the thawed pastry sheets into 1/8-inch thick. Cut each sheet to at least 9 rounds using the sharp 3-inches round cookie cutter. Coat each inside edges with a little water. Spoon 2 teaspoons of the filling into the center of each round. Fold each round in half to cover the filling, sealing the edges tightly. Arrange them onto the prepared baking sheet. Do the same with the remaining dough circles.
- Coat each pie with a little egg wash. Let it bake inside the preheated oven for 15-20 minutes until golden brown.

Nutrition Information

- Calories: 412 calories;
- Sodium: 162
- Total Carbohydrate: 26.4
- Cholesterol: 34
- Protein: 12.7
- Total Fat: 28.7

295. Miami Guava Pastries (Pastelitos)

Serving: 10 | Prep: 10mins | Cook: 20mins | Ready in:

Ingredients

- 1 tablespoon all-purpose flour, or as needed
- 1 sheet frozen puff pastry, thawed
- 1 egg
- 3 tablespoons water
- 3 tablespoons strawberry jam
- 1 (8 ounce) jar guava paste, or as desired

Direction

- Preheat an oven to 175 degrees C (350 degrees F). Coat a baking sheet lightly with flour.
- Onto a floured surface, fold the puff pastry into a thin sheet. Chop into squares of about the length of your hand and then put on the baking sheet prepared.
- In a bowl, beat together egg and water. Use the egg wash to rub each pastry square. Use a fork to stab each square several times.
- Bake for about 20 to 25 minutes in the oven until golden brown. Take out from the oven and allow to cool for a minimum of 10 minutes.
- In a bowl, combine together jam and guava paste until smooth.
- Make a large and vertical slit into each pastry. Pour one tablespoon of guava mixture into each slit and ensure the guava does not squeeze out when closed.

Nutrition Information

- Calories: 222 calories;
- Total Fat: 9.7
- Sodium: 68
- Total Carbohydrate: 31.9
- Cholesterol: 19
- Protein: 2.5

296. Mille Feuille (Napoleon Pastry Sheets)

Serving: 4 | Prep: 30mins | Cook: 25mins | Ready in:

Ingredients

- 1 (17.5 ounce) package frozen puff pastry dough, thawed
- 2 teaspoons white sugar, or as needed for dusting

Direction

- Set oven to 200° C (400° F) and start preheating. Line a silicone sheet on a baking tray.
- Split dough at the seams to make 4 squares; arrange on the prepared baking sheet. With the tines of a fork, score dough all over to avoid it rising too much while baking. Slightly sprinkle white granulated sugar over dough sheets.
- Use a sheet of parchment paper to cover, then wrap with 3 sheets of aluminum foil. Use another baking sheet to net to apply to the dough some pressure while baking.
- Put into the preheated oven and bake for 15 minutes; take out top pan and foil; peel gently to remove parchment paper. Bring pan back to the oven and bake for 10-15 minutes till the pastry is browned beautifully. (If wanted, bake for 7 minutes after removing cover. Flip sheets over then bake for 7 minutes longer till the other side is browned.)

- Remove to cooling rack, allow to cool entirely before cutting.
- With a sharp serrated knife, trim uneven edges off sheets to square the sheet with light sawing motion to avoid breaking the pastry. Slice each rectangle crosswise into 3 smaller rectangles of the same size. For each pastry, use 3 small rectangles.

Nutrition Information

- Calories: 683 calories;
- Protein: 8.9
- Total Fat: 46.7
- Sodium: 305
- Total Carbohydrate: 57.3
- Cholesterol: 0

297. Mini Beef Wellingtons With Red Wine Sauce

Serving: 6 | Prep: 30mins | Cook: 15mins | Ready in:

Ingredients

- 2 tablespoons vegetable oil
- salt and pepper to taste
- 6 (6 ounce) beef tenderloin filets
- 1 cup chopped fresh mushrooms
- 1/4 cup red wine
- 1 cup beef consomme
- 1 (3 ounce) jar foie gras pate
- 1 (17.25 ounce) package frozen puff pastry, thawed
- 1 egg, beaten
- 3 tablespoons butter
- 3 tablespoons all-purpose flour
- 2 tablespoons chopped green onion
- 1 cup beef consomme
- 1/2 cup red wine
- 2 tablespoons butter
- 2 tablespoons chopped fresh parsley

Direction

- Heat oil in a big skillet on medium-high heat; season filets with pepper and salt. Fry each side till browned to lock juices in. Remove from the skillet; put aside to allow to slightly cool.
- Put beef consommé, wine and mushrooms in the skillet; mix and cook on medium heat till mushrooms are tender. Transfer mushrooms to a small bowl using a slotted spoon; keeping the consommé. Mix the mushrooms and pate; if needed, add a little consommé to get a spreadable texture. Split the mushrooms among filets; spread on top. Refrigerate for 30 minutes.
- Preheat an oven to 200°C/400°F. On clean surface, lay out puff pastry; cut 2 5-6-in. rounds out for each steak. If you need more area, roll it out a bit thinner. Put a steak on a round; bring up edges around sides. Use the 2nd dough piece to cover the top, overlapping edges then pressing to seal into a package. Repeat with leftover steaks. Put the Wellingtons on a baking sheet; brush beaten egg on tops.
- Bake for 20 minutes for well done, 16 minutes for medium or 12 minutes for rare. Use meat thermometer to determine steaks' temperature for best results, with 60°C/140°F for medium doneness. Take out from the oven; let rest for 5 minutes.
- As steaks cook, make sauce: Melt butter in saucepan on medium heat. Mix flour in; cook, constantly mixing, till browned. Mix green onions in; cook for 1 minute till tender. Mix the leftover 1 cup of consommé and the reserved consommé in slowly; mix and cook till the sauce thickens. Lower heat to low; mix wine in. keep on simmering for 15 minutes till thick. Take off heat; mix parsley and butter in. Season to taste with pepper and salt.
- Serving: Cut every Wellington in half; put some sauce on the plate.

Nutrition Information

- Calories: 1027 calories;
- Total Fat: 65.2
- Sodium: 693
- Total Carbohydrate: 42.1
- Cholesterol: 212
- Protein: 59.9

---

298. Mini Mushroom And Goat Cheese Tarts

Serving: 2 | Prep: 20mins | Cook: 15mins | Ready in:

Ingredients

- 1/2 sheet puff pastry
- 3 tablespoons butter
- 1/4 pound mushrooms, sliced
- 2 cloves garlic, crushed
- 1/2 cup crumbled goat cheese
- 4 teaspoons finely chopped fresh parsley

Direction

- Preheat oven to 200°C/400°F. Prepare a baking tray with a light coating of grease.
- Lightly dust a work surface with flour, spread the puff pastry and cut into 8 squares. Prick several small holes on the squares using a fork. Transfer the squares to the baking sheet.
- Bake for 7 minutes. Take the tray out of the oven and use the backside of a spatula to flatten the squares, then return the tray into the oven. Bake for another 5 to 8 minutes, or until golden brown. Remove from the oven.
- While baking, place a skillet over high heat and melt the butter. Stir and cook garlic and mushrooms in the skillet for 5 to 7 minutes, or until the mushrooms are tender. Remove from the heat.
- Top mushroom mixture on each baked square evenly. Top mushrooms with crumbled goat cheese and sprinkle parsley.

Nutrition Information

- Calories: 630 calories;
- Total Carbohydrate: 31.1
- Cholesterol: 73
- Protein: 14.2
- Total Fat: 50.9
- Sodium: 458

299.   Mock 'Crookies'

Serving: 15 | Prep: 20mins | Cook: 20mins |Ready in:

Ingredients

- cooking spray
- 1 (17.5 ounce) package frozen puff pastry, thawed
- 5 tablespoons cream cheese, softened, or more as needed
- 30 chocolate sandwich cookies (such as Oreo®)
- 2 tablespoons confectioners' sugar, or as needed

Direction

- Let oven warm up to 375°F or 190°C. Coat two baking sheets with cooking oil.
- Slice each pastry into 15 rectangles to make 30 rectangles in total. Using your fingers, spread out the rectangles. In one side of each cookie, ladle half teaspoon cream cheese. Assemble every cookie with the cream cheese side down on one side of every pastry rectangles; press together the edges to seal. On each baking sheet, assemble 12 to 15 cookies.
- Let it bake in a warmed up oven for 18 to 22 minutes until it becomes golden brown. Let it stand to cool and then sprinkle with confectioners' sugar.

Nutrition Information

- Calories: 294 calories;
- Total Carbohydrate: 30.2

- Cholesterol: 5
- Protein: 3.8
- Total Fat: 18
- Sodium: 192

300.   Mom's Chicken Pie

Serving: 8 | Prep: 30mins | Cook: 30mins |Ready in:

Ingredients

- 1 pound fresh spinach
- 4 cups cooked chicken, chopped
- 1 cup sliced mushrooms
- 1 cup sour cream
- salt and pepper to taste
- 1 (17.25 ounce) package frozen puff pastry, thawed
- 1 egg, beaten

Direction

- Preheat the oven to 200 ° C or 400 ° F. In steamer on top of an-inch boiling water, put the spinach, and place on cover. Cook for 2 to 6 minutes, till soft. Let drain and allow to cool.
- In a 2-quarts casserole dish base, put the spinach. Top with chopped chicken to cover. Scatter with sliced mushrooms and add pepper and salt to season. Evenly scatter sour cream on the top. Top with puff pastry to cover.
- Puncture puff pastry in few areas to release steam. Brush beaten egg on top. In the prepped oven, bake till golden brown, for 20 minutes.

Nutrition Information

- Calories: 574 calories;
- Total Fat: 38.7
- Sodium: 349
- Total Carbohydrate: 31.6
- Cholesterol: 90

- Protein: 25.4

301. Mushroom Cheese Puffs

Serving: 8 | Prep: 10mins | Cook: 10mins | Ready in:

Ingredients

- 1 (8 ounce) package refrigerated crescent rolls
- 1 (8 ounce) can mushrooms, drained
- 1 cup shredded Cheddar cheese

Direction

- Preheat an oven to 190 °C or 375 °F. Slightly oil a cookie sheet.
- Roll out a crescent dough package and put on cookie sheet. Pinch seams together till sheet is form to a rectangle. Onto the dough, put the drained mushrooms and place grated cheese on top. Put another roll of crescent dough over, pinching the seams once more. Slightly press to flatten and pinch seams across but retaining a slit for steam to release.
- Let bake till golden brown for 10 minutes. Cut into 8 separate servings and serve right away.

Nutrition Information

- Calories: 167 calories;
- Sodium: 356
- Total Carbohydrate: 13.7
- Cholesterol: 29
- Protein: 6.8
- Total Fat: 9.4

302. Mushroom Pie

Serving: 12 | Prep: 20mins | Cook: 40mins | Ready in:

Ingredients

- 1 tablespoon olive oil
- 1 (10 ounce) package fresh mushrooms, sliced
- 1 large onion, chopped
- 4 slices bacon, chopped
- 3/4 cup heavy cream
- 1 cup shredded Swiss cheese
- salt and pepper to taste
- 1 teaspoon chopped fresh dill
- 1 (17.25 ounce) package frozen puff pastry, thawed
- 1 egg, beaten

Direction

- Preheat an oven to 175 ° C or 350 ° F.
- In a big skillet, heat oil on moderately-high heat. Put in bacon, onion and mushrooms; cook and mix till vegetables are soft, for 5 minutes. Lower heat to moderate, and put in dill and cream; cook and mix for an additional of 10 minutes. Take off from heat, and mix in cheese.
- Put a puff pastry sheet on a well-greased baking sheet, and add mushroom filling on the surface. Top with another sheet to cover, and pinch edges together to enclose. Create few holes using fork in top. Brush beaten egg on top.
- In the prepped oven, bake till golden brown, for 40 minutes. Let cool, then slice into squares and serve.

Nutrition Information

- Calories: 419 calories;
- Sodium: 230
- Total Carbohydrate: 21.7
- Cholesterol: 61
- Protein: 11.2
- Total Fat: 32.3

303. Mushroom, Leek, And Sausage Pot Pie

Serving: 6 | Prep: | Cook: 59mins | Ready in:

Ingredients

- 1 (17.5 ounce) package frozen puff pastry, thawed
- 2 links chicken sausage, halved lengthwise and cut into bite-sized pieces
- 3 tablespoons butter
- 4 carrots, cut into bite-sized pieces
- 1 leek, halved lengthwise and cut into bite-sized pieces
- 2 garlic cloves
- 1 (4 ounce) package mushrooms, quartered
- 3 tablespoons all-purpose flour
- 1 1/4 cups vegetable broth
- 1 tablespoon Dijon mustard
- 1 teaspoon ground cayenne pepper
- 1/2 teaspoon ground nutmeg
- salt and ground black pepper to taste
- 1 egg
- 1 tablespoon water

Direction

- Roll each puff pastry sheet out till they have an even thickness. Use a sharp knife to cut two 8-inches rounds from each sheet.
- Use the pastry rounds to line the sides and bottoms of the two 8-inches pie tins, reserving 2 pastry rounds for their tops. Arrange the pie tins and tops onto the baking sheet and place them inside the fridge.
- In a skillet, cook and stir the sausage over medium heat for 5 minutes until browned. Drain all the excess grease. Add the leek, carrots, butter, and garlic. Cook and stir for 5 minutes until the leek has softened.
- Mix mushrooms into the skillet. Cook for 8 minutes until tender. Mix in the flour for 1 minute. Slowly add the vegetable broth, and then followed by the cayenne pepper, pepper, salt, Dijon mustard, and nutmeg. Cook and stir for 5 minutes until the sauce is thick.
- Set the oven to 400°F or 200°C for preheating.
- Distribute the sausage mixture among the pie tins evenly. Use the pastry tops to cover them.
- In a small bowl, prepare the egg wash by mixing water and egg. Coat the pastry tops with the egg wash.
- Let them bake inside the preheated oven for 35 minutes until golden brown. Let them cool briefly for 10 minutes before slicing.

Nutrition Information

- Calories: 623 calories;
- Sodium: 600
- Total Carbohydrate: 49.6
- Cholesterol: 81
- Protein: 13.1
- Total Fat: 41.9

304. Napoleons

Serving: 20 | Prep: 1hours45mins | Cook: 15mins | Ready in:

Ingredients

- 1 1/2 (17.5 ounce) packages frozen puff pastry sheets, thawed
- 1/4 cup cornstarch
- 4 cups milk, divided
- 1/3 cup cake flour
- 7/8 cup white sugar, divided
- 3 eggs, separated
- 1 tablespoon butter
- 1 teaspoon vanilla extract
- 1 (12 ounce) jar apricot jam
- 3 cups sifted confectioners' sugar
- 1 tablespoon lemon juice

Direction

- Preheat an oven to 175°C/350°F.
- Roll 3 puff pastry sheets out to 1/8-in. thick,

each to same size. Prick with fork; put on baking sheets.

- In preheated oven, bake for 10 minutes till golden.
- Mix 1/2 cup milk and cornstarch with fingers till smooth in a medium bowl. Mix in 1/2 sugar and cake flour; beat in egg yolks. Put aside.
- Put leftover sugar and leftover milk on a rolling boil in a saucepan on medium heat. Mix in egg yolk mixture; mix then boil. Take off heat. Mix in vanilla and butter; cool.
- Heat jam till runny in the microwave/small saucepan.
- On a board, put 1 pastry sheet; spread cooled pastry cream to 1/2-in. thick. Put 2nd pastry sheet on cream; brush fruit glaze. Spread leftover pastry cream on glaze. Put final pastry sheet over; compress layers gently, using baking sheet to press.
- Icing: Beat lemon juice, confectioners' sugar and enough egg whites to create creamy consistency like cream soup. Color small frosting portion with red food coloring, working quickly. Frost sides and top of assembled pastry using white icing. Pipe parallel red icing lines over dessert; crosswise draw through icing with a knife/pick to create a traditional design. Before cutting to bars, let icing set.

Nutrition Information

- Calories: 405 calories;
- Cholesterol: 33
- Protein: 5.6
- Total Fat: 16.4
- Sodium: 133
- Total Carbohydrate: 60.5

305.   Nutella® Pastry Christmas Tree

Serving: 8 | Prep: 35mins | Cook: 12mins | Ready in:

Ingredients

- 1 (17.5 ounce) package frozen puff pastry, thawed
- 4 tablespoons chocolate-hazelnut spread (such as Nutella®), or more to taste, at room temperature
- 1 egg, lightly beaten

Direction

- Preheat the oven to 190°C or 375°F. Line parchment paper on a baking sheet.
- On a lightly floured area, unroll a sheet of puff pastry, making a big rectangle, and put on the prepped baking sheet.
- Score puff pastry lightly, resembling a Christmas tree or triangle with a broad bottom. On top of the triangle, smear chocolate-hazelnut spread in a thin layer using the back of a spoon.
- Unroll another puff pastry sheet into a big rectangle and put over the first one. Cautiously follow the form of the chocolate covered triangle beneath and cut out Christmas tree shape and the trunk. Remove extra pastry.
- To make tree trunk, cut 2 lines down the center of triangle lightly that is narrower at the top and gets wider towards the bottom. Into the triangle sides, cut branches with the trunk as guide.
- Twist branches away from you, trying to get in 2 turns on the lower branches. Keep moving up the tree, twisting away from you as you proceed.
- Slice one small star from the extra pastry; put on top of the tree. Brush beaten egg on tree and star.
- In the prepped oven, bake for 12 to 15 minutes till golden brown and puffy. Slightly cool for 5

minutes. Slip onto serving plate, using a parchment paper piece if necessary.

Nutrition Information

- Calories: 386 calories;
- Cholesterol: 23
- Protein: 5.8
- Total Fat: 26.2
- Sodium: 169
- Total Carbohydrate: 32.4

306.   Nutella® Star Bread With Puff Pastry

Serving: 8 | Prep: 15mins | Cook: 25mins |Ready in:

Ingredients

- 2 frozen puff pastry round sheets, thawed
- 5 tablespoons chocolate-hazelnut spread (such as Nutella®)
- 1 egg, lightly beaten

Direction

- Preheat the oven to 190 ° C or 375 ° F. Line parchment paper on a baking sheet.
- Unroll a sheet of puff pastry and put on prepped baking sheet.
- Onto the puff pastry, evenly scatter chocolate-hazelnut spread using back of spoon. Unroll another puff pastry sheet and put over.
- In the middle of puff pastry, put a Mason or glass jar facing down. Using sharp knife, cut the pastry making 4 even strips, pausing at glass border. Cut along every quarter once more, creating eight strips, and once more, finishing up with 16 even portions in all, while keeping the middle attach. Twist 2 portions apart from each other; drag outward and enclose seams together. Redo with the remaining portions till pastry looks much like a star.

- Brush beaten egg on top.
- In the prepped oven, bake till golden brown and puffy, for 25 minutes to half an hour. Cool partially for 5 minutes prior to serving.

Nutrition Information

- Calories: 391 calories;
- Cholesterol: 23
- Protein: 5.8
- Total Fat: 26.4
- Sodium: 168
- Total Carbohydrate: 33.2

307.   Olive Puffs

Serving: 12 | Prep: 20mins | Cook: 20mins |Ready in:

Ingredients

- 24 pimento-stuffed green olives
- 1 (17.25 ounce) package frozen puff pastry, thawed

Direction

- Set the oven to 400°F (200°C), and start preheating.
- Slice pastry into strips of about 1/2-inch wide and 6 inches long. Wrap each olive with a belt of pastry. Put on unoiled baking sheet.
- Bake in the oven for 20 minutes, until golden brown.

Nutrition Information

- Calories: 230 calories;
- Total Fat: 16.2
- Sodium: 265
- Total Carbohydrate: 18.3
- Cholesterol: 0
- Protein: 3

308.　Om Ali

Serving: 8 | Prep: 30mins | Cook: 30mins | Ready in:

Ingredients

- 1 (17.5 ounce) package frozen puff pastry sheets, thawed
- 1/2 cup chopped walnuts
- 1 cup chopped pecans
- 1 cup chopped hazelnuts
- 1 cup raisins
- 1 cup flaked coconut
- 1 1/4 cups white sugar, divided
- 4 cups milk
- 1/2 cup heavy cream

Direction

- Heat an oven to 175°C or 350°F. Grease a baking dish measuring 9x13-inch with butter.
- Arrange pastry sheets in baking dish; put dish in oven. Keep an eye. Once layer on top becomes golden and crunchy, take it out of oven. Proceed till every sheet cooked.
- Heat a broiler of oven.
- Mix quarter cup sugar, coconut, raisins, hazelnuts, pecans and walnuts in bowl. Tear cooked pastry to portions and mix in mixture of nut. Scatter mixture smoothly in dish measuring 9x13-inch.
- Boil half cup sugar and milk on moderate heat in medium-size saucepan. Add on top of nut mixture.
- Whip leftover half cup of sugar and heavy cream till firm peaks create. Smear smoothly in dish on top of nut mixture.
- Put the dessert below oven broiler for 10 minutes till surface turn golden brown in color. Serve while hot.

Nutrition Information

- Calories: 934 calories;
- Sodium: 215
- Total Carbohydrate: 87.4
- Cholesterol: 30
- Protein: 14.7
- Total Fat: 62.1

309.　Parmesan Puff Pastry Stars

Serving: 12 | Prep: 20mins | Cook: 15mins | Ready in:

Ingredients

- 1 (17.5 ounce) package frozen puff pastry, thawed
- 1/4 cup freshly grated Parmesan

Direction

- Preheat an oven to 175°C/350°F. Line parchment paper on baking sheet.
- Lightly dust flat work surface using flour. Unroll both of the puff pastry sheets; roll everyone to rectangle of same size. Brush a little water on a puff pastry sheet; sprinkle 1/2 parmesan cheese on. Lay 2nd puff pastry sheet over top and brush with water. Sprinkle leftover parmesan cheese. Cut about 12 2 1/2-3 1/2-in. stars using a big star cutter.
- Put starts on prepped baking sheet. Chill for 15 minutes in the fridge/5 minutes in freezer.
- In preheated oven, bake for 15-20 minutes till golden brown and puffed up.

Nutrition Information

- Calories: 232 calories;
- Total Carbohydrate: 18.5
- Cholesterol: 1
- Protein: 3.6
- Total Fat: 16
- Sodium: 127

310. Pasteles De Coco (Coconut Pastries)

Serving: 12 | Prep: 40mins | Cook: 10mins | Ready in:

Ingredients

- 1 (17.25 ounce) package frozen puff pastry (2 sheets), thawed
- 1 (15.5 ounce) can canned grated coconut in syrup

Direction

- Preheat the oven to 220 degrees C (425 degrees F). Use parchment paper to cover a baking sheet.
- Slightly roll out each sheet of pastry dough to thin it. Chop each sheet into 12 squares and then put half the squares onto the baking sheet prepared and leave at least half an inch between each square.
- Put a spoonful of coconut at the middle of each pastry square and then place a second pastry square on top. Seal in the coconut filling by pinching the dough on two sides.
- Bake the pastries in the oven for about 10 to 20 minutes until golden brown. Let to cool on a rack.

Nutrition Information

- Calories: 334 calories;
- Sodium: 107
- Total Carbohydrate: 37.8
- Cholesterol: 0
- Protein: 4.1
- Total Fat: 18.8

311. Pastry Wrapped Lamb Rack

Serving: 4 | Prep: 30mins | Cook: 15mins | Ready in:

Ingredients

- 1 tablespoon olive oil
- 1 small shallot, minced
- 1/2 cup fresh morel mushrooms, sliced
- 1/2 cup fresh oyster mushrooms, stemmed and sliced
- 2 tablespoons dry white wine
- 1 teaspoon ground cumin
- 1 teaspoon paprika
- 1 teaspoon dried oregano
- 2 teaspoons brown sugar
- 1 teaspoon garlic powder
- 1 teaspoon dried parsley flakes
- 2 teaspoons ground black pepper
- 2 teaspoons kosher salt
- 1 rack of lamb, trimmed and frenched
- 1 sheet frozen puff pastry, thawed
- 2 egg yolk, beaten
- 3/4 cup demi-glace
- 2 tablespoons butter
- 2 tablespoons chopped fresh parsley

Direction

- Heat olive oil on medium high heat in a skillet. Whisk in oyster mushrooms, morel and minced shallot; cook till mushrooms turn soft and lightly-browned. Add white wine, and cook till evaporated. Scrape mushrooms onto a plate, and put aside to cool down. At the same time, in a bowl, whisk the salt, pepper, parsley flakes, garlic powder, brown sugar, oregano, paprika and cumin together. Coat lamb rack with the spice mixture and put aside.
- Preheat the oven to 175 degrees C (350 degrees F). Use the aluminum foil to line the baking sheet and grease it slightly.
- Spread mushroom mixture evenly on one side of puff pastry. Slice a slit 2 in. away from one edge of puff pastry for each bone on lamb rack. Carefully poke bones through slits and wrap pastry around lamb rack, pressing edges of pastry together to seal them. Add to prepped baking sheet and use the beaten egg yolk to brush. Keep lamb in the refrigerator for 10 minutes prior to baking.

- Bake lamb in preheated oven for roughly 15 minutes or till pastry becomes puffed and golden-brown. Take out, and allow it to stand for 5 minutes prior to slicing. When lamb is resting, simmer demi-glace in a small-sized saucepan. Stir in butter till dissolved. Sprinkle demi-glace on sliced lamb chops, and drizzle with the chopped fresh parsley to decorate.

Nutrition Information

- Calories: 946 calories;
- Sodium: 2314
- Total Carbohydrate: 47.9
- Cholesterol: 212
- Protein: 42.1
- Total Fat: 63.9

---

312.   Pear And Blue Cheese Pastry Triangles

Serving: 36 | Prep: 35mins | Cook: 55mins | Ready in:

Ingredients

- 3 tablespoons butter
- 1 tablespoon olive oil
- 4 sweet onions, thinly sliced
- salt and pepper to taste
- 1 (17.5 ounce) package frozen puff pastry, thawed
- 2 firm pears, peeled, quartered, and sliced
- 3/4 cup crumbled blue cheese

Direction

- Start preheating the oven to 375°F (190°C). Use parchment paper to line 2 cookie sheet.
- Heat olive oil and butter over medium heat in a big frying pan. Mix onions into the butter and cook for 30-40 minutes until onions caramelize to a deep, golden brown and become tender. While the onions are cooking, toss regularly to prevent them from burning.

Once finished, use pepper and salt to season, put aside to cool down.
- Slice each sheet of puff pastry into 9 squares with a sharp knife. Slice each square into two diagonally to create 36 triangles. Put the triangles onto the prepared cookie sheet, put 1 teaspoon of blue cheese, pears, and the caramelized onions on top.
- Put in the preheated oven and bake for 20-30 minutes until the pastry is golden brown and puffed. Before serving, let it cool down to room temperature.

Nutrition Information

- Calories: 109 calories;
- Total Fat: 7.4
- Sodium: 81
- Total Carbohydrate: 9.2
- Cholesterol: 5
- Protein: 1.8

---

313.   Pesto Puff Pastry Pinwheel

Serving: 8 | Prep: 25mins | Cook: 25mins | Ready in:

Ingredients

- 2 sheets puff pastry
- 2 teaspoons all-purpose flour, or as needed
- 8 1/2 ounces ricotta cheese
- 8 1/2 ounces pesto

Direction

- Preheat oven to 200°C/400°F. Line a parchment paper on a baking tray. Dust the tray with flour lightly.
- On a flat work surface, lay puff pastry; cut a circle, around 12 inches, from each sheet of puff pastry. Place 1 pastry circle onto the baking sheet.

- Spread an even layer of ricotta on the pastry circle, then evenly top with a layer of pesto. Place the second circle on top. In the middle of the circle, place a small glass facing down.
- Starting from the edge of the glass, slice the circle into 4 equal quarters. Slice each quarter in half, then halve each of the eighths. There should be 16 equal strips. Remove the glass. Twist strips two times, two strips at a time, in the opposite direction and pinch the ends together. Continue with the rest of the strips, making a pinwheel shape.
- Bake for 25 to 30 minutes in the preheated oven, or until the pastry has browned.

Nutrition Information

- Calories: 535 calories;
- Total Fat: 39.9
- Sodium: 432
- Total Carbohydrate: 31.3
- Cholesterol: 20
- Protein: 13.6

314.   Pistachio Twists

Serving: 36 | Prep: 15mins | Cook: 15mins | Ready in:

Ingredients

- 1 (17.5 ounce) package frozen puff pastry, thawed
- 1 egg white, beaten
- 1/3 cup finely chopped shelled pistachios
- kosher salt to taste

Direction

- Preheat oven to 175°C/350°F. Line parchment papers on baking sheets.
- Unfold puff pastry sheets and brush egg white over the tops. Over the egg white wash, sprinkle salt and pistachios. Flip the sheets and repeat process of brushing with egg white and sprinkling with salt and pistachios. Slice

pastry into strips, 3 inches long and 3/4 inch wide using a sharp knife. Twist the strips two times and transfer them to the prepped baking sheet. Strips should not touch each other.
- Bake for 15 minutes in preheated oven, or until browned.

Nutrition Information

- Calories: 82 calories;
- Sodium: 52
- Total Carbohydrate: 6.5
- Cholesterol: 0
- Protein: 1.3
- Total Fat: 5.7

315.   Portuguese Custard Tarts Pasteis De Nata

Serving: 12 | Prep: 20mins | Cook: 20mins | Ready in:

Ingredients

- 1 cup milk
- 3 tablespoons cornstarch
- 1/2 vanilla bean
- 1 cup white sugar
- 6 egg yolks
- 1 (17.5 ounce) package frozen puff pastry, thawed

Direction

- Start preheating the oven to 375°F (190°C). Grease 12 muffin cups lightly and line puff pastry on sides and bottom.
- Combine vanilla, sugar, cornstarch and milk in a saucepan. Cook until the mixture thickens, stirring constantly. In a medium bowl, put egg yolks. Whisk half cup hot milk mixture slowly into the egg yolks. Put the egg yolk mixture gradually back to the remaining milk mixture, whisking constantly. Cook for 5 mins or until

thickened, stirring constantly. Discard the vanilla bean.

- Fill mixture into the pastry-lined muffin cups; bake for 20 mins in prepared oven until the filling has browned lightly on top and the crust turns golden brown

Nutrition Information

- Calories: 336 calories;
- Total Fat: 18.2
- Sodium: 114
- Total Carbohydrate: 38.7
- Cholesterol: 104
- Protein: 5

---

316.   Puff Pastry Bear Claws

Serving: 8 | Prep: 30mins | Cook: 15mins | Ready in:

Ingredients

- 1/3 cup superfine sugar
- 1/4 cup unsalted butter, softened
- 2 large egg yolks
- 1/4 teaspoon almond extract
- 1 cup ground almonds
- 1 tablespoon all-purpose flour
- 1 sheet puff pastry, thawed and rolled out into a 16x16-inch square
- 1 egg
- 1 tablespoon water
- 2 tablespoons sliced almonds, or to taste
- 2 tablespoons superfine sugar, or to taste

Direction

- Preheat an oven to 200 degrees C (400 degrees F).
- Use an electric mixer to beat butter and 1/3 cup superfine sugar together in a bowl for about 5 minutes until fluffy and light. Put in eggs yolks, then beat well; beat in the almond extract. Mix flour and ground almonds into

the butter mixture until the mixture attains a thick paste-like consistency.

- Slice the puff pastry into 8 pieces of equal size. Put one tablespoon of almond mixture in the lower middle of every piece. Then, fold down the top of puff pastry over filling and pinch the edges together to seal. Slice 3 half-inch cuts, equal lengths apart, at the bottom edge to form "claws". Place the pastries in baking sheet.
- In a bowl, whisk water and egg together. Brush the egg mixture onto each bear claw and drizzle with the sliced almonds and remaining 2 tablespoons superfine sugar.
- Bake for 15 to 20 minutes in the oven until golden brown and puffed.

Nutrition Information

- Calories: 354 calories;
- Total Carbohydrate: 30.3
- Cholesterol: 90
- Protein: 9.7
- Total Fat: 22.3
- Sodium: 88

---

317.   Puff Pastry Chicken 'N Broccoli Pot Pie

Serving: 12 | Prep: 35mins | Cook: 30mins | Ready in:

Ingredients

- cooking spray
- 4 cups diced deli rotisserie chicken
- 1 1/2 cups shredded Mexican cheese blend
- 1 cup mayonnaise (such as Hellman's®)
- 1 cup finely chopped broccoli florets
- 1/2 cup diced onion
- 1/3 cup finely chopped red bell pepper
- 2 cloves garlic, minced
- 3 tablespoons slivered almonds
- 3 tablespoons chopped fresh dill

- 1 (17 ounce) package frozen puff pastry, thawed
- 1 egg
- 1 teaspoon water
- 1 pinch salt

Direction

- Start preheating the oven to 375°F (190°C). Use cooking spray to spray the sides and bottom of a 9x13" baking pan.
- In a big bowl, mix together dill, almonds, garlic, red bell pepper, onion, broccoli, mayonnaise, Mexican cheese blend, and chicken.
- On a surface scattered with flour, roll the pastry sheets until all sides are longer than the bottom of the prepared pan by 3 inches. Put 1 sheet against the sides and on the bottom of the pan. Put the chicken filling evenly on the bottom crust. Put the second crust on top, tucking the ends between the bottom crust and the pan. Pinch crusts together to fasten.
- In a bowl, whisk eggs with salt and water, brush the top crust with this mixture. Slit vents into the top to release the steam.
- Put in the preheated oven and bake for 30 minutes until the top turns golden brown.

Nutrition Information

- Calories: 611 calories;
- Cholesterol: 96
- Protein: 26.3
- Total Fat: 46.8
- Sodium: 411
- Total Carbohydrate: 21.2

---

318. Puff Pastry Cinnamon Rolls

Serving: 12 | Prep: 15mins | Cook: 45mins | Ready in:

Ingredients

- 1 sheet frozen puff pastry, thawed
- 1 (8 ounce) package cream cheese, cubed
- 1 tablespoon butter
- 1 tablespoon ground cinnamon
- 1 tablespoon vanilla extract
- 1 (16 ounce) package cream cheese frosting

Direction

- Set oven to 375 0 F (190 0 C) and preheat. Use cooking spray to grease a 9x13 inch baking pan.
- Melt butter in a saucepan over medium heat. Put vanilla, cinnamon and cream cheese into pan, and stir until smooth. Take away from heat, and let it cool for 5 minutes.
- Spread over puff pastry with the cream cheese and cinnamon mixture. Form the puff pastry into a log, and pinch ends of the log together to hold the filling inside. Put roll in the greased pan.
- Put in the prepared oven and bake the roll for 35 to 40 minutes, or until golden brown. Take out of the oven, and spread over warm roll with cream cheese frosting. Serve while the roll is warm or at room temperature.

Nutrition Information

- Calories: 349 calories;
- Protein: 2.9
- Total Fat: 21.8
- Sodium: 186
- Total Carbohydrate: 36.1
- Cholesterol: 23

---

319. Puff Pastry Pinwheels With Bell Peppers, Cream Cheese, And Salami

Serving: 45 | Prep: 30mins | Cook: 20mins | Ready in:

Ingredients

- 1 tablespoon unsalted butter
- 1 red bell pepper, finely chopped
- 1 yellow bell pepper, finely chopped
- 1/2 pound peppered salami, finely diced
- 1 (8 ounce) container herb and garlic-flavored cream cheese
- 5 tablespoons freshly grated Parmesan cheese, or to taste
- 1 egg
- 1 teaspoon mild paprika, or to taste
- 1 (17.5 ounce) package frozen puff pastry, thawed

Direction

- Place a skillet over medium-low heat and heat the butter. Cook red and yellow bell peppers in the hot butter for 5 minutes, or until soft but not browned.
- In a bowl, mix together egg, Parmesan cheese, cream cheese, salami, and the bell peppers. Add paprika to season.
- On a lightly floured flat work surface, roll out both puff pastry sheets to 2 large rectangles. Leaving a 1-inch margin around the puff pastry borders, spread a layer of the bell pepper mixture. Tightly roll up the pastry and freeze in the freezer for 1 hour, or until the filling hardens.
- Preheat oven to 200°C/400°F. Line parchment papers on 2 to 3 baking sheets.
- Remove the puff pastry rolls from the freezer and slice the pastry into 1/2-inch thick slices. Arrange on the baking sheet, 2 inches apart.
- Bake on the center rack for 20 to 30 minutes in preheated oven, or until puffed up and lightly browned.

Nutrition Information

- Calories: 104 calories;
- Total Carbohydrate: 5.6
- Cholesterol: 15
- Protein: 2.5
- Total Fat: 7.8
- Sodium: 167

320.   Puff Pastry Pinwheels With Smoked Salmon And Cream Cheese

Serving: 15 | Prep: 10mins | Cook: 20mins | Ready in:

Ingredients

- 1/2 (17.5 ounce) package frozen puff pastry, thawed
- 1/2 (8 ounce) container herbed cream cheese
- 7 ounces sliced smoked salmon
- 1 sprig fresh dill, finely chopped, or to taste

Direction

- Use flour to lightly dust a flat work surface. Unroll the puff pastry and then roll out to form a rectangle. Lay a thin layer of herbed cream cheese onto the puff pastry. Add smoked slices of salmon to cover and drizzle with dill and leave a 1-inch border. Tightly roll up the puff pastry like a jelly roll and then use plastic wrap to wrap it. Chill for 15 minutes.
- Preheat an oven to 200 degrees C (400 degrees F). Line parchment paper onto a baking sheet.
- Cut the puff pastry roll into slices of 1/4-inch-thick and then spread onto the baking sheet.
- Bake for about 20-25 minutes at the center rack of the oven until puffed up and browned lightly.

Nutrition Information

- Calories: 132 calories;
- Sodium: 188
- Total Carbohydrate: 7.8
- Cholesterol: 10
- Protein: 3.8
- Total Fat: 9.2

321. Puff Pastry Pizza

Serving: 16 | Prep: 20mins | Cook: 25mins | Ready in:

Ingredients

- 1 (17.25 ounce) package frozen puff pastry sheets, thawed
- 2 tablespoons extra virgin olive oil
- 3 green onion, thinly sliced
- 1 tablespoon diced onion
- 1 clove garlic, minced
- 6 sun-dried tomatoes, chopped
- 2 teaspoons dried rosemary
- 2 cups shredded mozzarella cheese
- 1/4 cup crumbled Gorgonzola cheese

Direction

- Start preheating the oven to 400°F (200°C). On a large baking sheet, place both puff pastry sheets, then create 1 large sheet by pinching together in the middle. Bake about 15 mins.
- In the meantime, heat oil in a small skillet over medium heat. In oil, cook rosemary, tomatoes, garlic, onion and green onion for 5 mins, until onions become soft.
- Take the puff pastry out of the oven. Add garlic and onion mixture with mozzarella and Gorgonzola cheeses over the top. Place back to oven. Bake for 10 mins until cheese melts. Slice into 2-in. squares. Enjoy.

Nutrition Information

- Calories: 231 calories;
- Total Fat: 16.2
- Sodium: 205
- Total Carbohydrate: 14.8
- Cholesterol: 12
- Protein: 6.4

322. Puff Pastry Roast Beef Pot Pies

Serving: 6 | Prep: 25mins | Cook: 1hours | Ready in:

Ingredients

- 1 tablespoon olive oil
- 2 cups cubed beef stew meat
- 1 onion, diced
- 2 yellow potatoes, peeled and diced
- 2 carrots, diced
- 1 rib celery, diced
- 1 clove garlic, crushed
- 1/4 cup all-purpose flour
- 2 tablespoons butter
- 1 bay leaf
- salt and ground black pepper to taste
- 3 cups low-sodium beef stock
- 1 cup milk
- 1 sprig fresh rosemary
- 1/2 cup frozen peas
- 1 (17.5 ounce) package frozen puff pastry, thawed

Direction

- Preheat an oven to 175 ° C or 350 ° F.
- In a big stockpot, heat the olive oil on moderately heat; cook and mix the stew meat for 2 to 3 minutes, till browned. Put in the onion; cook and mix for 3 to 4 minutes, till onion is browned slightly. Put in the garlic, celery, carrots and potatoes; cook and mix for 3 to 4 minutes, till partially soft.
- Into the stew meat mixture, mix pepper, salt, bay leaf, butter and flour; cook and mix for 2 minutes till flour is dissolving and gravy is being created. On mixture of meat, add the beef stock, scratching food brown bits off base using wooden spoon; cook for 5 minutes, till gravy starts to thicken.
- Into the mixture of stew meat-gravy, mix rosemary and milk; keep cooking for 15 to 20 minutes, on low heat. Into the mixture, mix the peas.

- Into a cast iron 12-inches skillet or individual pot pie pans, put the mixture of stew meat-gravy; put puff pastry on top, fluting pastry sides down securely. Cover in aluminum foil.
- In the prepped oven, bake for 30 to 45 minutes, till pastry is golden and puffed.

Nutrition Information

- Calories: 834 calories;
- Total Fat: 52.4
- Sodium: 424
- Total Carbohydrate: 59.7
- Cholesterol: 76
- Protein: 30.3

323.   Puff Pastry Roll

Serving: 9 | Prep: | Cook: | Ready in:

Ingredients

- 1 (17.5 ounce) package frozen puff pastry, thawed
- 1 pound ground chicken
- 1/4 cup water
- 1 small onion, shredded
- 2 eggs
- 1/2 cup dry bread crumbs
- salt to taste
- ground black pepper to taste
- 1 tablespoon vegetable oil
- 2 tablespoons butter
- 2 tablespoons all-purpose flour
- 1 tablespoon soy sauce
- 1/2 packet dry onion soup mix
- 1 (8 ounce) can mushrooms, drained
- 1 cup water
- 2 tablespoons white wine

Direction

- Combine pepper and salt, eggs, grated onion, quarter cup of water and ground chicken

together. Stir in sufficient bread crumbs to create a moldable, soft mixture.
- In a big skillet, heat the oil, and the chicken mixture brown on moderate heat.
- Unroll puff pastry. Put the mixture along the lengthy pastry edge. Roll up, and fold ends beneath. Put on an unoiled cookie sheet.
- Bake till golden, for 12 to 15 minutes 220 ° C or 425 ° F.
- Meantime, make mushroom sauce. In small pot, liquify margarine or butter. Mix in flour. Put in white wine, 1 cup water, onion soup mix and soy sauce; mix till thick. Mix in mushrooms. Put on top of meat roll once serving.

Nutrition Information

- Calories: 591 calories;
- Protein: 12.5
- Total Fat: 27.9
- Sodium: 825
- Total Carbohydrate: 76
- Cholesterol: 48

324.   Puff Pastry Salmon

Serving: 6 | Prep: 15mins | Cook: 20mins | Ready in:

Ingredients

- 2 (12 ounce) skinless, boneless salmon fillets
- seasoned salt to taste
- 1/2 teaspoon garlic powder
- 1 teaspoon onion powder
- 1 (17.25 ounce) package frozen puff pastry, thawed
- 1/3 cup pesto
- 1 (6 ounce) package spinach leaves

Direction

- Start preheating the oven to 375°F (190°C).

- Add onion powder, garlic powder, and salt to salmon fillets for seasoning. Divide half spinach between 2 sheets of the puff pastry. Mound in middle. Top each spinach mound with a salmon fillet. Spread salmon fillets with pesto. Add the remaining spinach on top. Use water to moisten edges of puff pastry and fold to middle, then seal the seams.
- Bake for 20-25 minutes in the prepared oven, until salmon is cooked through and pastry is golden and puffed.

Nutrition Information

- Calories: 685 calories;
- Total Fat: 43.7
- Sodium: 529
- Total Carbohydrate: 38.9
- Cholesterol: 55
- Protein: 33.5

325.   Puff Pastry Shells

Serving: 4 | Prep: 10mins | Cook: 20mins | Ready in:

Ingredients

- 1 egg, beaten
- 2 tablespoons water
- 4 sheets frozen puff pastry

Direction

- In a small bowl, beat water and egg together.
- Use a 3-inch circle cutter to cut two circles on each puff pastry sheet. There should be 8 circles.
- Press a 2 1/2-inch circle cutter down the center of 4 of the circles to cut through. Top the un-cut circles with the cut circles. Brush egg mixture over the pastries.
- Bake for 20 to 25 minutes, or until golden and puffed.

Nutrition Information

- Calories: 1346 calories;
- Total Fat: 93.1
- Sodium: 618
- Total Carbohydrate: 108.8
- Cholesterol: 46
- Protein: 19.2

326.   Puff Pastry Waffles

Serving: 8 | Prep: 5mins | Cook: 3mins | Ready in:

Ingredients

- 1 (17.3 ounce) package frozen puff pastry, thawed
- cooking spray

Direction

- Line parchment paper on cutting board. Unfold puff pastry on cutting board. Cut every sheet to 4 even squares.
- Preheat a waffle iron following to manufacturer's instructions then grease using cooking spray.
- In preheated waffle iron, put 1 puff pastry square. Cook for 3-5 minutes till golden brown. Repeat with leftover puff pastry squares.

Nutrition Information

- Calories: 338 calories;
- Cholesterol: 0
- Protein: 4.5
- Total Fat: 23.4
- Sodium: 153
- Total Carbohydrate: 27.7

327. Puff Pastry With Spinach And Feta

Serving: 12 | Prep: 15mins | Cook: 30mins | Ready in:

Ingredients

- 1 (16 ounce) package frozen chopped spinach, thawed and drained
- salt and freshly ground black pepper to taste
- 1 pinch ground nutmeg
- 2 sheets frozen puff pastry, thawed
- 1 1/4 cups heavy whipping cream, or more to taste
- 1 (8 ounce) package crumbled feta cheese, or more to taste
- 2 cloves garlic, minced

Direction

- Using a sieve, drain the thawed spinach. Use your hands to press as much liquid out as possible. Season with nutmeg, pepper, and salt.
- Preheat oven to 175°C/350°F. Line parchment papers on two baking sheets. On each baking sheet, place 1 sheet of puff pastry.
- In a blender, blend together garlic, feta cheese, and cream until mixture smoothens.
- On the 2 puff pastry sheets, evenly distribute the spinach, leaving the borders of the puff pastry uncovered. Top the spinach with a layer of feta cheese mixture.
- Bake for 30 minutes in preheated oven, or until edges are lightly browned and the pastry is puffed up.

Nutrition Information

- Calories: 359 calories;
- Sodium: 335
- Total Carbohydrate: 19.9
- Cholesterol: 51
- Protein: 6.3
- Total Fat: 28.5

328. Pumpkin, Spinach And Barley Rolls

Serving: 6 | Prep: 30mins | Cook: 20mins | Ready in:

Ingredients

- 1/2 cup pearl barley
- 1 1/2 cups water
- 2 1/4 cups canned pumpkin
- 8 leaves spinach - rinsed, stemmed, and dried
- 1/2 teaspoon ground cumin
- 1/4 teaspoon chili powder
- salt and pepper to taste
- 1 (17.5 ounce) package frozen puff pastry, thawed

Direction

- In the medium pot, boil barley and water. Lower the heat to simmer, cover and allow it to cook for 15 minutes.
- Preheat the oven to 190 degrees C (375 degrees F).
- In the big mixing bowl, mix the pepper, salt, chili powder, cumin, spinach, barley and pumpkin.
- Lay out one sheet of the pastry and add half of pumpkin mixture along the middle horizontally. Roll pastry over mixture, and seal seams with a bit of water. Chop the stuffed pastry into 3 pieces. Arrange the pieces onto one cookie sheet. Repeat the process with the rest of ingredients.
- Bake at 190 degrees C (375 degrees F) till turning golden brown or for 20 minutes.

Nutrition Information

- Calories: 544 calories;
- Cholesterol: 0
- Protein: 9
- Total Fat: 31.7
- Sodium: 438
- Total Carbohydrate: 57.8

329. Quick Puff Pastry Apple Strudel

Serving: 8 | Prep: 15mins | Cook: 25mins | Ready in:

Ingredients

- 4 apples - peeled, cored, and chopped
- 1/2 cup raisins
- 3/4 cup white sugar
- 1/2 cup chopped walnuts
- 2 teaspoons ground cinnamon
- 1/2 (17.5 ounce) package frozen puff pastry, thawed
- 1 tablespoon all-purpose flour
- 1 egg, lightly beaten
- 1 tablespoon white sugar, or to taste

Direction

- Preheat an oven to 200°C/400°F.
- For filing, mix cinnamon, walnuts, raisins, 3/4 cup sugar and apples in a big bowl.
- Lightly flour a flat work surface. Unroll puff pastry; lightly sprinkle flour. Slightly roll out; mark to 3 even sections. Scoop filling in middle section; fold over left section. Brush using egg. Fold right section over like a letter; create shallow and diagonal cuts in top apple strudel layer. Brush with egg; sprinkle 1 tablespoon sugar over.
- In the preheated oven, bake for 25-30 minutes till apple strudel is golden and puffs up.

Nutrition Information

- Calories: 376 calories;
- Total Fat: 17.2
- Sodium: 87
- Total Carbohydrate: 54.1
- Cholesterol: 23
- Protein: 4.8

330. Quick And Easy Party Pinwheels With Cream Cheese And Ham

Serving: 24 | Prep: 15mins | Cook: 15mins | Ready in:

Ingredients

- 1/2 (17.5 ounce) package frozen puff pastry, thawed
- 1 (8 ounce) package cream cheese, softened
- 6 ounces deli-sliced ham

Direction

- Preheat the oven to 190 ° C or 375 ° F. Line parchment paper on a baking sheet.
- Lightly flour a flat work area. Roll out the puff pastry and unroll into rectangle. Scatter a thinnish layer of cream cheese on top of puff pastry. Top with slices of ham to cover, retaining an-inch margin. Tightly roll puff pastry up jelly roll style.
- Cut puff pastry roll into quarter-inch-thick pieces and lay on prepped baking sheet.
- In the prepped oven, bake on the middle rack for 15 to 20 minutes, till puffed up and slightly browned.

Nutrition Information

- Calories: 106 calories;
- Cholesterol: 14
- Protein: 2.7
- Total Fat: 8.4
- Sodium: 143
- Total Carbohydrate: 4.9

331. Raspberry Napoleons Dessert

Serving: 16 | Prep: 15mins | Cook: 10mins | Ready in:

Ingredients

- 1 (17.5 ounce) package frozen puff pastry, thawed
- 1 (8 ounce) package cream cheese, softened
- 1/2 cup white sugar
- 2 tablespoons 35% heavy whipping cream
- 1 teaspoon lemon zest
- 1 pint fresh raspberries
- 3 tablespoons confectioners' sugar, or as needed

Direction

- Preheat an oven to 175 ° C or 350 ° F. Line parchment paper on two baking sheets.
- On floured work area, unroll a sheet of puff pastry into quarter-inch thick. Slice into 16 squares. Turn onto a baking sheet and puncture entirely using fork. Redo with the rest of puff pastry sheet.
- In the prepped oven, bake for 10 to 15 minutes till slightly browned on surface and underside. Cool for 10 minutes.
- In bowl, mix lemon zest, heavy cream, white sugar and cream cheese. Combine using hand till shinny and smooth. Put dollop of cream cheese mixture on top of 16 squares. Scatter out mixture of cream cheese and top with raspberries to cover. Put the rest of the puff pastry squares on top and sprinkle confectioners' sugar over.

Nutrition Information

- Calories: 261 calories;
- Protein: 3.5
- Total Fat: 17.3
- Sodium: 118
- Total Carbohydrate: 23.7
- Cholesterol: 18

332.   Raspberry Pain Au Chocolat (Raspberry Chocolate Croissants)

Serving: 18 | Prep: 20mins | Cook: 18mins | Ready in:

Ingredients

- 1 (17.25 ounce) package frozen puff pastry, thawed
- 6 tablespoons chocolate hazelnut spread
- 3 tablespoons all fruit raspberry jam
- 1 egg, beaten
- 1/4 cup confectioners' sugar for dusting (optional)

Direction

- Preheat an oven to 200 degrees C (400 degrees F).
- Onto a lightly floured surface, unfold puff pastry sheets. Slice each one along the fold lines into thirds. Then, roll out each dough strip into about 16 inches long, then slice into thirds.
- Spread one half of each rectangle with some of the hazelnut spread to within half inch of edge. Spread half teaspoon of raspberry jam on top of the hazelnut spread. Coat the edges with egg, then fold over the other side to cover filling. Firmly press the edges to seal. Repeat this with the rest of the rectangles. Make 5 slits across the top of every pastry with a sharp knife, then put in baking sheets, two inches apart.
- Bake in the oven for about 18 minutes or until it turns golden brown. Let cool on racks. If you like, sprinkle with confectioners' sugar once cooled.

Nutrition Information

- Calories: 189 calories;
- Total Fat: 12
- Sodium: 76
- Total Carbohydrate: 18.1
- Cholesterol: 10

- Protein: 2.6

Serving: 12 | Prep: | Cook: |Ready in:

Ingredients

- 1 sheet frozen puff pastry, thawed but still cold (follow package directions)
- 8 ounces semisweet chocolate, cut in small dice
- 1 cup heavy cream
- 2 large egg yolks (if using raw eggs is a concern for you, substitute the yolks of 2 pasteurized eggs)
- Optional garnish:
- 1 cup heavy cream, whipped to soft peaks
- 1 cup raspberries

Direction

- Place the oven rack to lower-middle position and set oven to preheat at 425°. Put the pastry onto a working surface that is lightly floured and roll it out into a square with 12-inch sides. Fit it into a 9-by-1-inch round tart pan, do not stretch the pastry. Use the tip of your thumb to press around the edges to trim the excess pastry. Use a fork to prick across the pastry's surface.
- Use vegetable cooking spray to spray a 9-inch Pyrex-type pie plate's bottom side, then put it into the tart pan to prevent pastry from puffing too much. Bake till golden brown and crisp for about 20 to 22 minutes. Take off the pie plate and let the shell cool down to room temperature.
- In the meantime, on high power, microwave chocolate and cream in a Pyrex-type 1-quart measuring cup till cream can melt chocolate for about 3 minutes. (Or heat together the chocolate and cream in a double boiler.) Whisk it till smooth. Whisk the egg yolks in a small bowl. Whisk about a cup or so of the chocolate mixture slowly into the yolks (this way, they do not curdle). Whisk this mixture back into

333.   Rice Pie

Serving: 8 | Prep: | Cook: |Ready in:

Ingredients

- 2 cups fresh squeezed tomato juice
- 1 cup beef broth
- 1/4 cup butter
- salt to taste
- 1 cup long-grain white rice
- 1 cup drained canned peas
- 1 (15 ounce) can carrots, drained
- 1 (17.5 ounce) package frozen puff pastry, thawed
- 1 egg yolk, beaten

Direction

- In a big saucepan, mix salt, butter or margarine, broth and tomato juice. Let come to a full boil. Put in rice, and place cover. Lower heat to a simmer. Cook for 15 minutes, till liquid is soaked in. Mix in carrots and peas.
- Line a sheet of pastry on pie plate, 9-inch in size. Clip and crimp the edges. Into shell, scatter the rice mixture. Slice the rest of the dough into half-inch strips, and put on top of rice, in crisscross pattern. Clip and crimp edges. Brush egg yolk on pastry.
- Bake for 20 minutes at 175 ° C or 350 ° F.

Nutrition Information

- Calories: 515 calories;
- Sodium: 369
- Total Carbohydrate: 53.4
- Cholesterol: 41
- Protein: 8.5
- Total Fat: 30

the rest of the chocolate and stir till combined thoroughly.

- Transfer the chocolate filling into the tart shell. Let it cool down till filling has set. (Or loosely cover and refrigerate overnight. Bring it back to room temperature before serving.) Serve with whipped cream and raspberries (optional).

Nutrition Information

- Calories: 355 calories;
- Sodium: 66
- Total Carbohydrate: 22.1
- Cholesterol: 88
- Protein: 4.1
- Total Fat: 29.1

335.   Roasted Vegetables And Puff Pastry

Serving: 4 | Prep: 20mins | Cook: 30mins | Ready in:

Ingredients

- 1 onion, chopped
- 1 green bell pepper, chopped
- 1 red bell pepper, chopped
- 1 green chile pepper, chopped
- 1 clove garlic, chopped
- freshly ground black pepper to taste
- 1 tablespoon extra virgin olive oil
- 1 (14.5 ounce) can diced tomatoes, drained
- 1 (4 ounce) package feta cheese, crumbled
- 1/2 (17.5 ounce) package frozen puff pastry (1 sheet), thawed

Direction

- Preheat the oven to 200 ° C or 400 ° F. Grease a shallow pie dish or baking dish lightly.
- In prepped pan, put garlic, peppers and onion. Add freshly ground pepper to season, and scatter a bit of olive oil on top of them. In

prepped oven, roast till vegetable are done, for 10 minutes.

- Once vegetables are soft, take out of oven. Evenly scatter tomatoes on top of vegetables, and scatter feta cheese over. Unroll puff pastry, and put on top of vegetables.
- Bake till pastry turn golden brown, for 20 minutes. Take out of oven, put one tray above the dish, and then invert upside facing down to have a puff pastry underside with vegetables above. Serve right away while puff pastry is still crisp.

Nutrition Information

- Calories: 619 calories;
- Total Carbohydrate: 41.1
- Cholesterol: 67
- Protein: 17.1
- Total Fat: 42.9
- Sodium: 1156

336.   Russian Cabbage Pie

Serving: 8 | Prep: 15mins | Cook: 1hours10mins | Ready in:

Ingredients

- 3 tablespoons butter, or more to taste
- 1 small head cabbage, finely chopped
- 3 hard-boiled eggs, peeled and chopped, or more to taste
- 3 sprigs fresh dill, finely chopped, or to taste
- salt to taste
- 2 sheets yeasted puff pastry
- 1 egg, beaten

Direction

- Over medium-low heat, melt butter in a large skillet and add cabbage. Let to cook for about 30 minutes until it's softened but not browned. Take out from the heat and cool for about 10 to 15 minutes.

- Preheat an oven to 200 degrees C (400 degrees F).
- Combine the cooled cabbage with dill and hard-boiled eggs. Add salt to season.
- Line 1 sheet of puff pastry onto a pie plate and then add cabbage filling and leave some space around the edge. Then cover with another sheet of puff pastry and press the edges together. Use the beaten egg to glaze the top.
- Bake for 40 to 45 minutes in the preheated oven until turned golden brown.

Nutrition Information

- Calories: 431 calories;
- Total Fat: 30
- Sodium: 248
- Total Carbohydrate: 32.6
- Cholesterol: 114
- Protein: 8.7

---

337.   Salami Pinwheels

Serving: 24 | Prep: 15mins | Cook: 15mins | Ready in:

Ingredients

- 1/2 (17.5 ounce) package frozen puff pastry, thawed
- 6 ounces thinly sliced salami

Direction

- Preheat an oven to 190°C/375°F. Line parchment paper on baking sheet.
- Lightly dust flat work surface with flour. Unroll the puff pastry. Roll out to rectangle. Use salami slices to cover; leave 1-inch border. Tightly roll up puffy pastry, jellyroll style.
- Cut puff pastry toll to 1/4-inch thick slices. Put on the prepared baking sheet.
- In preheated oven, bake on middle rack for 15-20 minutes till puffed up and lightly browned.

Nutrition Information

- Calories: 83 calories;
- Protein: 2.4
- Total Fat: 6
- Sodium: 166
- Total Carbohydrate: 4.9
- Cholesterol: 7

---

338.   Salmon Pot Pie

Serving: 4 | Prep: 20mins | Cook: 40mins | Ready in:

Ingredients

- 3 cups clam juice
- 1 (3 ounce) salmon fillet, skin removed
- 1 tablespoon olive oil
- 2 tablespoons butter
- 1 carrot, peeled and diced
- 1 stalk celery, diced
- 1 small leek, diced
- 1 shallot, minced
- 3 tablespoons all-purpose flour, or as needed
- 1 cup heavy whipping cream
- 3 tablespoons chopped fresh dill, or to taste
- 1/2 lemon, juiced, or to taste
- salt and ground black pepper to taste
- 10 medium shrimp, peeled and deveined
- 1 1/2 ounces smoked salmon, chopped
- 1/2 sheet frozen puff pastry, thawed

Direction

- Preheat the oven to 220 ° C or 425 ° F. Oil 2 two-cup baking dishes.
- In small pot, simmer the clam juice. Into the clam juice, put salmon fillet; poach for 10 minutes till fish flakes effortlessly with fork. Transfer the salmon into plate; set poaching liquid aside.
- In skillet, heat butter and olive oil on moderate heat. Mix in shallot, leek, celery and carrot; cook and mix for 5 minutes, till vegetables are

soft. Into mixture of vegetable, mix flour; cook and mix for 5 minutes, till flour turn golden.

- Into mixture of vegetable, mix cream and the reserved poaching liquid; bring back to simmer and cook for 3 minutes, mixing from time to time, till sauce is thick. Into the mixture, mix lemon juice and dill; add pepper and salt to season.
- Separate salmon fillet into bite-size portions; distribute into prepped baking dishes. Top salmon with a third of the sauce to cover; into every dish, layer 5 shrimp. Top shrimp with a third of sauce to cover; distribute smoked salmon equally into every dish. Put leftover 1/3 of sauce on top.
- Unroll sheet of puff pastry on slightly floured area into 1/8-inch thick. Cut 2 pastry rounds, big enough to top baking dishes and put a round on top of every dish. On baking sheet, put dishes.
- In the prepped oven, bake for 15 minutes, till pastry is golden brown and risen. Let cool for 5 minutes prior to serving.

Nutrition Information

- Calories: 565 calories;
- Protein: 15.2
- Total Fat: 45.5
- Sodium: 687
- Total Carbohydrate: 25.1
- Cholesterol: 153

339. Salmon Wellington

Serving: 8 | Prep: 30mins | Cook: 45mins | Ready in:

Ingredients

- 1 tablespoon kosher salt
- 1 1/2 pounds salmon fillets
- 1 teaspoon chopped fresh thyme
- 1 teaspoon dried oregano
- 1 teaspoon chopped fresh basil leaves

- 2 teaspoons dried dill weed
- 1/2 cup Dijon mustard
- 1 1/2 cups mayonnaise
- 3/4 cup crumbled feta cheese
- 1 cup frozen chopped spinach, thawed and drained
- 1 (17.5 ounce) package frozen puff pastry, thawed
- 1 egg white, beaten

Direction

- Set oven to 375°F (190°C) to preheat.
- Sprinkle both sides of salmon with salt. In a small mixing bowl, combine mayonnaise, mustard, dill, basil, oregano, and thyme; smear mayonnaise mixture over fish, then scatter feta cheese over. Arrange spinach over feta cheese layer.
- Roll out the pastry large enough and wide enough to wrap around the salmon (about 1/4 inch in thickness). Position salmon the middle of the pastry and fold the pastry over the fish. Arrange the wrap on a baking sheet, seam side down. Create several small slits in the pasty to allow steam to release. Brush pastry with egg white.
- Bake for about 45 minutes in the preheated oven until pastry turns golden brown and fish is easily flaked using a fork.

Nutrition Information

- Calories: 843 calories;
- Total Fat: 66.2
- Sodium: 1803
- Total Carbohydrate: 34.2
- Cholesterol: 75
- Protein: 27.6

340. Salmon En Croute

Serving: 4 | Prep: 20mins | Cook: 53mins | Ready in:

Ingredients

- 2 tablespoons olive oil, divided
- 1/2 onion, chopped
- 1 cup chopped fresh mushrooms
- 2 teaspoons minced garlic, divided
- salt and ground black pepper to taste
- 1 cup baby spinach
- 1 tablespoon all-purpose flour, or as needed
- 2 sheets frozen puff pastry (such as Pepperidge Farm®), thawed
- 1 (1 1/2-pound) boned, skinned salmon fillet
- 1/2 teaspoon smoked paprika, or more to taste
- 1 egg, beaten
- Sauce:
- 1/2 cup mayonnaise
- 2 tablespoons fresh lemon juice
- 2 teaspoons Dijon mustard
- 1/2 teaspoon dried dill

Direction

- Over medium heat, heat one tablespoon of oil in a large skillet and add onion. Cook while stirring for about 5 minutes until translucent. Place in one teaspoon garlic and mushrooms and then cook while stirring for about 5 minutes until the mushrooms become soft. Add black pepper and salt to taste. In a small bowl, pour the onion and mushroom mixture.
- In the same skillet, heat the remaining one tablespoon of oil and then place in the remaining 1 teaspoon of garlic. Cook while stirring for about 30 seconds until fragrant. Place in spinach and then cook while stirring for 3 to 5 minutes until wilted. Add black pepper and salt to taste. Pour this mixture in another bowl.
- Preheat the oven to 175 degrees C (350 degrees F). Line parchment paper onto a glass baking dish.
- Dust the work surface using flour. Spread out one puff pastry sheet onto the work surface. Pour the onion and mushroom mixture evenly around the pastry and leave a 1/2-inch border. Place salmon at the center. Drizzle paprika on top of salmon and then add wilted spinach on top. Spread the second puff pastry sheet to cover. Roll over and crimp the edges to seal. Baste the top with beaten egg. Place in a baking dish.
- Bake for about 40 to 45 minutes in the oven until the pastry becomes golden. Take out and allow to sit for 5 minutes. Chop into four portions.
- In a small bowl, whisk together dill, mayonnaise, Dijon mustard, and lemon juice. Ladle the sauce onto four plates and top each with a piece of salmon.

Nutrition Information

- Calories: 1206 calories;
- Total Fat: 85.7
- Sodium: 653
- Total Carbohydrate: 60.8
- Cholesterol: 132
- Protein: 47.8

---

341.   Samosa Pot Pie

Serving: 8 | Prep: 20mins | Cook: 55mins | Ready in:

Ingredients

- 3 tablespoons salted butter
- 1 large sweet onion, chopped
- 2 cloves garlic, minced
- 1 teaspoon salt, divided
- 1/2 teaspoon ground black pepper, divided
- 1 1/2 cups chopped carrots
- 4 cups chopped yellow potatoes
- 1 cup whole milk
- 1 cup half-and-half
- 1 tablespoon ground coriander
- 1 tablespoon ground cumin
- 2 teaspoons curry powder
- 2 teaspoons garam masala
- 1 teaspoon ground ginger
- 1 1/2 cups frozen peas
- 1 sheet frozen puff pastry

Direction

- Preheat the oven to 200°C or 400°Fahrenheit.
- On medium heat, melt butter in a big stockpot. Cook and stir quarter teaspoon black pepper, sweet onion, half teaspoon salt, and garlic in hot butter for 10mins until the onion is translucent.
- Mix in carrots; cook and stir for another 5mins until the carrots are slightly soft. Mix in potatoes; stir.
- In a bowl, combine ginger, milk, garam masala, half-and-half, curry powder, half teaspoon salt, cumin, coriander, and quarter teaspoon pepper until the spices dissolve in liquid. Pour the mixture in the pot with vegetable mixture; boil. Mix in peas; cook for 2-3mins until the peas are warmed. Move to a 13-in by 9-in baking dish.
- Slice the frozen puff pastry lengthwise to three equal portions; place over the vegetable mixture.
- Bake for 40mins in the preheated oven until the vegetables are tender and the pastry is golden brown and puffed.

Nutrition Information

- Calories: 374 calories;
- Protein: 8.1
- Total Fat: 21
- Sodium: 479
- Total Carbohydrate: 40.1
- Cholesterol: 26

---

342.   Sausage Pinwheels

Serving: 16 | Prep: 15mins | Cook: 20mins | Ready in:

Ingredients

- 1 pound ground pork sausage
- 1 onion, finely chopped
- 2 stalks celery, finely chopped
- 1 tablespoon chopped fresh parsley
- ground black pepper to taste
- 1/2 (17.5 ounce) package frozen puff pastry, thawed

Direction

- Preheat the oven to 150 degrees C (300 degrees F).
- In a medium bowl, mix ground pork sausage, pepper, parsley, celery, and onion together.
- Next, roll a pastry sheet into a 12x8 inch rectangle. Scatter with 1/2 the sausage mixture. Then roll the pastry starting with one of the shorter sides. Wet with water. Use a moist fork to seal the edges. Cut the roll into approximately 1-inch slices. Repeat the process with the remaining sausage mixture and second pastry sheet.
- Flatten the roll slices onto a large baking sheet. Then bake for around 20 minutes, turning over after 10 minutes, until the pastry is golden brown and sausage is browned evenly. Allow to drain on paper towels and taste warm.

Nutrition Information

- Calories: 206 calories;
- Total Fat: 17.3
- Sodium: 232
- Total Carbohydrate: 8
- Cholesterol: 19
- Protein: 4.6

---

343.   Savory Puff Pastry Christmas Tree

Serving: 8 | Prep: 35mins | Cook: 20mins | Ready in:

Ingredients

- 2 tablespoons sun-dried tomato pesto
- 2 tablespoons soft goat cheese (such as Chavrie®)

- 2 sheets puff pastry
- 2 tablespoons freshly grated Pecorino-Romano cheese, divided
- 1 egg, beaten
- 1/2 teaspoon dried oregano

Direction

- Set an oven to 200°C (400°F) and start preheating. Use parchment paper to line a baking sheet.
- In a small bowl, stir goat cheese and sun-dried tomato pesto properly.
- On the prepared baking sheet, unroll a puff pastry sheet. To form a tree trunk, cut 2 about one-inch tall and wide strips at the bottom of the sheet away. To create a long triangular shape, diagonally cut to the top of the puff pastry sheet and take away excess pastry from either side.
- Cover all the way to the sides of the pastry with a thin layer of the pesto mixture. Dust over the top with a tablespoon of Pecorino-Romano cheese.
- Roll the second puff pastry sheet up and arrange at the vertex of the triangle. Gently unroll to the bottom. To match the first triangle, lightly press down and gently cut the sides away. Take excess pastry away.
- Slice 2/3-inches thick branches in the sides of the triangle from both sides; longwise from the trunk all the way up to the tip in the middle, leave a gap. Twist the branches away; try to twist the lower branches twice. Keep moving up the tree and twist away as you go.
- Brush beaten egg over the whole tree. Use the remaining 1 tablespoon of dried oregano and Pecorino-Romano cheese to dust.
- Bake in the prepared oven for around 20 minutes until deep golden brown. Allow to slightly cool on the baking sheet.

Nutrition Information

- Calories: 358 calories;
- Total Fat: 25
- Sodium: 184

- Total Carbohydrate: 27.6
- Cholesterol: 25
- Protein: 5.9

344.   Schweine Ohren (Pig's Ears)

Serving: 12 | Prep: | Cook: | Ready in:

Ingredients

- 1 (17.5 ounce) package frozen puff pastry, thawed
- 1 1/2 cups white sugar

Direction

- Preheat an oven to 200°C/400°F. Grease/line parchment paper on cookie sheet.
- On dry, lightly floured surface, unroll puff pastry sheets. Sheets should be 1/2-cm thick. Generously spread sugar on entire surface of every sheet. Tightly fold/roll up pastry from each sheet side to meet in center. It'll look like snails facing each other. Cut roll to 1-cm. slices like bread loaf. Lay out on the prepared cookie sheet, 2-cm. apart. In preheated oven, bake till golden brown for 10-15 minutes.

Nutrition Information

- Calories: 322 calories;
- Protein: 3
- Total Fat: 15.6
- Sodium: 102
- Total Carbohydrate: 43.4
- Cholesterol: 0

345.　　　Shrimp Scampi Cheesecake Appetizer

Serving: 12 | Prep: 45mins | Cook: 25mins | Ready in:

Ingredients

- 1 tablespoon olive oil
- 1 onion
- 6 teaspoons minced garlic
- 1 pound fresh shrimp, peeled and deveined
- 12 shells puff pastry, baked
- 4 tablespoons butter or margarine
- 3 (8 ounce) packages cream cheese, softened
- 4 eggs
- 1/2 cup heavy cream
- 16 ounces smoked Gouda, grated
- 2 teaspoons salt

Direction

- Preheat oven to 175°C/350°F.
- Place a large skillet over medium heat the oil. Sauté garlic and onions in the skillet until translucent, then set aside and allow to cool. Once cooled, pour liquid out and reserve the garlic.
- Save 12 pieces of shrimp for garnish and cut the rest of the shrimp into 1/2 inch pieces. Place a large skillet over medium-low heat and melt the butter; add the reserved garlic. Cook all the shrimp in the skillet until done, about 2 to 4 minutes.
- On cooled puff pastry shells, remove circles from the center and a small portion of the inside.
- Beat cream cheese in a medium bowl until creamy. Beat in 1 egg at a time until mixed thoroughly. Add salt, shrimp, onions, Gouda, and cream.
- Fill puff pastry shells with the filling.
- Bake for 20 to 25 minutes, or until the top of the filling is browned. Add chopped chives and a whole shrimp on each serving to garnish. Serve.

Nutrition Information

- Calories: 701 calories;
- Total Fat: 56.3
- Sodium: 1075
- Total Carbohydrate: 22.7
- Cholesterol: 248
- Protein: 26.8

346.　　　Shrimp Wellington

Serving: 4 | Prep: 15mins | Cook: 20mins | Ready in:

Ingredients

- 2 tablespoons olive oil
- 4 cups fresh spinach leaves
- salt and pepper to taste
- 1 sheet frozen puff pastry, thawed
- 4 jumbo shrimp, peeled and deveined
- 4 ounces crabmeat, drained and flaked
- 1/4 cup bechamel sauce
- 1 tablespoon chopped shallots
- 1 tablespoon chopped fresh tarragon
- 1 egg, beaten

Direction

- Prepare the oven by preheating to 400°F (200°C). Prepare a baking sheet that is greased.
- Put oil in a large skillet set on medium heat. Place spinach; stir and cook for approximately 3 minutes until wilted. Add pepper and salt to season. Strain off any extra liquid; reserve.
- On a clean surface, lay the sheet of puff pastry and slice into 4 squares. Use a fork to prick lightly.
- Combine tarragon, shallots, bechamel sauce, and crab meat in a medium bowl; stir until thoroughly combined.
- Slice prawns lengthwise then open them up to make a butterfly shape. In the center of each pastry square with the open side facing up, lay one shrimp. Fill every shrimp with an even amount of spinach and put a heaping

tablespoon of the crab mixture on top. Fold over pastry to form a triangle, then push the edges to seal. Transfer to a baking sheet, and use a beaten egg to brush with.

- Place in the preheated oven and bake for 15 to 20 minutes until golden brown. Serve warm.

Nutrition Information

- Calories: 502 calories;
- Protein: 20.1
- Total Fat: 33.5
- Sodium: 482
- Total Carbohydrate: 30
- Cholesterol: 129

347. Slow Cooker Guinness® Beef Stew

Serving: 8 | Prep: 30mins | Cook: 4hours15mins | Ready in:

Ingredients

- 1/2 cup all-purpose flour
- 1 teaspoon salt
- 1/2 teaspoon freshly ground black pepper
- 3 pounds boneless beef chuck, trimmed and cut into 1 1/2-inch pieces
- 1/4 cup vegetable oil
- 1 large yellow onion, coarsely chopped
- 1 (15 ounce) can Irish stout beer (e.g. Guinness®)
- 4 cloves garlic, chopped
- 1 (14.5 ounce) can beef broth
- 1 tablespoon chopped fresh parsley
- 2 sprigs fresh thyme
- 2 bay leaves
- 1 pound round red potatoes, halved
- 3 carrots, cut into 1-inch chunks
- 1 (17.5 ounce) package frozen puff pastry, thawed and cut into quarters (optional)

Direction

- In a shallow dish, combine pepper, salt and flour; put beef slices. Toss to coat every piece equally. For later use, save leftover flour mixture.
- In a big non-stick skillet, heat oil; cook, mix coated beef, work in batches till all sides are browned, 10 minutes for every batch. In a slow cooker, put cooked beef.
- Cook and mix onion for 5 minutes with the same skillet used for beef, till golden. Put garlic and beer; boil for a minute. Using a wooden spoon, scrape browned bits from base of the pan. Into the slow cooker, add onion mixture.
- Into beef mixture in slow cooker, stir bay leaves, thyme, parsley and beef broth.
- Cook on Low for 2 and a half to 3 hours till beef is nearly tender. Scatter in the leftover flour mixture; mix nicely. Put carrots and potatoes.
- Cook for an hour on High till potatoes are soft.
- Preheat oven to 200°C or 400°F.
- On baking sheets, set puff pastry; using a fork, prick every piece multiple times.
- Bake for 10 minutes in the preheated oven till crispy and golden. Into individual dishes, spoon stew; put pastry square on top.

Nutrition Information

- Calories: 738 calories;
- Total Fat: 48.5
- Sodium: 678
- Total Carbohydrate: 47.2
- Cholesterol: 77
- Protein: 27.7

348. Spicy Garlic Cheese Puffs

Serving: 6 | Prep: 20mins | Cook: | Ready in:

Ingredients

- 1 egg yolk

- 2 teaspoons Dijon mustard
- 1 teaspoon water
- 1 clove garlic, pressed
- 1 sheet frozen pre-rolled puff pastry sheet
- 1/3 cup CRACKER BARREL Shredded Habanero Heat Cheese, divided

Direction

- Heat the oven to 400 °F.
- Mix water, mustard and egg yolk till incorporated; mix in the garlic. On slightly floured area, roll pastry sheet making rectangle, 14x10-inch in size; halve lengthwise. Brush some of egg mixture lightly.
- Scatter 3 tablespoon cheese on a pastry piece. Cover using the leftover pastry piece, egg side facing down. Using rolling pin, roll slowly to enclose; brush with 1/2 of the rest of egg mixture. Beginning at a lengthy side, roll up securely; slice crosswise into 2 dozen slices.
- On a baking sheet coated with cooking spray, set 2-inche away, cut sides facing down; pat lightly. Brush with the rest of egg mixture; scatter the rest of cheese.
- Allow to bake for 12 to 14 minutes or till golden brown. Serve at room temperature or while warm.

Nutrition Information

- Calories: 233 calories;
- Protein: 3.4
- Total Fat: 16
- Sodium: 143
- Total Carbohydrate: 18.7
- Cholesterol: 34

---

349. Spinach Pie With Pancetta

Serving: 8 | Prep: 20mins | Cook: 28mins | Ready in:

Ingredients

- 3 tablespoons extra-virgin olive oil
- 1/2 large red onion, diced
- 2 cloves garlic, minced
- 1/4 cup cubed pancetta
- 1 (10 ounce) box frozen chopped spinach - thawed, drained and squeezed dry
- 3 tablespoons feta cheese
- 4 (1 ounce) slices Provolone cheese
- 1 sheet frozen puff pastry, thawed
- 1 egg white

Direction

- Preheat the oven to 350°F (175°C). Coat an 8-inch pie plate slightly with oil.
- Put olive oil in a skillet and heat it up over medium heat. Put in the red onions and sauté for about 5 minutes or until translucent and soft. Add in the pancetta and garlic and let it cook for about 8 minutes or until the pancetta is crispy. Lower the heat to low setting. Stir in the feta cheese and spinach. Remove the skillet from heat.
- Cover the bottom of the prepared pie plate with a layer of Provolone cheese. Spread the spinach mixture evenly on top of the Provolone cheese layer. Put a sheet of puff pastry on top and cut off the edges to let it fit on the pie plate. Use a brush to coat the top of the puff pastry with egg white.
- Place in the preheated oven and bake for about 15 minutes until the top is golden brown in color. Before serving, let it cool down for 1 hour.

Nutrition Information

- Calories: 314 calories;
- Total Carbohydrate: 16.7
- Cholesterol: 17
- Protein: 8.9
- Total Fat: 23.8
- Sodium: 319

350. Spinach Rolls With Puff Pastry

Serving: 36 | Prep: 20mins | Cook: 25mins | Ready in:

Ingredients

- 2 tablespoons vegetable oil
- 1 clove clove garlic, minced, or more to taste
- 1 (10 ounce) package frozen chopped spinach, thawed and drained
- salt to taste
- 1 (4 ounce) package crumbled feta cheese
- 3 sheets frozen puff pastry, thawed
- 1 egg, beaten
- 1 tablespoon milk
- 2 tablespoons sesame seeds

Direction

- Place a skillet over medium heat and heat the oil. Add garlic and cook for 1 to 2 minutes, or until fragrant. Stir in spinach; cook for 3 to 5 minutes, or until warmed through. Add salt to season and mix thoroughly. Transfer to a bowl, add feta cheese and mix.
- Preheat oven to 200°C/400°F. Prepare two greased baking sheets.
- Dust a work surface lightly with flour and lay 1 sheet of puff pastry. Slice lengthwise in half. Using a rolling pin, roll out 1 of the halves wide enough to fold twice lengthwise. In a small bowl, mix together milk and egg.
- In the center of the puff pastry, spread 1/6 of the spinach mixture lengthwise. Roll one side to cover the filling and brush egg-milk mixture on the other side, then seal pastry by rolling the brushed side over.
- Brush the egg-milk mixture over the top of roll and sprinkle sesame seeds on top. Slice into 6 small rolls. Repeat process with the remaining pastry. Transfer the small rolls to the prepped baking sheets.
- Bake for 20 to 25 minutes in preheated oven, or until the rolls are golden and puffed.

Nutrition Information

- Calories: 133 calories;
- Sodium: 97
- Total Carbohydrate: 9.7
- Cholesterol: 7
- Protein: 2.5
- Total Fat: 9.5

351. Steak And Kidney Pie I

Serving: 8 | Prep: 30mins | Cook: 1hours30mins | Ready in:

Ingredients

- 1 pound beef tenderloin
- 1 pound beef kidney
- 1 cup all-purpose flour for rolling
- 4 cups water to cover
- 1 tablespoon all-purpose flour
- 1 to taste salt and pepper to taste
- 1 (17.5 ounce) package frozen puff pastry, thawed

Direction

- Cut meat into 1-in. cubes; roll in seasoned flour. Cover meat with enough water in a saucepan. Cook for 3 hours till meat is tender. Remove meat; leave liquid in pan.
- Use 1 tbsp. flour to thicken gravy; season to taste with pepper and salt. Put meat back in pan; put into pie dish. Let cool.
- Get a small portion of pastry; roll into 1-in. wide strips. Moisten pie dish's edges; press pastry around the rim. Roll out rest of the pastry to size of the dish. Moisten strip pastry; cover using pastry.
- Bake till nicely browned, about 15-20 minutes at 230°C/450°F.

Nutrition Information

- Calories: 570 calories;

- Sodium: 343
- Total Carbohydrate: 40.5
- Cholesterol: 260
- Protein: 24.4
- Total Fat: 33.9

352.   Steak And Kidney Pie With Bacon And Mushrooms

Serving: 8 | Prep: 50mins | Cook: 3hours | Ready in:

Ingredients

- 1/2 pound beef kidney
- 1 tablespoon vegetable oil
- 1/4 cup all-purpose flour
- salt and pepper to taste
- 1 pound beef for stew, cut in 1 inch pieces
- 4 slices thick sliced bacon, cut into 1 inch pieces
- 1 medium onion, chopped
- 1 (6 ounce) package sliced mushrooms
- 1/2 cup beef stock
- 1/2 cup red wine
- 4 large potatoes, peeled, cut into 1-inch chunks
- 2 tablespoons butter
- 1/2 cup milk
- 1 (17.25 ounce) package frozen puff pastry, thawed
- 1 egg, beaten with 2 teaspoons water

Direction

- Split the kidney in half then take the skins and tubes off. Rinse using cold water then pat to dry. Dice the kidney into 1/2 cubes. Use a big and heavy pot and pour in the vegetable oil, set the heat to medium high. Season the flour with salt and pepper using a bowl. Mix the kidney and stew meat in the flour then shake the excess off. Sear the meat in the hot oil until it becomes brown then remove. Add the bacon to the pot. Cook the bacon until it becomes crisp. Add in the mushroom and onion and cook for 2 minutes to soften. Pour the beef

stock in, browned meat and the wine. Let it boil while stirring constantly for about 5 to 10 minutes. When it start thickens, lower the heat and simmer for one and a half to two hours or until the meat becomes tender. Take it away from the heat and let it cool to room temperature.
- Put the potatoes in a sauce pan then fill it with water just enough to cover the potatoes. Heat over high heat until it boils. Lower the heat to medium low and let it simmer for 20 minutes until it tenders. Drain the water out then mash with milk and butter. Add salt and pepper to taste. Set aside to cool.
- Prepare the oven and preheat to 375°F or 190°C.
- Place one sheet of puff pastry into a 9-inch pie dish and press it. Trim the edges to make it fit. Fill with cooled meat mixture. Top it with the mashed potatoes about an inch thick then take the remaining sheet of puff pastry and place it on top. Trim the excess pastry around the edges then flute the edges using a fork. Apply the top with beaten egg.
- Let it bake in the preheated oven between 20 to 25 minutes or until crust becomes golden brown.

Nutrition Information

- Calories: 767 calories;
- Total Fat: 42.6
- Sodium: 539
- Total Carbohydrate: 65.9
- Cholesterol: 190
- Protein: 27.9

353.   Steak N Ale Pie

Serving: 4 | Prep: | Cook: | Ready in:

Ingredients

- 1/2 (17.5 ounce) package frozen puff pastry, thawed
- 1 tablespoon lard
- 1/2 pound cubed beef
- 1/4 pound carrots, diced
- 1/4 pound turnips, diced
- 1/2 pound peeled and cubed potatoes
- 1/4 pound onions, diced
- 1 cup water
- 1 cup bitter ale
- 1 tablespoon cornstarch
- 1/4 cup cold water
- salt and pepper to taste

Direction

- Start preheating the oven to 375°F (190°C).
- Put a big frying pan on high heat. Add lard, and then meat. Toss to blend the meat, and sauté just until the meat turns brown on all sides. Take away from heat. In a 1-quart baking plate, put the meat. Add onion, potatoes, turnip, and carrots. Stir thoroughly.
- In a small saucepan, add 1 cup of water and ale. Simmer it. Combine 1/4 cup of cold water and cornstarch until smooth. Gradually add the cornstarch mixture into the simmering ale mixture, stirring continually. Keep simmering until the mixture thickens. Sprinkle pepper and salt to taste. Put the mixture on vegetables and meat. Cut the puff pastry to fit the top of the filling.
- Put in the preheated oven and bake until the pastry turns deep golden brown, about 45-50 minutes.

Nutrition Information

- Calories: 587 calories;
- Cholesterol: 34
- Protein: 16.1
- Total Fat: 34.4
- Sodium: 221
- Total Carbohydrate: 48.7

354.   Strawberry Napoleons

Serving: 8 | Prep: 25mins | Cook: 15mins | Ready in:

Ingredients

- 1 (3.5 ounce) package instant vanilla pudding and pie filling
- 1 cup cold 2% milk
- 1 1/2 cups non-dairy whipped topping, thawed
- 1/2 (17.25 ounce) package frozen puff pastry, thawed
- 1 pint fresh strawberries, thinly sliced
- 1/4 cup confectioners' sugar

Direction

- Heat oven to 400°F (200°C). Mix cold milk and pudding mix; fold in whipped topping. Chill before using.
- On a lightly floured, cool surface, unfold pastry. Slice into three strips along the fold marks, then slice each strip into four pieces equally. Put 2-in. apart on a baking sheet.
- Bake in the heated oven for 15 mins, or until golden brown. Take out of baking sheet, let rest to cool.
- Divide pastries into two layers, putting aside the 8 tops that is best looking. Arrange dollops of pudding mixture over 8 bottom layers evenly. Top each with a layer of strawberries, a little pudding, and other pastry layer. (A little bit of pudding mix over the berries will act as a glue.) Distribute remaining pudding mixture and strawberries on top evenly, finish with leftover pastry layers (the best looking ones). Scatter with confectioners' sugar.

Nutrition Information

- Calories: 301 calories;
- Sodium: 268
- Total Carbohydrate: 37
- Cholesterol: 2

- Protein: 3.7
- Total Fat: 15.9

355. Stuffed Fish In Puff Pastry

Serving: 8 | Prep: 45mins | Cook: 35mins | Ready in:

Ingredients

- 1/4 cup butter
- 1 cup finely chopped onion
- 1 cup minced celery
- 1 tablespoon chopped fresh parsley
- 8 ounces crabmeat
- 8 ounces shrimp, peeled, deveined and minced
- 1/4 cup dry vermouth
- salt to taste
- ground black pepper to taste
- 1/4 teaspoon hot pepper sauce
- 1/2 cup bread crumbs
- 1 (17.5 ounce) package frozen puff pastry sheets, thawed
- 2 pounds flounder fillets
- 2 egg yolks, beaten

Direction

- For the stuffing: In a large saucepan, melt margarine or butter on medium-low heat. Sauté parsley, celery, and onion just until all vegetables become tender. Combine in vermouth, shrimp, and crabmeat. Flavor with the hot pepper sauce, pepper, and salt; cook until the shrimp is done the cooking (it will turn pink). Combine in a little of breadcrumbs at a time. Stop adding bread crumbs once the mixture holds together properly. Taste, and if needed, add more seasoning including hot pepper sauce, pepper, and salt. Put aside the mixture to allow it to cool.
- Grease a baking sheet using non-stick cooking spray.
- Roll a sheet of puff pastry on a flat surface. When rolled, the puff pastry needs to be 1/3-

1/4 inch in thickness and large enough to top with the fish and still remain puff pastry on the sides. Place one fish fillets over the puff pastry. Spread evenly on top of the fish fillet with the stuffing mixture. Arrange the rest of fillet on top of the stuffing. Trim the pastry around the fillets to about the shape of a fish. Retain the trimmings.
- Roll the second sheet of puff pastry to roughly 1/3-1/4 inch in thickness. Drape the second sheet on the stuffed fillets and ensure there is enough top sheet to tuck beneath the bottom sheet of the puff pastry. Trim the top sheet of pastry roughly 1/2 inch larger the bottom one. Brush water underside the top pastry sheet, then tuck beneath the bottom sheet of puff pastry and press lightly to encase the stuffing and fish package totally. On the greased baking sheet, arrange the sealed packet, allow to cool for 10-15 minutes.
- Roll out pastry scraps while chilling the packet. Slice out 'lips', an eye, and fins from the scraps. Use a little water to attach cut-outs to the chilled package. Make indentations in puff pastry with an inverted teaspoon to resemble fish scales but don't puncture pastry. Let the whole package chill.
- Set an oven to 220°C (425°F) and start preheating while chilling the package.
- Take the fish out of the fridge and brush egg yolks over the package. Measure the thickness of the package on the thickest part. Bake for 15 minutes, then turn down the heat to 175°C (350°F) and bake the fish for 10 more minutes per inch of the measured thickness. Place a thermometer to insert in the package to check the doneness, the fish will be done cooking once the temperature achieves 70°C (140°F).

Nutrition Information

- Calories: 613 calories;
- Total Fat: 32.8
- Sodium: 490
- Total Carbohydrate: 36.5
- Cholesterol: 189

- Protein: 39.4

Serving: 12 | Prep: 30mins | Cook: 9mins | Ready in:

Ingredients

- 1/3 cup gyoza dipping sauce
- 2 teaspoons granulated sugar
- 1 clove garlic, minced
- 1/2 teaspoon sesame oil
- 1/4 teaspoon crushed red pepper flakes
- 1 sheet frozen puff pastry, thawed
- 1 tablespoon all-purpose flour
- 2 (5 ounce) cans Bumble Bee® Solid White Albacore Tuna in Water, drained
- 1/3 cup finely diced fresh mango
- 1 tablespoon chopped green onion
- 2 tablespoons minced green bell pepper
- 1/2 tablespoon toasted sesame seeds (optional)

Direction

- In a small saucepan over medium heat, combine red pepper flakes, toasted sesame oil, garlic, sugar, and gyoza dipping sauce; cook until reduced by half. Remove from the heat. Set aside.
- Preheat oven to 200°C/400°F.
- Lightly dust flour over a work surface and place a defrosted puff pastry sheet. Dust top with flour and roll out the pastry slightly until it forms an 11 x 13-inch rectangle. From the 11-inch side, cut 4 even strips; and from the 13-inch side, cut 6 even strips, making 24 even rectangles.
- Form cup by placing each rectangle on the hole of a mini muffin tin and pressing the dough down the middle of muffin tin. (If necessary, bake in batches basing on the size of mini muffin pan while skipping every-other hole in the muffin tin to prevent the excess dough sticking out of the tin from touching each other.)
- Bake pastry cups for 8 minutes; then remove from the oven, use a fork to punch the puffed-

356.   Super Easy Hazelnut Pastries

Serving: 34 | Prep: 5mins | Cook: 15mins | Ready in:

Ingredients

- 1 (17.25 ounce) package frozen puff pastry, thawed
- 11 tablespoons chocolate hazelnut spread
- 1/2 cup chopped hazelnuts (optional)
- 6 teaspoons powdered sugar

Direction

- Preheat an oven to 220 degrees C (425 degrees F). Coat a baking sheet lightly with grease.
- Onto a lightly floured surface, unfold puff pastry, then roll out into a rectangle of approximately 20x9 inches. Spread the pastry with chocolate hazelnut spread, then sprinkle hazelnuts all over the top.
- Roll long sides of pastry rectangle towards the middle; dampen where they meet in the middle with water to hold in place. Slice into about half-inch slices with a sharp knife, then arrange in the baking sheet; dust with powdered sugar.
- Bake for about 10 to 15 minutes in the oven until they turn golden brown.

Nutrition Information

- Calories: 116 calories;
- Sodium: 40
- Total Carbohydrate: 10.2
- Cholesterol: 0
- Protein: 1.6
- Total Fat: 7.9

up center down. Return to the oven and bake until the cups are lightly golden brown, about 3 more minutes. Remove from the oven and, once again, use a fork to punch down the center to form a hole for the filling. Before removing the cups from the tin, allow to cool completely.

- Add sweet bell pepper, mango, and tuna in a medium bowl, toss lightly until well combined. With a small spoon, spoon the filling into each pastry cup. Drizzle reserved sauce on the filling, garnish with toasted sesame seeds and chopped green onions.

Nutrition Information

- Calories: 153 calories;
- Total Carbohydrate: 11.8
- Cholesterol: 11
- Protein: 7.2
- Total Fat: 8.1
- Sodium: 249

358. Thanksgiving No Turkey Turkey

Serving: 10 | Prep: 35mins | Cook: 1hours10mins | Ready in:

Ingredients

- 2 (1 pound) loaves multigrain bread
- 2 tablespoons margarine
- 2 carrots, minced
- 2 large stalks celery, minced
- 1 onion, minced
- 1/4 cup chopped fresh parsley
- 1 teaspoon crumbled dried sage
- ground black pepper to taste
- 5 1/2 teaspoons egg replacer (dry)
- 1/2 cup water
- 1/2 cup vegetable broth
- 2 (16 ounce) packages chicken-style seitan, cut horizontally into 1 inch thick strips

- 1 cup garbanzo bean gravy
- 1 (17.5 ounce) package frozen puff pastry, thawed

Direction

- Tear bread into 1-in. cubes; put into a large bowl. Allow the bread to dry in the bowl for at least 8 hours, uncovered.
- Place a large skillet on medium-high heat; melt margarine. Stir in onion, celery and carrots. Cook while stirring for around 10 minutes, or till the onion is golden brown and softened. Scrape the onion mixture into the bowl of the dried bread; flavor with pepper, sage and parsley. In a small bowl, whisk vegetable broth, water and egg replacer together till smooth. Transfer over the bread cubes; gently fold till evenly combined. Allow to sit for 30 minutes so that the bread can absorb the liquid.
- Set the oven at 400°F (200°C) and start preheating. Use aluminum foil to line a baking dish; use non-stick cooking spray to coat.
- Brush both sides of seitan with gravy; arrange overlapping slices on foil in a row, mounding in the center. Press the stuffing mixture around the seitan to cover. Lightly wet hands and press into a neat oval. Unroll pastry sheets to 1/16-in. thickness; arrange to form a large rectangle, overlapping slightly. Seal the edges with dabs of cold water. Drape the pastry over the mound; trim any excess away from the bottom. Cut out decorative shapes (apples, leaves, etc) with scraps. Attached with dabs of cold water.
- Bake for 1-1 1/4 hours, or till the pastry turns deep golden brown. Use aluminum foil to cover the pastry if it begins to brown too much.

Nutrition Information

- Calories: 716 calories;
- Total Fat: 24.9
- Sodium: 1124
- Total Carbohydrate: 81.7

- Cholesterol: 0
- Protein: 42.6

359. Tuna Tart With Mushrooms And Artichokes

Serving: 9 | Prep: 20mins | Cook: 30mins | Ready in:

Ingredients

- 1 cup thinly sliced onions
- 2 tablespoons butter, divided
- 1 (17.5 ounce) package frozen puff pastry, thawed
- 1 tablespoon all-purpose flour for dusting
- 1 egg, beaten
- 1 cup button mushrooms, quartered
- 2 tablespoons red wine
- Salt and black pepper to taste
- 1 (5.2 ounce) package herb and garlic-flavored cream cheese
- 2 tablespoons heavy cream
- 1 (5 ounce) can Bumble Bee® Solid White Albacore Tuna in Water
- 1 (7.5 ounce) jar marinated artichoke hearts, drained and chopped
- Chopped fresh parsley (optional)
- Chopped fresh chives (optional)

Direction

- Set the oven to 400°F (200°C), and start preheating.
- In a non-stick skillet, put 1 tablespoon of butter then add onions. Cook for half an hour over low heat until onions get light brown.
- In the meantime, on a lightly floured piece of parchment paper, unfold 1 sheet of pastry and roll to shape into a rectangle of 10x12 inches and put on a baking sheet. Gently brush the beaten egg over the whole pastry rectangle.
- Unfold the other pastry sheet and cut off four 1 inch strips from the longest side. To form a thicker edge, arrange each strip along each edge of the egg-washed pastry. Get rid of

unused pastry. Lightly brush the beaten egg over the strips. Put the remaining egg aside. Use a fork to pierce the pastry inside formed edges several times.
- Bake the pastry in the oven for 8 minutes, rotate pan and keep baking for 8 more minutes. Take pastry out of the oven and cool slightly.
- Melt 1 tablespoon butter in a separate pan; then add pepper, salt, wine and mushrooms. Cook over medium heat until most of the liquid is absorbed and mushrooms are tender.
- While cooking mushrooms, whisk the cream, herb cheese and remaining beaten egg until smooth. Slowly distribute cheese mixture over pastry. Spread evenly tuna, artichokes, mushrooms and onions over the cheese mixture.
- Put back in the oven and bake for 20 minutes, or until the cheese mixture is set and the crust turns brown.
- Take it out of the oven and garnish with a sprinkle of snipped chives or snipped parsley. Slice evenly into 9 pieces and serve.

Nutrition Information

- Calories: 452 calories;
- Total Fat: 31.7
- Sodium: 406
- Total Carbohydrate: 30.7
- Cholesterol: 55
- Protein: 10.4

360. Ultimate Ham Cups

Serving: 9 | Prep: 15mins | Cook: 23mins | Ready in:

Ingredients

- 1/4 cup butter
- 1/4 cup all-purpose flour
- 1 cup milk
- 1/4 teaspoon ground nutmeg

- 1/8 teaspoon ground white pepper
- 1/8 teaspoon cayenne pepper
- salt to taste
- 1 cup diced smoked ham
- 1 cup diced smoked mozzarella cheese
- 1/2 cup sweetened dried cranberries
- 1/2 cup slivered almonds
- 1 sheet frozen puff pastry dough, thawed
- 1 teaspoon melted butter, or as needed

Direction

- Preheat oven to 200°C/400°F.
- Place a saucepan over medium heat and melt 1/4 cup of butter. Add flour and whisk until fully combined. Pour in milk and bring to a slow boil. Whisk for 3 to 5 minutes, or until mixture thickens. Add salt, cayenne, white pepper, and nutmeg. Remove pan from the heat and allow the filling to slightly cool. Add almonds, cranberries, mozzarella cheese, and ham.
- Lightly dust flour on a work surface and roll out the puff pastry. Brush melted butter lightly on the puff pastry. Slice into 9 even squares. Gently stretch the squares to enlarge. Place into muffin cups, buttered side-down. Fill cups with even amount of filling.
- Bake for 15 minutes in preheated oven, or until golden brown. Allow to slightly cool.

Nutrition Information

- Calories: 356 calories;
- Protein: 9.7
- Total Fat: 25
- Sodium: 382
- Total Carbohydrate: 23.3
- Cholesterol: 32

---

361.   Umm Ali

Serving: 8 | Prep: 10mins | Cook: 30mins | Ready in:

Ingredients

- 1 (17.25 ounce) package frozen puff pastry, thawed
- 5 cups milk
- 1 cup white sugar
- 1 teaspoon vanilla extract
- 1/4 cup raisins
- 1/4 cup slivered almonds
- 1/4 cup pine nuts
- 1/4 cup chopped pistachio nuts
- 1/4 cup sweetened, flaked coconut

Direction

- Preheat an oven to 200°C/400°F; unroll puff pastry sheets. Put on baking sheet flat. In preheated oven, bake for 15 minutes or till golden brown and puffed.
- Break puff pastry to pieces; put in big bowl. Add coconut, pistachios, pine nuts, almonds and raisins; toss to distribute. Put in 9x13-in. glass baking dish; evenly spread.
- Put milk in saucepan; mix vanilla and sugar in. Heat till hot yet not boiling; put on mixture in baking dish.
- In preheated oven, bake for 15 minutes. Put oven on broil; broil to brown top for 2 minutes. Take out of oven; stand for 5 minutes then serve warm.

Nutrition Information

- Calories: 605 calories;
- Total Fat: 32.7
- Sodium: 237
- Total Carbohydrate: 67.2
- Cholesterol: 12
- Protein: 12.4

---

362.   Vanilla Slice

Serving: 16 | Prep: 10mins | Cook: 20mins | Ready in:

Ingredients

- 1 (17.25 ounce) package frozen puff pastry, thawed
- 1 cup white sugar
- 1/2 cup custard powder
- 3/4 cup cornstarch
- 5 1/4 cups milk
- 1/4 cup butter
- 2 egg yolks
- 1 teaspoon vanilla extract
- 1 cup confectioners' sugar
- 1 tablespoon milk
- 1 dash vanilla extract

Direction

- Set the oven to 400°F (200°C) to preheat. Unfold puff pastry sheets, and put it flat onto baking sheets. Bake until slightly browned and puffed or for 10 to 15 minutes. Put aside.
- In a large saucepan, mix the cornstarch, sugar and custard powder. Stir in milk just enough to form a paste, slowly stir in the rest, which will prevent forming lumps. Put in the butter. Cook over medium heat, mixing occasionally until thick. To keep a smooth texture, you may need to use a whisk. Cook and mix frequently when the mixture comes to a simmer for 2 minutes. Take off from the heat, and mix in the vanilla and egg yolks.
- Line a 9 inches baking dish with aluminum foil. Put one of the prepared pastry sheets on the bottom of the dish. Put the custard filling in an even layer on top of the pastry, and put the other sheet on top.
- To make an icing, stir the 1 tablespoon of milk with confectioners' sugar, and a dash of vanilla. Put on top of the pastry evenly. Chill until the custard layer is set. Take off from the pan and cut.

Nutrition Information

- Calories: 358 calories;
- Sodium: 130
- Total Carbohydrate: 47.5
- Cholesterol: 40
- Protein: 5.3
- Total Fat: 16.6

---

363. Vegetarian Sausage Rolls

Serving: 12 | Prep: 20mins | Cook: 25mins | Ready in:

Ingredients

- 1 tablespoon vegetable oil
- 1/3 cup chopped onion
- 1/2 carrot, finely shredded
- 1/2 cup dried bread crumbs
- 2 meatless patties (such as Morningstar Farms® Grillers®)
- 1 egg, lightly beaten
- 1 sheet frozen puff pastry, thawed
- 1 tablespoon milk
- 2 tablespoons poppy seeds

Direction

- Preheat an oven to 200°C/400°F; line parchment paper on baking sheet.
- Heat vegetable oil in skillet on medium heat then add carrot and onion; mix and cook for 5 minutes till soft.
- Put onion and carrot into food processor then add breadcrumbs. Coarsely chop meatless patties; add to food processor. Pulse for 4-5 times till combined. Add egg; pulse a few more times.
- Put puff pastry on lightly floured surface; slightly roll out. Across pastry, add 3 rows of the meatless patty mixture; use pizza wheel to cut into 3 sections. Press pastry edges together; to seal, roll over.
- Brush milk over pastry tops; prick with a fork. Sprinkle milk with poppy seeds. Use pizza cutter to cut rolls into 2-in. pieces; put on prepped baking sheet.
- In preheated oven, bake for 20 minutes till pastry is golden brown and puffed.

Nutrition Information

- Calories: 169 calories;
- Total Fat: 10.6
- Sodium: 134
- Total Carbohydrate: 14
- Cholesterol: 16
- Protein: 4.6

364.   Veggie Rose Tart

Serving: 8 | Prep: 30mins | Cook: 1hours | Ready in:

Ingredients

- 1 sheet frozen puff pastry, thawed
- 1 1/2 cups ricotta cheese
- 1 1/2 tablespoons ricotta cheese
- 1/2 cup cubed fresh mozzarella cheese
- 1 egg
- 1/4 cup grated Parmesan cheese
- 1 pinch ground nutmeg
- 1 sprig fresh thyme, leaves stripped
- salt to taste
- 6 carrots, assorted colors
- 2 zucchini (courgettes)
- 2 tablespoons olive oil

Direction

- Preheat an oven to 175°C/350°F.
- Gently press puff pastry onto sides and bottom of 9-in. tart tin. Trim extra pastry off; discard. Line parchment paper on pastry; fill with dried beans/ceramic pie weights.
- In preheated oven, bake pastry crust for 15 minutes till light golden in color. Remove from oven and remove pie weights and parchment paper.
- Put oven temperature on 200°C/400°F.
- Mix salt, thyme, nutmeg, parmesan cheese, egg, mozzarella cheese and 1 1/2 cup and 1 1/2 tbsp. ricotta cheese in a bowl. Put filling in crust; smooth top out.

- Lengthwise slice zucchini and carrots using a vegetable peeler/mandolin to thin strips.
- Spread zucchini and carrot strips on microwave-safe plate; cook for 1-2 minutes till slightly soft in microwave.
- Tightly roll 1 vegetable strip to rosebud shape. To make full rose shape, wrap another of same vegetable strip around; repeat with leftover strips. Put zucchini and carrot roses on filling in decorative pattern, alternating colors then brush olive oil.
- In preheated oven, bake for 40 minutes till zucchini and carrot roses are tender, filling is firm and pastry is golden brown.

Nutrition Information

- Calories: 265 calories;
- Total Fat: 18.2
- Sodium: 190
- Total Carbohydrate: 19.5
- Cholesterol: 32
- Protein: 6.4

365.   Wild Mushroom Puff Pastry

Serving: 8 | Prep: 25mins | Cook: 10mins | Ready in:

Ingredients

- 1 tablespoon olive oil
- 1 shallot, minced
- 1 pound assorted wild mushrooms, sliced
- 2 cloves roasted garlic, minced
- 1 cup grated Parmesan cheese
- 1 bunch fresh thyme, leaves stripped and chopped
- salt and black pepper to taste
- 1/2 cup heavy cream
- 1 (17.25 ounce) package frozen puff pastry, thawed

Direction

- Preheat an oven to 400 °F.
- In a big skillet, heat olive oil over medium-high heat. Put the shallot; cook and mix for 5 minutes till soft. Reduce heat to medium-low and put the mushrooms. Cook and mix for 15 minutes till mushrooms reduce by 1/2. Mix in thyme, Parmesan cheese and roasted garlic. Season with pepper and salt to taste. Mix in cream. Take off from heat and let mushroom mixture to cool. As it cools, it will thicken.
- Onto floured surface, unroll pastry sheet and gently roll into 12x15-inch square. Slice into 18 squares, 3-inch in size. In the middle of every square, put a mounded teaspoon of mushroom filling. Fold pastry on top of filling to create a triangle. Using a fork, firmly pinch edges together to seal.
- Allow to bake till golden brown for 12 to 16 minutes. Serve at room temperature or while hot.

Nutrition Information

- Calories: 484 calories;
- Total Fat: 33.8
- Sodium: 361
- Total Carbohydrate: 33.4
- Cholesterol: 31
- Protein: 11.2

Index

Quince 4,98

R

Raspberry 3,4,5,7,43,48,72,97,114,116,219,220

Rhubarb 4,5,88,114,115,116

Rice 7,221

Ricotta 3,4,5,44,66,115

S

Sage 3,28

Salad 3,4,32,80

Salami 7,213,223

Salmon 3,5,7,31,106,120,123,124,214,216,223,224

Salsa 166

Salt 49,69,76,77,126,132,139,237

Satsuma 110

Sausage 3,5,6,7,9,28,44,45,144,165,197,205,226,239

Savory 3,5,7,29,121,122,226

Sesame seeds 108,165

Shallot 3,31

Sherry 47,89,93,94

Sorbet 4,98

Sorrel 5,126

Soup 6,177

Spinach 3,5,6,7,8,120,126,127,168,181,218,230,231

Squash 3,5,10,20,122

Steak 6,7,187,231,232

Stew 7,229

Stilton 5,105

Strawberry 5,7,128,233

Sugar 3,5,9,45,47,86,90,116,129

Swiss chard 130

Syrup 4,87,93,138

T

Tabasco 195

Taco 3,33

Tapenade 5,133

Tea 208,236

Thyme 5,6,139,174

Tofu 5,132

Tomato 3,4,5,45,46,70,95,104,118,132,133

Truffle 92

Turkey 5,6,7,134,191,236

V

Vegetable oil 140

Vegetables 7,222

Vegetarian 6,7,171,239

W

Waffles 7,217

Walnut 4,5,75,78,130,137,138,154

Wine 6,201

Worcestershire sauce 30,45,60,150,157,183,194,198

Wraps 3,8

Z

Zest 6,174

Conclusion

Thank you again for downloading this book!

I hope you enjoyed reading about my book!

If you enjoyed this book, please take the time to share your thoughts and post a review on Amazon. It'd be greatly appreciated!

Write me an honest review about the book – I truly value your opinion and thoughts and I will incorporate them into my next book, which is already underway.

Thank you!

If you have any questions, **feel free to contact at:** _author@tempehrecipes.com_

Kathy Terry

tempehrecipes.com

Printed in the USA
CPSIA information can be obtained
at www.ICGtesting.com
LVHW071101051223
765741LV00013B/681